Carlos Smaniotto Costa · Ina Šuklje Erjavec
Therese Kenna · Michiel de Lange
Konstantinos Ioannidis · Gabriela Maksymiuk
Martijn de Waal (Eds.)

CyberParks – The Interface Between People, Places and Technology

New Approaches and Perspectives

Editors
Carlos Smaniotto Costa
Universidade Lusófona
Lisbon, Portugal

Ina Šuklje Erjavec
Urban Planning Institute
of the Republic of Slovenia
Ljubljana, Slovenia

Therese Kenna
University College Cork
Cork, Ireland

Michiel de Lange
Utrecht University
Utrecht, The Netherlands

Konstantinos Ioannidis
aaiko arkitekter
Oslo, Norway

Gabriela Maksymiuk
Warsaw University of Life Sciences
Warsaw, Poland

Martijn de Waal
Amsterdam University of Applied Sciences
Amsterdam, The Netherlands

https://doi.org/10.1007/978-3-030-13417-4

Acknowledgement and Disclaimer
This publication is based upon work from COST Action TU1306, supported by COST (European Cooperation in Science and Technology).
The book reflects only the authors' views. Neither the COST Association nor any person acting on its behalf is responsible for the use, which might be made of the information contained in this publication. The COST Association is not responsible for external websites referred to in this publication.

COST

This publication is based upon work from COST Action TU1306, supported by COST (European Cooperation in Science and Technology).

COST (European Cooperation in Science and Technology) is a funding agency for research and innovation networks. Our Actions help connect research initiatives across Europe and enable scientists to grow their ideas by sharing them with their peers. This boosts their research, career and innovation.

www.cost.eu

Preface

This book presents different challenges related to public open spaces and people, the relationships between them and possible roles of digital technology in this relationship. It is a book about a phenomenon that is increasingly being in the centre of sciences and strategies – the penetration of digital technologies in the urban space and related different approaches, methods, empirical studies, open questions and concerns. It brings together research work results, ideas, discussions and experiences of different participants of the Project CyberParks, fostering knowledge about the relationship between information and communication technologies and public spaces supported by strategies to improve their use and attractiveness (www.cyberparks-project.eu), that was founded by the H2020 European Programme Cooperation in Science and Technology (COST) in the period of April 2014 to April 2018 (https://www.cost.eu/actions/TU1306).

As a network, CyberParks opened opportunities for participants with different professional experiences and backgrounds, coming from 31 different countries to gather and explore, from different perspectives, the emerging challenge that digital technology advancements and their increasing pervasiveness pose to the production and use of public open spaces. Such endeavour called for interdisciplinary research, in order to advance fundamental understanding on issues that go beyond the scope of a single field of research practice.

As the main outcome of the CyberParks Project, this book aims at fostering the understanding about the current and future interactions of the nexus people, public spaces and technology. It addresses a wide range of challenges and multidisciplinary perspectives on emerging phenomena related to the penetration of technology in people's lifestyles – affecting therefore the whole of society and, with this, the production and use of public open spaces. CyberParks coined the term "cyberpark" to describe the mediated public open space, that emerging type of urban space where nature and cybertechnologies blend together to generate hybrid experiences and enhance quality of life. The latter issue – enhancing quality of life – has been a crucial aspect in the project, as the lure of technology should not be in place towards creating high-tech places but rather places that are inclusive and responsive. In a cyberpark, ICT and their devices are a driving force, media and tool, which act as a mediator between users and the virtual and real worlds. And that in turn could fuel a greater attachment of people to places. As a new space typology and/or as a new layer, a cyberpark has the potential to attract people to spend more time outdoors, to challenge new ways of outdoor activities and as interfaces to support new ways of co-creation. A cyberpark calls to generate innovative solutions, and thus encourage also new investment, and spur economic growth. These should be reasons enough to create more mediated public open spaces – an assumption that was widely reflected in the Project and is now widely addressed in the chapters of this book.

The concept of cyberpark, a complex system at the crossroads of different disciplines, is approached from different aspects and points of view – all aiming at developing a systematic understanding of how people use media, senseable and locative technologies in their appropriation of places, and at making sense out of a place's new intangible properties.

This book represents our own experiences of this journey, in a given timeframe and financial support for networking. Given the high interdisciplinarity of the CyberParks issues, it called for the need of a structured dialogue and a common understanding between the disciplines. From the perspective of cyberparks, technology can be used to "engage" users as co-creators of the production and management of public spaces. However, it is relevant to state that the technology penetration alone will not raise an active contribution for increasing the quality, inclusiveness and responsiveness of public spaces – as the digital/virtual world is not a substitute of the physical place. Technology must be coupled with "human" knowledge, towards preserving and increasing the different benefits, functions and "interpretations" of a public space, and towards avoiding the sameness, and bland and uninteresting places. In this process, technology in a constant development assumes an important role in shaping the future. Hence, the digital technologies and tools must be better understood and shaped in order to be properly used in transforming public spaces into more inclusive and responsive places. This leads us to the next question of whether augmented reality and senseable places will bring more people outdoors, increase the use of public places and connect people with nature. In short, does technology provide meaningful structures for sustained actions towards increasing quality of urban life?

COST Action CyberParks: A Think Tank

The CyberParks Project has focused its attention on information and communications technology (ICTs) as an active interface between the production of knowledge about the use of urban public space (research purposes) and guidance for interventions (policies and design practices). The penetration of technology in people's life and the use of the city is transforming our physical living space into a meditated and hybrid place. The digital development poses a societal challenge with reflections on social practices and on planning and design approaches to public spaces. This, in turn, might also challenge the future development of ICTs and their devices. Four years ago we embarked on an expedition marked by the rapid transformation of the urban landscape, growing of pervasive and ubiquitous computing, improved data interpretation technologies and a corresponding explosion of data, etc. The CyberParks initial idea grew to 88 researchers from 31 countries (as of April 2018). CyberParks understands itself as a research platform on the relationship between ICT and the production of public open spaces, and the relevance of both to sustainable urban development. As a COST Action, CyberParks had limited researching and working activities but they were also flexible enough to face the challenges and to provide the financial means to the ideas that arose and discuss them – and financing is a crucial issue in research that takes up challenges and innovation in urban development and is not a target of creating new markets. Five working groups were tasked with dealing with relevant issues (digital methods, urban ethnography, conceptual reflection, designing a cyberpark and dissemination activities) aiming at providing insights and enhancing the conceptualisation of the mediated space and of the social practices under the influence of technology.

The COST framework financed the costs for the setting up of meetings and conferences, the organisation of scientific exchanges of short duration, training schools, and publications and dissemination activities. The flexible structure and the simple implementation and management initiatives enabled CyberParks to organise ten working groups meetings in different European cities, send 28 researchers for short scientific missions, and organise two conferences, a midterm in Malta in April 2016 and the Final Conference in Berlin in 2018. CyberParks was fortunate to count on the commitment of the participants, who in every single initiative demonstrated great motivation, dedication and vigour. The great commitment has also been a challenge for the management, as not all participants could always be invited. The COST enabled CyberParks to also organise capacity-building initiatives besides the aforementioned short missions, four different training schools tackling different issues and in different cities (Thessaloniki, Amsterdam, Lisbon and Nicosia) could be organised, in these training schools 77 young professionals widely discussed the issues with invited tutors. These training schools, linking up high-quality scientific networks across Europe, thus paid particular attention to young researchers in offering a discussion forum and networking opportunities tailored to their requests.

CyberParks, grasping the idea of the mediated and hybrid place, investigated the shape and scope of ICT impacts and the opportunities digital technology and mobile devices created to improve the legibility and liveability of public spaces, as well as new forms of integrating people's needs into urban design processes – on these issues participation in several international conferences and publications could be organised. All these publications are open source and available on the Project's website as part of the concept of sharing knowledge. Sharing knowledge is a step towards CyberParks leading issues: to use ICT to transform our cities into more human environment, rather than just more high-tech and to understand that "smartness" should be people friendly and a democratic process. Place-making, co-creation and inclusiveness to be helped through the advances in technology are seen as an opportunity to bring people together to engage with the production of public spaces and to create and support opportunities and capacities for people to transact with others for a common good.

Book Structure

The chapters of this book originate from different writing teams, organised across the five CyberParks' working groups. A call for chapters was launched by an Editorial Board organised to coordinate the production of this book. The Editorial Board members were also responsible for the peer review process, and this ensured double reviews per chapter. The two reviewers were selected according to the chapter topics. In a final process the chapters were again reviewed by the Editors-in-Chief, who with the Editorial Board members structured the chapters into the four parts. Each part was coordinated by two editors who guided the development of the chapters, and now present and discuss them in the introduction of each part. This editorial approach (peer review process, international and interdisciplinary writing teams) reflects the accentuated internationality and multidisciplinarity of the CyberParks Project. Although this book is not the place to discuss the influence of new technologies on a general basis, it does, however, focus on the ability of digital technology to enhance communication and interaction with (potential) users, as a way to transform the production and uses of public spaces into an interactive process, enabling creative community participation and empowerment.

By casting light on this emerging urban phenomenon – the mediated public space – this book presents as pioneer case the relationship of people and technology with places. It illuminates paradigm shifts, introduces new concepts, visions and future trends, addresses challenges, new approaches, innovative tools and adaptive research methodologies, and it provides arguments for policy design and challenges practices for future planning of public open spaces. The spirit of internationality and in particular of transdisciplinarity is the common thread in this book. It is a witness of an intensified co-operation among the partners and the critical discussions to facilitate the advancement of knowledge.

Altogether 24 chapters, prepared by international writing teams, are arranged under the four broad themes:

- Part I explores the concept of CyberParks, its theoretical background and how the notion of the mediated place evolved.
- Part II centres its focus on socio-spatial practices towards increasing the knowledge of people and their relations with the space, since it is people who bring life to public spaces.
- Part III focuses on programming and activating cyberparks, on what has to be done to turn mediated spaces into places for learning, gaming and to make use of the potential of public spaces to increase the resilience of cities.
- Part IV dealing with technological challenges and research methodologies addresses the potential of technologies to increase the understanding of the relationship between people and places.

The issues addressed are preliminary in nature and are intended to provide starting arguments for further investigation in this field, in particular because of the accelerating development of technology and constant changes in opportunities for the adoption of devices and technology-based new products and services. The constant and accelerated development creates a challenging environment to study the social, cultural, political and urban impacts of digital technology advancements. The overarching intention behind introducing concepts, perspectives and methods is not to generate a comprehensive inventory on the interaction of technology into the urban space but above all to initiate a debate carefully considering crucial factors such as people, methods and methodologies in the production of public spaces. The quest remains in how to translate the technical development into more liveable and people-friendly environments.

Outlook and Acknowledgements

We wish to thank the chapter editors for their engagement with the CyberParks Project and with this book, the authors for their contributions, both together ensure that this book increases the understanding of the manifold relationships between public spaces and new technologies, their role in shaping public behaviour and sense of the common along with insights to enhance and take forward some key conceptual theoretical and methodological debates in the urban development and beyond. We hope that CyberParks, its findings condensed in this book, and the issues it explores can push forward the discussion around delivering safe, inviting and inspiring public spaces for all. We hope that the discussion started within the Project will last and will be transformed into action, empowering people with the knowledge and tools to support the social and physical changes needed to transform the urban environment into a more liveable and responsible space. We must be ready to nurture the innovation that the future holds – the future of the urban environment depends very much on actions taken today.

Finally, we want to thank the COST Programme for the trust placed in the CyberParks network.

October 2018

Carlos Smaniotto Costa
Ina Šuklje Erjavec

Contents

Part I The Unveiling Potential of Cyberparks

Edited by Carlos Smaniotto and Ina Šuklje-Erjavec

1.1

The Rationale of CyberParks and the Potential of Mediated Public Open Spaces

Carlos Smaniotto Costa[1(✉)] and Ina Šuklje Erjavec[2]

[1] Interdisciplinary Research Centre for Education and Development CeiED, Universidade Lusófona, Lisbon, Portugal
smaniotto.costa@ulusofona.pt

[2] Urban Planning Institute of the Republic of Slovenia UIRS, Ljubljana, Slovenia
inas@uirs.si

Abstract. Cybertechnologies are changing the world, both in terms of sociability and subjectivity, and consequently how people experience the city, appreciate urban landscape and nature, along with the way people interrelate to each other and with the space. The penetration of ICT into urban landscapes has increased the open space typology, adding a concept of 'cyberpark' to it – the public open space where nature, society, and cybertechnologies blend together to generate hybrid experiences and enhance quality of urban life. A cyberpark evolves through different ways of the implementation and use of digital technologies into a new type of a connectable, real-time responsive, sharing and integrating public place, in which, the physical dimension of a space becomes a more dynamic and blurred form of interaction This calls for understanding such hybrid spaces as more than a simple new spatial unit of urban tissue. This chapter proposes a conceptual framework for a better understanding of inter weaving between physical and virtual spheres in public open spaces and addresses the results of the COST Action CyberParks. It explores, in terms of policy-making, urban planning and design, the numerous challenges and opportunities created by digital and mobile technologies. The efforts of this work are thus centred on the potential of ICT to increased possibilities for new uses and elements or even types of urban open spaces, as an important added value to the quality of life, inclusiveness, responsiveness and attractiveness of the city. In critically addressing opportunities, the chapter shall seek to question and challenge, the more 'traditional' understanding of what makes a good public place. In doing so, it shall attempt to provide pointers towards a re-conceptualised view of urban space design/production and (planning) control/guidance.

Keywords: Public open spaces · Digitally mediated spaces · Hybrid spaces · Urban landscape · Urban design

C. Smaniotto Costa et al. (Eds.): CyberParks, LNCS 11380, pp. 3–13, 2019.
https://doi.org/10.1007/978-3-030-13417-4_1

1 Digital Technology and Urban Landscape

The rapid and pervasive development of digital and mobile technologies is drastically influencing everyday life of the average citizens, changing behaviour and interests. The digital development, as stated by Castells (2004) is not limited to a technological paradigm but comprises a broad process of computerisation of thought, knowledge, culture and social organization, and these in turn affect the physical and social urban landscape. The proliferation of smartphones and ubiquitous Internet access are changing the way people work, learn and communicate. These also reflect in the way people use, perceive and experience the city, along with the way they spent their leisure time. It seems that people, especially the young generation, are attaching a growing importance to be permanently connected, as the studies of Bocci and Smaniotto (2017), Menezes et al. (2017) organised within CyberParks evidence. Young generation growing up in the digital age are linked to social media, smart phones and apps, and they use and perceive them almost as new, additional senses. No doubt that technology yields the enormous benefits that were not available in the recent past but also confronts urban development with new societal and spatial design challenges. Furthermore, new technologies are opening new opportunities for the production and management of urban spaces, creating new forms of use as well as for research on public open spaces.

The CyberParks Project addresses the need for a conceptual framework for the production of mediated public spaces in urban development - different approaches and concerns are tackled in this book. The Project coined the term cyberpark to define a new aspect of public open spaces, now intertwined in diverse ways by technologies. This intertwining creates a dynamic environment and gives rise to the phenomenon of mediated open space - where physical and the digital coexists and complement each other. The cyberpark concept defines a digitally mediated public open space as space where nature, society, and cybertechnologies blend together to generate hybrid experiences, opening new possibilities of use and enhancing quality of urban life. To be responsive as possible, a cyberpark is often characterised by the use of sensor technologies in a connectable space, accessible to the public through ubiquitous technologies used in sociable and sharable ways[1]. A cyberpark thus enables to cross borders and to extrapolate the real world with the virtual world. It creates new ways of immersion, use and management of public open spaces, and by adding new angles of perception and involvement. By attaching a meaning to the public spaces, a cyberpark contributes to the mutation of a space into a place. In this respect, a number of key issues relating to spaces, public spaces and places need to be addressed as a background frame.

2 Public Open Spaces in the Core of Research

The work in a multidisciplinary atmosphere and tackling different aspects of the digital development, as in CyberParks, make the call to create a common ground for understanding. Although it is not the intention to widely discuss a series of issues, there are

[1] This definition was developed by Working Group 4 (Designing CyberParks).

terms that merit further assessment to be understood in the scope of the Project and this book. In CyberParks, urban landscape is considered as a complexity of various aspects, forming different visible features of a city, as a result of land take by humans. It includes a vast variety of natural, semi-natural and man-made/artificial environments. From CyberParks' perspective the special focus has been on publicly accessible spaces. For the project use the public open space is understood in its broadest sense: It is a type of land use, the unbuilt space or space free of large built structures, planned, designed and managed in public interest with particular purpose, in general by a city council. The adjective *public* connotes a space that is generally open and accessible to people on equal terms. The typology of public open spaces includes spaces for mobility, recreation, for the merit of their environmental benefits, and to address ecology and biodiversity, and public health. Among them are streets and walkways, squares, plazas, market places, parks, green spaces, greenways, community gardens, playgrounds, waterfronts, etc., each one playing different but vital roles in a city. A city with a wide range of open space typology is more likely to be able to open different possibilities for use and to fulfil equivalently the different needs, preferences and expectations (responsiveness) of different users' groups (inclusiveness), and welcoming atmosphere for all, not only in physical, but also in psychological and social senses, forming territorial identity and image (Šuklje Erjavec 2010). Henceforth, the term *public spaces* will be used, independent of different connotations and features they might have.

Public spaces are widely recognised as a crucial aspect of sustainability and people friendly development of cities and play a relevant role for the quality of urban life. There is a consensus that the creation of healthy, attractive and sustainable urban environment not only depends on the presence, distribution, interconnection and accessibility to open spaces, but also their usability in terms of attractiveness, responsiveness, and inclusiveness. A growing body of research indicates their environmental, social, cultural and economic values and benefits (GreenKeys 2008). For CyberParks, the social quality of an open space is in the centre of attention, as they allow people to gather together, in planned and serendipitous ways, to interact with other people, with the community and the environment. An open space enables people to be in public, to practice sociability on neutral ground, in green spaces to contact with nature, providing them the ground for a variety of every day and occasional activities and experiences. An open space is thus the place for communication, interaction, connection and encounters, for inhabitants and visitors, as well as place to express cultural diversity. The social interactions are important for defining a sense of place, for contributing to people's physical, cultural, and spiritual well-being (Šuklje Erjavec 2010), for the personal development and social learning, and for the development of tolerance (Larice and Macdonald 2013). This is an interesting line of though as it suggests, as Amin (2006) argued that the free and unfettered socialising in an open public space encourages forbearance towards others, pleasure in the urban experience, appreciation for the shared commons, and an interest in civic and political life.

Public spaces can be regarded as the soul of a city. Their qualities validate the assumption that they reflect the attention and care by councils of the public realm. As it is in public spaces that some of the best and the worst characteristics of urban life and society are created, observed and reproduced (Šuklje Erjavec 2010). In fact, one of the main factors that determines the appropriation of a place and the resulting people's behaviour in this place, is the intrinsic connection between urban design, and more in particular the design of public spaces. Carmona et al. (2010: 106) aptly pointed out, that human behaviour in the public realm is largely influenced by the amenities and facilitates provided. The design and elements provided in a public space provide opportunities for staying, doing activities and interactions - enhancing community life, or alternatively their absence does not enact such actions. If public spaces are not located where people need them, if they are not safe and easy to access, if do not meet the needs and expectations of people no one will use them. How can people value an old tree if there is none there, or stay and enjoy the sunshine if there no benches to sit? Such aspects are relevant if the call for getting people to be outdoors, and to lead to an active and healthy lifestyle is to succeed. Quite conversely and for sure not future-oriented is the development in several American cities as Crawford (2017) reports, where benches are being teared out from the urban landscape as an effort to not offer opportunities for vagrancy and crime, so homeless people and loiterers cannot settle. Such development, that could be called anti-design is for sure bad for publicness and urban life.

Such development made raise to tackle the concern on inclusiveness. No doubt, urban societies are facing concerns due to expanding social diversification, what blurs and dilutes the concept of cohesive society (Holland et al. 2007), and this makes the design of public places meant to be for all in such society more difficult and challenging. Inclusiveness has to do with offering adequate and balanced opportunity for all in the appropriation of public spaces. In fact, the concentration of unwanted, disadvantaged and vulnerable groups in public spaces creates a sense of insecurity and entrapment, turning communication often difficult, as different social groups use different languages and have different attitudes and frameworks (Madanipour et al. 2014). And these also make interactions more difficult.

Different appropriation patterns of children, teenagers and adults, diverging expectations of women and men regarding public spaces, as well as dissimilar aesthetic preferences depending on social groups (Löw 2015) put pressure on the design, production and maintenance of public spaces. In Western Europe, inclusiveness calls above all for making public realm more age-friendly. Tackling such differences should however be at the same time taking the challenge for creating new opportunities. This includes the analysis of practices of negotiating the urban environment, what in the end leads to shaping civic and political culture. This argument endorses again a wide range of typology of public spaces, as the more different spaces (with different sizes and features) provided, the more opportunities people have to appropriate and enjoy, enlivening in this way the urban environment. Jacobs (1961) also recognises that "cities have the capability of providing something for everybody, only because, and only when, they are created by everybody", and this "created" must be a result of deliberated, pro-active urban policy.

CyberParks is addressing potentials of new digital technologies to open new opportunities for improving inclusiveness of public open spaces from several aspects. Another paramount issue related to the public space is the place-responsive concept. It is related to the inclusiveness, as a public space being inclusive should meet the need, preferences and expectations of users but also introduces a dynamic time-change frame for a nowadays rapid changing society. Responsiveness is another aspect considered a crucial in CyberParks. It addresses the people friendliness of the urban landscape and it should go beyond recreation (Turner 2004) creating "places" for new needs and activities, new way of uses and experiences (Thompson 2002). Therefore, a public space with its own logic and dynamism, must be able to cope with changes over time, and has accordingly to be able to respond to these changes. The technological advancements are undoubtedly developing a new wide range of possibilities of real time and place responsiveness, in different ways, aspects and intensities, challenging open space planners, designers and managers to use them within their co-creation processes and design solutions.

CyberParks' understanding of public spaces indicates a complex and multi-faceted perspective, blending the physical characteristics of the space with attached values, memories, stories, art, etc. The addition of such attachments, be them individual or collective, is the enabler of turning a space into a place (the aforementioned mutation). While space is related to something abstract, devoid of a substantial meaning, *place* refers to how people are aware of, and attracted to a certain piece of space. A place is thus the result of a process of identification between people and a space, which holds a creative tension between deep experience and critical awareness.

Such broader perception of public open space as a cumulative and undivided resource is the vital basis for its strategic planning, design and management, and now to be enhanced by technology. For the sake of clarity and simplicity, and because it best captures what people care most about, CyberParks adopted the concept of public open space as drawn broadly to recognise the intersection of built-social as well as virtual environment and their influences in the socio-spatial practices. Thus, the typology of public spaces addressed by CyberParks encompasses both physical space and the virtual meeting places in form of social media, those however devoted to public spaces concerns.

3 The Potential of Digitally Enhanced Public Spaces: Cyberpark's Added Values

In a mediated public space, as CyberParks advocates, technology is at the same time the fuel that drives a paradigm shift to combat the previously mentioned threats. This raises the questions, which are also simultaneous challenges: What are the possible benefits of enhanced public spaces? How cyberpark's value differs from a non-mediated public space? How to respond with innovative solutions that are smart and interactive, while helping and attracting people to establish an active and healthy lifestyle? Is it necessary to develop new elements, equipment or new design approaches? The answers take the production of open spaces out from previously easily demarcated planning sciences, to an interdisciplinary domain, where it can benefit from synergies. As already noted, use of ICT as a part of public open space development is a challenge to (re) invent, experiment, stimulate certain processes, programmes, usages, and social interactions within public spaces, these opportunities are explored in the forthcoming chapters.

Public space getting mediated, is developing a new layer of use, perception and functioning, is becoming a place of extension and emplacement, i.e. a finitely real public space is becoming by grids and networks enhanced. The penetration of ICT makes more than a clear-cut distinction of the physical to the virtual world, it transforms the public space in dualities, as open and isolated, universal and particular, juxtaposed and disaggregated, collective und individualized, raising heterotopias, the places of otherness (Patricio 2017). The point it that the interrelations between digital technology and cities are being mostly discussed within technology-driven visions, smart cities policies with particular emphasis on digital infrastructure, urban data, energy and mobility issues are playing a decisive role. Increasingly, however, more authors emphasise the importance of people-oriented aspects, especially if the goal is to improve inclusiveness and responsiveness of urban fabric. Backed by a people's centred approach CyberParks concentrates the efforts primary on opportunities and positive aspects of the technology pervasiveness. Equitable use, flexibility and innovation in appropriation of public spaces, design applications, perceptive information, sensitive (senseable) environments are issues that guided the Project. It collected and systematised several examples of the penetration of technology into public spaces, these are available in the Pool of Examples[2]. With the Pool CyberParks seeks to increase the understanding of the benefits of technology to enhance places in order to achieve an added value (i.e. new outdoor experiences, new possibilities of use, new types of spaces).

A growing body of research is concerned with the challenges and threats of technology. Reports about technology addiction, interpersonal communication and interaction difficulties, loneliness in a hyperconnected world, sedentary life styles, etc. increasingly call our attention, reminding that people are losing the contact to each other, with the environment and nature, and becoming prisoner of technology[3]. Yet, it is a positive aspect that technology (still) needs user's engagement. Technology meets sooner or later face to face with people, and what people do (or don't) retains ultimate, as this ensures often that technology works (or not). However, some authors recognize missing of the required "user engagement", some of the mentioned reasons are: technology gap/divide (the society is not ready for this new technology or people do not have access to it), reward (people are unable to see the point of this new technology, it is not clear the immediate reward for using it), trust (the lack of trust on the provider or the share/use of data, cybersecurity). These issues raise the ultimately question, of the value of the technology if it doesn't help to make cities more inclusive, and public spaces more responsive. Thus, development and use of the technology cannot be isolated from social and cultural spheres and influences. It must be re-regarded as a tool or (a set of tools) only developed to facilitate, support and enable a sustainable way of life. In fact, the growing technology pervasiveness is creating new forms of social interactions and practices, mediating experiences, transforming (sensory) experiences and opening novel possibilities of engagement, resulting in more awareness on the environment conditions and quality of life. What seems for the

---

[2] The Pool is available at www.cyberparks-project.eu/examples, and enables the searching, navigating and adding new examples.

[3] Kristen Houghton: "Prisoner of Technology Escapes" in her blog on Mar 27, 2015. https://www.huffingtonpost.com/kristen-houghton/prisoner-of-technology-es_b_6541452.html.

moment, to be a superficial interaction, could become the embryo of bringing more people, especially the young ones (the future users of public spaces, and decision makers) more intensively and more connected with the places. To achieve this need calls to build sustainable digital-physical bridges.

Another issue to consider is that even "good" technologies will do little good if they are misapplied or even mature too late to help avert unsustainable and hostile urban environment. This is further exacerbated by the exceptional speed of the development of technology, which is very difficult to harmonize in time with changes in society and possible paces of spatial planning and development. Studying and building a theory on the planning, environmental and social impacts of ICTs, as well as their political, economic and cultural contexts, is not an easy task. Technical and technological progress is breath-taking, and the pace keeps accelerating, but this in turn, results in new interrelations and interactions of people to and in public spaces.

To understand really the nexus people, places and technology it is important to understand the difference of the time-change frame of each of the 3 factors in the nexus. The space itself is the most permanent element of the three thus providing the frame of physical reality. It also requires, especially in the form of greenspaces that are also very dependent of natural processes, a long-term planning and strategic development approach. Processes of deliberate change of place to meet new need and values of society are usually very slow, always little behind. Urban development reality shows that time is needed for the society to transform new needs and opportunities into demands, values and decisions. The gap in the dynamics to react to changes in the nexus people, places and technology is one of the greatest future challenges to be addressed and solved in the future of cyberparks development. Public spaces can be the stress-resilient factor against the volatility of the technological advances. Thus, the linchpin remains the space.

CyberParks, identifies the technology as a great enabler for engaging with people, recognises also that technology alone is never the solution. It cannot replace the "traditional" aspects that are important for people in the use of public spaces as social cohesion, mental and physical activities and contact with nature. However, the use of technology as a supporting tool for increasing attractiveness, variety, inclusiveness and responsiveness of open spaces may be of great added value for their quality and important step further to the sustainable and people friendly cities in the future.

It is the contention of the discussion to position the cyberpark, the hybrid space, not only a as key for a more sustainable and inclusive development, but mainly for opening opportunities towards making urban development interactive. Yet, the real public space demand and play a major role. Being locally rooted they offer a common ground for transforming the use and production of public spaces based on co-creation and interactive activities. Social media, for example, supports in a low-priced way the interaction with a broad range of people, and this can result in increased interest in civic and political life in the community. Additionally, ICT and mobile devices increased the ways with new tools and methods of analysing the human spatial behaviour (Aurigi 2013). These goals increase perspectives but also show the multi-faced character of a public space.

4 Approaching the Cyberparks Concept - Overview of Chapters

The first part of the book aims at broadening perspectives; it addresses different background aspects related to the cyberpark concept. The chapters provide multidisciplinary arguments and views for a better understanding the challenges of interaction between new digital technologies, public open space design and people for future urban development. In the chapter 1.2 **Heterotopic Landscapes: from Green Parks to Hybrid Territories**, **Catarina Patrício, Christoph Breser and Konstantinos Ioannidis** discuss the cyberpark concept from philosophical aspects. They look at public spaces beyond their physical manifestation, through the principles of the heterotopia and the non-place theories. The authors alert that a cyberpark by combining the physical dimension and image with an information layer result into the hybrid construct, and point out that a hybrid-place that contains the super modern potential needs to be further explored.

The estimated impact of new technologies on the future urban development if further explored in the chapter 1.3 **Cybercities: Mediated public open spaces - is it a question about interfaces**, **Stefan Zedlacher, Anna Khromova, Eva Savina Malinverni, and Preben Hansen** argue that the key focus of adding technology to public spaces must be the quality of the interfaces. In a mediated space, so the authors, the place itself is covered with information about itself, its history, as well as advertising, marketing, etc. They point out that in cyberspace the ICT is opening the possibility to provide personalised information and real time responses. In this context, the interfaces become of paramount importance, on different levels, changing also the role of the urban planner. On the other hand, **Aleksandra Djukic, Thanos Vlastos and Viera Joklova** in the chapter 1.4 **Liveable Opens Public Spaces – from Flaneur to Cyborg** discuss the aspects of quality of public open spaces, their cultural aspects and questions of functionality, social role and liveability. The authors address the challenges of the future development and needs of future urban society with the special focus on the walkability of place.

The last chapter addresses aspects of multidisciplinarity and the understanding of cyberpark by experts. **Paschalis Arvanitidis, Konstantinos Lalenis, Georgios Artopoulos and Montserrat Pallares-Barbera**, in their chapter 1.5 **Exploring the concept of cyberpark: what the experts think** discuss an analysis on how the concept of a cyberpark is differently perceived by the participants of the CyberParks Project, as they have a wide range of expertise background. The authors address the commonalities and differences of experts' views regarding both the mediated and the not mediated public open spaces. This chapters contributes to further delineate the scope of a cyberpark, mapping out its characteristics and dimensions.

5 CyberParks' Key Findings

Strengthening the link of the nexus people, places and technology, aiming at increasing the quality of environment is the linchpin and hallmark of CyberParks. The interaction between people, places and technology raises a series of conceptual complexities, extrapolating the socio-spatial knowledge in place. The experience in CyberParks shows that the potential for a transdisciplinary research with a people's driven approach has still significant potential for the future. On the one side, there is a wealth of evidence that engaging people provoke real and sustainable changes in quality of life and in the urban environment (Šuklje Erjavec 2010; GreenKeys 2008). On the other side, technology is enabling new forms of space appropriation and attachment. As Smaniotto Costa et al. (2017a, b) acknowledges, in the process of appropriation, technology can be the fuel that keeps the attachment in motion, generating innovative ways not only of use but also the production of public spaces. Further, as the authors state, technology is shaping and will continue to shape people's perceptions and social interactions, and probably the emergence of social and political thoughts, which will reflect not only in the way people use urban spaces but also on their needs and requirements regarding the design and quality of these spaces. This in turn, stresses the role of governance, as the decision-making and participatory processes must be updated to a mediated world and real-time information systems, as further discussed in the forthcoming chapters.

On the flip side, the lure for technology and the fast-paced technological innovation we are experimenting nowadays calls for being attentive and be aware of the risks of a growing reliance in technology - especially for social interactions and the provision of personal data. Although accessing technology brings lots of reward and huge benefits the ultimately satisfying answer to the question what the impact of the mediated space is to transform the urban environment more inclusive and responsive cannot be answered yet. The mediated space and cyberpark are issues therefore that will be on our minds for a long time to come. Among the rewards the technological innovation is bringing about as tackled in this book, the hyperconnectiveness enables the development of new process, methods and tools of co-creation, amalgamating the dual reasoning of local and global. Public spaces call for a devoted approach to the environment where they are attached and to a process riddled with conflict. It is in such duality that the real and the virtual worlds blend, both in their symbolic function and social significance. Even in the mediated space there is a constant negotiation of space, now aggregated with digital inputs, meanings and significances.

The blur of global and local calls also for being attentive to place attachment, which is the emotional bond between people and place, and is a main concept of place-responsiveness. This calls for local programmes responsive to the users, addressing the social dimension of technologies along with environmental resilience, further addressed in this book. This places high demands and calls for creating a learning environment. A place-responsive approach should provide the space for outdoor education programmes. CyberParks demonstrated that this is viable and sustainable achievement and fits well with research needs. Public open spaces bear material and immaterial features, also the mediated space consists of both – more precisely physical and virtual dimensions. The material and immaterial features are not inseparable but once technology intertwined the space, technology becomes itself also a spatial dimension, which is not fully explored yet. Today and even more so in the future public spaces have to meet the needs of people and be able to accommodate changes. Technology can be a key to success.

CyberParks' pledge is for more nature and not less technology. The mediated places also need people – real people sharing and interacting in the same space, and not the remote presence of them. Therefore, the call of CyberParks is towards a multi-disciplinary perspective on preparing the urban environment to be more inclusive, responsive, and with them more sustainable and resilient. These issues are the common thread, that running through the whole CyberParks Project are reflected in this book.

These findings are preliminary in nature and are intended to provide a starting point for further investigation in a field across disciplines. CyberParks casted its net far and wide in a bid to capture insights of relevance, drawing on evidence from across a range of disciplines and policy arenas. Further studies could include investigation via self-reporting measures that involve subjects as social justice, co-creation and social reporting. This would need to be supported with a broad policy context associated with funding. Getting research funding is a perennial obstacle, especially for exploratory issues. However, further research should endeavour to establish a relationship between the locational of support structures, public appropriation of these structures and the relationship with quality of life. It may also be viable to investigate the different types of digital structures and to determine which are more attractive to the public, more sustainable, responsible and inclusive.

CyberParks, as an exploratory project, delivers with this book key findings that reflect the brief period covered by the Project. There remain more questions than answers regarding the experiences and consequences of the penetration of technology into public open spaces. CyberParks should be reviewed in some years ahead.

References

Amin, A.: Collective culture and urban public space. CCCB (2006). http://www.publicspace.org/en/text-library/eng/b003-collective-culture-and-urban-public-space

Aurigi, A.: Reflections towards an agenda for urban-designing the digital city. Urban Des. Int. **18** (2), 131–144 (2013). https://doi.org/10.1057/udi.2012.32

Bocci, M., Smaniotto Costa, C.: Insights on the use of public spaces: leisure behaviours of young professionals and the role of digital technologies. In: Smaniotto Costa, C., Ioannidis, K. (eds.) The Making of the Mediated Public Space - Essays on Emerging Urban Phenomena. CyberParks Project, pp. 109–119. Edições Universitárias Lusófona, Lisbon (2017)

Carmona, M., Tiesdell, S., Heath, T., Oc, T.: Public Places Urban Spaces, the Dimensions of Urban Design. Architectural Press, Oxford (2010)

Castells, M.: Informationalism, Networks, and the Network Society: A Theoretical Blueprinting, The Network Society: A Cross-Cultural Perspective. Edward Elgar, Northampton (2004)

Crawford, A.: Cities Take Both Sides in the 'War on Sitting'. CityLab, 20 October 2017. https://www.citylab.com/design/2017/10/cities-take-both-sides-in-the-war-on-sitting/542643

GreenKeys Project: GreenKeys @ Your City – A Guide for Urban Green Quality. IOER, Dresden (2008). www.greenkeys-project.net

Holland, C., Clark, A., Katz, J., Peace, S.: Social Interactions in Urban Public Places. The Policy Press, Bristol (2007)

Jacobs, J.: The Death and Life of Great American Cities. Random House, New York (1961)

Larice, M., Macdonald, E. (eds.): The Urban Design Reader, 2nd edn. Routledge, Abingdon (2013)

Löw, M.: Managing urban commons: public interest and the representation if interconnectedness. In: Borch, C., Kornberger, M. (eds.) Urban Commons: Rethinking the City, pp. 109–126. Routledge, New York (2015)

Madanipour, A., Knierbein, S., Degros, A.: Public Space and the Challenges of Urban Transformation in Europe. Routledge, New York (2014)

Menezes, M., Smaniotto Costa, C., Ioannidis, K.: Interconnections among ICT, social practices, public space and urban design. Revista da Associação Portuguesa de Sociologia **11**, 6–21 (2016)

Patricio, C.: Smart cities and the re-invention of the Panopticon. In: Smaniotto Costa, C., Ioannidis, K. (eds.) The Making of the Mediated Public Space - Essays on Emerging Urban Phenomena. CyberParks Project, pp. 55–64. Edições Universitárias Lusófona, Lisbon (2017)

Smaniotto Costa, C., Bahillo Martínez, A., Álvarez, F.J., Šuklje Erjavec, I., Menezes, M., Pallares-Barbera, M.: Digital tools for capturing user's needs on urban open spaces: drawing lessons from Cyberparks project. In: Certomà, C., Dyer, M., Pocatilu, L., Rizzi, F. (eds.) Citizen Empowerment and Innovation in the Data-Rich City. Springer Tracts in Civil Engineering, pp. 177–193 (2017a). Springer, Cham. https://doi.org/10.1007/978-3-319-47904-0_11

Smaniotto Costa, C., Bovelet, J., Dolata, K., Menezes, M.: Building a theory on co-creating a Cyberpark. Lessons learnt from the COST Action CyberParks and the Flussbad Project, Berlin. In: Smaniotto Costa, C., Ioannidis, K. (eds.) The Making of the Mediated Public Space - Essays on Emerging Urban Phenomena. CyberParks Project, pp. 165–174. Edições Universitárias Lusófonas, Lisbon (2017b)

Šuklje Erjavec, I.: Designing an urban park as a contemporary user-friendly place. In: Marušić, B.G., Nikšič, M. (eds.) Human Cities - Celebrating Public Space, pp. 39–51. Stichting Kunstboek, Oostkamp (2010)

Thompson, C.W.: Urban open space in the 21st century. Landsc. Urban Plan. **60**(2), 59–72 (2002)

Turner, M.A.: Urban Parks as Partners in Youth Development. Washington, D.C. (2004). https://doi.org/10.1037/e688712011-001

1.2

Heterotopic Landscapes: From GreenParks to Hybrid Territories

Catarina Patrício[1(✉)], Christoph Breser[2], and Konstantinos Ioannidis[3]

[1] Universidade Lusófona e CECL/ICNOVA, Lisboa, Portugal
catarinapatricioleitao14@gmail.com
[2] Graz University of Technology, Graz, Austria
christoph.breser@tugraz.at
[3] aaiko arkitekter, Oslo, Norway
konionn@aaiko.no

Abstract. This chapter develops an interest in clarifying the meaning of cyberparks through an interrogation beyond its material preconditions. A cyber-park, as *a fold in space* generated by a hybrid emergent form of co-mediated space, is a disjunctive combination: it presupposes an encounter between open public urban places and the use of ICT tools. Outstretched beyond its physical manifestation as a place of encounter, a «heterotopic» reading might reveal that the subject is displaced in many different ways, from the analogue to the digital landscape, and from the specificity of the local to the universal of the global web. It is in such transferences that several worlds blend, both in its symbolic function and social significance. Impacts of such «Other Spaces» on the nature of human being's behaviours can be critically reflected by the consideration of the social role of ICTs as tools of alienation through reinforced governances. Hence the question of creating «non-places» arouses, affording both a consensual appropriation process and the representative commodity networks, that henceforth includes natural, technical and human aspects and at the same time constitutes hybrid identities at the interfaces of its users, subjects, objects and places.

Keywords: Heterotopia · Non-place · Technology · Experience · Hybrid-place

1 Setting «Other Spaces» as a Place Theory

Heterotopias are considered to be aporetic spaces: open and isolated, universal and particular, juxtaposed and disaggregated, collective and individualized. A heterotopia is a place of otherness inasmuch as it raises a certain ambiguity on similitude and emancipation, alienation and resistance. In this regard Edward Soja said it is «*frustratingly incomplete, inconsistent, incoherent*»[1] in spite of him devoting an entire chapter to it in

[1] Under the influence of Lefebvre Soja also said: «narrowly focused on peculiar micro-geographies, near-sighted and near-sited, deviant and deviously apolitical» (Soja 1996: 162). However, it seems improbable to read them as an alternative space-taking program when after all they are the outline of an analytic. Even though heterotopias are an interruption of space continuity, this doesn't mean an entire intervention program.

C. Smaniotto Costa et al. (Eds.): CyberParks, LNCS 11380, pp. 14–24, 2019.
https://doi.org/10.1007/978-3-030-13417-4_2

«Thirdspace» (Soja 1996). The term arises for the Social Sciences[2] in «Des espaces autres», a conference given by Michel Foucault in 1967 in the *Cercle d'Études Architecturales*, published only twenty years later[3]. It is a raw work left in abeyance, perhaps even abandoned by Foucault, but powerful if we confront the public space with the new mediations, plus the so called «Internet Galaxy»[4]. Although the web renders possible the exploration of Foucault's diverse notion *heterotopia*, this chapter works with it to reflect on the potential of the possible engagement of technology with space.

«*Des espaces autres*» is divided in two parts: initially, Foucault sketches some considerations about the mutations that the idea of space suffered in the western experience, dealing with the notion of space in its abstract sense – undifferentiated and absolute. In a second moment, Foucault approaches a heterotopology, focusing on the nature of place, which emerges concretely and *locus* of differentiation[5].

But why space? If the nineteenth century allowed itself to be hallucinated by time (Foucault 1984: 752), through its *relativity* and how it *revealed* the History[6], with the experience of *duration* and *simultaneity – recall Bergson's work – for the twentieth century the priority is to think of space. In the moment when the Earth is wired and orbited by satellites, the Earth re-emerges as absolute. Foucault realizes it well, seeking to situate space in the Western History, even before the age of networks. Although presenting a somewhat panoramic view, it is evident to perceive how a mutation is operated in the way one is in the space with each technical breakthrough.*

The archaic space, located sometime up to the Medieval Age, corresponded to the hierarchical set of places that differed according to the seminal oppositions between *sacred* and *profane*, *guarded* (known) and *open* (unknown). The paradigm of the *space of localization* was dominant (Foucault 1984: 753). It concerned some kind of a primitive panic about human impotence when facing the brutality of nature, death and void. This space expands with Galileo and with the discovery of an "infinite space and infinitely open one" (753). The *space of localization* is then dissolved giving rise to the *space of expansion*.

Currently, it is the problem of *emplacement* that shatters the preceding spatial orders precisely because the relation of propinquity between points or elements prevails and it can be described as "ramifications"[7]. Foucault reveals the reticulate nature of

---

[2] It was already used in medical sciences to characterize, for example, the abnormal location or displacement of a tissue or of an entire anatomical structure.

[3] Published in *Architecture, Movement, Continuité,* no. 5, currently compiled in *Dits et écrits*: 1954–1988, vol. IV, Paris, Gallimard, 1994, pp. 752–762. Foucault only authorized the publication of this text in 1984, months before his death.

[4] Cf. Manuel Castells (2001) *The Internet Galaxy*. Oxford University Press.

[5] This differentiation between space and place is, however, imprecise. For further information Cf. Edward S. Casey (1997) *The Fate of Place: A Philosophical History*. Berkeley: University of California Press.

[6] Here we recall first Einstein and the Theory of Relativity, then Hegel and Marx.

[7] Emphasis is given to the priority of space in the age of networks: «In a still more concrete manner, the problem of place or the emplacement arises for mankind in terms of demography. This problem of the human emplacement is not simply the question of knowing what relations of vicinity, elements, should be adopted in this or that situation in order to achieve this or that end. We are in an epoch in which space is given to us in the form of relations between emplacements». (Foucault 1984, 753–4).

space, and how this is offered to us in the form of *emplacement relationships*. Yet, to discover the network is to discover the whole world scrutinized and mapped, thereby perceiving how space is finite and how it is impossible to expand. The limit of extension is the great anxiety of the twenty-first century at a time when the world population is already surpassing the 7 billion people. Thus, smart cities are idealized to manage the urban space in the face of such challenge. Even cloud storage assumes servers, and those are based on the ground. This absolute relay on space also imposed certain sensitivity towards place. No wonder, therefore, that the *site* has become a fetish object – both in the anthropology of the progressive disappearing, taking for instance Augé's *Non-Lieux* (1992) or Jane Jacobs' iconic *Death and Life of Great American Cities* (1961) and subsequent critiques to the process of gentrification. In contemporary art the same interest arouses – with *Site-Specific* or *Land-Art* usage of place, either in the ethnographic *turn* marked in the 1990s[8] or even with the current obsession with the archive[9].

Returning to "Of Other Spaces", Foucault wants to analyse spaces that have the odd property of being *in connection* with all the others, perhaps even contesting them. They are of two types: utopias and heterotopias. Utopias are *emplacements* by direct or inverted analogy with society, but without real place; "*it is society itself perfected*" (Foucault 1984: 755), or perfected by force as in the case of dystopias. However, they do not exist anywhere. Real spaces *in connection* with other spaces are *heterotopias*.

Foucault unfolds his heterotopology into six principles. The first, *heterotopias of crisis, is found in all cultures, however in its archaic form (Foucault 1984, 756): it is reserved for individuals who are in a state of physical crisis – pregnant women, adolescents, menstruating women, elderly. In societies where one lives in the light of modernity, Foucault sees these heterotopias gradually replaced* by *heterotopias of deviance* (757): specific places where individuals, whose behaviour is not based on normal or healthy behavioural patterns, are targeted.

As a second principle of heterotopias listed by Foucault are those whose meaning suffers mutations through time. The categorization is resumed, and the only example given is the cemetery, which in pre-industrialized societies is located in the heart of the city and in post-industrial societies it is sent to the periphery. The strangest thing is that at the moment when public life is secularized, there is a growing concern with the packing case and the pileup of the individual's body, whereas previously, when the cemetery was in the centre of the city, bodies were commonly buried in mass graves. From here we can shed some more light in a rather elusive dimension: that heterotopias are in fact in a process of constant becoming; they do not crystallize but rather depict themselves as *snapshots* of a current condition. In fact, there is a general illusion of permanence in space, and that is unverifiable. Any attempt to control and fix it led to conflicts.

---

[8] Also manifested in cinema, with Jean Rouch or António Reis's ethnofictions, to name a few. For the aspiration to fieldwork in contemporary arts see Hal Foster' "The Artist as Ethnographer", in which the *novelty of the Art* is based on a *drive* for the cultural context. Cf. H. Foster (1996) «The Artist as Ethnographer» in *The return of the Real: The avant-garde at the end of the century*, The MIT Press.

[9] Cf. Foster (2004): «An Archival Impulse» in October 110, Fall 2004, pp. 3–22.

The third principle is one of the most important parameters to be retained: «The heterotopia has the power to juxtapose in a single real place several places, several emplacements that are in themselves incompatible» (Foucault 1984, 758). In this way works the verticality or the overlapping of several plans, some of them incompatible. It is an important feature when we talk about the new media – as a matter of fact, the example given is the projection rectangle of the cinema (the rectangular screen). But it is also the garden:

«*The garden is a rug where the whole world comes to accomplish its symbolic perfection, and the rug is a sort of garden that is mobile across space*». (Foucault 1984, 758-9)

The fitted carpet is a portable garden ... just as we now carry the whole world inside a smartphone. That is, what the smartphone performs is a technical achievement of what, once, was already trapped in a carpet: the whole world. And so, floating (surfing the internet), just as when one imaginatively does with the flying carpet – a kind of suspension occurs in time. It is possible for the subject to immerse himself in this mobile *micrography* of the world and to mediate the dialectic between the traditional/physical and the symbolic/augmented. However, this kind of mediation is performed by a succession of displacements: as the four parts of the world were displaced within the territory of the garden that constitutes the microcosm, the subject is similarly displaced within the digital landscape that, in a sense, constitutes a treatise on the future of the man/space/information relationship.

In the fourth principle Foucault presents the *heterochronies*, that is, heterotopias that are related to chunks of time. They are suspensions in the experience of temporality, ideally linear. By introducing temporality here, one that is different from space's constitutive term *permanence*, we can propose a different kind of association with human activity: the possibility of ephemeral, ever-changing and variable meanings and the absence of solid conceptions – a limitation that applies in Foucault's Persian traditional garden. Fairs, thematic festivals, fake environments that condense slices of culture, or in pure accumulation, such as libraries and museums. And what about the internet if we think of the cloud as a mega archive?[10] Being both a pedestrian-in-a-cyberpark and an internet-user renders possible a navigation experience through a mega archive while walking in a green public park.

The fifth principle is on the permeability of its limits. Heterotopias are simultaneously isolated and penetrable. *There,* the inside and outside are not stable categories. It is said that you are in a heterotopia, but maybe you are already out of it. Or to access it, one must go through certain rites of passage—one has to decline a password or your identity to enter a certain circle when navigating in the internet. Edward Soja explanation strengthens the connection between heterotopias and non-places. Following Soja, «[...] *implicit in this heterotopian regulation of opening and closing are working*

---

[10] Both, a methodological and technical solution for connecting physical and digital archive with on-site objects had been presented during the international conference of the COST Action TU1306 CyberParks in Valletta/Malta in 2016 and is printed in: Breser, C., Zedlacher, S., Winkler, R. (2017) *The Principle of Geotagging. Cross-linking archival sources with people and the city through digital urban places.* Antoine Zammit and Therese Kenna (Eds): Enhancing Places through Technology. Lisbon: Lusófona University Press, pp. 208–213.

powers, of what Foucault would later describe as "disciplinary technologies" that operate through the social control of space, time, and otherness to produce a certain kind of "normalization"» (Soja 1996: 161). New forms of sensibility and of engagement are shaped and reflected by new media, but they also suppose new and more complex forms of alienation, surveillance and governance.

Finally, Foucault evokes the *heterotopias of compensation*. They have an inclusive function in relation to the space that is left *outside*: sometimes because they *denounce that space itself is also a space of dream and illusion, sometimes because they constitute a progress – which may even be radical. At one extreme, Foucault places the "brothels", at the other the Jesuit villages in the colonies. Then concludes, inconclusively and abruptly, with the example of the ship, a floating piece of space: «[...] the heterotopia par excellence. In civilizations without boats, dreams dry up, espionage replaces adventure, and the police the pirates*» (Foucault 1984: 762), perhaps because when moving along the signifying chain of heterotopia – and thus floating in a space within space – the production of symbols is also challenged. Heterotopia can thus be seen as a signifying supplement for the product of the enhanced interactions between perception and imagination, a mechanism of displacement from the outside: a "tool" to move from fantasy and hallucination to the underlying order of physical space.

Thus, as shown before, heterotopias are an evanescent and non-static terrain. It is a fold in space. A certain ambiguity leaves it opened precisely because it is a combinatory ground. Heterotopias can be read as marginal sites, but only because they threaten to corrupt the closures and certainties of space as a field of continuous and smooth representation. Foucault said in *Les mots et les choses* (1966) that utopia affords consolation due precisely to its *smoothness*[11].

Now, think of the mirror. It is a hybrid terrain, an arch-medium point between utopia and heterotopia – «A placeless place» – hence its utopian characteristics because it «enables me to see myself there where I am not» (Foucault 1984, 754). In addition, it is also a heterotopia because it does present, or practice a counteraction or refusal of the position that I actually occupy (754). The mirror leads us to an ontological inquiry into the nature of the presence, there where the absence is also played. Maybe in the heterotopia of the mirror we can find, radicalizing, the experience of the body in the digital era. Of that hybrid body that sails in *hetero-affection*[12].

2 The Non-place Theory

The attempt to set the «Thirdspace» (Soja 1996) and «Other Spaces» (Foucault 1984) as a Place-Theory regarding *cyberparks* so far, needs – as a counterargument – further the confrontation with the negation of place by itself, as a result of an exponential increase of using technology and human's introversion at the same time. When Marc Augé published his *non-place* theory in 1992, yet at this time the Smartphone had not

[11] Heterotopias disturb because «they secretly undermine language»: they *break, entangle,* desiccate, *hold, contest and undo*, «they dissolve our myths and sterilize the lyricism of our sentences» (Foucault, The Order of Things, p. XIX).

[12] CF. Jacques Derrida (2000) *Le Toucher, Jean-Luc Nancy*, Paris Galilée.

been invented and the Internet had not been opened to commercial use.[13] The conceptual background of this theory could not have been influenced so by these two basic developments for today's use of ICTs. His theory has been recently mentioned in several discussions, but so why is it also important for our reflection on the concepts of cyberparks and the use of ICTs?

One interesting aspect of this theory deals with individualization and introversion as a kind of social change, long before we have got used to our mobile devices and long before a discussion of their impacts on our lives have been critically started. The social roles of such medial apparatuses as well as the question about how they changed our behaviours have to be discussed therefore exhaustively as a next step of a deeper understanding for Augé's theory and for the quality of a cyberpark. The term «supermodernity» (Augé: 1994, 39ff.) arouses to characterize the second half of the 20th century—the increasing excess of objects information and events in time and space. Industrial mass productions led to an ever-growing consuming world, while new mass transport infrastructures changed experience of extension. Non-places, such as highways, supermarkets, airports, etc., are logistical platforms that assist the circulation of subjects and objects. The definition of a non-place however bases mostly on anthropological studies of human behaviours in a network of practices or moving elements in space – mainly based on Michel de Certeau's definition of space (1980). Augé's theory is largely influenced by a delineation of the anthropological term of place, thus its *identity, relations* and *history*. A non-place refers to the absence of these aspects, but mostly by missing recognition of human interactions; there relations are constantly being constituted newly and managed by its «instructions of use»: directions, advices, instructions and prohibitions.

3 Cyberparks as *Non-places*?

The last decades, in a digital landscape in which the materiality and physicality of things give place to the impression drawn from protocol-based representations (computational images, animations or texts), we impose upon space a topological dislocation technique that has, quite literally, a reversible logic. In an interesting way, and from Arnheim's perception-and-response to the analogue stimuli evolving conception, the digital dimension brings in a significant effect on this traditional process retaining at the same time its humanist terms – that is the active and personal aspects found within. The heterotopic displacement, reacting to the loss of the analogue materiality, seems to inaugurate a reversed way: from the observer's responses to data elements, the mind is challenged to construct a posteriori perceptual content in the imaginary register, or better a trace to use a rather influential laconic term for this theoretic study. As mentioned earlier, this content is not as deterministic as its precedent analogous one, but can constantly resurface in alternative versions based on an exchange of conscious and

[13] In 1992 the Internet has just been introduced as the *World Wide Web* the Swiss *Tim Berners-Lee*, for one year, but has been finally opened to commercial use by the *U.S. National Science Foundation (NSF)* only in 1995. The first Smartphone '*Simon Personal Communicator'* has been invented in 1994 by *BellSouth* and *IBM*.

unconscious thought. However, the questions to be asked evenly concerning cyberparks are the following: Are Information and Communication Technologies (ICTs) able to transform non-places into places by enhancing the quality of *identity, relations* and *history*, or inversely do they promote parks becoming non-places? Which roles do ICTs play in the eyes of Augé's 'supermodernity'—do we speak about tools of alienation through reinforced governances or are these tools made for liberating their users through the support of their individualisation as well as their emancipation?

The question of cyberparks becoming a non-place through ICTs leads firstly to a reflection on the conceptual background of Augé's theory. His pre-smartphone and pre-internet understanding of 'supermodernity', obviously seems to be a further step, a superlative of modernity, that is historically influenced by a futuristic understanding of modernity – but with a different connotation. When he speaks about 'supermodernity' as excesses of information, time and space his historical understanding of modernity partially seems to follow the idea of Filippo Tommaso Marinetti – but in a negatively way. In the *'manifesto del futurismo'* of 1909 Marinetti glorifies speed and technologies, and refuses history, moral and any institutional knowledge[14]. Regarding the many different movements of the beginning 20th century, Augé's 'supermodernity' bases just on a reduced and basically negative connoted sight on some social phenomena of what modernity is seen today – as well as just on some (anthropological) aspects of places too.

It is unarguable that industrial progresses have enormously been determining social changes since the 19th century and the digital turn now offers even more by influencing people's behaviours. But what Augé actually does not consider is the existence of neither hybrid nor heterotopic places (Reisinger 2013) and history. So, it might be a difference of understanding for identity-based attributions that could be seen as a consensual appropriation process by the users (Fade: 2008) that were always related to each other what makes it difficult to define such non-places at all. This way of interpretation leads us further to see ICTs not as tools of a supermodern concept any more, that speed up cognitive processes and enlarge extent spatial experiences as an expense of remaining qualities and human interactions. But in this context ICTs serve as intermediaries that do not have any functional role, but constitute within new identities, such as a hybrid identity in a network between users and subjects in place.

4 ICTs as Intermediaries of Hybrid Spaces

Like in physical public open spaces, the space of the CyberParks combines an image or spatial layout with its overlapped information layering into a hybrid construct. However, reminding the anthropological definition of place, that must enclose *identity, relation* or *history*, are ICTs dealing with one of these aspects? Such a dualistic concept of place or non-place tempts us to see technical progresses proportional opposite to

---

[14] Le Figaro, 20th February 1909, pp. 6–8. *"Noi siamo sul promontorio estremo dei secoli[!].. Perchè dovremmo guardarci alle spalle, se vogliamo sfondare le misteriose porte dell'Impossibile? Il Tempo e lo Spazio morirono ieri. Noi viviamo già nell'assoluto, poichè abbiamo già creata l'eterna velocità onnipresente."*

interpersonal progresses, as the following statements: *The use of ICTs prevents us to speak with each other*, or: *The excess amount of virtual offers interferes our social life.* By seeing ICTs as part of an intermediary network, communication has just been shifted to another space, which yet could not be considered by Augé. Ignoring moral assessments of personal interacting - that by the way would be an aspect of a non-place - it should be noticed that ICTs transform a place not into a non-place but into a Hybrid-Space, in which elevated forms of interactions still take place. This alternative understanding for the relation between the technical and the social does not recognise them separately any more. But is this construct an oxymoron?

5 The Possibility of an *Experienced* Hybrid-place

Hybrid places as described above have become part of the cultural development not only of our public open spaces' heritage but also of our own elevated mechanisms of thinking and understanding space and place. The rising number of online cutting-edge technologies that undertake the task of dislocating place from the analogue of coordinate relations to the digital landscape and virtual reality of categorical relations[15] is a demonstration of this mode of hybrid terrain. The analogue of space, being a park or a square, is a timeless patrimony. It is a constitutive dimension that seems to deeply preserve itself to heterotopia as an *engenderment* of the materiality and physicality of its form. It is the traditional medium, Foucault's Persian garden in other words, by which the logic of space's symbolic systems in the poetic world of Gaston Bachelard, are transformed into material variations, allowing thus the reasoning human mind be attached to the sensible world. The analogue is the forefather; that necessary element which social aspects are tied up with in order to lend themselves to further dialectical investigations that extend beyond the practical function of space's form. It is the common starting point from which we are infused in even more complex conceptions of either geometric or symbolic order - to mention one example, Rudolf Arnheim's symbolic readings of forms seized upon the field of the analogue and its visual qualities as a way to project them "as images of the human condition" instead. The relation between the technical and the human seems an oxymoron. But a more careful approach can remove this arbitrary viewpoint. The question about the oxymoron blending and the roles of ICTs in cyberparks as tools of alienation through reinforced governances or for liberating people through the support of their individualisation and emancipation can be answered shortly by defining those medial apparatuses as intermediaries that change our identities to hybrid identities in place for which we cannot speak about non-places any more. But we can talk about places neither! In a 'modern' way of thinking - that might refer to futuristic concepts too - we would have seen ICTs influencing our behaviours and enhancing the quality of places. (Super)modernity as increasing excesses of information, time and space has become suitable for the separation of time

[15] Support for the workings of the coordinate and categorical relations as well as their correspondences to the analogue and digital can be found in studies on the representation of the visual information in subject's mind. See *Hugdahl and Westerhausen. (2010). The Two Halves of the Brain: Information Processing in the Cerebral Hemispheres*: MIT Press.

and space, the separation of nature and technology, the social and the non-social. In a non-modern way (Latour 1997) that ontologically does not distinguish between human beings and non-human beings, between natures and technologies we see them constantly creating new, hybrid identities. In exclusion of a (super-)modern understanding that differences between the social, technology and nature it is difficult not to overcome the awareness of being governed through one of those actors. When Latour speaks about the missing possibility of controlling 'the other', such as the other (virtual) space, the other culture or even the changing climate as a common challenge (Latour 1997, p. 192), we are asked to reassemble what modernity divided. Then we definitely cannot see ICTs as separate tools with a mandate for directions, advices, instructions and prohibitions too, but as parts of new common identities that are not governed nor by the user neither by technology.

In this way a cyberpark is neither a place nor non-Place but a *hybrid-place*, where *relations, history* or *identity* are constantly being constituted newly by a consensual appropriation process between all the actors – humans and non-humans. This emerging form of appropriation can be seen as the human's dateless quest for meaning and reason – within the hybrid form itself this time. It does not matter if there is Internet or a smart phone available. Neither technology nor nature enhance the quality of place nor increase possibilities for human interactions so. Interactions and thus the assessment for increasing the quality of places can accordingly start with a differentiated understanding for the roles of nature and technology, that see them not as parts of a common space but as parts of a common identity that create non-dualistic networks including hybrid or even heterotopic places too.

Nowadays, ICT mediated formations are useful dimensions to outdoor experience. They can certainly be seen, on one hand, as "decorative follies" for the public open space, but, on the other, they work in the field of emerging and new forms of topos' sense. From the previous, it became noticed that the distinction between the *Euclidean* space and the *Hetero* topos was critically touched by Foucault. From this starting line and point of view, technologically mediated spaces as hybrid terrains function differently from Euclidean spaces. A critical approach beyond the utilitarian features of outdoor digitally accessed and retrieved information and an exploration on the influence of such features on *what remains after* the end of the experience – that is, the memory of hybrid spaces – seems to become a necessary tool in understanding the range of a cyberpark as mediated spaces *beyond* their Euclidean discipline and as relevant to the meanings constructed and apprehended during their spatial experience.

6 Conclusion

Here, we have to admit that the above question made already a valuable contribution to the previous discourse on non-place; and now will continue to preserve its immense value within this last one. It somehow shows that meaning-ascription, being an intrinsic part of the mnemonic function of human experience, retains a significant role to hybrid spaces as well. A cyberpark, as all other similar immaterial artefacts that feed from virtuality and the digital dimension, cannot escape from it. Moreover, a cyberpark will use meaning ascription regularly.

While from 2014 to 2018 the TU1306 CyberParks Network envisioned the future of open green spaces, the possibility of introducing their heterotopic dimension has been considered either through the Euclidean perspective (in which it makes little sense) or simply taken at the word of ICT developers and programmers. The possibility of a cyberpark to carry and construct different kinds of meanings as compared, at least, to the analogue space itself contains a plethora of heterotopic undertones, or as it is sometimes argued, *supermodern potential*, that needs to be further explored. The Network suggested that human, space and digital environment can perfectly co-exist; and that the contact between them can extend far beyond the narrow field of "seeing" and "perceiving". This is a phenomenological plane initially sketched out by the TU1306 Network acknowledging that many of the aspects out of CyberParks intermediary network are issues submerged to a mneme/meaning dialectic. They are interpretative entities of the lived, perceived and conceived hybrid reality. We thus claim that cyberparks are, in a sense, symbol-systems themselves giving "*concrete expression to concepts of values, meanings and the like*" (Rapoport 1977: 192) through technology.

The COST Action CyberParks attempted to explore further the argument that the intermediary dimension of such systems has practical applications in the design strategy for experiencing non-places pertaining to questions like ''can mediated places deliver up a meaning?" or ''can digital landscapes conciliate symbolic signs with peculiar urbanistic issues?" Questions whose answers are not useful to be presented dogmatically here, but at least were implied by the structural technique of the *apparatus* itself. Resorting to Ricoeur (2004), cyberparks are, after all, nothing but symbols in a fundamental level, which are systems of relationships that relate the human condition with space and elements of the digital and immaterial world.

The digital moment has passed. Roy Ascott

References

Augé, M.: Non-lieux. Introduction à une anthropologie de la surmodernite. Éd. du Seuil, Paris (1994)

Bachelard, G.: The Poetics of Space. Beacon Press, Boston (1994)

Cresswell, T.: Place: A Short Introduction. Blackwell, Oxford (2004)

De Certeau, M.: L'Invention du Quotidien, vol. 1. Arts de Faire, Paris (1980)

Foucault, M.: Dits et écrits: 1954–1988, vol. IV, pp. 752–762. Gallimard, Paris (1994)

Latour, B.: Nous n'avons jamais été modernes. Essai d'anthropologie symétrique. Éditions La Découverte & Syros, Paris (1997)

Le Figaro, 20th February 1909, pp. 6–8. "Noi siamo sul promontorio estremo dei secoli!.. Perchè dovremmo guardarci alle spalle, se vogliamo sfondare le misteriose porte dell'Impossibile? Il Tempo e lo Spazio morirono ieri. Noi viviamo già nell'assoluto, poichè abbiamo già creata l'eterna velocità onnipresente."

Rapoport, A.: Human Aspects of Urban Form: Towards a Man-Environment Approach to Urban Form and Design. Pergamon Press, New York (1977)

Reisinger, N.: Vom Stationsplatz zur Shopping Mall. Der Bahnhof als Ausdruck eines veränderten Lebensgefühls. In: Morscher, L., Scheutz, M., Schuster, W. (Hrsg.) Orte der Stadt im Wandel vom Mittelalter zur Gegenwart. Beiträge zur Geschichte der Städte Mitteleuropas, vol. 24, pp. 313–329. StudienVerlag, Wien, S. (2013)

Ricoeur, P.: The Rule of Metaphor. Routledge, New York (2004)

Soja, E.: Thirdspace: Journeys to Los-Angeles and Other Real-and-Imagined Places. Blackwell, Oxford (1996)

1.3

Cybercities: Mediated Public Open Spaces - A Matter of Interaction and Interfaces

Stefan Zedlacher[1(✉)], Anna Khromova[2], Eva Savina Malinverni[2], and Preben Hansen[3]

[1] Institute of Art History, University Graz, Graz, Austria
office@zedlacher.at

[2] Facoltà di Ingegneria, Università Politecnica delle Marche, Ancona, Italy
khromova.anyu@gmail.com, e.s.malinverni@univpm.it

[3] Department of Computer and Systems Sciences (DSV), Stockholm University, Stockholm, Sweden
preben@dsv.su.se

Abstract. In the near past, sources of information about public open spaces were: people, the place itself and historical archives. Accordingly, the information could be obtained by interviewing the visitors, by reading some poorly equipped signs on monuments or by research in libraries. Today, a new source appeared: The place itself covers its own information by the mean of the growing of the ICT (Information Communication Technologies). In addition, the information can be personalised in a way each people can access it individually. Ten years ago, a left-over newspaper on a park bench was a compact piece of information. Today, the newspaper resides on a smartphone in our pockets. In the future, the park bench will still be there, but dramatically changed to an IoT (Internet of things) object, bringing information to the people. Therefore, there is the need to re-think the park bench as an interface. A simple, fundamental point is: the quality of the interface rules the quality of the information. With a special focus on the latter, this chapter discusses how the classical model of the city is enhanced with the senseable city concept and how digital information influences, adopts, transforms and re-configures different objects in urban areas.

Keywords: Mediated spaces · Interfaces · Design methods · Senseable city

1 Introduction

In his 2002 motion picture Minority Report, based on the same name novel by Philip K. Dick from 1990, the director Steven Spielberg leads his main actor through a public open space (POS). In this 20-seconds scene, the actor gets, while escaping from prison, a lot of personalised advertising while the people around him are informed that he is a volatile criminal. The whole place with its infrastructure (screens, entrances, etc.) seems to be real-time responsive to the (fictional) situation - even to the operations elsewhere, shown in the scenes before and after. The phenomenon is the change of the POS to an innovative cyber one, in agreement to new concepts like smart city (Gibson et al. 1992;

C. Smaniotto Costa et al. (Eds.): CyberParks, LNCS 11380, pp. 25–37, 2019.
https://doi.org/10.1007/978-3-030-13417-4_3

Hollands 2008). To answer the question "Which interactions is a POS in Cyber Cities capable for?", the analysis of city planning processes is a good starting point.

2 Theoretical Framework

In agreement with the vision shared by George Kubler in his book "The shape of time" the city design can be interpreted as a series of ideas in the history of human thinking, divided into four groups (Barnett 2016): Modern city design (Chandigarh), Traditional city design (Rome, Paris), Green city design (Surabaya) and System city design (Dubai). The main idea is that these listed concepts are not opposed to each other or mutually exclusive, rather they interplay with each other, being each one periodically more or less important (according to the duty of the project).

2.1 The Intelligent City Concept

The intelligent city concept is incorporated in the smart city, e.g. a city that is affected by technology, and also the self-organising city, which is without technologies but has a strong flexibility of the urban structure. The paradigm of smart city concept is based on interlacing the technological systems and human intelligence with the aim of better results and improved productivity. In the intelligent city concept, two types of approach can be identified: the top-down and the bottom-up. Both of them are aimed to support human needs by the mean of technology, but while the first one proposes solutions coming from the head of any organisation centre, the second one directly comes from the final users. Both types of systems have four components: Sensors, Collected data, Predictive models and Interfaces.

Here, a main difference between fiction and the real world arises: The fictional story from the introduction only takes the top-down city-concept in account. Talking about the top-down approach, the target is organising urban facilities in the cities to get better response for collective needs (energy management system, traffic control and incident management). The Bjork Ingals Group proposed to BMW to organise a competition having the title: The city of the futures (B. I. Group 2017). The winner of the project presented how people and cars can share space without frightening each other. The intelligence resides both in the vehicle and in the environment through sensors and lightning. Basically, the self-driving car informs the environment about its intentions, e.g. to sensors hidden in the pavement. Then, the latter creates a safe zone called area of influence for pedestrians, where no vehicles are allowed to enter. It has to be remarked how such a smart streets concept can make public open spaces safer for citizen. Passing to the bottom-up approach, it can be sufficient to integrate intelligent systems, that make the city perform better, instead of fundamentally rethinking the city design. Interfaces are the key component for this integration. Bottom-up examples like Copenhagen Wheel (Superpedestrian 2018) or Stuttgart's Luftdaten (2018) demonstrates that it is not necessary to adjust the city with new static sensors. Equipment that are already around (bicycles, clothes, baskets) could be used for data collecting process as a Mobile Sensors. Additionally, equipping bicycles with sensors effectively turns a city into an interface that collects data in real-time. The integration of such kind of bottom-up intelligence in the city and its surfaces could upgrade the quality of citizen life.

The paradigm of Self-organising city concept performs a kind of urban play-ground where planners use techniques that don't impose a preconceived plan: the citizen freely share their ideas and projects with each other and, mostly important, with planners. The city is seen as an organism that doesn't need to follow any human master plan for growing and functioning. The role of the planners is to guide the existing self-organising concepts in the urban environment. Tracing back this concept to the idea of Metabolism in the '60s, a Japanese group of architects (e.g. Kisho Kurokawa's Helix City Project) fused ideas about architectural mega-structures with those of organic biological growth (taking inspiration from the recently discovered DNA). Continuing the chronological time-line, the Hungarian architect Yona Friedman made his contribution in designing a mobile architecture that he called a Spatial Infrastructure (Friedman 1956). In that experimental project the user plays a key role in the city design process. The citizen was allowed to freely use the mobile city's structural system according to his needs and wishes, which is perfectly in line with the self-organising city concept. In the same period the rising of cybernetics in the field of communication and technology impacted on the architects' methods and visions (Pask 1969). The main concept is based on the notion that intelligence lies in its capacity to learn from feedbacks. That new vision shifts the role of planner in the design process and opens the necessity to bring new technologies that can help machines to react to a real-time stimulus. By applying this concept to the planning process, an interesting question arises: Could the cities and their buildings learn from their usage and auto-correct themselves into an optimal configuration and anticipating future uses? Also, computer programmes as the SimCity series games (Jonathan Burnett) or the MVRDV Function-mixer (Hartog 2006) shown a good example of how technologies bring new visions in urban planning. The virtual simulation of urban environment explores the use of computer-generated scenarios for having a support in taking decisions and planning solutions. This involvement helps people, municipalities and communities to find optimal configurations. But, projects from the intelligent (smart) concepts are mainly top-down and ignoring the existence of interfaces at all. Although they have sensors, predictive models and collected data which are also parts of the fictional city concept from Minority Report.

2.2 The Cyborg-Society and the Senseable City Concept

"*Permit man's existence in environments which differ radically from those provided by nature as we know it*" (Clynes and Kline 1960: 29–33) was the starting point for rethinking the concept of the human body and its extensions and possibilities. This new way of thinking gave the perspective for the first cyborg project: "*cyborg is a hybrid capable of more than either the biological or the mechanical system alone can do, with a correspondingly expanded range of possible habitation*" (Ratti and Claudel 2016: 42–49). The tools and all innovations people have been aware, allowing humanity to survive in extreme conditions that they otherwise could never adapt. Serving as an additional option to the biological presence defines us as a kind of cyborg. "*Human progress was marked by the gradual externalization of functions, from stone knives and axes that extended the capacity of the hand to the externalization of mental functions with the computer.*" (Picon 2004: 114–121). If in the past the innovations were created as an enhancement of the physical body, today they are mainly used as an extension of the possibilities of the mind: "… *digital technologies have become a dynamic extension of our bodies and minds, demanding a constant and two-way cybernetic exchange in a way that our traditional (one-way) extensions, such as clothing or axes, have never done*" (Ratti and Claudel 2016: 42–49). Interesting aspects appeared, as the deep natural involvement of technological system into human environment. "*We […] are provided with two types of bodies … the real body which is linked with the real world by means of fluids running inside, and the virtual body linked with the world by the flow of electrons*" (Ito 1997: 132). Smartphones became the strongest connection between the two bodies and so recognised as an interface. It additionally extends humans memory and logical capacities in such a marked way that the person is not considered a simple human anymore but kind of an upgraded version of it: a post-human. "*A new entity that is born with technology rather than acquiring it … where each individual's mental and social existence is enable, sustained and improved by technologies.*" (Ratti and Claudel 2016: 42–49).

The main technology mentioned are the so-called smart-devices. They are changing the way people think about a city and its infrastructure in a radical way: thanks to the rising of digital networks what before was passive is now active, so every aspect of an urban reality should now be able to be interfaced with smartphones. In simple words, a modern city should give the post-humans an environment suitable for them. With the rising of smart-devices still both methods from the intelligent city in the senseable city concepts, could be found. But with different notion:

- Tracking as the top-down method where the information is gathered and visualized for decision-makers, stakeholder, city council or researcher (Ratti et al. 2007).
- Interaction as the bottom-up example with, e.g. QR codes (Foth et al. 2015). The interaction includes human to human, human to companies (marketing) or authorities (information) or human to machine while the layer that carries the QR code is differently (i.e. cloths, streets, buildings, etc.)

The senseable city concept pushes further the interactivity of this innovative way of thinking about POS. In a short period, places became a breathing, living entity acting on a large-scale with the inhabitants (what we previously defined as cyborgs). The latter will create, plug into and interact with this new entity, and so, digital spaces will be naturally interacted and above all spontaneously born onto POS. This reality was, among others, mentioned and explained by Mark Weiser, ac-cording to which the interfaces would find no places anymore since everything will be intimately absorbed into the city. Allowing then a complete merging between the digital and the physical spaces a "*new way of thinking about computers in the world, one that takes into account the natural human environment and allows the computers themselves to vanish into the background.*" (Weiser 1991: 1). Another realisation of the senseable city concept can be found in the so-called boards, e.g. interactive screens disseminated all along the cities (Fig. 1) where POS infrastructure are transformed into intercommunicating interfaces, away from smart-phones. Basically, these new generation billboards are in effect web browser applications capable of all the tracking and advertising functionalities known from any desktop website. So, what was oriented towards a single user before is now becoming public: a desktop browser turns to a public display where advertises take place, all integrated into the POS. This scene of the 2002's Minority Report became reality.

In summary, the senseable city concept can be resumed as the "*Technology recedes into the background, and interaction is brought to the fore. Buildings and public open spaces can be simple-rather than voluptuous and shocking – but even more integrally vibrant and living*" (Ratti and Claudel 2016: 62–73).

Fig. 1. Graz city information terminals (Source: authors. 2017)

3 Interaction Design and Interfaces

Although, as widely discussed in the previous sections, the city of the future completely neglects the necessity of having an interface between citizen and spaces (since the digital and the physical domains are perfectly interlaced between each other), nowadays they still are of fundamental importance since the progress is still making the first steps toward such reality. A brief overview of the basic concepts of interactions and of the various kinds of interfaces will been given in the present section.

3.1 Basic Concepts of Interaction

One of the aims of interaction design is to create an interface that makes efficient and user-friendly for a user to interact, operate and manage a digital or physical electronic device. Basically, this means that there should be some kind of input to achieve the desired output. Within interaction, there are several crucial and important concepts that need to be considered in a design process, in which the interaction between a human and a device (physical or digital) is a vital component. Interaction and design for interaction in physical or blended (Benyon 2014: 420–425) POS may also be viewed and understood as explicit interaction or implicit interaction. Explicit interaction usually builds on the classical desktop screen-based interaction metaphor. This often result in that the human need to cope with different technological issues in order to achieve a certain goal. In contrast, implicit interaction design puts the human in the foreground and the technology in the background. These are important aspects of interaction in (blended) mediated spaces since that may have the possibility to entangle and embed into our daily activities in both urban and rural environments. Some important concepts are that may apply to design of POS, mediated or not:

- **Dynamics** – This concept refers to indications of current and changing modes and states and how a device, components or system adapts to different contexts, situations, tasks, people etc. (Buxton 2010; Löwgren and Stolterman 2004).
- **Temporality** – It refers to the concept of time. In design it can concern, for example, the extension over time, the duration of an interaction, the immediacy of the interaction activity, the delays and pauses within an interaction, the segmentations of an interaction, the separation and connection of several interaction sequences, the pace and rhythm of an interaction, and the periodicity (Buxton 2010; Löwgren and Stolterman 2004).
- **Interactivity** – The interactivity generally refers to how users and (digital and physical) artefacts initiate and respond to different actions including action openings, turn-taking by humans but also by tasks of a device, and closures (Löwgren and Stolterman 2004).
- **Sequentiality** – One very important aspect of designing for interaction refers to how interactions are ordered and structured; the flow of different actions and tasks to be accomplished, how courses of events are planned and how much freedom, control, guidance, support etc. are built into activities with the service, components or system (Benyon 2014; Löwgren 2002).
- **Context of use** – This concept refers to placing the planned activities, objects, services or system in specific social and physical contexts which exemplify the artefact in use (Gedenryd 1998; Ozenc et al. 2010; Suchman 1985).

Different interaction design qualities are defined by Lim et al. (2007: 246) as something that appears only in (inter)action: "*The interaction gestalt also has to be designed in a way that will evoke the desired user experiences. The designer has to anticipate how a certain gestalt will be experienced by a user, and that anticipation has to be translated back into ideas on how the gestalt should be shaped*". In interaction design in general, Lim et al. (2007) define different qualities that may apply for the context and situation in which people interact in POS. The authors also talk about the "*…the interaction gestalt…*" that it need to be considered and approached in the design process as well. The "gestalt" is very important since it is to evoke the desired user experience. This means that the designer needs to anticipate how users in a POS can experience a certain gestalt. So, when designing for interactions, this anticipation needs to be translated back into ideas on how a "gestalt" should be shaped and formed. Löwgren (2002) proposes to think about interaction design in terms of specific use qualities. Use qualities are certain properties of a digital design that are experienced in its use situation or context. According to the author, such qualities transcend the specific design. At the same time, it offers a certain language to be used when talking about design. Furthermore, the author suggests a set of qualities that design of public open spaces needs to consider: motivation, interaction per se, social aspects of the object or systems, structural qualities, meaning-making.

3.2 Types of Interfaces

The role of a user interface is to give to the final user a dedicated platform to control generic software (that, in turn, has been defined on hardware). Although in the recent past the concept of interface was limited to the engineering world, nowadays, thanks to the use of sensors in multiple fields (applications in medicine, architecture, landscape planning etc.), it has to be used and understood in a broader meaning. The way users interact with interfaces depends on the interface in use. While the most common one has been for decades the simple textual command line interface, nowadays a huge variety of interfaces are available, where all the senses of the human body have been exploited. Generally speaking, the available kinds of interfaces are:

- **Voice User Interface (VUI)** - In this first kind of interface, the human voice is the vehicle through which the information is carried from the user to the software. Various challenges are currently being addressed in the developing of such interfaces, all more or less related to the voice recognition issue, that allows a more functional voice-controlled interface. In turn, the interaction re-quired with this kind of interface is quite natural since it doesn't require any-thing else than the vocal command of the user.
- **Tangible User Interface (TUI)** - As the name suggests, this kind of interface is based on a physical medium that stands between the user and the software. The latter can be a door, a spoon, or in general an available object in an urban space. Although the TUIs are relatively new, numerous examples can be found in museums, architecture (Wang et al. 2017a), furniture and clothing, and this remarks the importance of such a kind of interface. An interesting aspect regards the experience that the user gets from the just introduced interface: the more playful and active way of interacting facilitates a more creative and learning effect (Wang et al. 2017b).
- **Natural User Interface (NUI)** - While a TUI exploits tangible objects to create a way of communication between the software and the user, a NUI reaches the same result making use of gesture (Li et al. 2016) and eye-interaction. This results in a more natural way of interacting.
- **Brain Computer Interface (BCI)** - Finding its place in the borderline of the scientific progress, the BCI is probably the most interesting and appealing kind of interface that can be found today. The interaction between the user and the software is here carried out by the mean of electric impulses running through the brain and collected by the mean of electrodes. The BCI will make possible to control robotic arms, machines etc. in a large variety of application areas (medical, industrial, etc.).

Such kind of innovation will, in addition, help many people with disabilities in improving their life in a huge number of situations.

- **Cross-Object User Interfaces (COUI)** - Cross-objects user interfaces is a literally new term that describes user interfaces spatially distributed across object surfaces in the physical world and the virtual reality in a similar way. In contrast to tangible user interfaces, COUIs are inhabited in physical or virtual objects in flexible ways and are compatible with multiple and different interaction methods (Sun et al. 2018; Li et al. 2017).

Starting with the smartphone in the previous chapter we hopefully verified with this chapter the huge variety of possible interfaces for the POS. In the next chapter we combine the city design methods mentioned, the types of interfaces and the evolution of POS to a possible explanation.

4 The Ternary Structure of a POS and Its Scientific Rationalities Interpretation

According to the city design methods previously explained, the reality of a POS has changed over the last decades. They are not interpreted as physical spaces, but rather as entities that embrace different dimensions into the same system. In fact, according to the vision of Stanley Milgram (Milgram et al. 1992), space is made not only of physical characteristics, but it has also a mental image that lives in human mind. One step further in Philip K. Dick's vision from Minority Report, it is a visual, digital representation of an individual view on a common base (the POS).

A simple yet effective way to describe POS is the ternary system of Nature, Culture and Geist (Khromova et al. 2016), where:

- Nature is the environment in its essential form, i.e. without any human interference.
- Culture is any expression of human's creativity, that can be differentiated into tangible (materials and artefacts) and intangible (values, traditions, beliefs, etc.).
- Geist is the source of human's creativity itself; it defines human's goals, objectives and lines of action that modify the nature towards the realization of what we defined culture (Fig. 2).

To understand this complex approach of POS, the three-different kind of scientific rationalities (Stepin 2008) will be introduced: the classical, non-classical and post-non-classical. The first kind of scientific rationality, the classical rationality, deals with what we may call simple systems, where all properties of its parts define the whole system. They are delimited against external components like space and time and their elements are causal deterministic. Such systems are essentially a mechanical combination of their components, whose interactions are completely neglected. Essentially, "*the classic rationality approach analyses it by simply considering the properties of its different sections for then adding them up together to get the global overview of the set*" (Khromova 2018: 28–33). For example, McLuhan's (1964) vision of a social system made only of unidirectional interaction between the mass of people and the source of

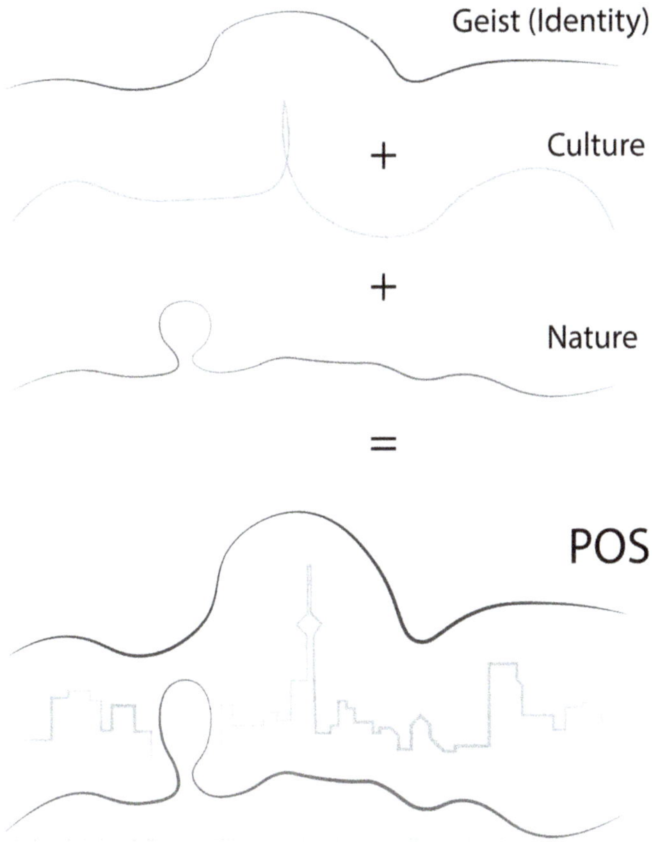

Fig. 2. The public spaces ternary structure: Geist, Culture and Nature (Source: authors)

information (as television or radio) is efficiently described by the mean of the just introduced first kind of rationality.

When dealing with large systems including autonomous subsystem having a huge number of interactions between each other, the classical rationality approach becomes obsolete. It leads to the second kind of scientific rationality, the non-classical. With an integrated "control-block" the system has a build in feed-back loop for its elements and subsystems. The feedback of each element runs into a simple programme whose output determines the behaviour of the system. This ongoing reproduction of organised elements could be found in society (social objects), nature (organisms) or populations of any kind. The whole is more than its individual parts. A multicellular organism provides one of the best examples of a right application of the non-classical rationality. Nowadays design of POS is strongly related to the non-classical rationality concepts since the aim in creating harmony by considering all the components of the POS itself (Khromova 2018).

The last kind of scientific rationality, defined as post-non-classical, relates to systems evolving themselves through self-regulating. This kind of system is "characterized by the development that leads from one self-regulation type to another. Each newly developed level causes back effects on earlier formed ones and restructures them, the system thus acquires a new integrity. The system changes as new levels emerge, with new relatively autonomous subsystems being formed there. Openness, exchange of energy and information with the surrounding are key attributes of complex, self-developing systems. A modern city with its services exemplifies it. The self-regulating aspect is represented by the huge variety of different agencies such as the communal office, the land registry office, services for the city, etc., whose usefulness would vanish without a proper interaction with all other public authorities such as health services, police stations, etc. The post-non-classical rationality finds its applications in many recent projects aimed to update the city. One of the best examples is given by the Futurecraft project (Ratti and Claudel 2016), where planners don't provide anymore a fixed, pre-conceived and so strict indication about what their vision of the city-design of the future will be. Basically, conditions, scenarios and consequences are shared and discussed. This method supports public debates and spreads ideas and alternatives where people construct new values and guides to POS design. By turning classical design of urban space upside-down, planners (not exclusively) called this approach mutations. Such mutations will then grow, evolve and finally end up in creating tangible artefacts (pre-interfaces) in the reality of the city. An example implementing the post-non-classical method is the Trash Track project from MIT senseable city lab, "*where cheap tags equipped with GPS localization are applied to rubbish and a full-scale urban demonstration was created to test it. As a result, subsequent discussion and debate has led to systemic improvements by waste management companies, start-up companies that produce trash trackers, and, most importantly, citizens where inspired to reduce waste and to recycle*" (Ratti and Claudel 2016). Switching back to our topic of interest, a synergetic urban landscape like a POS equipped with ICT may be represented by the post-non-classical scientific rationality.

One should also notice that, according to what has been said and to the examples that has been given, the three proposed approaches for describing and interpreting a generic system don't abolish nor replace each other. Contrarily to what one can think, the post-non-classical vision, although clearly more complete in respect to the classic one, is not always the best choice since sometimes its complexity can be completely avoided, resulting in a much immediate and practical interpretation of the system under investigation.

5 Conclusions

With the ternary system of public spaces, the co-existence of bottom-up and top-down methods in senseable city systems are proven. Which one of the scientific rationalities (between the classic, non-classic and post-non-classic) is more suitable to a POS equipped with ICT strongly depends on the attitude of the planner. This fact also remarks how each new type of rationality doesn't imply the rejection of the previous one, but only completes our set of tools for analysing any kind of system, from the simplest ones (where the classic kind of rationality is preferred) to the more complex ones (where the post-non-classical is often the right choice). The tools could be part of the interfaces.

Currently, interfaces that support tracking and interaction are not reduced to smartphone. Rather they harness IoT and possibly change to tools for analysing and interaction. We have also shown that the interfaces, beside mobile devices, are deeply underdeveloped in their usage for a cyberpark, compared with their possibilities. But, comparing Mark Weiser's vision for computer[s] for the 21st century (Weiser 1991), the have developed further. The way disseminating information from the cyberspace to the user, i.e. the interfaces and their different types, is being a real-time connection between city-planner and all the other components of the cyber-area. The role of city-planners (and their computers!) in a senseable city has to be redefined.

Further work has also to be done in order to deeply investigate what may be the weak points of the conception of cyberparks, such as the growing information pollution and peoples experience with the (digital) urban environment. According to that, the political structures and decision-making process must be updated to a real-time information system. Therefore, additional efforts should also be put in realizing a structure where individuals can choose how much they want to be involved in the cyber dimension, according their needs and comfort. The ground level for this structure could be the total absence of the cyber interaction and a balanced synergy between personal will and pre-built scenarios. Realtime, reactive POS, by the way described in the beginning, are possible, but nevertheless they lack the connection between their users, their inherent systematics and the quality of interfaces. Minority Report with the vision of Philip K. Dick is only a shadow of today's capabilities.

References

B. I. Group, 17 September 2017. http://audi-urban-future-initiative.com/blog/bjarke-ingels-group. Accessed 21 Aug 2017

Barnett, J.: City Design: Modernist, Traditional, Green and Systems Perspectives. Routledge, New York (2016)

Benyon, D.: Designing Interactive Systems: A Comprehensive Guide to HCI and Inter-Action Design. Addison Wesley, Harlow (2014)

Buxton, B.: Sketching User Experiences: Getting the Design Right and the Right Design. Morgan Kaufmann, San Francisco (2010)

Clynes, M.E., Kline, N.S.: Cyborgs and space. Astronautics **14**(9), 26–27 (1960)

Foth, M., Brynskov, M., Ojala, T.: Citizen's Right to the Digital City: Urban Interfaces, Activism, and Placemaking. Springer, Singapore (2015). https://doi.org/10.1007/978-981-287-919-6

Friedman, Y.: (1956). http://www.yonafriedman.nl/?page_id=225. Accessed 13 May 2018

Gedenryd, H.: How Designers Work - Making Sense of Authentic Cognitive Activities. Cognitive Science, Lund (1998)

Gibson, D.V., Kozmetsky, G., Raymond, W., Smilor, R.W.: Smart Cities, Fast Systems, Global Networks. The Technopolis Phenomenon. Rowman & Littlefield, Lanham (1992)

Hollands, R.G.: Will the real smart city please stand up? City **12**(3), 303–320 (2008)

Hartog de, H.: MVRDVs 3D urban design, 10 November 2006. https://www.archined.nl/2006/10/mvrdv%C2%92s-3d-urban-design. Accessed 3 May 2017

Ito, T.: Tarzans in the media forest. In: 2G, no. 2, p. 132 (1997)

Khromova, A., et al.: Is the mediated public open space a smart place? Relationships between urban landscapes and ICT, The Cost Action TU 1306 CyberParks. SCIRES-IT (SCIentific RESearch) and Information Technology, pp. 17–28 (2016)

Khromova, A.: Are the Urban Parks becoming Cyberparks? The Developing of Public Open Spaces: ICT tools to support the landscape planning process (Unpublished thesis) UNIVPM (2018)

Li, X.A., Hansen, P., Lou, X., Geng, W., Peng, R.: Design and evaluation of cross-objects user interface for whiteboard interaction. In: Streitz, N., Markopoulos, P. (eds.) DAPI 2017. LNCS, vol. 10291, pp. 180–191. Springer, Cham (2017). https://doi.org/10.1007/978-3-319-58697-7_13

Li, X.A., Lou, X., Hansen, P., Peng, R.: On the influence of distance in the interaction with large displays. IEEE J. Disp. Technol. **12**(8), 840–850 (2016)

Lim, Y., Stolterman, E., Jung, H., Donaldson, J.: Interaction gestalt and the design of aesthetic interactions. In: Proceedings of the 3rd Conference on Designing Pleasurable Products and Interfaces, pp 239–254. ACM Press, New York (2007)

Löwgren, J., Stolterman, E.: Thoughtful Interaction Design - A Design Perspective on Information Technology. The MIT Press, Cambridge (2004)

Löwgren, J.: The use qualities of digital designs. complete draft 1.0, 21 October 2002. http://citeseerx.ist.psu.edu/viewdoc/download?doi=10.1.1.196.4873&rep=rep1&type=pdf. Accessed 13 June 2018

Luftdaten, 12 January 2018. https://luftdaten.info. Accessed 23 May 2018

McLuhan, M.: Understanding Media: The Extensions of Man. McGraw-Hill Book Company, New York (1964)

Milgram, S., Sabini, J.E., Silver, M.E.: The Individual in a Social World: Essays and Experiments. McGraw-Hill Book Company, New York (1992)

Ozenc, F.K., Kim, M., Zimmermann, J., Oney, S., Myers, B.: How to support designers in getting hold of the immaterial material of software. In: Proceedings of the 28th Annual CHI Conference on Human Factors in Computing Systems, Atlanta, Georgia, 10–15 April, pp. 2513–2522 (2010)

Pask, G.: The architectural relevance of cybernetics. Architectural Design, September issue No 7/6, 494–496 (1969)

Picon, A.: Architecture and the virtual: towards a new materiality? Praxis **6**, 114–121 (2004)

Ratti, C., Claudel, M.: The City of Tomorrow: Sensors, Networks, Hackers, and the Future of Urban Life. Yale University Press, New Haven (2016)

Ratti, C., Sevtsuk, A., Huang, S., Pailer, R.: Mobile landscapes: graz in real time. In: Gartner, G., Cartwright, W., Peterson, M.P. (eds.) Location Based Services and TeleCartography. Lecture Notes in Geoinformation and Cartography, pp. 433–444. Springer, Heidelberg (2007). https://doi.org/10.1007/978-3-540-36728-4_31

Stepin, V.S.: Types of systems and types of scientific rationality. SATS **9**, 27–43 (2008)

Suchman, L.A.: Plans and Situated Actions - The Problem of Human Machine Communication. Xerox, Palo Alto (1985)

Sun, L., Zhou, Y., Hansen, P., Geng, W., Li, X.: Cross-objects user interfaces for video interaction in virtual reality museum context. Int. J. Multimedia Tools Appl. May 2018 (2018, forthcoming). https://doi.org/10.1007/s11042-018-6091-5

Superpedestrian, 21 March 2018. https://www.superpedestrian.com/tech. Accessed 5 June 2018

Wang, Y., Luo, S., Liu, S., Lu, Y., Hansen, P.: Crafting concrete as a material for enhancing meaningful interactions. In: Kurosu, M. (ed.) HCI 2017. LNCS, vol. 10271, pp. 634–644. Springer, Cham (2017a). https://doi.org/10.1007/978-3-319-58071-5_48

Wang, Y., et al.: AnimSkin: fabricating epidermis with interactive, functional and aesthetic color animation. In: Mival, O., Smyth, M., Dalsgaards, P. (eds). Proceedings of the 2017 Conference on Designing Interactive systems, Edinburgh, UK, pp. 397–401 (2017b)

Weiser, M.: The computer for the 21st century. Sci. Am. **265**(3), 94–104 (1991)

1.4

Liveable Open Public Space - From Flaneur to Cyborg

Aleksandra Djukic[1(✉)], Thanos Vlastos[2], and Viera Joklova[3]

[1] Faculty of Architecture, University of Belgrade, Belgrade, Serbia
adjukic@afrodita.rcub.bg.ac.rs

[2] Department of Geography and Regional Planning, National Technical University, Athens, Greece
vlastos@survey.ntua.gr

[3] Slovak University of Technology, Bratislava, Slovakia
viera.joklova@stuba.sk

Abstract. Open public spaces have always been key elements of the city. Now they are also crucial for mixed reality. It is the main carrier of urban life, place for socialization, where users rest, have fun and talk. Moreover, "Seeing others and being seen" is a condition of socialization. Intensity of life in public spaces provides qualities like safety, comfort and attractiveness. Furthermore, open public spaces represent a spatial framework for meetings and multileveled interactions, and should include virtual flows, stimulating merging of physical and digital reality. Aim of the chapter is to present a critical analysis of public open spaces, aspects of their social role and liveability. It will also suggest how new technologies, in a mixed reality world, may enhance design approaches and upgrade the relationship between a user and his surroundings. New technologies are necessary for obtaining physical/digital spaces, becoming playable and liveable which will encourage walking, cycling, standing and interacting. Hence, they will attract more citizens and visitors, assure a healthy environment, quality of life and sociability. Public space, acting as an open book of the history of the city and of its future, should play a new role, being a place of reference for the flaneur/cyborg citizen personal and social life. The key result is a framework for understanding the particular importance of cyberparks in contemporary urban life in order to better adapt technologies in the modern urban life needs.

Keywords: Liveability · Walkability · Mixed reality · Quality of life · Cyborg

1 Introduction

Real reality, Amplified reality, Augmented reality, Mediated reality, Augmented virtuality, Virtualized reality, Virtuality. These are versions of a real world which is enriched by the accelerating influence of a new digital world. A new reality, or meta-reality, which appears to be both complex and attractive, is created, particularly for young people. Digital world is penetrating almost in every aspect of the 'real' life. The result is a mixed reality which could make our everyday life pleasant, educating and inspiring for addressing consciously and responsibly the problems of the planet. It will also provide

C. Smaniotto Costa et al. (Eds.): CyberParks, LNCS 11380, pp. 38–49, 2019.
https://doi.org/10.1007/978-3-030-13417-4_4

conditions for helping us to communicate, to meet and to coordinate our coexistence. Mixed reality will bring future sustainable city closer to its citizens. They will no more act as passive spectators but rather as active players and participants for the city's development. Mixed reality will contribute to the implementation of a user centred planning for cities belonging to everybody, with no exclusions. They will be liveable, accessible and fair, true public cities with fewer inequalities and socially cohesive.

Public spaces are the right environment to enjoy with all the senses. Images, sounds, colours and smells are qualities that can be felt because the attention doesn't focus on how to avoid cars but freely turns to what really touch the heart of the user. They offer a richness of experience, possibilities for action and leisure (Stevens 2007). Furthermore, open public spaces are places of collective presence, communication, gatherings and celebrations, or political rallies. Lefebvre's pointed that "the city is the imprint of the society in space", by which he perceives space as a product of thought and action, but as well as an instrument of control and expression of power (Lefebvre 1991). Everyday routine takes a break in public spaces. They are places of rest, places where work stops, where you can chat without an agenda, where kisses and hugs deserve a place. Public spaces are places of pauses where the mind and body relax. What differentiates open and closed public spaces is that visitors to the former are there without a specific reason, they are not oriented towards a certain activity, they simply relax, look around at passers-by. In open public spaces, one can find again his/her freedom, which the function and aesthetics of closed spaces has taken away from him/her. It is a fact that, since antiquity and until today, architecture tried to integrate man from the open to the closed space, in order to discipline and control his thoughts and emotions. Naturally, modern architecture is today bare of ideology and symbolism, as is our era, its only aim is functionalism and to impress. The result is in stereotyped industrialised products and places, without an identity.

Open public spaces are only attractive for users if there is a certain concentration of people. When an osmosis between open spaces and the city occurs – it is an osmosis of the human presence in the streets with the human presence in public spaces. This way, public spaces being connected with the movement of pedestrians and cyclists in the streets, give them the opportunity for some pauses, meetings and mutual experiences with their visitors. In the second half of the 19th century, trade gained great importance in the cities again. This time it becomes part of the fun and lifestyle of the higher strata of civil society. Open public spaces, especially those with shopping activities, became the most important places in the city for leisure time. The open public spaces were reviving and becoming places of gathering. At the same time, at the beginning of the 20th century, large shopping centres, partially or completely covered open public spaces, were developed mainly in Western European countries, providing comfort from weather conditions (such as arcades in Paris in the late 19th century and many department stores in the cities of Europe). The appearance of department stores was preceded by exhibitions (Gandl 2007). The protected areas of department stores become a prototype for the middle class to purchase and spend free time. In contrast to that, spending time on the street, connected with the cultural urban phenomenon, the flâneur, who is an unconscious youth, artist or writer, with bohemian behaviour, that conducts days in cafes and on the street with a cynical view of the world around him, was first proposed by Charles Baudelaire in 1863. In the middle of the 19th century, spending time or gathering on the street was incriminated and was considered immoral for women. "The presence of unprotected women on the streets represents a threat to male power and male weakness. Despite the fact that men in power did everything to limit the movement of women in cities, it is impossible to completely remove them from open public places. Women continue to gather in the city centre and within factories" (Watson and Gibson 1995: 61).

Unlike open-air public space, shopping at a department store has been considered acceptable. Department stores could fulfil the most of their wishes. They were, in fact, closed worlds - small towns. They influenced the closure of small shops and contributed to the formation of a new zone of the city, a "pleasure zone", as the customer was characterized as someone who is looking for satisfaction, material goods, performances and public life (Rappaport 2000).

In the first half of 20th century, after the proclamation of the Athens Charter of 1933, the avant-garde of architecture and urbanism, led by Le Corbusier, Gropius and Jacobs advocated for a radical transformation of the city. They insisted on a transformation with a thesis that "chaotic and disordered cities with many social problems should be rationally rearranged and clearly organized, with a dominant influence of technology" (Bridge and Watson 2002). The strongest influence on these attitudes had Le Corbusier, who insisted on introducing the legibility and transparency in urban areas. Implementation of these values would be carried out by uniform zoning (zoning plan). Emphasizing the importance of urban open space as a "large central open space that allows spectacular order and vitality" (Forty 2004: 140), the social value of the street is negated, as well as its historical and cultural value, significance and architecture. Followers of modern architecture were advocated for abolishing of the social function of the streets. Furthermore, they were trying to invent and create such a form that would be fully able to replace the street with a new infrastructure built for cars and not for the human presence. Certain architects and theorists of architecture and urban planning did not agree with such theses. Christopher Alexander was an opponent of this "street theory", believing that the streets should be shaped and arranged in such a way to keep the passers-in as long as possible. Jane Jacobs emphasized the central role of the streets (especially commercial) in establishing the urban life of the community, arguing that multifunctionality is supported by the mechanism of "self-regulation of street life" and that thus increases the level of security (Jacobs 1995). Mies van der Rohe, as a supporter of functionalism in architecture, observed that the social values and construction technology should be placed before form and that all structures and facilities should be subordinate to their function and purpose of (Forty 2004: 165).

Theorists-rationalists, Lash and Friedman, believed that the streets should have an exclusively traffic function and serve to the fastest way of transport of people and goods from one point to the other (Lash and Friedmann 1992). These thoughts were also the imperatives of modernist planning and consumer capitalism, who sought to transform the symbolic shopping streets into functional spaces that maximize consumption and facilitate transit (Fyfe 1998). The ideology of fascism has supported ideas (called neo-classical) about straight and wide avenues that would provide a fast flow of traffic and a sufficient amount of sunshine and ventilation. They should be designed in accordance with the principles of public morality dictated by the state. One of the most famous projects realized during the fascist period is the reconstruction of Via del Mare in Rome (Kostof 1973). These principles were implemented also in Brasilia in 1960, where only high-speed avenues were constructed, as well as cul-de-sac residential streets, while the social dimension of the streets was completely neglected. Walking was undervalued in the same way that the historical city was scorned worldwide. The objection against the latter didn't concern its architecture but its public character. The construction of many shopping centres in the prefixes of US cities, and also in West European cities was supposed to replace trade at main or local streets. Practically, shopping malls have become surrogates of the shopping streets of the city centre (Crawford 1992).

In 1980's open public spaces were in a focus of architects and urban designers again. The urban concepts of car free cities and New Urbanism have been launched and influenced the concepts of planning and designing of open public spaces. The urban design has been oriented towards the users' needs trying to achieve "more collective and more responsible city". Walking and cycling have been again observed as an 'active' type of transport, as they obviously serve the important values of quality of life. After the signing of the Alborg (1994), most European cities, signatories of this treaty, plead for upgrading sustainable mobility and favouring pedestrian and bicycle movement, with the goal to promote sustainable urban development. This is additionally based on the launching of numerous initiatives and activities throughout Europe which promote pedestrian movement.

2 Cultural Aspects of Open Public Spaces

Cultural aspects of open public spaces are result of the overlapping of morphological and functional characteristics. These characteristics create the identity of the open space. Cultural context as the main factor of identity is an unavoidable part of collective memory with its incorporated signs (Djukic 2011).

2.1 Morphological Framework of Open Public Spaces

The physical character of space is the product of a physical form, or as Kropf says, "*The most important part of our perception of the character of space is the physical fabric of the place*" (Kropf 1996; Hall 1996). He adds that the previous thesis is an axiom of urban design, urban morphology and landscape architecture, and that, in essence, this concept has now been rehabilitated as a valid planning method. Cullen (1961), while exploring the psychological and emotional aspects of the experience of urban ambiance, also pointed to the importance of the perception of morphological characteristics of the city by the user, while passing along the streets and paths. As users of open spaces, we mostly observe objects that define them as part of a wider field of view. Most often, we rarely enter these objects, but after leaving this scene, even if we move fast, along our movement, we can easily bring judgment about the character and quality of that space (Bentley et al. 1985).

In a study that examined the positive effects of urban design (done by the CABE - Commission for Architecture and Built Environment and DETR 2001), in the section dealing with urban design, the quality of open public space is measured by the number of users and their flow through the selected space. It is concluded that the number of users is directly dependent on the physical characteristics of the subject area (urban structure, the relationship between the block, the street and the plot, the intensity of the activity, the type of objects, the facade, the details and materialization, the street front and the streetscape/landscape).

2.2 Functionality

Open public spaces are used by different protagonists, often of subtle values and views. However, managing these spaces is extremely complex and produces a series of problems (Sennett 1974). These problems are mostly related to the conflicts between activities and their intensity, as well as the regime of functioning (Djukic 2011). Open public space has the function of moving, gathering and retaining users (pedestrians, vehicles). On the one hand, the content of the activity indirectly influences the character of the place, and on the other hand the formed physical structure determines the functions and defines the contents in objects that are built along its boundaries (Djukic 2011). The current physical structure determines the future physical structure that will take its place in the future. In the book The Death and Life of Great American Cities, (Jacobs 1961), the author deals with the phenomenon of urban life and highlights the significance of the streets and open public spaces for the livelihoods of cities, comparing them with the heart of the city. She also noted that the key role of open public space is in accepting pedestrians and in their animation (both the local population and the visitor). The basis of vital life in the street is the diversity of both physical forms and functions and activities in it. Furthermore, the quality of the physical structure of the city refers to its connection with functions (primarily in the ground), the dimension of the blocks (primarily the shredding), the position of the front door (direct access to ground floor facilities), possibility of choosing the path for pedestrian traffic, etc. (Djukic 2011).

The concept of Jane Jacobs was supported by the group of professors from Bartlett School of Architecture and Planning in 70's. One of the results of this research was the space syntax method (B. Hillier and J. Hanson) which was focused on the social and physical aspect of open urban spaces. Space syntax uses quantitative methods (counting of pedestrians and vehicles) to get connections between the built space, the functions and liveability of open public spaces. In this way, the urban vision of Jacobs was confirmed on several occasions and the space syntax authors have come up with two very important conclusions: that it is necessary to study the space first, and then start with the design, and that the intensity of the network of pedestrian movements has the main role to its significance. In later research (80's of the 20th century), Hillier identified types of street networks that support the life of open-air urban spaces experimentally (based on everyday experiences, behaviours, events, and especially between psycho-spatial quality, pedestrian movements, possible encounters, informal and formal social structures), in a world which enables us to understand the dynamics of open spaces.

2.3 Cultural Context as a Result of Morphological and Functional Characteristics

Anthropologists believe that textual and collage metaphors were crucial in the creation of culture, and that the world was established by the principle of symbols, myths and rituals, which certain groups connect in appropriate circuits ideology (Ellin 1999; Levi-Strauss 2001; Geertz 1964). Similarly, sociologist Suttles (1973) claims that communities were formed differently, because they were educated by different people, and that the task of the anthropologist was to decipher the messages they left recorded in the cities. This multifaceted space, with respect to multiculturalism and multi-ethnicity, is one of the foundations of modern thought in the field of urban design of open public spaces. Therefore, we can claim, that cultural heritage carries a spiritual message of its time and we cannot observe it outside the temporal and spatial framework. Open public spaces were formed in different periods of time, with different cultural and socio-political frameworks, from different social strata, in different ways. Different social groups were even excluded from public spaces in particular periods and cultures (in ancient Greece, free women were forbidden to walk freely in open public spaces, in New York in the 19th century "women and children were subjected to short-term arrests if they were without male escort. The streets were perceived as a place of sexual danger." (Fyfe 1998). In the 19th century, up to this day, the open public spaces were considered as a place of conflicts, and the streets were regarded as a place of sexual danger and scene for political events (public protests and political struggles). The cultural context implies socio-cultural characteristics of the ambience, and therefore the open public spaces are the parts of the city that its inhabitants are the most often identified with.

At the same time, open public spaces are the main city stage for the social events (Djukic 2011). Observed from the sociological aspect, the problem of the modern city is in the inability of its citizens to identify themselves with the environment in which they live, which affects the psycho-physical state of the individual. This problem is a consequence of citizens' dissatisfaction with the exaggerated insistence of architects and urbanists in a universal language or style in architecture, which negates historical experiences and local traditions. According to Baudrillard, the "aesthetics of break-in" was fashionable with previous patterns of fashion and social behaviour, while at the same time nurturing "the destruction of traditional forms". The discontent of the inhabitants caused by their inability to identify with certain urban areas (usually new residential areas) has sometimes culminated, leading to the alienation of individuals and various social deviations (suburbs of Paris, housing estates for social housing in England). Good architecture does not usually include good open spaces on which it is leaning, and good open public spaces, squares and streets can be framed with quite average architectural achievements.

Many authors refer to the "soul of the city", which is considered as a structural connection between the city and its inhabitants, and which as a historical category marks memory. Halbrouck pointed to the interaction between the city and its inhabitants, stressing the fact, that groups of people who have settled some space, adapt and change that space to their own ideas, but at the same time they adapt themselves to the space, closing within the boundaries they have formed (Djukic 2011). The picture of the external environment and the character of the relationship that the group has built up among each other, have a significant effect on the image that this group forms on itself. (Boyer 1995). Christina Boyer states that the unity between the past and the future is in the very idea of a city which permeates them, "as memory recalls the life of one person", and in order to realize the idea, it must shape reality, but it must also be shaped in its own way. These processes, which are recorded in individual urban units, monuments and our performances and the experiences of integrally possessing identities and continuity, explain in part the reasons for embedding bribes into the foundations of the city (Boyer 1995). According to Jung, the most important urban spaces and myths about them are inherited from our predecessors. We borrow them from the image of collective consciousness. And the Norbert-Schulz theorist emphasises familiarity, as a sense of belonging to some space, which is formed even in our childhood and which we carry in ourselves for the rest of our lives. It enables us to feel more comfortable in a certain area, to get better and to accept it as an integral part of our own memory image.

Physical forms are the product of cultural and social reflections on the one hand and individual aspirations of investors and architects on the other. However, open public spaces without users, activities and social contacts, are as scenes without actors and performances (Djukic 2011). The complexity of the relationship between the form and the open public space stems from the cultural and sociological patterns, but also from the inherited physical frames. It is difficult to determine what is older - the form or function, and what is necessary to start first, to activate the second.

3 The Qualities of Open Public Spaces – Toward Liveable City

Liveability is one of the key factors of the quality of the urban environment. Renowned Dutch architect, urban planner and humanist Jan Gehl, who was the creator of vital public spaces with human scale in cities like Copenhagen, New York and Melbourne, said: "Urban design is all about the human dimensions. Not about cars, industry or business. The quality of life has to be on the first place, followed up by space and buildings – other way round it does not work. If people perceive positively the city for their life, everything else will come gradually".

Walkability, as one of the factors of liveability, can be defined as a measure of how friendly an area or a city is. The idea of "walkable" neighbourhood conjures up a pre-19th century, holistic view of health and well-being, combining notions of citizenship, civic life, democracy, resiliency, spiritual health, beauty, and social justice (Kashef 2016). The walkable neighbourhood has been associated with trust and social engagement (Leyden 2003) as well as sociability (Brown and Cropper 2001). Some people have negative perceptions on walking whether it's because they don't feel safe, or the pedestrian network is not adequate developed, absence of sidewalks, or because of climate comfort (usually thermal). One of the most important benefits of walking is improved quality of life. It could provide that city become a better place to live by helping people become healthier, encouraging social cohesion, decrease air pollution and provide people who do not drive a car an easy and safe walk to their destination.

At the very core of good urban design is a deep understanding of how residents live in the apartment block, district, neighbourhood, city and region. Quality of life is currently a new differentiator, cities compete in quality of life, providing its residents in habitability and liveability. Once the sufficient level to ensure the health, housing, employment, education, services and security is achieved, the quality of habitability is directly connected with the feelings of happiness and fulfilment of meaning of life. The most vulnerable part of the population must be taken into account, children, pensioners, economically, socially or physically disadvantaged. Liveable cities provide the full potential of possibilities and opportunities for people's lives and meaningful development of their families.

The concentration of pedestrians is one of the key factors for a successful walkable - neighbourhood and a city. According to many authors there is a strong connection between the experiences of urban space and presence of people using it (Gehl 2010; Jacobs 1995; Lynch 1974; Hiller and Henson 1984). It is related with the people's activities, cognitive experiences and also depends on the way people interact between each other. In that regard, Whyte considers that the number of the people in urban space is not the only important fact, it should include time they spend in the place, as well as the fact if they come alone or in groups (1980). Quality space and critical mass of users are prerequisites for processes in which small events can blossom (Jacobs 1995) and on the other hand, it is the main precondition for successful public space.

Walkability is defined by Abley and Turner (2011) as the degree that the urban environment is friendly to its users. According to Leslie et al. (2006) walkable is the place which, due to its characteristics, encourages people to walk. As Litman (1999) argues these characteristics are safety, convenience, comfort and the quality of pavements. For Hess and Farrow (2010) walkability is measured according to the attractiveness of pedestrians. Pivo and Fisher (2011) define the same parameter as the degree that inhabitants of an area are encouraged to reach by foot their close destinations. Walkability depends on the population density of an area, the mixite of land uses, the connectivity of the networks, the distance of principal destinations, the width of pavements, the distance between successive crossings, the topography of the urban landscape, the feeling of safety, the aesthetics of architecture etc. Walking and standing are the two sides of the same coin.

How to make our cities walkable is a crucial issue for Sustainable Urban Mobility Plans. These are the 21st century Combined Urban and Transport Plans which replace conventional planning. Their purpose is to reduce speeds and the number of cars in the streets, to enhance walking and cycling and to increase the role of public transport (Fig. 1). The vision for the city of tomorrow is to transform the streets in places to live and to socialize. This is a huge infrastructure and technological challenge (Vlastos 2014).

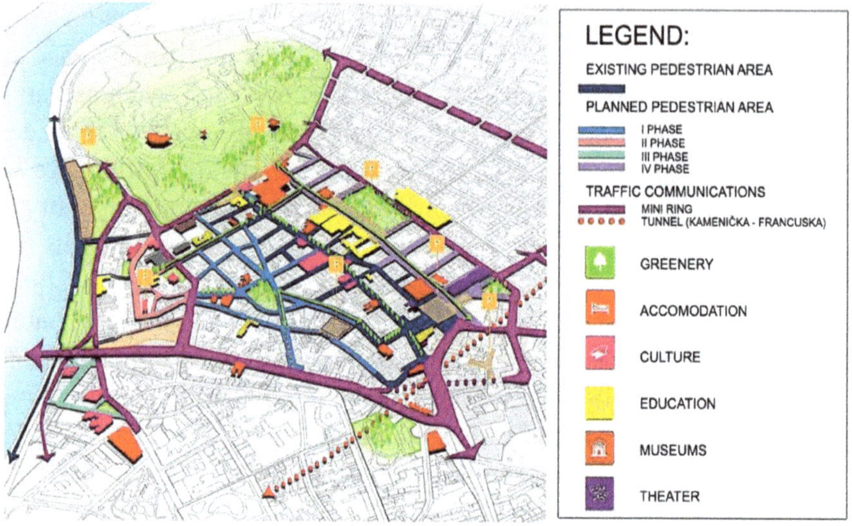

Fig. 1. Plan for widening the pedestrian network (car-free streets) within the historical center of Belgrade. Source: author Ana Delipara, in Folic M., Vukmirovic M (2016) "Projekat IME: Identity_Mobility_Environment of the City of Belgrade". City of Belgrade Communication Office, Belgrade.

4 Future of Open Public Spaces or Are the Cyberparks for Cyborgs?

What is the future of open public spaces? How they can become more vibrant and how they contribute to the liveability of a city? Although citizens in surveys which had been done in Belgrade during 2005 and 2016 have been concerned about the decrease of the quality of open public spaces, especially of the parks, the number of the open public space within the cities usually remains the same. Furthermore, some open public spaces are changing in a positive way, as it concerns technology. During the last three decades, ICT becomes the crucial part of our everyday life. ICT systems in cities, providing and ensuring low-cost internet access in open public spaces, are an indicator of development and the well-being of citizens (Djukic and Aleksic 2016). As Souza e Silva (2006: 262) has already pointed out, contemporary cities are 'hybrid spaces' where ICT, overlapping physical urban and information space, create hybrid space. People use social networks on everyday basis and interact in both the physical and virtual realms, gathering formally or informally in order to exchange information and knowledge, disseminate practice and experiences, and erase various kinds of limitations (Stupar and Djukic 2014). Citizens are also becoming interactive participants in the process of collaborative planning and design of the spaces they use. While the main role of an open public space is still to provide physical social contact between people - a place where they can rest, recreate and enjoy the environment – e-networks have opened up additional channels of communication and diffusion and become a new tool for the continuous development of such locations (Stupar and Djukic 2014). Users acting as consumers of places can use ICT to participate as active contributors to the process of urban design or as critics of open urban space.

'A cyborg is a cybernetic organism, a hybrid of machine and organism, a creature of social reality as well as a creature of fiction' (Haraway 1991: 149). Cyborgs use provided data and function according to them. Is the cyborg-flâneur a modern flâneur who adapts to a new technology? Mitchell introduced the cyber flâneur in 1996 in his writings 'I am an electronic flâneur. I hang out on the network … The keyboard is my café' (p. 7). Cyborg flâneur explains how citizens use and inhabit the hybrid space. He is searching for pleasure and joy, while involving in activities associated with flaneur (games, virtual tours, online shopping, sharing social or Facebook status, virtual contacts with others) which allow the illusion of a certain freedom in hybrid space – virtual reality.

5 Conclusions and Future Developments

The street has a history. Going out onto the street we leave behind us our private space and become part of the public and social sphere. Far from the protection of the private, we let go, we are open and free to communicate. We could easily avoid this by quickly getting into our car or a taxi. Instead, we are transported into a different world. Walking and cycling combine the personal and collective experience. The street is also an open public space where should be space for the citizens to stand and being present. Qualities of the street like accessibility, safety, comfort, attractiveness are crucial for liveability and social cohesion. Implementation of ICT's in open spaces and streets is crucial to enhance the above qualities. ICT's turn open spaces into digital places which are environments of socialization that compete with physical places. Technology is a new experience, and among other things, it is an urban game – playable city – which can transfer you anywhere, to any city. With augmented reality applications on the internet Cyborg-flaneur will live the city directly or indirectly, autonomously or collectively. He could even play with it. New communication technology will contribute greatly in this direction. Tomorrow's digital public city, a city of information, exchange, dialogue, meeting and playing will constitute a social field of liveliness and inspiration.

Cyberparks will become a new real and simultaneously digital world of places where the community will be connected with the local and the wider. In these places the live and digital exchange of information will be combined, and new social and political experiences will be acquired. The planet is becoming more unified, financially and culturally and is developing explosively under the umbrella of a new social digital public space of communication and exchange, which is the internet. In reality tomorrow, this will become our new home. Internet will be present everywhere, we will all share the same information and distance will count for nothing when it comes to exchange. As travellers on the web and citizens of the world we will know a lot about it since we will move intensively and therefore, we will be informed about everything that is happening. We will become more conscious about dangers the planet faces. The open public spaces of the city of tomorrow will be places for people prepared to discuss and find collective solutions. Cyborg-flaneur will be the citizen of tomorrow searching for pleasure and joy and solutions for surviving in our complex new world.

References

Abley, S., Turner, S.: Predicting Walkability. NZ Transport Agency, Wellington (2011)

Alborg, C.: Charter of European cities & towns towards sustainability (1994). http://ec.europa.eu/environment/urban/pdf/aalborg_charter.pdf

Bentley, I., Alcock, A., Murrain, P., McGlynn, S., Smith, G.: Responsive Environments – A Manual For Designers. Butterworth Architecture, Oxford (1985)

Bridge, G., Watson, S.: A Companion to the City. Blackwell Companion to Geography, Oxford (2002)

Boyer, M.C.: The City of Collective Memory. The MIT Press, Massachusetts (1995)

Brown, B.B., Cropper, V.L.: New urban and standard suburban subdivisions: evaluating psychological and social goals. J. Am. Plan. Assoc. **67**(4), 402–419 (2001)

CABE: The Value of Urban Design: A Research Project Commissioned by CABE and DETR. Thomas Telford, London (2001)

Crawford, M.: The world in a shopping mall. In: Sorkin, M. (ed.) Variations on a Theme Park: The New American City and The End of Public Space, pp. 3–30. Hill and Wang, New York (1992)

Cullen, G.: Townscape. Architectural Press, New York (1961)

De Souza e Silva, A.: From cyber to hybrid: mobile technologies as interfaces of hybrid spaces. Space Cult. **9**(3), 261–278 (2006)

Djukic, A.: Keeping the Identity of the Main Streets in Vojvodina Towns in the Process of Urban Renewal (Doctoral dissertation, unpublished). Faculty of Architecture, Belgrade (2011)

Djukic, A., Aleksic, D.: Mixed reality environment and open public space design. In: Vanista Lazarevic, E., Vukmirovic, M., Krstic-Furundzic, A., Djukic, A. (eds.) International Academic Conference: Places and Technologies 2016: Keeping up with Technologies to Improve Places- Cognitive City, pp. 761–769 (2016)

Ellin, N.: Postmodern Urbanism. Princeton Architectural Press, New York (1999)

Fyfe, R.N.: Images of the Streets. Routledge, London and New York (1998)

Forty, A.: Words and Buildings. Thames & Hudson, London (2004)

Gandl, S.: Glamur. CLIO, Belgrade (2007)

Gehl, J.: Cities for People. Island Press, Washington (2010)

Geertz, C.: Ideology as a cultural system. In: Ideology and Discontent, vol. 5 (1964)

Hall, A.C.: Design Control: Towards a New Approach. Butterworth Architecture, Oxford (1996)

Haraway, D.: Simians, Cyborgs and Women - The Reinvention of Nature. Free Association Books, London (1991)

Hess, P.M., Farrow, J.: Walkability in Toronto's High-Rise Neighbourhoods. University of Toronto, Toronto (2010)

Hiller, B., Henson, J.: The Social Logic of Space. Cambridge University Press, Cambridge (1984)

Jacobs, J.: The Death and Life of Great American Cities. Vintage Books, New York (1961)

Jacobs, A.: Great Streets. MIT Press, Massachusetts (1995)

Kashef, M.: Urban liveability across disciplinary and professional boundaries. Front. Arch. Res. **5**(2), 239–253 (2016)

Kostof, S.: The City Shaped – Urban Patterns and Meanings Through History. Thames and Hudson, London (1973)

Kropf, K.: Urban tissue and the character of towns. Urban Des. Int. **1**(3), 247–263 (1996)

Lash, S., Friedmann, J.: Modernity and Identity. Blackwell, Oxford (1992)

Lefebvre, H.: Writings on Cities. Blackwell, Oxford (1991)

Leslie, E., Butterworth, I., Edwards, M.: Measuring the walkability of local communities using geographic information systems data. In: Walk 21-VII, Melbourne, Australia (2006)
Levi-Strauss, C.: Myth and Meaning. Routledge, London (2001)
Leyden, K.M.: Social capital and the built environment: the importance of walkable neighbourhoods. Am. J. Public Health **93**(9), 1546–1551 (2003)
Litman, T.A.: Traffic calming benefits, costs and equity impacts. Victoria Transport Policy Institute, Victoria (1999)
Lynch, K.: Image of a City. The MIT Press, Massachusetts (1974)
Mitchell, W.J.: City of Bits: Space, Place and the Infobahn. MIT Press, Cambridge (1996)
Pivo, G., Fisher, J.D.: The walkability premium in commercial real estate investments. Real Estate Econ. **39**(2), 185–219 (2011)
Rappaport, E.D.: Shopping for Pleasure: Woman and the Making of the London's West End. Princeton University Press, Princeton (2000)
Sennett, R.: The Fall of Public Man. Faber & Faber, London (1974)
Stevens, Q.: The Ludic City: Exploring the Potential of Public Space. Routledge, New York (2007)
Stupar, A., Djukic, A.: Vis-à-vis communication? The digital and physical spaces of interaction in the contemporary city. In: Schrenk, M., Popovich, V., Zeile, P., Elisei, P. (eds.) International Scientific Conference "REAL CORP 2015 - Plan Together - Right Now - Overall: From Visions to Reality for Vibrant Cities and Regions", pp. 687–693 (2014)
Suttles, G.: The Social Construction of Communities. University of Chicago Press, Chicago (1973)
Vlastos, T.: Les limites de la marche. Recherche – Transports – Securité, **30**, 35–45 (2014)
Watson, S., Gibson, K. (eds.): Postmodern Cities and Spaces. Basil Blackwell, Oxford (1995)
Whyte, W.H.: The Social Life of Small Urban Spaces. Conservation Foundation, PPS, New York (1980)

1.5

Exploring the Concept of *Cyberpark*: What the Experts Think

Paschalis Arvanitidis[1(✉)], Konstantinos Lalenis[1], Georgios Artopoulos[2], and Montserrat Pallares-Barbera[3]

[1] University of Thessaly, Volos, Greece
parvanit@uth.gr, klalenis@prd.uth.gr
[2] The Cyprus Institute, Nicosia, Cyprus
g.artopoulos@cyi.ac.cy
[3] Universitat Autònoma de Barcelona, Cerdanyola, Spain
montserrat.pallares@uab.cat

Abstract. The chapter aims to provide a contextualisation of the *cyberpark* concept as this is perceived by a wide range of experts in public space and information technologies. To do so it makes use of a questionnaire survey conducted with the participants of the CyberParks COST Action, which collected their views on a number of aspects concerning both the mediated and the not mediated public open spaces, such as: their elements and qualities, the facilities they should offer, the activities they should facilitate, the type of space and location that are most suitable to accommodate them, their appropriate size and manner for their development, their target user group and other aspects of their configuration. The analysis brings out the commonalities and differences in experts' views regarding the mediated and the not mediated public open spaces, and, as such, it contributes to specify further the *cyberpark* concept, mapping out its characteristics and dimensions. This should enrich the ongoing dialogue within the literature and facilitate interactions between relevant, yet fragmented, scientific disciplines in the area to inform the production and appropriation of both mediated and the not mediated public open spaces.

Keywords: Experts · Views · Diversity · Survey

1 Introduction

The idea of a technologically augmented public open space (POS) has been seen in a very positive way by some people, but with scepticism by others. People perceive parks, plazas, squares, etc. as places to enjoy for leisure, sometimes for work, but rarely as places specifically designed to bring together the 'real' with the 'virtual' and to offer digital interaction and cyber experiences to people. This chapter gets involved in this discussion and attempts to elucidate the concept and characteristics of such a space, termed as '*cyberpark*' (Smaniotto Costa et al. 2017). To do so, the chapter makes use of a survey conducted with various experts on the issue. These are the participants of the COST Action TU 1306 CyberParks. The questionnaire that is used has collected

C. Smaniotto Costa et al. (Eds.): CyberParks, LNCS 11380, pp. 50–66, 2019.
https://doi.org/10.1007/978-3-030-13417-4_5

their views on a number of *cyberpark* and public space aspects, aiming to bring out the commonalities and differences in their opinion and, as such, to explore the idea and specify the peculiarities and characteristics of *cyberpark*, in comparison to POS which are not enhanced with information and communications technology (ICT). Analysis of these data is very important given the variety in scientific backgrounds and training of these people (including social scientists, artists, urban designers, information technology professionals, communication specialists, etc.) and consequently the diversity of their views regarding what a *cyberpark* might actually be.

In a nutshell, the chapter aims to provide, in a more systematic, organized and structured way, a contextualization of the various dimensions of the ICT mediated POS, vis-à-vis POS that are not enhanced with technology, which emerge due to different perspectives, disciplines, backgrounds, etc. of the related experts. Of course, this chapter is not a conclusive piece of work on the issue; it simply presents a first attempt to explore the terrain and to introduce new elements from the expert's perspectives in understanding the concept of *cyberpark* and the important role ICTs play to POS in the twenty first century.

2 From CyberParks (COST Action) to *Cyberpark* (Concept)

COST Action CyberParks participants have different cultural/national backgrounds and professional experience (in research, policy making, urban design, arts, etc.), and come from various scientific fields (ICTs specialists, spatial planners, urban developers, geographers, sociologists, anthropologists, economists, communication professionals, etc.), having different education and viewpoints on the issues of production, use and management of POS. This is certainly an advantage for a COST Action, since it provides a stimulating environment for sparking ideas, synergies and cross-fertilisation between different scientific disciplines, but it brings out the diversity that exists in the terminology, perspectives and, perhaps, understanding of what *cyberpark* is or it should be like.

At the beginning of the CyberParks project the concept of *cyberpark* was relatively vague; a subtle idea that new technologies are able to play an important part in the development of POS into intelligent spaces, where urban (mainly natural) landscape and digital environment blend together to provide services that enhance the quality of life. It is interesting to observe the evolution of the constituent concepts, the interpretations given, and the focus placed by the participants as the project went through. At the kick-off meeting of the project (Brussels on April 2014) the main objective was to:

> *...create a research platform on the relationship between information and communication technologies (ICTs) and the production and use of public open spaces, and their relevance to sustainable urban development. The impacts of this relationship will be explored from social, ecological, urban design and methodological perspectives.*

This lead, in a second CyberParks meeting (in Barcelona on November 2014) to the provision of the following working definition concerning *cyberpark*:

> *A cyberpark is a designed ecosystem of living processes and technologies. It comprises an outdoor green or blue space interacting with a digital intelligent environment. It usually contains living beings, plants, trees, and water features, many of which are integrated with computerised sensors, haptic technologies and virtual objects. Its features can vary widely. For example: It can be used for a range of purposes such as exercise, leisure, social interaction, relaxation and many other activities. It may be public or private. It can be found in urban, suburban, rural, coastal and wilderness areas. It can consist of a large area of land not covered with buildings, roads, or sports facilities, or a dedicated small area in such places as streets, squares, buildings (courtyards, roofs), or disused thoroughfares like the New York Highline. It can also be a beach, ocean, lake, river, or wetland.*

We see that the concept evolves to perceive *cyberpark* not simply as a technologically blended place, but as an ecosystem; the definition deepens on the specifics of the constituent elements, such as outdoor green or blue space; it highlights the ICT connection; it sets forth the diversity of virtual object present in a *cyberpark*; and emphasizes the flexibility of the concept, to be seen as a working definition which could serve different objectives and agents, from academics to public and private institutions and users. In time, the many understandings of the concept started converging to a more concise meaning of what a *cyberpark* is:

> *A cyberpark is a new type of urban landscape where nature and cybertechnologies blend together to generate hybrid experiences and enhance quality of life. The attributes of a Cyberpark (referenced from the Smart Cities initiative) could be defined by the use of sensor technologies in a connectable space, accessible to the public through ubiquitous technologies used in sociable and sharable ways where the virtual is made visible or augments the landscape. ICT can be used in this context to give or gather information, to aid co-creation of space, to allow crowd sourcing of information and opinions, and to allow affective sharing or self-monitoring of activities. Hardware may be embedded in the environment in the form of responsive sound or lighting systems, control systems, kinetic objects or artworks, passive sensor technologies and display systems. We recognize that the use of such affordances will be qualified by such considerations as the time of day, the duration of the visit, the weather and temperature, location, season, individual or group engagement, age, gender, purpose of visit and the topology and size of the space. (Agora* 2017*)*

Currently, it is important to emphasize the complexity of the *cyberpark* concept and its relation to quality of life in which "the virtual is made visible or augments the landscape." In this sense work is needed to identify *cyberpark's* specific characteristics and peculiarities that distinguish it from the general category of POS. These are attempted in the following section.

3 Exploring the Understanding of the *Cyberpark* Concept

3.1 Research Concept and Methodology

This section discusses how CyberParks Action participants perceive the notion of *cyberpark* and its dimensions, vis-à-vis other, more conventional, POS, i.e. POS that are not enhanced with technology. Data was collected through a questionnaire survey that explored a number of issues, such as: the elements and qualities of both *cyberpark* and POS, the facilities they should offer, the activities they should facilitate, the type of space and location that are most suitable to accommodate them, their appropriate size and manner for their development, their target user group and other aspects of their configuration.

Established studies in the area, such as the one by the Project for Public Spaces[1], have observed that in order to be relevant and occupied (i.e., be sustainable and alive), a POS must:

- Encourage the sociality and socialisation of its users, by being hospitable, friendly, interactive, multi-thematic, collective, familiar, etc.
- Offer a variety of uses and related activities, by being pleasant, lively, unique, useful, local and sustainable.
- Provide comfort and an attractive image, by being safe, clean, “green”, providing places to sit and rest but also paths for walking, being pleasant, encouraging intellectual pursuits, being attractive and showcasing local historical moments.
- Be accessible and hospitable to all, by providing continuity with the urban fabric, proximity, connectivity, being easily readable and recognisable, convenient, and by not excluding any social group.

These considerations have been taken into account for the construction of the questionnaire that contributed to this chapter. Also, the authors acknowledge that POS, with its complexities, indeterminacy, and abundance of possible interactions, when it is accessible by the wanderer, local or tourist, offers a sensual experience. This became a point of entry for the development of both CyberParks and *cyberpark*, as it is further discussed in other chapters of this book. The enriched appropriation of citizens to public space and to data overlaid on physical space, and most importantly, the enhanced capacity for both individual and collective action for the management of the POS, are considered some of the added values over conventional public space.

The questionnaire developed consists of three parts containing 24 questions where participants were asked to choose from a list of options and to evaluate specific characteristics of both *cyberpark* and not mediated POS, on a scale of 0 (denoting strong disagreement, negative opinion, etc.) to 10 (denoting strong agreement, positive opinion, etc.). In particular, the first part of the questionnaire informs the participants on the purpose of the research and ensures the anonymity of participation. The second part gathers socio-demographic information, such as gender, age, nationality, discipline of specialisation, and occupation. Finally, the third part records views regarding the number of *cyberpark's* and POS's aspects examined. Survey questions were pre-tested in a pilot study enabling fine-tuning of the instrument.

[1] The Project for Public Spaces is a non-profit organisation for study, design and education with the goal of creating sustainable active public and collective spaces for the strengthening of community. The organisation was founded in the United States in 1975 and since then has studied more than 3,000 communities in 43 countries; see <http://www.pps.org/about/>.

The survey was conducted in April 2017 during the CyberParks' Working Groups Meeting. Questionnaires were distributed in person by the members of the research team and asked to be completed on the spot. In order to increase response rate and quality, participants were given the choice of their responses to be recorded by the researcher, or, should they wish, to complete the questions by themselves on their own time. Questionnaires were collected, validated, and then coded and analysed to generate a number of statistics illustrating the respondents' answers on the issues raised.

3.2 Composition of Respondents

From a targeted population of 48 experts that participated in the Ancona meeting of the project (where our data were collected), 44 validated questionnaires were acquired (91.7%). The gender composition of the respondents was about 63.6% male and 36.4% female. The average age was about 47 years, with the youngest expert being 30 years old and the oldest 69. The respondents are from 22 countries all over Europe and Israel, but higher participation was from Italy (5 respondents), Portugal (5), Spain (5), Poland (3) and Sweden (3) (see Fig. 1). The vast majority of the respondents (90.0% of the sample) hold a PhD, whereas the rest have completed postgraduate studies (9.1%). Their knowledge base is informed by 13 academic disciplines (Fig. 2), ranging from spatial planning and urban design, to information technology and various social science subjects (sociology, anthropology, economics, etc.). Most of the participants are academics (67.4%), some work in the private sector (16.3%), others in the public sector (11.6%) and a few are freelancers (4.7%).

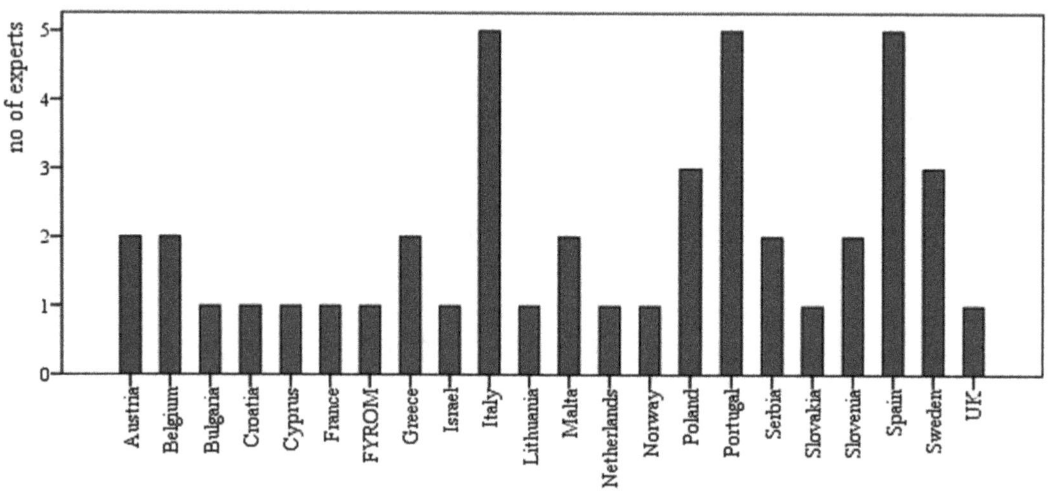

Fig. 1. Origin country of respondents

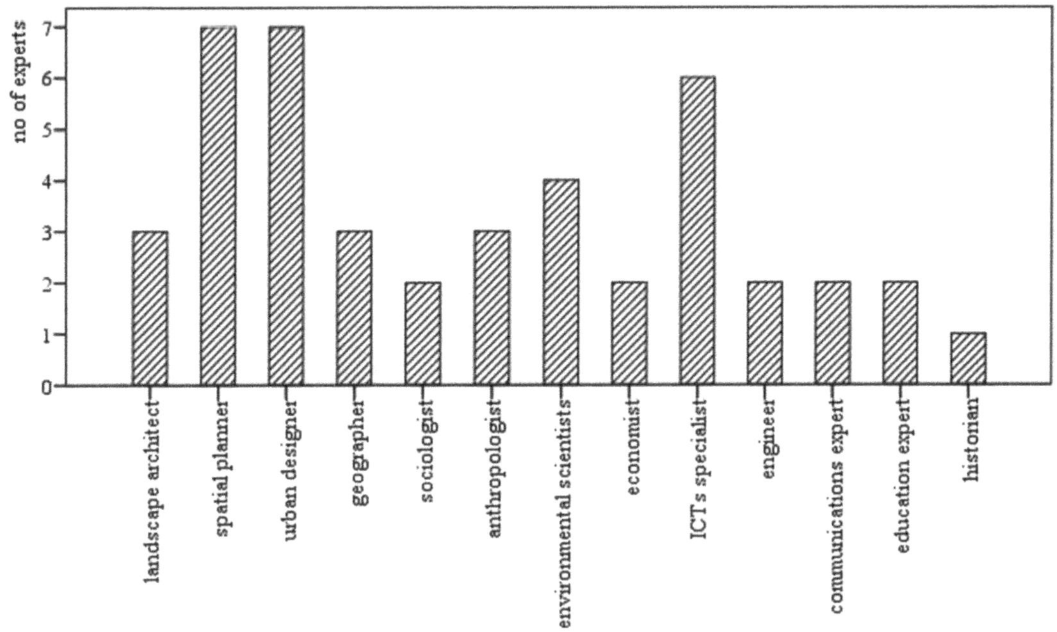

Fig. 2. Specialization of respondents

3.3 Analysis

Firstly, the participants were asked to specify which one of the three constituent elements, that is, space, people and technology, is the principal feature of *cyberpark* and POS. As Fig. 3 shows, experts regard that people is the central element of both, but whereas in POS technology plays a rather minimal role, in *cyberpark* this becomes the second most important component, followed by space, which comes last in array.

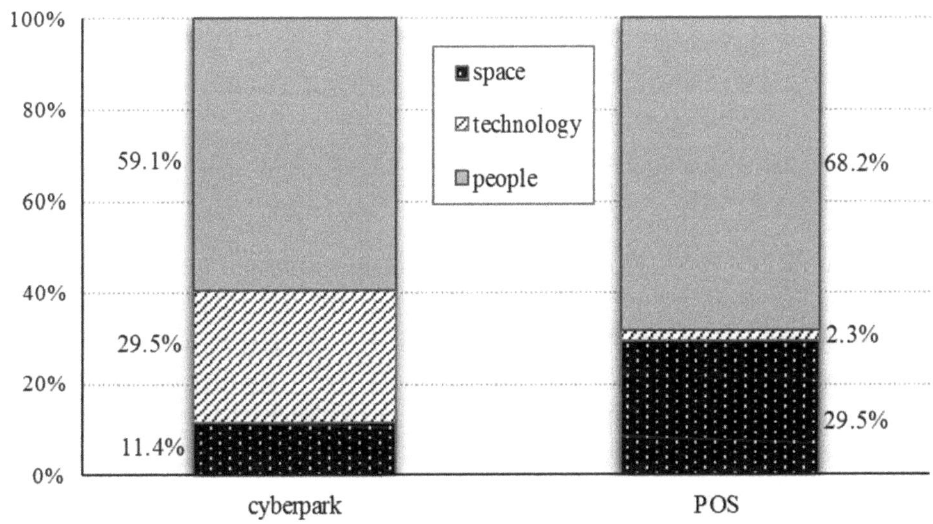

Fig. 3. Importance of constituent elements

In addition, participants were invited to identify five keywords that best define the concept of *cyberpark*. Their responses are classified on the basis of the three constituent elements and are presented in Table 1 below. As becomes evident, from the 53 keywords provided by the experts, information and communications technologies (ICTs) constitutes the distinctive one that characterises *cyberpark* (identified by 23 people). Public space (here mentioned for short as POS) is the second one (identified 14 times), followed by enhanced and interactive space (both identified 9 times). Digital and inclusive space, come next, along with cooperation and community (8 times). Figure 4 offers a visualisation of these data, where the importance of each keyword (in terms of the times it has been identified) is represented by its different size in the graph.

Table 1. *Cyberpark* keywords

Space	*People*	*Technology*
POS (14)	Inclusive (8)	ICTs (23)
Enhanced (9)	Cooperation (8)	Interactive (9)
Innovative (7)	Community (8)	Digital (8)
Hybrid (7)	Communication (4)	Wi-fi (5)
Open (5)	Well-being (4)	Virtual (4)
Green (6)	Connectivity (3)	Apps (3)
Quality space (2)	Experience (2)	Information (3)
Facilities (2)	Free (2)	Augmented (2)
Modern (2)	Users (2)	Smart (2)
Added value	Work (2)	Important (2)
Diversity	Planning (2)	Inevitable
Dynamic	Activities	Sensors
Functionality	Bottom-up	Valuable
Glocal	Enabling	Energy provision
Heterotopia	Engagement	
Heuristic	Identity	
Temporarity	Learning	
Accessibility	Playing	
Security	Resilience	
	Story-telling	

Next, respondents were asked to identify the most important qualities of the spaces under investigation. Figure 5 presents the results. We see that information transmission is perceived to be the most important quality of *cyberpark* (a feature that is ranked very low in conventional POS), followed by safety and space quality, both of which are regarded as quite important qualities of good POS. Interestingly, the existence of natural environment and greenery is regarded as an essential quality of POS, but not that much of a *cyberpark*.

Fig. 4. Word-cloud of *cyberpark* keywords

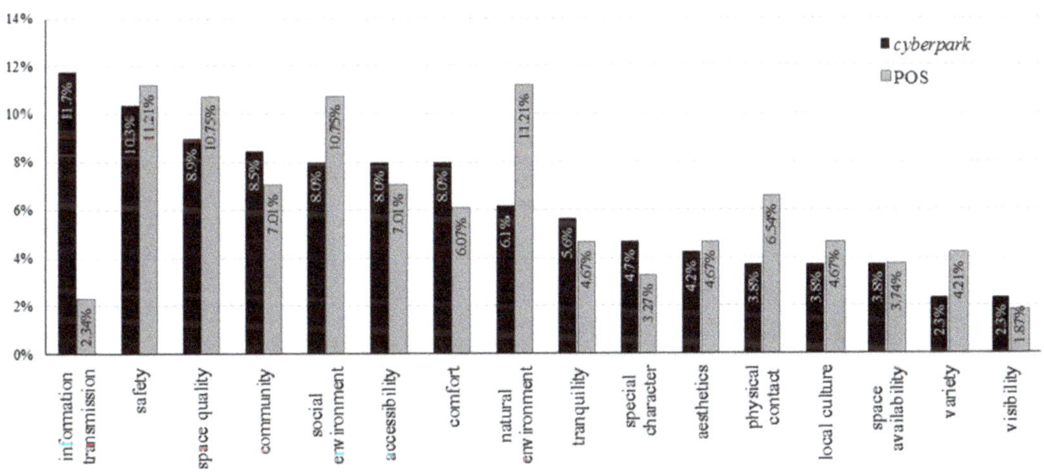

Fig. 5. Qualities of spaces

From a list of facilities that public spaces could offer, experts were asked to choose those that are most necessary to *cyberpark* and to POS. As Fig. 6 illustrates, internet facilities, interactive information and places to work are essential for *cyberpark*, and of rather low importance to POS. In turn, places to sit and facilities for visitors in general, including facilities for specific groups (such as disadvantaged citizens or children), are regarded as most important for POS.

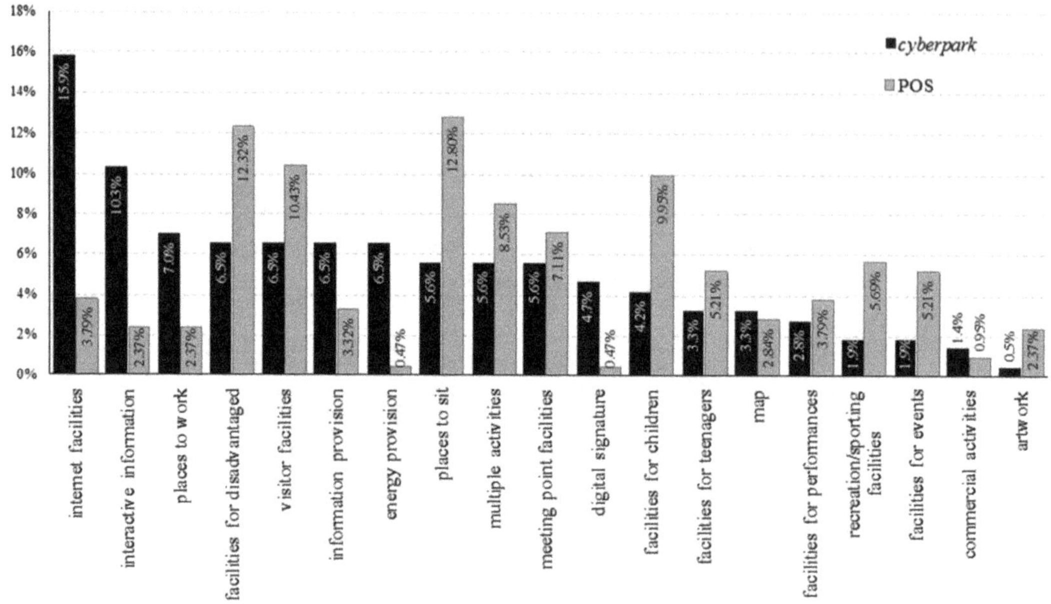

Fig. 6. Facilities provided

Turning to the activities that the public spaces under examination should facilitate, experts indicated that relaxing, socializing and communicating with people constitute the most important functions that a *cyberpark* should offer (Fig. 7). The first two are also the two main activities that POS also facilitate, along with strolling and leisure. Interestingly, educational, work and communicate facilities are ranked quite high in *cyberpark* (fourth, fifth and third, respectively), but very low in POS, which are mainly appreciated for their recreational and leisure role.

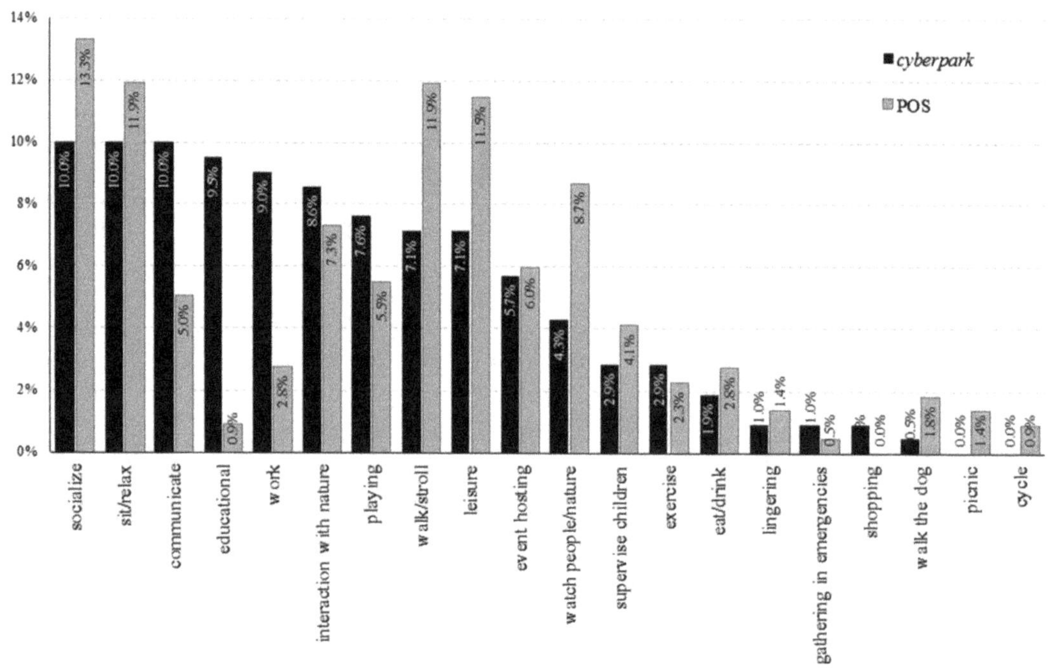

Fig. 7. Facilitated activities

The next question asked respondents to assess what types of places are best for each of the spaces examined. Figure 8 presents the findings. We see that mainly parks, followed by squares, historic sites and river banks and canals, are the most suitable places for deploying both *cyberpark* and POS, whereas cemeteries, parking-spaces and sport-fields are the least appropriate for both. Spaces that are regarded as suitable to host a *cyberpark*, but are not that appropriate for POS, are leftover or vacant spaces (ranked fifth), as well as bus and railway stops and stations (ranked eight). In turn, experts believe that places which could better accommodate a *cyberpark*, rather than conventional POS, are institutional public spaces (like, university campuses, libraries, church and school yards), internalized 'public' spaces (such as, interior of shopping/leisure centres and retail space), and any other space with public access. We note with interest that CyberParks experts do not confine *cyberpark* to outdoor locations.

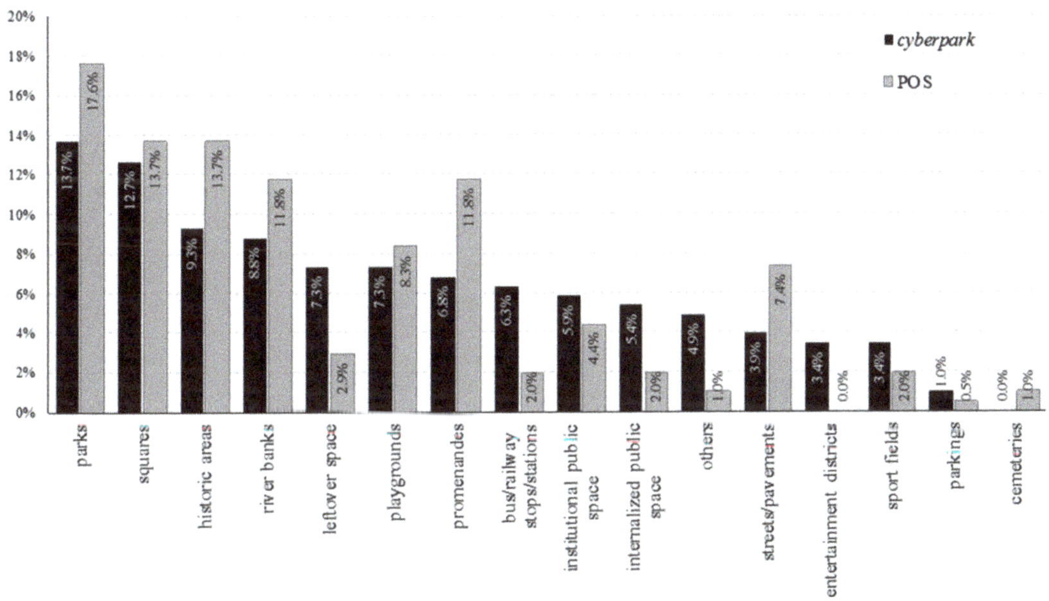

Fig. 8. Suitable spaces

Next, we asked the specialists to specify, which locations are best for a *cyberpark* vis-à-vis POS. As Fig. 9 illustrates, city centre and downtown are most appropriate places for *cyberpark*. City centre is also a good location for POS in general; however, downtown locations are not regarded as suitable. Third in line comes sites within neighbourhoods, which is seen as a quite good location for the development of all POS as well.

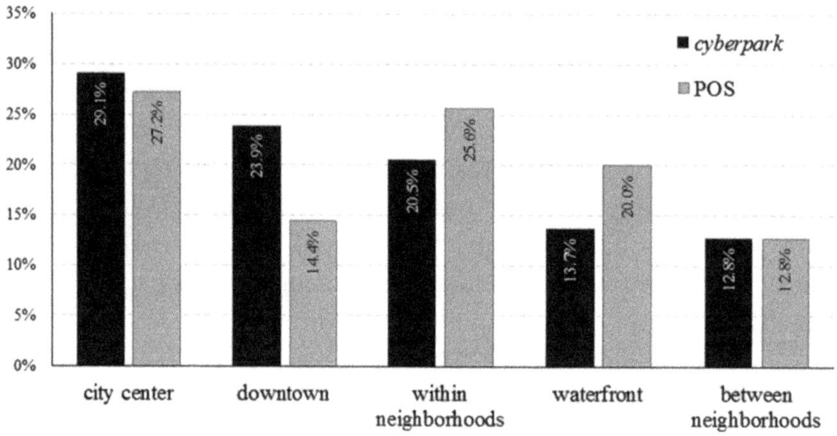

Fig. 9. Suitable locations

The appropriate size of both *cyberpark* and conventional POS was another issue explored with the experts. As Fig. 10 makes evident, medium and small size spaces are most appropriate for a *cyberpark*, whereas for POS medium to large size should be sought. Of course, what constitutes small or large size of space is a relative and rather subjective measure (which might differ between different disciplines or exerts), however the answers we received provide an indication that size could be a characteristic that distinguishes *cyberpark* from conventional POS.

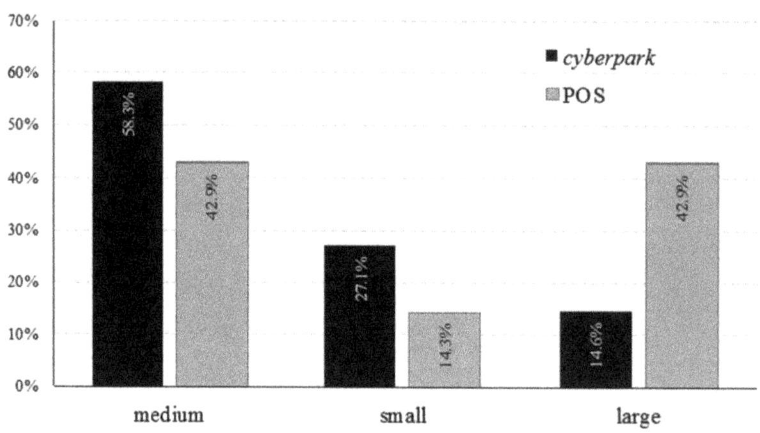

Fig. 10. Suitable sizes

Figure 11 presents the results concerning the target population of both *cyberpark* and POS. We see that city dwellers are the main target group of both spaces. Moreover, a *cyberpark* should focus on servicing tourists and visitors (ranked second), and the youth (ranked third), whereas POS should primarily target local residents living nearby. Intriguingly, we also see that elderly people is a legitimate target group for POS, but are not regarded that can take advantage of the special facilities that a *cyberpark* can offer.

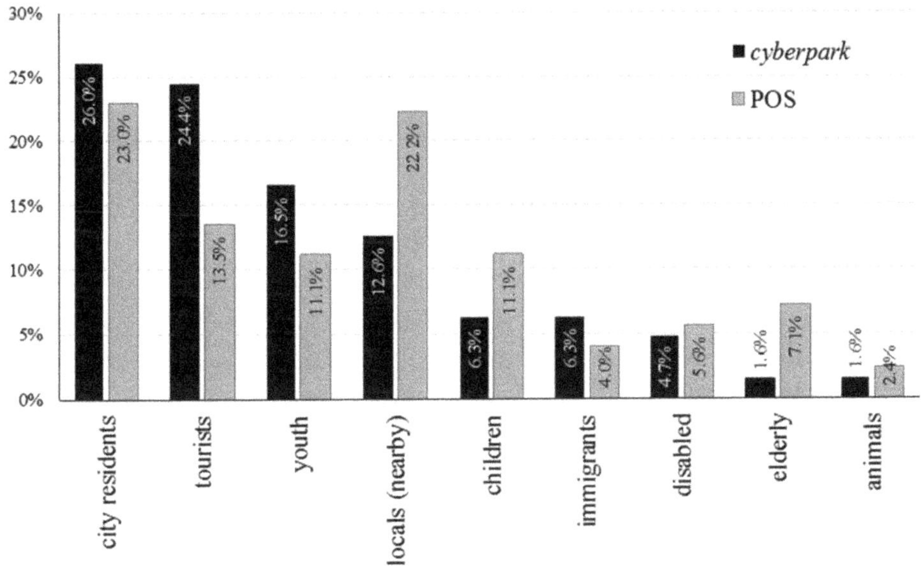

Fig. 11. Target population

The development and maintenance of public space constitutes a major issue, especially during the times of economic crisis, where local authorities are facing increased financial problems and difficulties. The question that follows examines who the experts reckon should bear the costs of providing and maintaining the spaces under investigation. Four options were given: the users of the spaces, all citizens, the local authorities with the municipality, and the private sector. As Fig. 12 depicts, the vast majority of experts agree that local authorities should undertake such costs, for the development and maintenance of both *cyberpark* and POS. However, in contrast to POS, experts seem to be open to other sources of finance when the question turns to *cyberpark*. Interestingly the 13.6% of the respondents regard that the private sector could contribute to the provision and maintenance of *cyberpark* and 9.1% is willing the users themselves to bear part of these costs.

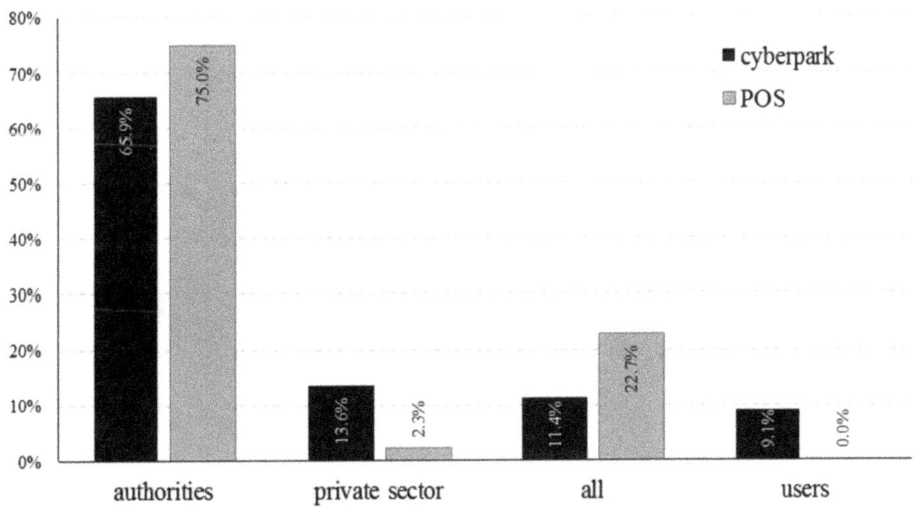

Fig. 12. Provision and maintenance

The final set of questions explored the views of experts on various characteristics of *cyberpark*. In particular, the participants were asked to evaluate a number of statements concerning the value and specific aspects of *cyberpark* development, using an eleven-point Likert scale, ranging of 0 (strongly disagree) to 10 (strongly agree). The statements were the following: (1) *cyberparks* are essential to a city, (2) they are costly to create, (3) they are costly to maintain, (4) they increase the welfare of the citizens, (5) controlled access should be applied, (6) security cameras should be used, (7) entrance fees should be applied, and (8) the users should contribute financially to their creation and maintenance. Table 2 presents the results. We see that the majority of experts believe that *cyberpark* places are quite important to the city (mean: 6.7, with most of respondents favouring the highest values); although they are costly in their development and maintenance (means respectively 6.3 and 6.0) they increase substantially the citizens welfare (mean: 7.3). When the question turns to issues of security, experts seems to be somewhat divided; although many are sceptical on applying security cameras and access control (most respondents are favouring the lowest values), there are a few who feel that such an approach would overall benefit *cyberpark* spaces (as the high standard deviation reveals). As regards the application of entrance fees and financial contribution by the users, respondents are rather reserved to both (means 1.5 and 2.1, respectively), corroborating the previous finding that *cyberpark* is essentially a public good and the local authorities should be those to bear its costs.

Table 2. Views on aspects of *cyberpark* provision

	0 (%)	1 (%)	2 (%)	3 (%)	4 (%)	5 (%)	6 (%)	7 (%)	8 (%)	9 (%)	10 (%)	N	Mean	Stand. dev.
Essential to a city	0	0	2.4	2.4	7.1	28.6	7.1	7.1	28.6	2.4	14.3	*42*	*6.7*	*2.1*
Costly to create	0	2.4	4.9	9.8	7.3	22.0	7.3	7.3	9.8	17.1	12.2	*41*	*6.3*	*2.6*
Costly to maintain	0	0	11.9	4.8	7.1	19.0	11.9	16.7	16.7	0	11.9	*42*	*6.0*	*2.4*
Increase welfare	0	0	0	2.4	2.4	14.6	17.1	14.6	22.0	7.3	19.5	*41*	*7.3*	*1.9*
Control access should be applied	16.7	9.5	16.7	2.4	2.4	19.0	7.1	4.8	7.1	9.5	4.8	*42*	*4.2*	*3.3*
Security cameras should be applied	23.3	11.6	2.3	2.3	2.3	18.6	7.0	2.3	14.0	7.0	9.3	*43*	*4.5*	*3.6*
Entrance fees should be applied	54.8	19.0	0	2.4	7.1	11.9	0	2.4	0	2.4	0	*42*	*1.5*	*2.3*
Users should contribute financially	46.3	12.2	7.3	7.3	7.3	2.4	12.2	0	2.4	2.4	0	*41*	*2.1*	*2.6*

4 On *Cyberpark* and Public Spaces

As mentioned above, the CyberParks Action defines *cyberpark as "... a new type of urban landscape where nature and cyber technologies blend together to generate hybrid experiences and enhance quality of life. ... ICT can be used in this context to give or gather information, to aid co-creation of space, to allow crowd sourcing of information and opinions, and to allow effective sharing or self-monitoring of activities"* (Agora 2017). This conception underlines the unique character of a *cyberpark*, functioning as a distinct entity and offering more than the mere sum of its major components, i.e. 'cyber' and 'parks'. Having this in mind, it is worth probing into the views of CyberParks participants[2] as concerns the main characteristics, conditions and functions of this new hybrid space. Such an exercise is quite important for the formation of a theoretical notion that aspires to adequately persuade policy makers, local authorities, and the public, in order to be effectively implemented and well accepted by stakeholders.

Bearing the above in mind, it is useful to distinguish the "points of agreement", or "strong points" of experts concerning the notion of *cyberpark*, and compare it with equivalent points concerning POS in general. As "points of agreement" or "strong points" we refer to the responses of various questions, which scored 20.0% or more in frequency, compared to the rest of the responses to the specific question. For *cyberpark*, these were:

- *Importance of constituent elements*: people (59.1%)
- *Cyberpark keywords*: Technology/ICT (43.4%), Space/POS (26.4%)
- *Suitable locations:* city centre (29.1%)
- *Suitable sizes:* medium (58.3%)
- *Target Population:* city residents (26.0%), tourists (24.9%)
- *Provision and maintenance*: authorities (65.9%).

In the categories of *Qualities of space*, *Facilities provided*, *Facilitated activities*, and *Suitable spaces* there were no responses which clearly dominated the opinions of experts.

At the same time, looking at the equivalent responses for the POS, the same categories of questions gather high percentages of most preferred responses, and furthermore, the first preferences of these categories were the same as in *cyberpark*. More specifically:

- *Importance of constituent elements*: people (68.2%)
- *Suitable locations:* city centre (27.2%)
- *Suitable sizes:* medium (42.9%)

[2] All CyberParks participants are considered, by definition, to be experts on the issues examined here (i.e. the relationship between POS and ICTs), since this is a prerequisite form their participation in the COST Action. However, as discussed, CyberParks participants might understand and approach *cyberpark* slightly different, due to their different scientific discipline, theoretical background, occupation, nationality, etc.

- *Target Population:* city residents (23%), locals (22.2%), which is almost double than tourists (13.5%)
- *Provision and maintenance:* authorities (65.9%).

In *Qualities of space*, *Facilities provided*, *Facilitated activities*, and *Suitable spaces* there were no responses which clearly dominated the opinions of experts (as was the case in *cyberpark*).

The category of *Cyberpark keywords* had no equivalent in POS. One could note, though, a sign of contradiction in experts' responses in this category, compared to the ones in *Importance of constituent elements*. So, although *people* are recognized as the most important element for *cyberpark*, in comparison to *space* and *technology*, the most "favourite" keywords belong to the categories of *technology (ICT)* and *space (POS)*. At the same time, keywords of the category of *technology* gathered 61 preferences, the *space* category 54, and the category of *people* 45 preferences.

In the categories of no responses of high occurrence (*Qualities of space*, *Facilities provided*, *Facilitated activities*, and *Suitable spaces*), coincidence of the same answers in the first places of preferences in *cyberpark* and POS was recorded in *Facilitated activities* [*socialize* with 10% of opinions in *cyberpark* (sharing the first place with *relax* and *communicate*) and 13.3% in POS], and in *Suitable spaces* (*Parks* with 13.7% of opinions in *cyberpark* and 17.6% in POS), while in *Qualities of space*, *safety* was a close second (10.3%) in *cyberpark* [first being *information transmission* (11.75%)], and first (11.21%) in POS (with the same percentage of opinions with *natural environment*).

Conclusions drawn from the above are that for experts, a *cyberpark* retains the "strong" characteristics of POS. It is worth noticing that, besides these common "strong" characteristics there were no other "strong" ones, either solely for a *cyberpark* or for POS. So, for experts, a *cyberpark* has to share significant common ground with POS, and ideally, both should have *people* as the most important constituent element, they should be in the *city centre*, being of a *medium size*, having *city residents* as their *target group*, and having *authorities* (municipality, etc.) responsible for their *provision and maintenance*. Experts also tend to think, in lower percentages, that both *cyberparks* and POS should be *safe*, with *socializing* as the most important *facilitated activity*, and preferably in *parks*.

Looking for elements distinguishing *cyberpark* space from conventional POS, there were no coincidences in the first three categories of facilities of high occurrence in responses between *cyberpark* and POS in the category of *Facilities provided*, and – expectedly so – *internet* was the prime preference for the former with 15.9% of responses, with *places to sit* being the prime equivalent for the latter with 12.5% of responses. The responses of high occurrence in this category (*internet*, *interacting information*, and *places to work* for *cyberpark*, and *places to sit*, *facilities for disadvantaged*, and *facilities for visitors* for POS) show a differentiation of the character of *cyberpark* from this of POS, the former being more "informatic" with the latter being closer to social values and aspects. This is perhaps the reason why experts see suitable places for *cyberparks* to be leftover spaces, bus/railway stations and stops and internalised public spaces of rather medium to small sizes. Moving to the *Accommodated activities*, *cyberpark's* role is perceived in facilitating communication, education and work, whereas POS is appreciated mainly for its recreation and leisure aspects. As such, it is not surprising that in the categories of *Target population*, *elderly people* are almost ignored in *cyberpark* (presumably because this group is expected to use ICT at a lesser degree than young people[3]) whereas in *Provision and maintenance*, the *private sector* is seen as a possible provider of *cyberpark* in a much higher percentage that the equivalent in POS. This is also verified in the category of *Cyberpark keywords* where *ICT*, *POS*, *interactive*, and *enhanced* were considered as better characterizing a *cyberpark.* As discussed above, all these belong to the categories of *technology*, and *space*, while the category of *people* gathered keywords with lower preferences of the former.

5 Conclusions

This chapter comes to provide, in a more systematic and organized way, a contextualization of the various dimensions of the *cyberpark* concept, which emerge due to different perspectives, disciplines, backgrounds, etc. of the 84 experts involved in the CyberParks COST Action. We believe that such analysis would enrich the ongoing dialogue within the respective scientific community, and facilitate interactions between relevant, yet fragmented, research in various scientific areas and countries. From the analysis we conducted, a number of points drawn should be highlighted.

First, *cyberpark* is perceived as a specific type of POS, characterised by enhanced provision of information technology that advance modern life. However, as any type of POS, *cyberpark* is a space aiming to serve the needs of real people, by combining recreation and leisure along with connectivity, interaction and community development. Second, although most POS areas are suitable for the deployment of a *cyberpark*, such spaces might be more relevant in specific sites and locations that best serve its purpose. Leftover spaces, bus and railway stops and stations, institutional public spaces and internalized 'public' spaces in downtown and city centres seem to be appropriate such locations. Third, *cyberpark*, though a bit costly in development and maintenance (due to the ICT element that it adds to the conventional POS), are appreciated for adding value to modern cities. On these grounds, local authorities should opt for their provision and should bear these costs as it is argued that these *cyberpark* spaces would increase citizens' welfare and the quality of urban life overall.

[3] This might be due to lack of dexterity or need on the part of the elderly to use ICTs, at least as compared to the younger generations. Surely, it seems that technology, from computing to cell phones, is not designed having the elderly in mind.

References

Agora Cyberparks (2017). http://cyberparks-project.eu/agora/forums/topic/extended-definition-based-on-discussion/. Accessed June 2017

Smaniotto Costa, C., Martínez, A.B., Álvarez, F.J., Šuklje-Erjavec, I., Menezes, M., Pallares-Barbera, M.: Digital tools for capturing user's needs on urban open spaces: drawing lessons from cyberparks project. In: Certomà, C., Dyer, M., Pocatilu, L., Rizzi, F. (eds.) Citizen Empowerment and Innovation in the Data-Rich City, pp. 177–194. Springer, Cham (2017). https://doi.org/10.1007/978-3-319-47904-0_11

Part II Socio-Spatial Practices

Edited by Therese Kenna and Gabriela Maksymiuk

2.1

Socio-Spatial Practices: An Introduction and Overview

Therese Kenna[1(✉)] and Gabriela Maksymiuk[2]

[1] University College Cork, Cork, Ireland
t.kenna@ucc.ie
[2] Warsaw University of Life Sciences, Warsaw, Poland
gabriela_maksymiuk@sggw.pl

1 Introduction: Socio-Spatial Practices

We are now firmly in a digital era and technologies are ever-present. Since the introduction of new digital technologies and ICTs, such as smart phones, the literature has presented some contrasting analyses of the socio-spatial practices and impacts that have resulted from the uptake of new technologies in urban public spaces. On one hand, there is a particular set of debates that have expressed concerns that the introduction of digital technologies, especially personal ICTs, is leading to a greater withdrawal from urban public spaces. For example, the work by Hampton and Gupta (2008) and Hampton *et al.* (2010) examined uses of ICTs in urban public spaces. They concluded that people who were using technology in public spaces were not actively engaged in the public spaces and were merely "silent spectators". This allowed for a 'public privatism' and created concerns for a widening of the gaps between public and private and a decline of public spaces. These sorts of findings create concerns for the diminishing value of public space in a traditional sense, for the declining significance of public spaces in the digital era, and for the potential of ICTs to generate and increase social inequalities, as well as reduce opportunities for encountering 'others' in the city.

Somewhat contrary to such studies are a number of recent examples of the ways in which social media, smart phones and other platforms are used to encourage physical gathering in public squares, citing examples such as the Arab Springs, anti-austerity protests in Europe, and the Occupy movement that quickly spread globally (Dieter and van Doorn 2013). In these instances, the gatherings in public spaces can be recorded through video and photography and uploaded in real time to the Web, transforming individuals into a collective to address political issues (Dieter and van Doorn 2013). What emerges as apparent then, following Willis (2007, p. 160), is that wireless communication technologies such as smart phones can enable 'multiple social realities' to occur in a single place. While we are witnessing evidence of the potentials for ICTs, like smart phones, to create new social spaces, this is primarily through the use of social media and technologies to create new political functions for citizens and public spaces via gathering and protest.

The contrasting perspectives offer a snapshot of some the ways in which new technologies, especially ICTs, are thought to be transforming the nature of social

C. Smaniotto Costa et al. (Eds.): CyberParks, LNCS 11380, pp. 69–75, 2019.
https://doi.org/10.1007/978-3-030-13417-4_6

relationships and of socio-spatial practices in urban public spaces. One criticism that has emerged from some of the recent research is directed towards the inadequacies that current social research methods present when researching in the digital era. Digital and online methods are now increasing in popularity, albeit in limited ways. Social networking sites such as Facebook and Twitter are being used to conduct social research and as such are opening up the production of knowledge and new ways of understanding. In particular, online spaces, such as Twitter and Facebook, are being increasingly used as digital data sources for researchers where content analysis of the data, that is publicly available on such sites, is being performed (see Dowling *et al.* 2015). Latham (2014, p. 111) noted how social media technologies and websites have become a rich source of data, with things like Twitter forming 'micro-diaries' of lived experience. Latham notes, however, that researchers are only beginning to explore the potential of social media technologies to generate electronic diaries of everyday lives. That is, the use of digital spaces and social media platforms for research activities and as data gathering spaces is relatively new. A paper by de Freitas (2010, p. 640) that reviewed current research on the implications of ICTs for the city and everyday social life, noted that the increasing prevalence of digital realities opens up new opportunities for imaginative research techniques such as interviews conducted via social networking sites or real-time archiving of field-notes in 140 characters or less on Twitter, which can be additions to the more established research methods for social sciences researchers. A recent article by De Jong (2014) reflected on the use of one online space, Facebook, as a site for storytelling in research. De Jong's (2014, p. 1) research with festival participants used the online space of Facebook. This research project ultimately concluded that Facebook "has the potential to allow for different ways of knowing that cannot be ascertained in more orthodox research spaces". As De Jong (2014) argued, there is a strong need to re-imagine the ways in which various online spaces may be incorporated as sites for methodologies (p. 2). The Chapters in Part II contribute to these emerging literature and debates by offering novel perspectives on both research methods for analysing the socio-spatial practices in urban public spaces in the digital era, and empirical data into emerging socio-spatial practices and outcomes.

Beyond these two sets of debates, there is emerging research and literature on the ways that ICTs can be used in urban professions, such as urban planning and design. Here, the research to-date is exploring the potential opportunities that might exist when ICTs are used in urban planning, especially for the ways in which ICTs can lead to more user-friendly or people-centred urban spaces, as well as more inclusionary urban planning, design and development processes, that are bottom-up, rather than top-down, and open to diverse socio-spatial practices. ICTs in urban environments deal with several issues, i.e. citizen activism, governance or urban planning. For all these issues, ICTs give a possibility for 'electronic' versions of activities or actions that traditionally had been organised in physical realities. Thus nowadays, we face a specific duality of virtual and physical as, for example, citizen activism can take the form of e-activism, governance can be changed with e-governance and even democracy can be outlined as e-democracy. The case studies and examples showing that new technological solutions increase in general the participation and public engagement in urban issues are numerous, but at the same time there are contrary opinions that omnipresent new technologies can cause the exclusion of some users. The findings of research performed by Yeh (2017) on participation with Taiwanese citizens, reveal that they are willing to accept and use the ICT-based smart city services, and that the access to 'e-services' resulted in higher quality of life being achieved. Also, work by Soomro et al. (2017) presenting results from an EU FP7 project called 'urbanAPI', in which 3 different ICT applications addressing diverse aspects of participatory urban governance were tested in four countries, show that the studied applications are useful tools especially for: enhancing spatial planning assessments, activating public participation and 'communicating proposed plans to different stakeholders and identifying key development issues which can provide crucial inputs in planning and decision making processes' (p. 419). On the other hand, according to recent findings of Ertiö and Bhagwatwar (2017) nowadays citizens are more interested and capable to use and benefit from online platforms that facilitate urban planning. Furthermore, Mueller et al. (2018) argues that even though the last decades in urban design research are characterised by a focus on smart cities, actualised through advanced technological aspects of cities, nowadays we are aware that a good infrastructure and sustainable energy supply do not make liveable cities alone, but we also need a citizens' input and feedback. This approach of harnessing information from urban users is greatly enhanced by ICTs and is essential for reaching a responsive city (p. 181). The recent Swedish studies show that the outdoor mobile augmented reality tools facilitate on-site multi-stakeholder urban design and gathering of crowdsourced data, and thus 'mobile and cloud-based computing technologies open up possibilities for multi-stakeholder inclusion in urban planning' (Imottesjo and Kain 2018, p. 1). However, as stated above quite opposite findings are also present. For example, the Finnish study on the appropriation process of two public computing infrastructures in the City of Oulu, a municipal WiFi network and large interactive displays, showed that while the use of the WiFi network has grown steadily, the use of the displays has been declining (Ylipulli et al. 2014). Positioned within these recent debates and the emerging literature, the Chapters in Part II offer some discussions and case study research into the ways new technologies, such as Twitter and participatory GIS, can offer urban planning and design professionals useful tools for understanding social behaviours, attitudes and diverse socio-spatial practices, which will ultimately enable more inclusive design, planning and decision-making processes, as well as more inclusionary urban public spaces.

2 Urban Ethnography

The chapters in Part II are also the result of the working group on urban ethnography in the CyberParks COST Action TU1306. The aim of this working group was to bring together knowledge about the uses of new technologies in public spaces and to create new understandings of the relationships between public spaces and social behaviour in the digital era, in order to understand how to best connect technology with public spaces for socially sustainable outcomes. The working group was concerned with theoretical and methodological approaches, as well as novel research findings. The leading questions for the working group were: What is known about the relationship between new media use and spatial practices? What do people want from public space?

Does this differ by socioeconomic status, gender, age? What technological developments are most likely to enhance current user behaviour or develop new user behaviours? Essentially, the improvement, through Information and Communication Technologies (ICT), of the quality of urban life, the inclusion and social participation in the design of public open spaces (POS), and the development of tools for studying and supporting urban planning, were basic goals for the working group.

3 Overview of Chapters

The Chapters in this section of the book fall into three broad categories. Firstly, are those concerned with the generation of novel empirical data on the emerging socio-spatial practices resulting from the increased uptake of ICTs within urban public spaces. Secondly, are papers that focus on the need for methodological development to be able to capture the new socio-spatial practices in the digital era. Finally, there are two papers that focus on the contributions of ICTs and new technologies to urban professionals.

The first chapter 2.2 by **Marluci Menezes, Paschalis Arvanitidis, Therese Kenna and Petja Ivanova-Radovanova** is entitled '**People-space-technology: an ethnographic approach**'. This chapter is concerned with ethnographic research methodologies in the digital era. In particular, this chapter questions the utility of current ethnographic approaches and develops a new framework to guide researchers undertaking research relating to peoples use of technology in urban space. The authors argue that in the digital era, ethnographic research is required to capture, explore and understand the cyber-social phenomena and dynamics in a multifaceted, hybrid, triangulated and cross-referenced way, which makes the research more complex and perhaps more stimulating. By providing an integrated framework for the analysis of the relationships between people, space and technology, the authors of this Chapter argue that the ethnographic approach is enriched, as is our knowledge of socio-spatial practices in urban public spaces.

Following this, in chapter 2.3 **Paschalis Arvanitidis, Therese Kenna, and Gabriela Maksymiuk** explore university students use of ICTs in university public spaces, entitled "**Public space engagement and ICT usage by university students: an exploratory study in three countries**". The research in these locations examined how university students perceive and use the public spaces on their university campuses, and how they now use personal technologies, such as smart phones, within these spaces. Importantly, the research in this Chapter is based on data that was collected from an online questionnaire, and thus new digital methods were used in this study. The research is conducted in three geographic locations: University College Cork in Cork (Ireland), the University of Thessaly in Volos (Greece), and the Warsaw University of Life Sciences in Warsaw (Poland), which has allowed for novel insights into the differences and similarities that arise in these differing contexts.

The work presented by **Marluci Menezes, Paschalis Arvanitidis, Carlos Smaniotto Costa and Zvi Weinstein** entitled '**Teenagers' perception of public spaces and their ICTs practices**' (chapter 2.4) focusses on a cohort of the population who are deemed to be tech-savvy and thus heavily intertwined in the debates about the new socio-spatial practices in urban public spaces in the digital era. In this chapter, the authors shed light on the perceptions and practices of adolescents, as obtained via structured interviews with teenagers living in Hannover (Germany), Lisbon (Portugal), Tel Aviv (Israel) and Volos (Greece). The study is small-scale and offers some preliminary results that are argued to be indicative of possible wider trends and attitudes. In particular, the authors articulate how young people from distinct sociocultural contexts perceive and use both public spaces and digital technologies, and thus they identify teenagers emerging socio-spatial practices.

The chapter 2.5 by **Montserrat Pallares-Barbera, Elena Masala, Jugoslav Jokovic, Aleksandra Djukic and Xavier Albacete** is entitled "**Challenging methods and results obtained from user-generated content in Barcelona's urban open spaces**". This chapter examines user-generated content from Twitter users in Barcelona, Spain. The research examined the spatial signatures that result from the twitter uses in different public open spaces in Barcelona. It is argued that the analysis of the data offers insights into new social behaviours that are emerging in public spaces and of a range of multifunctional uses within the public spaces. The authors argue that user-generated content (UGC) provides useful resources for academics, technicians and policymakers to obtain and analyse results in order to improve lives of individuals in urban settings. They argue, similar to the emerging debates in the literature noted in the introduction, that there are new methodologies and new data sources, such as Twitter, that can offer new insights into socio-spatial practices in urban public spaces and thus these new insights can better inform urban planning practice.

The final chapter 2.6 in Part II by **Antoine Zammit, Therese Kenna and Gabriela Maksymiuk**, entitled "**Social implications of new mediated spaces: the need for a rethought design approach**", examines the ways in which ICTs can be utilised as tools for enhancing urban planning and design process for more inclusionary urban public spaces. In this Chapter, case studies are presented from three European urban contexts – the UK, Poland and Malta – where research has been conducted into the use of participatory digital mapping for citizen participation in urban planning and design. Here, ICT tools such as PGIS, or SoftGIS, are discussed for their abilities to engage a wider range of social groups in planning and design processes than might be obtained through more traditional methods of participation, such as written submissions or face-to-face meetings. Ultimately, new technologies have allowed for an expansion of the tools and methods available for participation in urban planning and design processes, thus allowing urban professionals to have access to a greater range of socio-spatial practices and behaviours. This will essentially allow for the design of more inclusive urban public spaces, designed with a diverse range of social groups and users in mind.

Each of the chapters in Part II offer new contributions to knowledge relating to the use of digital technologies in urban public spaces, the methodologies for understanding the new relationships and practices, and the applications of new technologies in the design of urban public spaces. Chapters 2.2 and 2.5 present strong arguments for the need for new research methods to analyse the people-space-technology triad. Chapters 2.3, 2.5 and 2.6 offer examples of the ways in which digital methods can be used to analyse new socio-spatial practices and attitudes in urban public spaces. Beyond the methodological contributions, the work in Chapters 2.3, 2.4 and 2.5 all offer new insights into the lived experiences of new technologies in urban public spaces, albeit through small-scale pilot studies and preliminary analyses. Importantly, the work in Chapters 2.3 and 2.4 has strongly argued for the need to develop research that spans different social and cultural contexts, as this enables us to reveal the differences and similarities that can occur in the uses, perceptions and relationships between technology, people and urban space. Further, the work in chapters 2.5 and 2.6 highlight the ways that new technologies can be harnessed for urban design and planning, by using tools such as Twitter and PGIS to understanding a wider range of socio-spatial practices than traditional methods might allow, and ultimately allow for a more inclusive planning and design process and outcome. In all, the chapters in Part II contribute to emerging debates in the literature.

References

Ertiö, T.-P., Bhagwatwar, A.: Citizens as planners: harnessing information and values from the bottom-up. Int. J. Inf. Manage. **37**(3), 111–113 (2017)

De Freitas, A.: Changing spaces: locating public space at the intersection of the physical and digital. Geogr. Compass **4**(6), 630–643 (2010)

De Jong, A.: Using Facebook as a space for storytelling in geographical research. Geogr. Res. **53** (2), 211–223 (2014)

Dieter, M., van Doorn, N.: Urban Social Spaces: Tactical Media in the Hybrid City'. New Media Theories - Research Essay (2013)

Dowling, R., Lloyd, K., Suchet-Pearson, S.: Qualitative methods 1: enriching the interview. Prog. Hum. Geogr. **40**, 1–8 (2015)

Hampton, K.N., Gupta, N.: Community and social interaction in the wireless city: Wi-Fi use in public and semi-public spaces. New Media Soc. **10**(6), 831–850 (2008)

Hampton, K., Livio, O., Sessions Goulet, L.: The social life of wireless urban spaces: internet use, social networks, and the public realm. J. Commun. **60**, 701–722 (2010)

Imottesjo, H., Kain, J.H.: The urban cobuilder – a mobile augmented reality tool for crowd-sourced simulation of emergent urban development patterns: requirements, prototyping and assessment. In: Computers, Environment and Urban Systems (2018). https://doi.org/10.1016/j.compenvurbsys.2018.05.003

Latham, A.: Using diaries to study urban worlds'. In: Ward, K. (ed.) Researching the City: A Guide for Students. Sage, London (2014)

Mueller, J., Lu, H., Chirkin, A., Klein, B., Schmitt, G.: Citizen design science: a strategy for crowd-creative urban design. Cities **72**(Part A), 181–188 (2018)

Soomro, K., Khan, Z., Ludlow, D.: Participatory governance in smart cities: the urban API case study. Int. J. Serv. Technol. Manage. **23**(5/6), 419–444 (2017)

Willis, K.: Sensing place – mobile and wireless technologies in urban space. In: Meier, L., Frers, L. (eds.) Encountering Urban Places: Visual and Material Performances in the City. Ashgate, Aldershot (2007)

Yeh, H.: The effects of successful ICT-based smart city services: from citizens' perspectives'. Gov. Inf. Q. **34**(3), 556–565 (2017)

Ylipulli, J., Suopajärvi, T., Ojala, T., Kostakos, V., Kukka, H.: Municipal WiFi and interactive displays: appropriation of new technologies in public urban spaces. Technol. Forecast. Soc. Chang. **89**, 145–160 (2014). https://doi.org/10.1016/j.techfore.2013.08.037

2.2

People - Space - Technology: An Ethnographic Approach

Marluci Menezes[1(✉)], Paschalis Arvanitidis[2], Therese Kenna[3], and Petja Ivanova-Radovanova[4]

[1] National Laboratory for Civil Engineering – LNEC, Lisbon, Portugal
marluci@lnec.pt
[2] Department of Economics, University of Thessaly, Volos, Greece
parvanit@uth.gr
[3] Department of Geography, University College Cork, Cork, Ireland
t.kenna@ucc.ie
[4] Association for Integrated Development and Sustainability, Sofia, Bulgaria
petjaivanova@gmail.com

Abstract. CyberParks aims at advancing knowledge on the relationship between information and communication technologies and the socially sustainable production and usage of public open spaces. Such research necessitates a solid methodological base. Urban ethnography brings together a number of perspectives and approaches to deal with cultural and social aspects of urban life, and as such it is able to provide an integrated methodological framework for the study of technology-public space relationship. The ethnographic approach means, by definition, an in-depth, micro-scale look at the phenomena under concern. However, the technological dimension makes the relationship between people and space more complex. This is not simply because an additional layer of analysis is added; it comes as a result of the emergence of multiple connections between the real and the virtual. From an ethnographic perspective, this requires the researcher to capture, explore and understand the cyber-social phenomena and dynamics in a multifaceted, hybrid, triangulated and cross-referenced way. This makes ethnographic research much more complicated but more interesting as well. The current chapter attempts to outline such an analytical framework to guide empirical research on the issues. This framework draws on the public space literature and adds the technological dimension brought in by the CyberParks project. We argue that this enriches the ethnographic approach providing a more integrated framework for the analysis of the relationship between people, space and technology.

Keywords: Ethnographic perspective · Methodological framework · Micro-scale · Social hybrid dynamics · Cyber phenomena

C. Smaniotto Costa et al. (Eds.): CyberParks, LNCS 11380, pp. 76–86, 2019.
https://doi.org/10.1007/978-3-030-13417-4_7

1 Introduction: Capturing the Social Cyber Phenomenon in Urban Public Spaces

The improvement, through Information and Communication Technologies (ICT), of the quality of urban life, the inclusion and social participation in the design of public open spaces (POS), and the development of tools for studying and supporting urban planning, constitute basic pursuits of the CyberParks project. Certainly, all these presuppose and necessitate a clear and coherent view of the relationship between people, space and technology, and the dynamics of their links. Questions that come to the fore include: What kind of public spaces, people, practices and needs are we talking about? How does the introduction of ICT affect both space and people? How are POS design, planning and usage affected by the osmosis of the real with the virtual? What kind of new experiences, discourses, practices and expectations would emerge in such world?

Ethnography is a methodological perspective that can shed light on all these questions. This is due to its ability to explore "understudied regions of society" and to "illuminate the unknown" (cf. Didier Fassin, in Low 2016: 2), placing emphasis on people and their preferences, practices and experiences. Such oriented ethnography can provide a base to the study of socio-spatial questions, and the development of knowledge about the people-space-technology relationship. In that direction, we follow Low (2016) to conceive space as a site of culture, to draw on the notion of spatialization[1] that takes under proper consideration the multiple, translocal and unequal social processes of production and construction of space[2], and to use ethnography as an approach for the understanding of people's living within space.

The notion of spatialization of culture (Low 2016) allows us to consider that people create spaces through their bodies and behaviours, discourses, emotive and affective aspects, as well as through their mobility and trajectories. Space is thus embodied and endowed with meanings, just as everyday patterns, movements, and trajectories occur in specific places and landscapes. Thus, ethnography of socio-spatial questions is oriented towards capturing place making. In summary, these issues contribute to the reciprocal incorporation of the material and the experiential.

However, constituting ICT as a tangible dimension of the social (Castells 2001) leads to the emergence of complex socio-spatial experiences, generating a multiplicity of connections (and disconnections) between real-real and virtual-real. This is not simply because an additional layer of analysis in added, giving rise to a dualism between the real and the virtual. In fact, the complexity is the result of the emergence of new relationships between the real-real and the real-virtual, in which cybernetic reality increasingly becomes a tangible dimension of the social. From an ethnographic perspective, this requires the researcher to capture, explore and understand the cyber-social

---

[1] By spatialization we mean the physical, historical, affective and discursive production and localization process of social relations, institutions, representations and practices in space.

[2] By social production of space, we consider the factors – social, economic, ideological and technological - that contribute to the creation and materialization of a setting. The social construction of space is here considered as the phenomenological and symbolic experiences that take place in space, being mediated by the change, conflict and control process (Low 2000a, b).

phenomena and dynamics in a multifaceted, hybrid, triangulated and cross-referenced way. It should be pointed out, however, that the methodological perspective advocated here is not ethnography of the virtual space. It is rather an approach to capture the richness of the relationship between people, space and ICT. In other words, we are interested here in an ethnographic analysis of socio-spatial issues related to urban public spaces, taking into proper account the technological element and the changes it leads to. That is, in particular, it is intended to finding ways to help answer questions, such as: What is known about the relationship between new media use and spatial practices? What do people want from an ICT enhanced public open space? How do these requirements differ by socioeconomic status, gender and age? What technological developments are most likely to enhance current user behaviour or develop new user behaviours?

On these grounds, the current chapter provides introductory methodological and applied guidance for doing ethnography with a focus on the triptych people-space-technology. In achieving this objective, the arguments presented here place emphasis on the following aspects: (1) the ethnographic issues that the CyberParks project presents and the challenges they put to the scholar of the contemporary urban phenomenon; and synthetic explanation of what an ethnographic approach means, emphasizing the importance of capturing the phenomena under study from a micro-scale and a close and deep perspective; (2) an ethnographic analytical perspective seen through the lenses and objectives set by the CyberParks project, namely: to bring more people into POS; suggest urban design responses that are closer to people's needs and interests; increase people's participation in the design of POS; improve the planning and urban design processes; and to develop an ethnographic analytical framework on the main dimensions about which specific studies will be carried out.

2 Ethnographic Perspective to Capture the Cyberpark Phenomenon

The urban ethnographic perspective to CyberParks analysis aims to advance understanding of the relation between space-people-technology and its dynamics, through cultural and sociological fieldwork and by employing various theoretical and methodological approaches. In particular, it brings together knowledge about the use of new ICT in POS, enhances understanding of POS and of human behaviour in the context of new media, and offers advice for appropriate ways in employing technology within public spaces. To do so, researchers should observe uses of technology within space as well as behaviours in space of all people, including those using and those not using technology. But in what sense can an ethnographic perspective help us to clarify and understand the people-space relationship and its links with technology?

The first aspect to consider is the unquestionable influence of ICT in the growing, accelerated and unequal transformation of society and, as such, of urban contexts. What, in the first instance, hinders the design of public spaces in a manner that is more inclusive, participative, healthy and connected with the needs and desires of the people? That is, there is a lack of knowledge about the relation between people-space-technology in order to think and to create POS that are more suitable to people, despite the fact that there is a proliferation of studies in the contemporary public space literature. This is because the majority of such studies are of a macro-analytical nature and, in many cases, the design of space is privileged to the detriment of the understanding of the relationship between people and space, even if digital technologies are included in this connection. What we argue is that in order to capture and better understand the socio-spatial issues with proper emphasis on the ICT dimension, it is important to carry out smaller, more intensive and comprehensive studies, and pervade by dense descriptions.

The above, we advocate, provides a more precise approximation and increases the possibility of producing useful practical (and theoretical) knowledge of the relationship between people-space-technology. The adoption of an analytical prism close to and within the social practices in public space can even be an important contribution to answer the many questions that arise in the context of living, thinking and acting in the city. This is because, this approach of 'close and inside' can also be associated to the idea of proximity and assiduity with the study contexts; it makes possible to detect sociocultural regularities and patterns, but it also contributes to overcoming the most visible expressions of the contemporary city, in large part associated with its multiple fragmentations and transformations. Such a perspective collaborates to recognize space as a significant reference for people and on that basis enables us to capture the social daily rhythms of space use and appropriation, and explore how these dynamics define behavioural scenarios, routes, points and landscapes. This, in other words, resonates the importance of micro-geographies (Barker and Shoggen 1973; Wicker 1979; Rapoport 1980; Low 2000a, b). We believe that the role of micro-geographies and the local context are both within the leading factors for urban development on different scales, including national, international or EU level, such as the differences of existing local institutions' policy frameworks could cause differences in the development of urban policy processes (Dukes 2010) and the difference in knowledge on public needs and preferences at the local level, which could lead to difficulties in applicability of modern technologies in public open space, relating to the needs of the public (Radovanova and Radovanov 2017). There is, therefore, a role that ethnography can play in capturing practices, always in transformation, but which define a variety of socio-spatial contexts. This is through the close approach to socio-spatial phenomena, which helps us to capture subtleties and distinctions (Geertz 1973). But, on the other hand, from a set of ethnographic experiences, the analysis should be complemented by a more distanced approach. This contributes to giving meaning to what is not yet part of integrated body of knowledge (cf. Lévi-Strauus, in Magnani 2009: 153).

3 Cyberpark: What Can Be Analysed from an Ethnographic Perspective?

An ethnographic approach to the people-space-technology triptych presupposes attention to the three poles, privileging the study of the relationship between them. Rather than considering social actors, spatial contexts and ICTs as separate elements, disseminated and subjugated to a macro and homogeneous urban order, it is essential to explore the dynamics through which the three constituent elements of the triptych are related, generating specific meanings, places and landscapes.

We are interested in going further from previous analyses in the field which, having an interest in answering certain objectives, do not correspond to what is primarily intended by an ethnographic approach. In the close and inside ethnographical approach, the objective is to provide a framework that contributes to awareness and guide scholars in capturing and understanding the less well-known aspects, though often seemingly obvious, singularities, patterns, etc., of the people-space-technology relationship. From a multidimensional point of view, the ethnography will be of interest to reconcile different levels of interpretation and scales of analysis: from the daily experiences of people in living spaces to those of a socio-historical nature; from social practices, discourses and representations, to aspects of the production and circulation of images and imagery; from planning ideologies to intervention techniques and urban design. In the idealized ethnography design, we suggest here (see Fig. 1) that the relations someone might intend to study, pivot around five linked points or questions of interest: Who are the users? How do they use the space? When do they use the space? Where, i.e. which places do they use? and What do users do (and what artefacts they use) in the spaces?

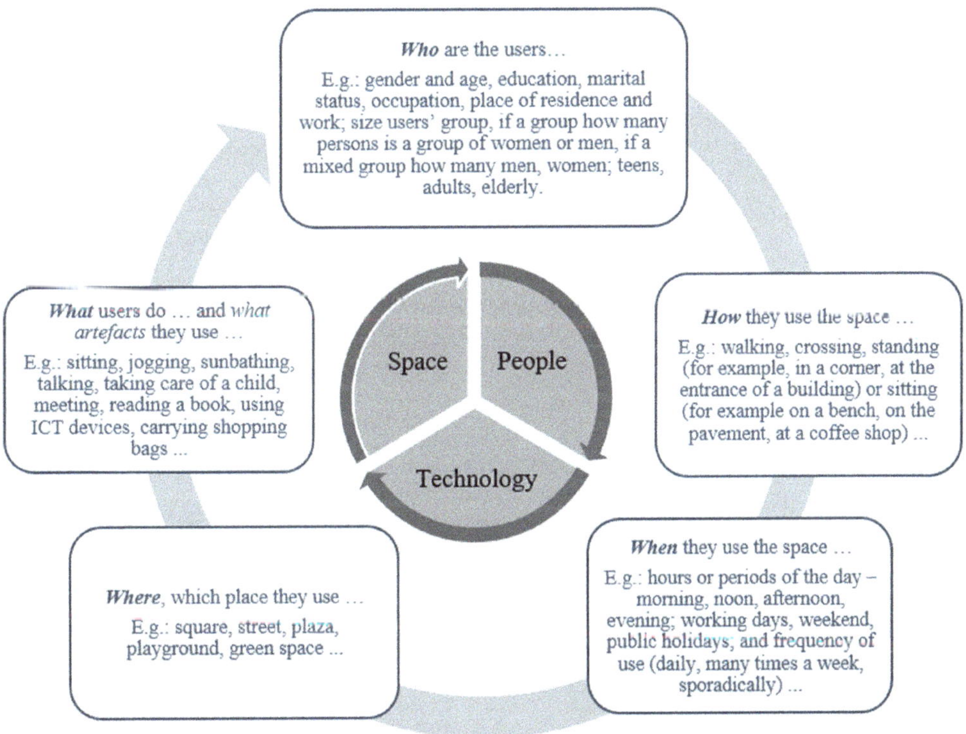

Fig. 1. CyberParks ethnographic approach: capturing the relationship between people-space-technology. Source: adapted from Menezes and Smaniotto Costa (2017)

Through ethnographic methods, the aim is to capture the relations between everyday micro-geographies in the use and appropriation of space, the use (or not) of technological artefacts and objects, the practices and socio-spatial representations, and the established relations between spaces, behaviours and environments in the constitution of urban places and landscapes (Menezes and Smaniotto Costa 2017)[3]. These relations are still central to understanding the meaning of lived spaces and the constituted spatialities considered important for urban design and planning as envisaged by the CyberParks project.

Having this general framework in mind, Fig. 2 presents the main dimensions research should address providing also the specific content (or objectives) of each dimension. In particular, we argue that the triptych people-space-technology can be ethnologically analysed along three dimensions, all of which keep the human element to the forefront while exploring the nexus of the other two (i.e. POS and ICT). The first dimension concerns the use and appropriation of POS by people.

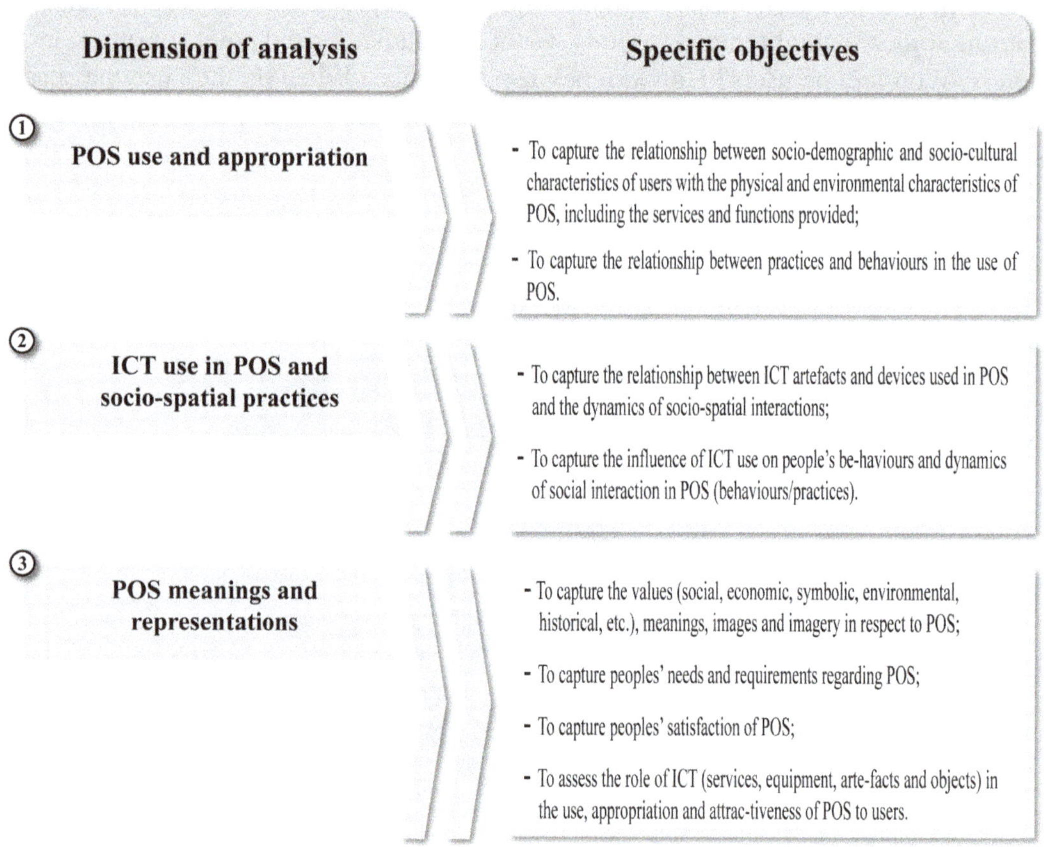

Fig. 2. Dimensions that capture the intersections between POS and ICT. (Objective: to identify the role of people-space-technology aspects of interactions).

Figure 2 focuses on the relationships between the socio-demographic characteristics of the users, on the one hand, and the physical, spatial, environmental and functional characteristics of the POS on the other, and it aims to capture the richness of deployed

---

[3] Of course, the realization of an ethnography is not alien to the more specific subjects and interests of the researchers, nor to their theoretical and conceptual options, which should be presented and discussed, which then defines the techniques and instruments to be used (and that can be many, for example, observation, interviews, questionnaires, photographs, behavioural maps, etc.).

behaviours and practices in the use and appropriation of POS. The second dimension brings into play the ICT element, placing emphasis on the way it affects space and social practices. In particular, it focuses on the relationships between ICT usage (of devices, artefacts, etc.) in POS and the dynamics of their interaction, aiming to capture the effect ICTs have on people's behaviour and practises in POS. The last dimension concentrates on meanings and representations of these relations. It aims to capture the richness of values, images and meanings (social, economic, symbolic, environmental, etc.) people attach to POS vis-à-vis their needs and levels of their satisfaction, and to evaluate the contribution of ICT (services, equipment, artefacts, etc.) in the fulfilment of those needs and the enhancement of POS attractiveness to the public.

Having identified the main dimensions of inquiry, the next step is to specify the variables of analysis and the kind of information that needs to be sought. Figures 3, 4 and 5 present these for the first, second and third dimensions respectively. It should be noted that our intention here is not to provide a full check-list of the relevant variables and information required, but rather to eclectically outline indicative aspects in order to convey our rationale and to clarify our perspective.

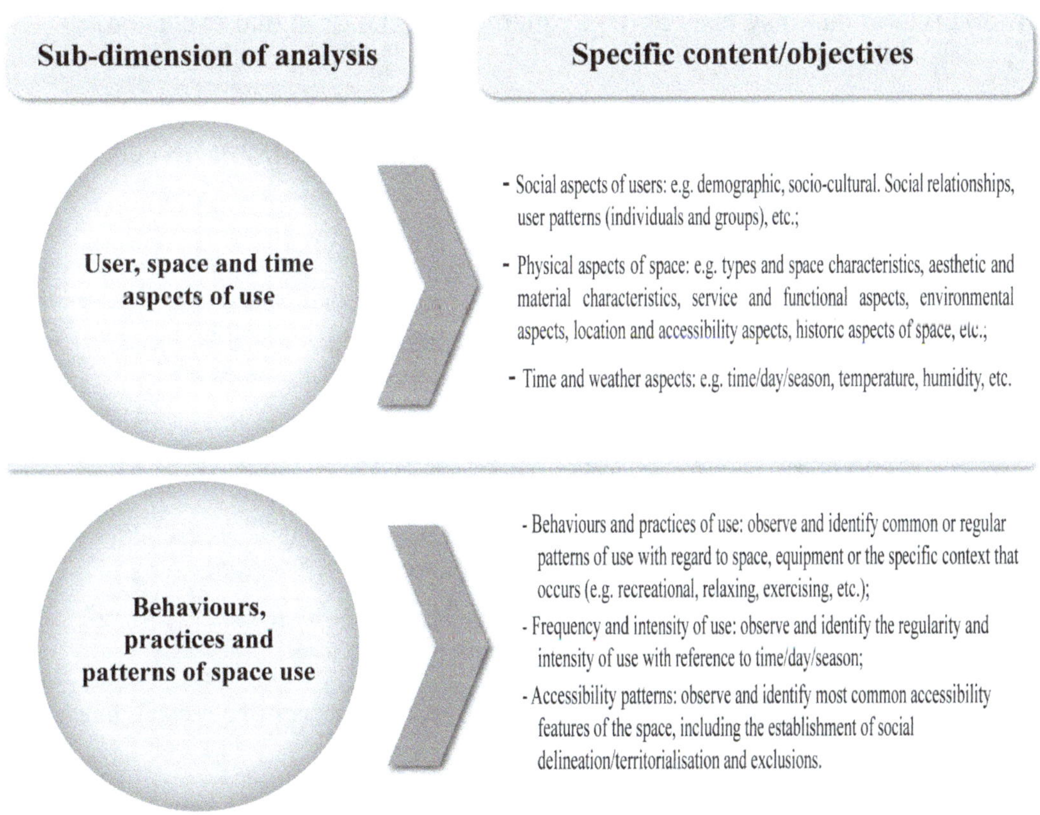

Fig. 3. Aspects that capture POS social use and appropriation (the first dimension).

The framework provided in this chapter has to be seen as holistic view towards public open space development within the scope of "triptych" approach for better understanding people-space-technology relationships. With regard to the first dimension of our approach, we envisage two sets of variables that need to be considered (see Fig. 3). The first concentrates on the social aspects of the users and the physical and temporal elements of their POS use. Information that needs to be collected concerns: the socio-demographic characteristics of the users (age, gender, education level, etc.), which provide the profile of the users, socio-cultural attributes (e.g. lifestyle) to allow for a description of the way users use the POS; social relationships (e.g. level of socialisation), which delineate the relationships between users in the POS; and use patterns (e.g. aspects of exclusion or heterogeneity); which outline the ways space is used and appropriated. In regard to the physical aspects of space, one needs to examine the location and accessibility characteristics of the POS, the composition of space (e.g. shadowed-sunny places), its service and functional characteristics (e.g. equipment, facilities and services available) and its environmental elements (vegetation cover, flora and fauna, etc.). The temporal element, finally, concerns the time of the study (hour, day and season) and the weather characteristics associated with it (temperature, humidity, etc.). The second set of variables we suggest concentrates on the practices and behavioural patterns of space usage. These concern the ways that space is used by the visitors (walking, strolling, sitting, exercising, etc.), the pattern of their accessibility, the frequency, regularity and intensity of the use, and the degree of territorialisation that may emerge (e.g. patterns of social or digital exclusion).

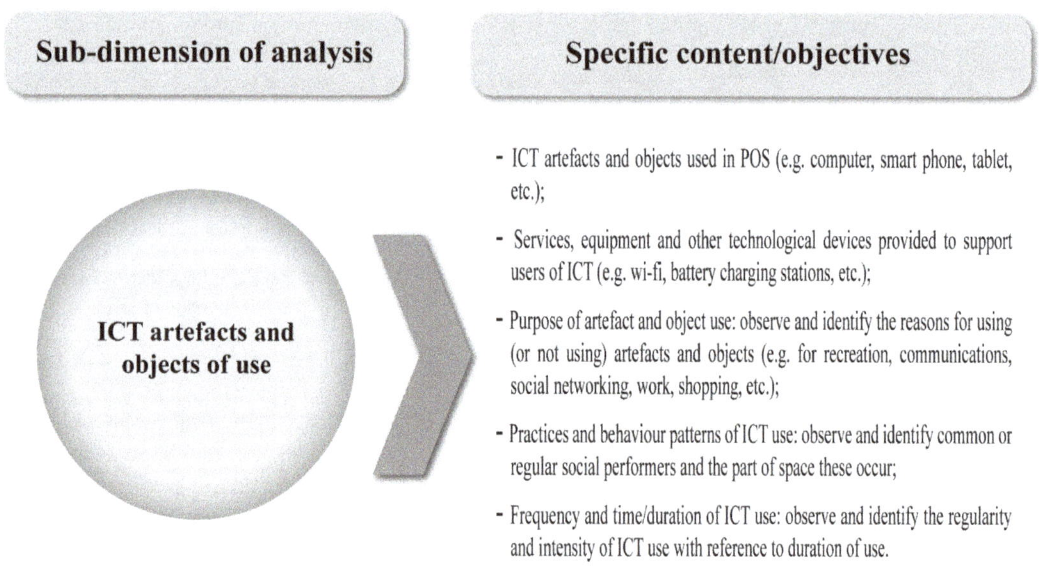

Fig. 4. Aspects that capture POS-ICT use and socio-spatial practices (the second dimension).

Moving to the second dimension of our framework, we place emphasis on ICT artefacts and objects of use (see Fig. 4). Here researchers need to record the types of devices and applications visitors used (smart phone, laptop, etc.), the artefacts, equipment and facilities the space provides to users (e.g. Wi-Fi access, furniture to electrically charge devices), the purpose of device and artefact use (e.g. for recreation, communication, work), the patterns of such use, and finally, the frequency and timing of the ICT use.

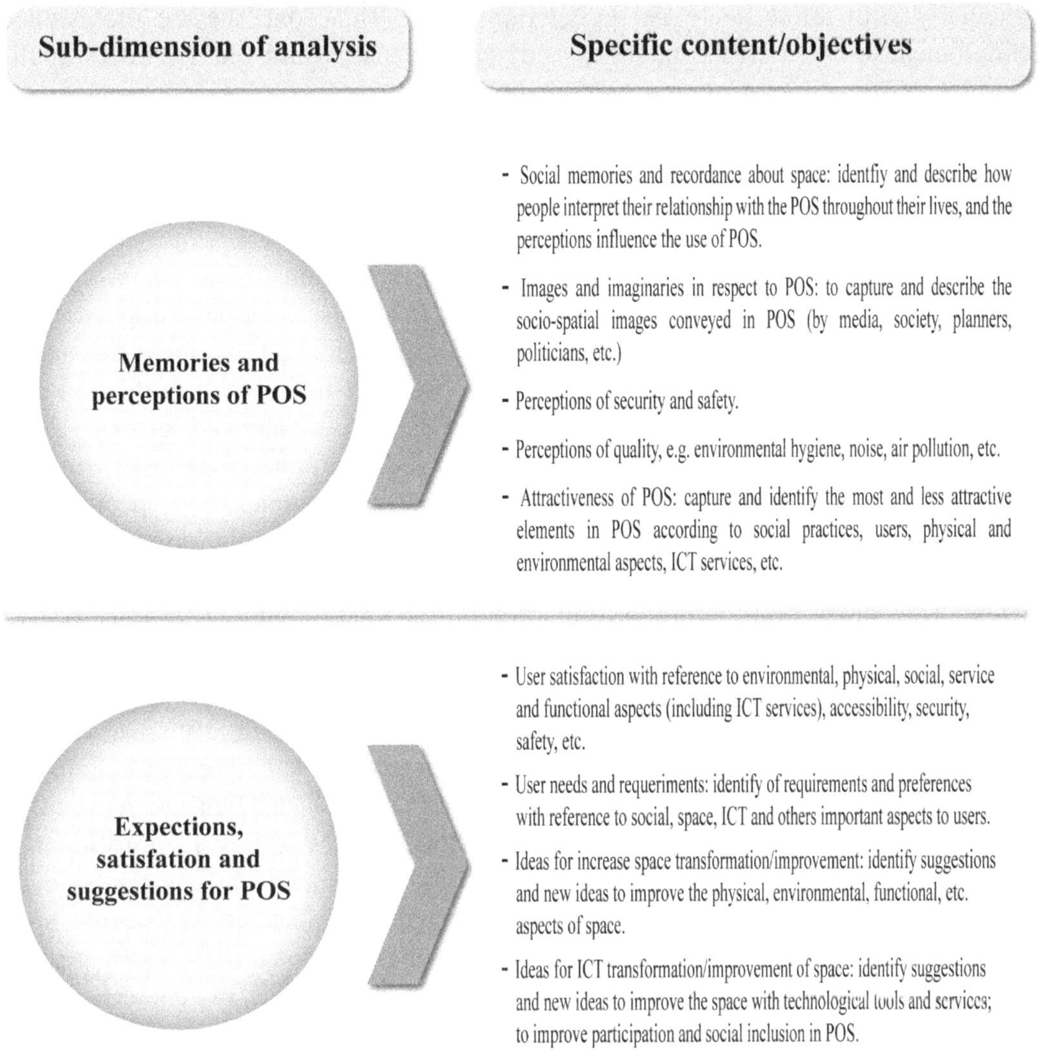

Fig. 5. Aspects that capture the POS social meaning and representations (the third dimension).

In the third dimension of our approach we perceive two key sets of variables that need to be examined (see Fig. 5). The first refers to the memories and perceptions of space, and the second to users' needs and levels of their satisfaction. With regard to the former, information that needs to be collected concerns: the social memories and meanings space connotes (i.e. how people perceive space and their social relationships in space); the images and imaginaries space conveys to different types of users and actors involved (e.g. planners, politicians, etc.); perceptions of security, safety and quality of space (noise, pollution, etc.); and, elements of space attractiveness to users (physical, environmental, digital, social, etc.). Turning to the second set of variables in this dimension, aspects that need to be considered include the level of users' satisfaction from all elements of space (physical, environmental, social, digital, functional, security, etc.), as well as their needs and their requirements. Last, but not least, users could and should provide the researcher with their ideas and suggestions of how space can be improved (in all of its aspects: physical, environmental, functional, etc.) and particularly with reference to its digital dimension. This concerns the provision of technological tools, artefacts, facilities and services that would improve POS quality and enhance social inclusion and participation.

4 Discussion and Conclusions

Given that a cyber reality has become a tangible dimension of the social world, it makes it more complex to conceptualise, capture and analyse socio-spatial phenomena, namely the social uses and needs of urban public space. This, on the one hand, implies that we need more agile and interdisciplinary approaches to research in this field. On the other hand, the broad dimension, continuous and accelerated growth of the cybernetic phenomenon, in parallel with urban transformation processes, require the production of more focused knowledge (micro-scale) with attention to specific situations and to people. The ethnographic perspective, although not the only available to such kind of inquiry, helps, to a great extent, to analyse and understand all such aspects. This stems from its proper emphasis on the spatio-temporal character of the social phenomena, enabling to formulate and further develop more comprehensive theories. We also strongly argue for the need to continually place people at the centre of our analyses, to best understand the people-space-technology triad. Thus, we advocate for a people-centred approach to research that seeks to understand the ways people use POS, ICTs and engage in a range of social behaviours within such spaces. As such, we feel that the framework presented in this Chapter makes a novel contribution to knowledge in this field and enhances our ability to achieve various goals in our explorations of contemporary understandings of the interactions between people, space and technology. One further aspect of our thinking that remains crucial to any research project, is a recognition that investments in, and developments of, CyberParks, are context specific and that CyberParks occur differently in different geographic locations, and will serve different purposes, as well as have different forms and functions within these locations. The inherent versatility of different locations calls for more call detailed and comprehensive studies to be carried out, as well as comparative research.

In this sense, the ethnographic framework we attempted to assemble in this article can be used for both the development of scientific knowledge on contemporary urban phenomena and for the provision of advice in urban design and planning. Certainly, such a framework cannot incorporate (and definitely we did not intend to do so) all aspects that can (or should) be studied in the context of the relationship between people, space and technology. That would be extremely difficult (if even possible) given the variety of disciplines, theories and perspectives involved, let alone that such an endeavour would be contrary to the spirit of the ethnographic approach itself. Yet, we attempted to pinpoint and incorporate elements we regarded as essential and pertinent to the aspects that emerged during the CyberParks project. What we wish to see is how this framework approach will continue to illustrate the value of cyberparks to different stakeholders, partners and politicians to ensure that it continues to form part of the discussion of planning delivery mechanisms and lead to wider establishment of a modern type of public open space, along with the more traditional forms of landscape investments.

References

Barker, R., Shoggen, P.: Qualities of Community Life. Jossey – Bass Publishers, London (1973)

Castells, M.: The Internet Galaxy: Reflections on the Internet, Business and Society. Oxford University Press, New York (2001)

Dukes, T.H.: The role of local context: explaining the policy process of the URBAN programmes in Amsterdam and the Hague. Urban Res. Pract. **3**(3), 159–176 (2010)

Geertz, C.: The Interpretation of Cultures. Basic Books, New York (1973)

Low, S.M.: On the Plaza – The Politics of Public Space and Culture. University of Texas Press, Austin (2000a)

Low, S.M.: Culture in the modern city: the microgeographies of gender, class, and generation in the Costa Rican plaza. Horiz. Antropol. **6**(13), 31–64 (2000b). https://doi.org/10.1590/s0104-71832000000100003

Low, S.M.: Spatializing Culture: The Ethnography of Space and Place. Routledge, New York (2016)

Magnani, J.G.C.: Etnografia como prática e experiência. Horiz. Antropol. **15**(32), 129–156 (2009). https://doi.org/10.1590/S0104-71832009000200006

Menezes, M., Smaniotto Costa, C.: People, public space, digital technology and social practice: an ethnographic approach. In: Zammit, A., Kenna, T. (eds.) Enhancing Places Through Technology, pp. 167–180. Edições Universitárias Lusófonas, Lisbon (2017). ISBN 978-989-757-055-1. http://cyberparks-project.eu/sites/default/files/publications/cyberparks_enhancing placestechnology.pdf

Radovanova, P., Radovanov, A.: Urban development in respect to social media – the applicability of the Amsterdam city in other European cities. In: Zammit, A., Kenna, T. (eds.) ICiTy: Enhancing Spaces Through Technology, pp. 129–138. Edições Lusófonas, Lisbon (2017)

Rapoport, A.: Cross-cultural aspects of environmental design. In: Altman, I., Rapoport, A., Wolhwill, J.F. (eds.) Environment and Culture, pp. 7–46. Plenum, New York (1980)

Wicker, A.: An Introduction to Ecological Psychology. Brooks/Cole Publication, San Francisco (1979)

2.3

Public Space Engagement and ICT Usage by University Students: An Exploratory Study in Three Countries

Paschalis Arvanitidis[1(✉)], Therese Kenna[2], and Gabriela Maksymiuk[3]

[1] University of Thessaly, Volos, Greece
parvanit@uth.gr
[2] University College Cork, Cork, Ireland
t.kenna@ucc.ie
[3] Warsaw University of Life Sciences, Warsaw, Poland
gabriela_maksymiuk@sggw.pl

Abstract. The new mobile information and communications technologies expand human connectivity to reconfigure public spatialities and to give rise to novel needs for, and practices of, public space usage. The research in this chapter focuses on university students to explore how they perceive and use the public space of university campuses and how they use personal information and communications technologies in it. This allows for an identification of emerging patterns and practices of university public space usage, along with preferable characteristics, designs and ways of management. Data are collected from three case studies, the University College Cork in Cork (Ireland), the University of Thessaly in Volos (Greece), and the Warsaw University of Life Sciences in Warsaw (Poland), enabling us to spot similarities and differences in the above trends, that would be attributed to culture and local conditions and lifestyles.

Keywords: University public space · Information and communications technologies · University students · Cross-cultural analysis

1 Introduction

One dominant and momentous trend is emerging as a defining hallmark of the contemporary era: the rapid global diffusion of personal information and communications technologies (ICTs), including mobile and smart phones, personal laptops and tablets devices (see Graham 2002). This rapid diffusion and uptake of personal ICTs presents a new societal challenge for cities of increasing diversity and inequality as social life in the city becomes increasing (yet perhaps unevenly) mediated by personal digital devices. The introduction of mobile personal digital technologies – such as mobile phones and personal laptops and tablets – is transforming the ways in which people use and engage with urban public space, as well as encounter others within those spaces

C. Smaniotto Costa et al. (Eds.): CyberParks, LNCS 11380, pp. 87–108, 2019.
https://doi.org/10.1007/978-3-030-13417-4_8

and engage in social interactions and activities. While it is widely held that the introduction of ICTs has resulted in significant changes to the organisation of cities, public spaces and everyday social life (Graham 2002; Aurigi and de Cindio 2008), it remains that there is little research into the exact nature of the socio-cultural transformation resulting from personal ICT usage in the city and urban public spaces.

The current chapter draws on a wider research project undertaken by the research team aiming to investigate how university students engage with personal ICTs and urban public spaces, especially within a university campus, or what we call, University Public Spaces[1] (UPS), as a way of engaging with critical debates concerning young people's social and digital engagement and encounter. This was performed through a comparative study in three different geographical regions of Europe (North, South, East) to ascertain differences based on geographical and cultural context, via the development of new digital social science research methods (online questionnaires). More specifically, the chapter is guided by the following objectives:

1. To explore the perceptions and attitudes of university students towards UPS. This objective included questions such as: What types of UPS do students use and engage with the most? How do university students use UPS? What features or attributes of the UPS do they value the most? Are they willing to participate in UPS management and maintenance?
2. To explore perceptions, attitudes and patterns of ICT usage among university students. This objective involved a series of sub-questions, such as: How intensively do university students use ICTs? What kind of devices and services are used? What activities do university students engage in whilst using ICTs? How they make use of ICTs when they are in UPS?

For the needs of the chapter, we reflect on preliminary analysis of the data to offer some initial observations regarding university student use of ICTs and UPS in universities at three European cities: Cork (Ireland); Volos (Greece); and Warsaw (Poland). Following this introduction, the chapter moves to explore some of the key literature in this field of research relating to ICT usages in urban public spaces, as well as on university campuses. This is followed then by a discussion of our research methodology, an introduction to our case studies, and preliminary analysis of the data. The chapter concludes with a discussion of the key findings.

2 New ICTs and the Usage of UPS

The proliferation of personal ICT devices has led scholars (predominantly in communication studies, as well as urban studies) to speculate about their exclusiveness, their perceived contributions to increasing privatisation and privatism in urban society

---

[1] UPS is a kind of semi-public space, in the sense that it is owned or controlled by a public institution and it is partially, but not entirely, visible to and open to the use of the general public. Such spaces include, for example, university gardens, green spaces, walkways and entrance ways to university buildings (outdoor spaces), as well as indoor spaces such as student centers, refectories, or common areas within university buildings like the library.

(i.e. their role in widening the gap between the public and private realms), their contribution to the reduction of encounters with 'others' or the stranger and reduced chance encounters (Hampton et al. 2010; Hampton and Gupta 2008; Hatuka and Toch 2014; Leyshon et al. 2013). For example, Hampton et al. (2010) studied people's use of Wi-Fi on personal mobile devices in public and semi-public spaces in a number of North American cities. This work found that although the availability of Wi-Fi in public spaces increased peoples use of such spaces, they were found not to be active participants in the social activities of the public spaces (i.e. they were 'silent spectators'). The research concluded that the use of wireless internet on personal mobile digital devices in these spaces afforded a public privatism whereby people engaged in private personal activities and their private social networks whilst in public space, thus they were not active participants in public space. Further, the work of Leyshon et al. (2013) examined how young people locate themselves in the city through their use of GPS-enabled mobile phones. This research was partly concerned with the role of GPS-enabled mobile phones in young people's way-finding and exploration through the city. While the study found that the young people were less like to 'get lost' in the city and had greater confidence in exploring new places as a result of their GPS-enabled mobile phones, they also found that the mobile devices proved a distraction from their surroundings in that they were less inclined to observe or engage with the surrounding urban environment. Findings, such as those from the aforementioned studies, create concerns for the diminishing value of public space in a traditional sense, for the declining significance of the city and urban spaces in the digital era, and for the potential of ICTs to generate and increase social inequalities, as well as reduce opportunities for encountering 'others' in the city (Valentine 2008). It is generally these themes that the undertaken research sought to explore in relation to university students and their uses of public spaces on the university campus.

Boren (2014) noted that there were now more mobile devices globally than people, making the mobile phone one of the fastest diffusing technologies in history with over seven billion mobile devices in global circulation. According to Leyshon et al. (2013), young people own many of these mobile devices and, as such, there are ongoing investigations into how new technologies are 'changing young people's behaviour, social relationships, attention spans, time expenditure and privacy' (pp. 587–88). Given that young people are thought to be one of the most 'tech-savvy' segments of society with almost constant connectivity to digital devices, as well as constituting a significant target market for tech company products and innovations, we focussed our research on young people, mostly notable university students (predominantly aged 18–25).

There have been very few studies of how students actually use, perceive and evaluate campus green spaces (Speake et al. 2013), and furthermore there have been no research of how students use ICTs within university public spaces. Among topics discussed in previous studies related to campuses, there are: campuses studied as public spaces (Gumprecht 2007), campus green spaces and their positive influence on quality of life (McFarland et al. 2008) and campus as a tool for promotion of university (Griffith 1994). In his research, Gumprecht (2007), for instance, outlines that attractive and lively campuses enhance students' experience of academic life, create memories and build loyalty among fellow students. Griffith (1994), in turn, reports that a choice of university often depends on the prospective student's perception of the campus.

The studies of Speake et al. (2013) explored students' perceptions and use of university campus green spaces - the case study of Liverpool Hope University. Their findings reveal that the vast majority of students both use and is pleased about green spaces, and believe there are important for the image of the university and make an essential component of the campus environment. Besides, the authors of this study underline that university campuses need various types of green spaces in order to satisfy the multifarious needs of students. However, they haven't considered applying of ICT as example of such solutions, yet. In terms of social functions, the campus was described by surveyed students as place for "meeting people", "chatting with friends", "waiting for classes" or "simply for socialising" (Speake et al. 2013: 24). Furthermore, among most popular activities undertaken by students in UPS, the authors of quoted paper list: relaxation, eating or drinking, studying or sport.

3 Exploring ICT and UPS Usage in Three Case Studies

3.1 Research Concept and Methodology

This section discusses how university students perceive and report to use UPS and ICTs in three case studies across Europe: The University College Cork in Cork, Ireland, the University of Thessaly in Volos, Greece, and the Warsaw University of Life Sciences in Warsaw, Poland. Data were collected through an online questionnaire survey that explored students' views, attitudes, stances and behaviours towards UPS and ICTs, examining a number of issues, such as: the qualities and facilities available in UPS, the ways and intensity of UPS use, the social interactions taking place, the student's willingness to contribute to UPS management, the kind of ICT devices and services used, the intensity of their use and the activities students engage in through ICTs.

The questionnaire used consists of seven parts containing 56 questions of all kinds: measurement, dichotomous, ordinal, as well as Likert-type ones scaled from 1 (denoting strong disagreement, negative opinion, etc.) to 5 (denoting strong agreement, positive opinion, etc.). In particular, the first part of the questionnaire informs the participants on the purpose of the research and ensures the anonymity of participation. The second part records views regarding the condition of the UPS they use most (qualities, facilities, etc.) and the way these are used (intensity, activities, social interactions, etc.). The third and fourth parts assess respectively how students use ICTs generally in their life and in particular when they are in UPS (devises, services, ways of use, etc.). Part five examines aspects of UPS management and the willingness of students to get involved in this. The sixth part examines the social life of the students and their stances towards other people and institutions. Finally, the last part gathers socio-demographic information, such as gender, age, nationality, discipline of study, and economic status.

The survey took place in the second quarter of 2017. Questionnaires were distributed electronically by the research team, via Google forms, to university students. Apart from the initial invitation to participate in the research, students were notified two more times (through emails) to complete the developed questionnaire. This increased substantially the response rate and the quality of the survey. Responses were then put together, validated, coded and analysed to generate a number of statistics illustrating the respondents' answers on the issues raised.

3.2 Description of the Cases

University College Cork (UCC) is the second largest tertiary education institution in the Republic of Ireland and the largest higher education institution in Cork city. UCC has approximately 20,000 full-time students, which includes 14,000 undergraduate students and 4,000 Masters and PhD students (www.ucc.ie, 2017). Physically, UCC is a large campus to the western edge of the city centre of Cork. The main campus boasts a number of UPS, such as the main student centre, the amphitheatre, president's garden and various boulevards and spaces within buildings (Fig. 1). UCC recently introduced high-quality free Wi-Fi throughout the University Campus, via EduRoam, so students, visitors and staff have access to high-quality internet at all times.

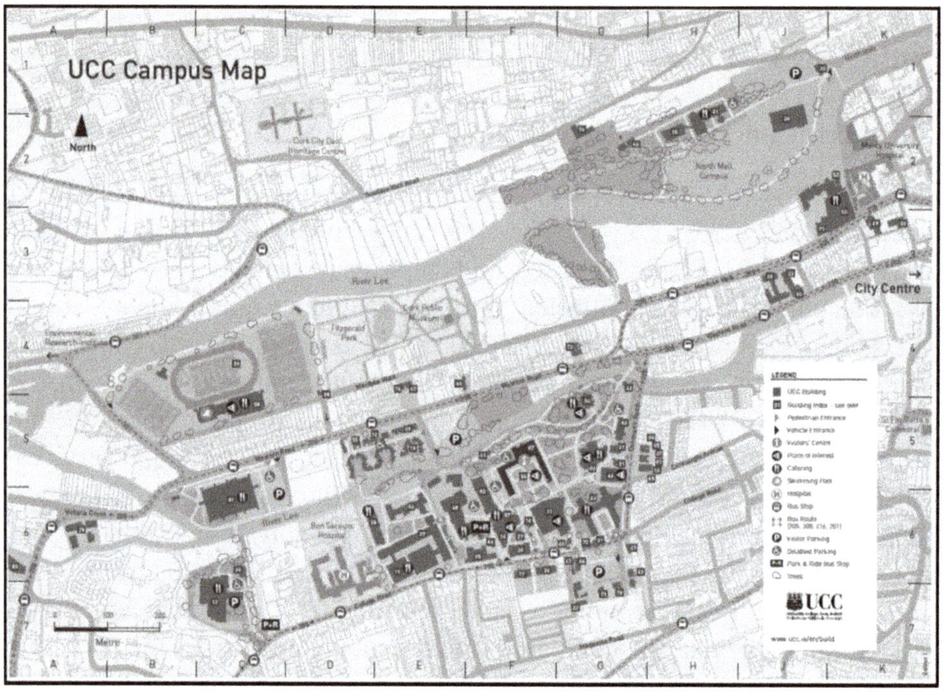

Fig. 1. Map of the UCC campus (Source: https://www.ucc.ie/en/media/academic/languagecentre/UCC_campus_map_Edition1_2010-new.pdf; Accessed on 1st July, 2017)

The University of Thessaly (UTH) is one of the new public universities in Greece having been founded in 1984. It is comprised of eighteen Departments organized in six Schools. UTH has more than 10,000 undergraduate students, 1,500 postgraduate and 1,000 PhDs (www.uth.gr, 2017). The University is located in central Greece (in Thessaly region), operating campuses in five cities: Volos, Larisa, Trikala, Karditsa and Lamia. The administration and most of the Departments (twelve of them) are deployed in Volos, and UPS is scattered all over the city (Fig. 2). UTH provides high-quality free Wi-Fi throughout its campuses and buildings, so all academic community and visitors have access to high-quality internet at all times.

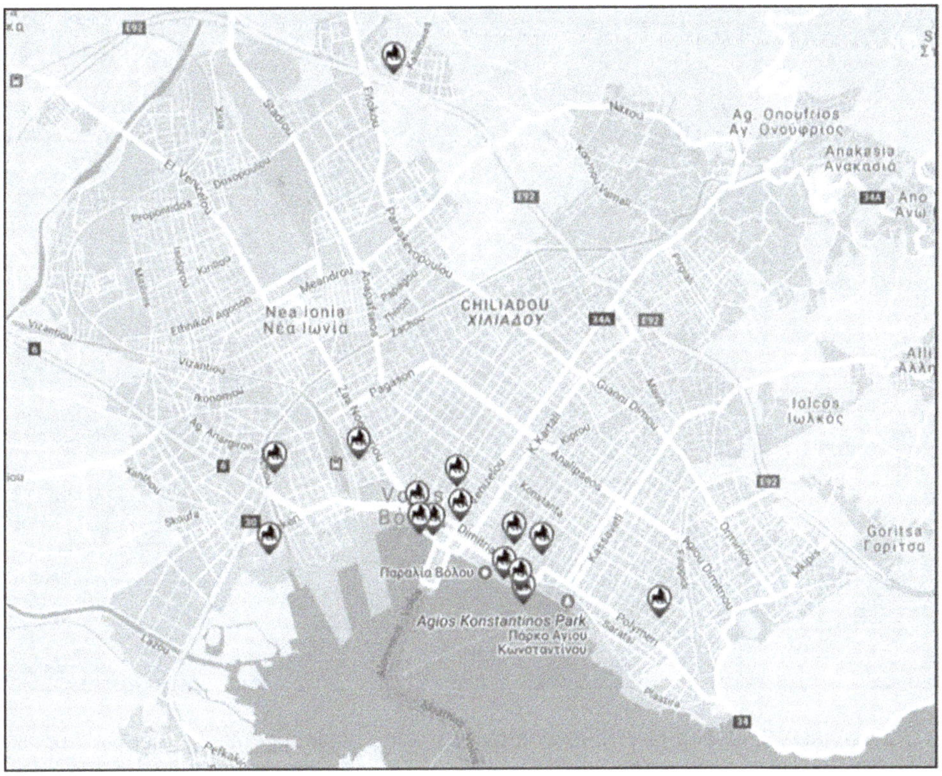

Fig. 2. Map of the UTH locations in Volos city (Source: own construction)

Warsaw University of Life Sciences (WULS) is the oldest and the largest life sciences university in Poland and the third largest higher education institution in Warsaw (in terms of number of students). WULS has approximately 25,000 full-time students and 1,200 academics (www.sggw.pl, 2017). The university campus is located in the southern part of Warsaw and it covers an area over 70 hectares, which makes it the biggest university campus in Warsaw. The campus is divided into 2 parts - the Old Campus, which is a historical park with an arboretum and Neo-Renaissance architecture and the New Campus, where new university buildings, students' dormitories and sport centre are located. The WULS campus consists of a wide array of public spaces and recreational facilities, such as an old park and arboretum, vast lawn areas for picnics, a grill zone and faulty courtyards (Fig. 3). WULS very recently introduced a free Wi-Fi in selected parts of the campus and buildings provided by EduRoam, and in the near future the whole campus area is planned to be covered by a high-quality internet at all times.

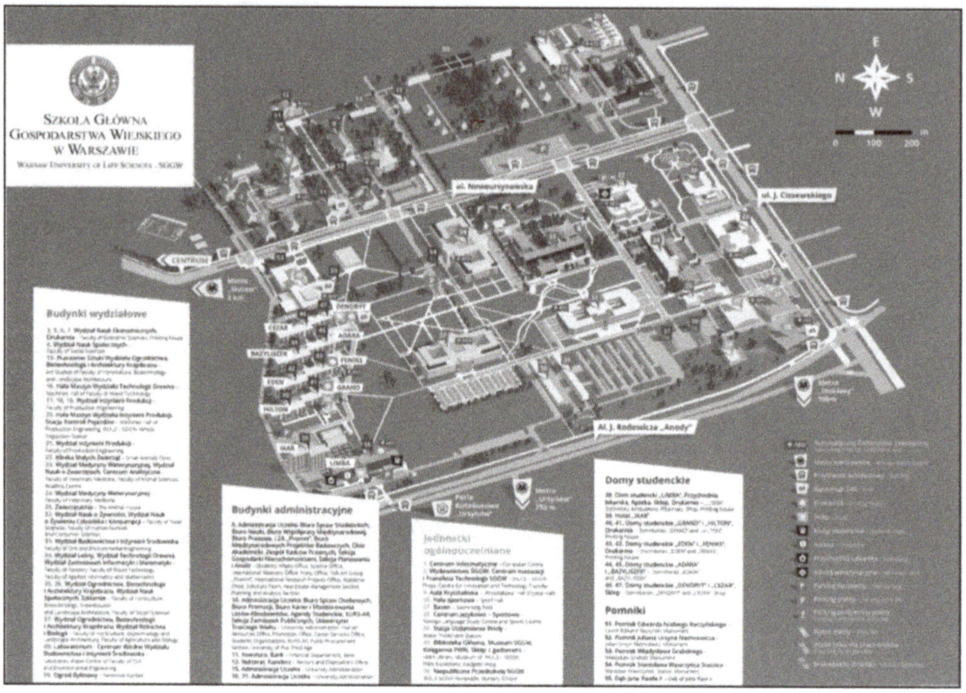

Fig. 3. Map of the WULS campus (Source: http://www.sggw.pl/en/contact__/sggw-campus#prettyPhoto; Accessed on July 2nd, 2017)

3.3 Composition of Respondents

A total of 172 responses were received, of which 168 (97.7%) were valid. Of those, about 41.4% were from students of THU (Greece), 32.0% of WULS (Poland) and 26.6% of UCC (Ireland) (see Fig. 4). The nationality of the respondents was mainly Greek, Polish and Irish, but there were few originating from other countries too (see Fig. 5). Their gender composition was about 68.9% female and 26.9% male, whereas a 4.2% of the students selected the option "prefer not to say" (see Fig. 6). The average age of our sample was about 22.7 years, with the youngest being 19 years old and the oldest 47. Their chosen subjects of study were various, though the majority were students of economics, landscape architecture, geography, spatial economy and arts (see Fig. 7). The respondents' economic conditions were, on average, about moderate to low (Fig. 8).

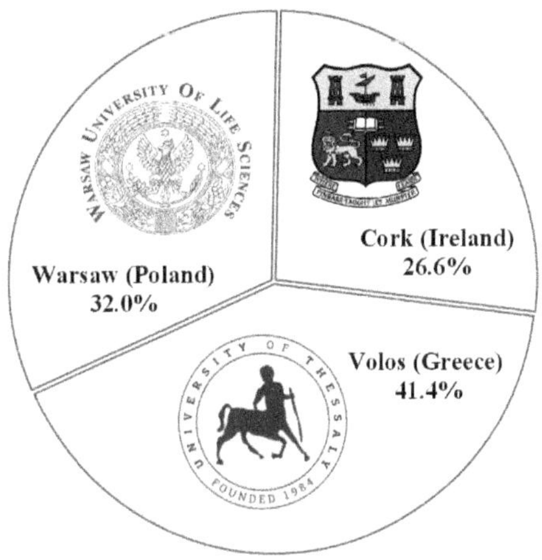

Fig. 4. Origin country of respondents

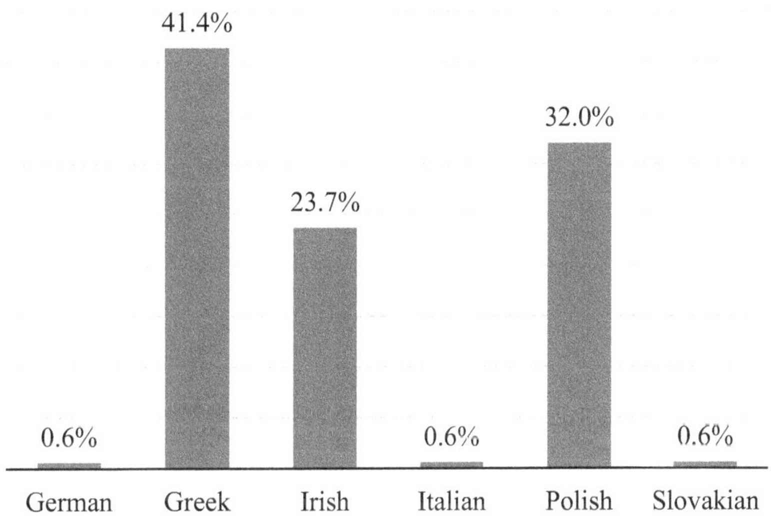

Fig. 5. Nationality of respondents

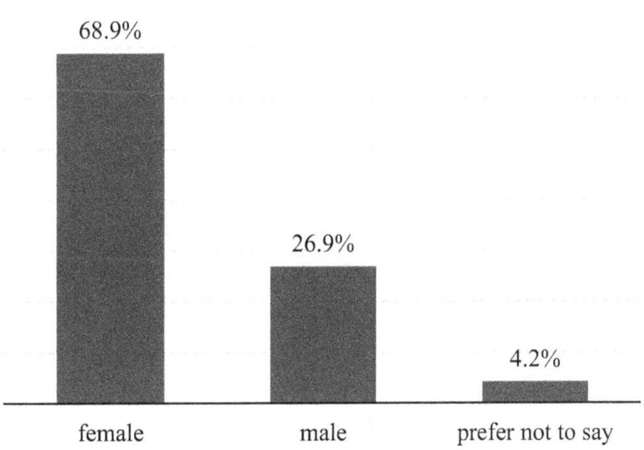

Fig. 6. Gender of respondents

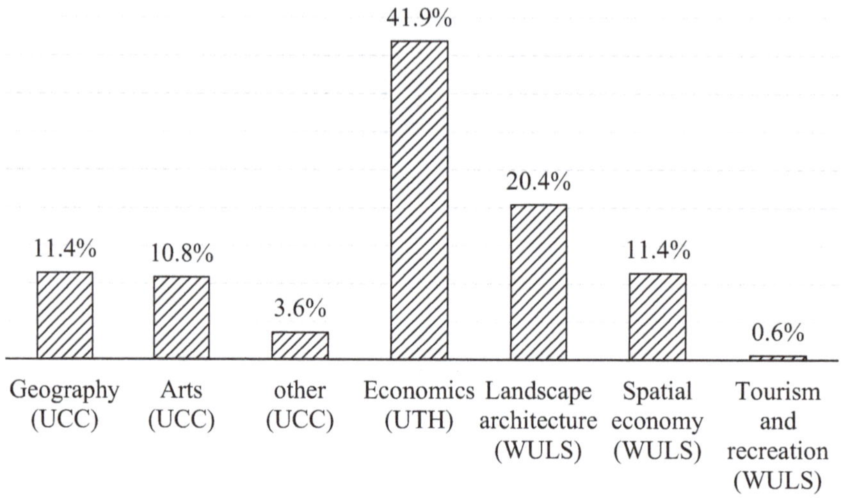

Fig. 7. Field of study of respondents (major)

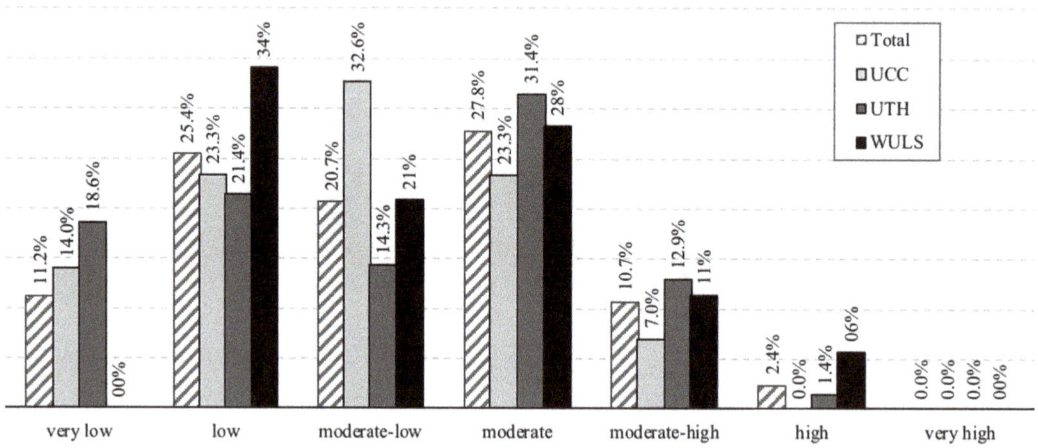

Fig. 8. Economic condition of respondents (income)

3.4 Analysis

On a scale of 1 (least positive) to 5 (highly positive), students were firstly asked to evaluate a number of qualities with reference to the UPS they use most, these are: their aesthetics, natural environment (greenery), safety, tranquillity, overall space quality (e.g. cleanness), the vigour of their social environment, whether they provide a sense of community and whether they have a unique or special character. Figure 9 presents the results (average scores) both for the total sample and for each specific case, making clear that UPS in all universities examined are in general of good quality (most quality scores are above 3). At a rather medium level to all UPS is tranquillity, perhaps due to the fact that these places are quite lively and busy urban spaces. In Greece, UPS seems to suffer from low quality natural environment (greenery), something that is typical to all cities in the country in general (Arvanitidis and Nasioka 2017). However, Greek students seems to be quite happy with the overall quality of space.

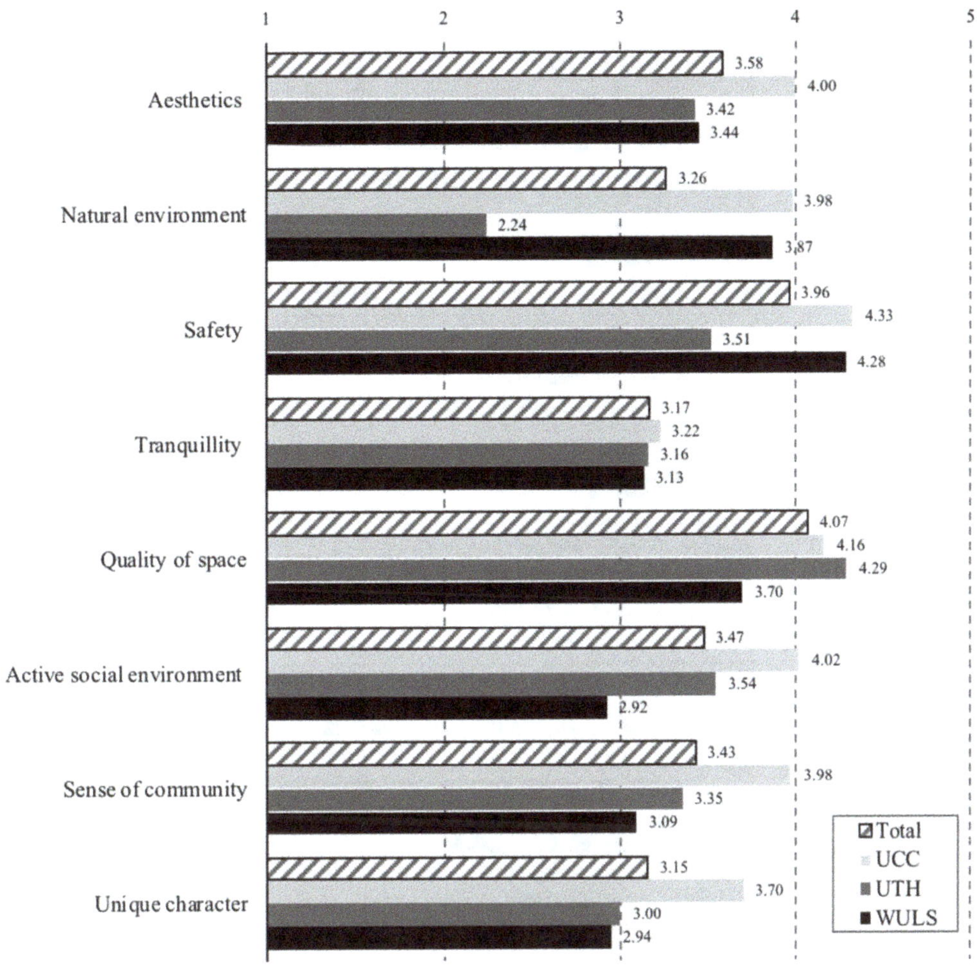

Fig. 9. Qualities of UPS

The next question examined the facilities that UPS offer. In particular, students were asked to assess (on a scale of 1 to 5) whether the UPS they use most provides quality facilities for visitors (e.g. toilets, parking, etc.), places to sit and work, internet facilities, places with interactive information, facilities for energy provision, facilities for recreation and commercial activities (e.g. refectory, vending machines), and maps. Figure 10 depicts the average scores acquired (both for the total sample and each case study). In general, we see that a low assessment of UPS in WULS is made in terms of adequate places to work and of spaces with interactive information, that latter of which is also the case in both UCC and UTH. Recreational facilities are of shortage in Volos' UPS. Internet provision facilities are valued quite highly in UCC but rather low in WULS. Overall, comparing the three case studies, it seems that the students of UCC are the most contented with the UPS of their university, something that can be attributed to the overall design of the university space.

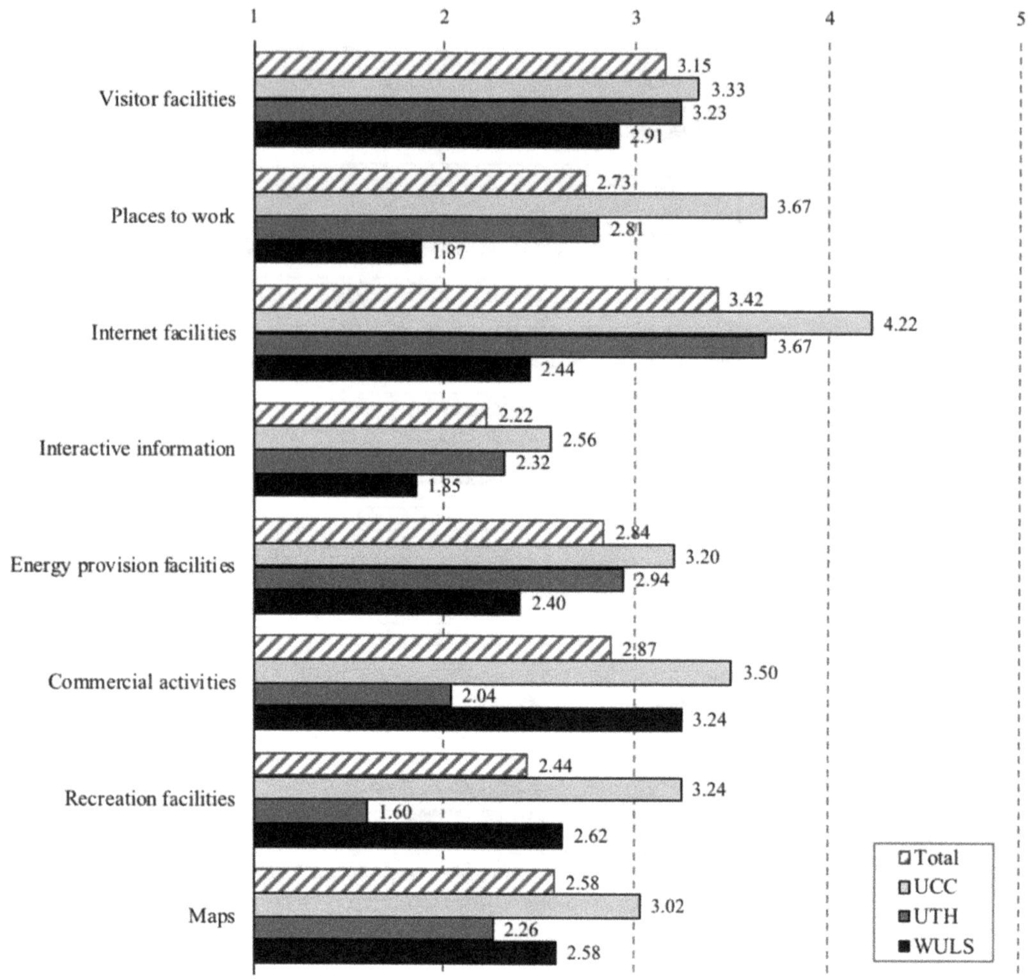

Fig. 10. Facilities of UPS

The following question attempted to gauge how content students are with UPS. We asked them to specify (on a scale of 1 to 5) whether the UPS they use most are appreciated by their peers, whether they think that UPS advance the quality of student life, the degree of their overall satisfaction they receive, and whether they believe that there are improvement that need to be made in UPS. Figure 11 illustrates the findings. As can be seen, all students are generally quite happy with the UPS they use (all average scores are above 3). As before, the most satisfied are the students in Cork. Students in Warsaw are happy too, but to a lesser degree, highlighting the need for UPS improvements.

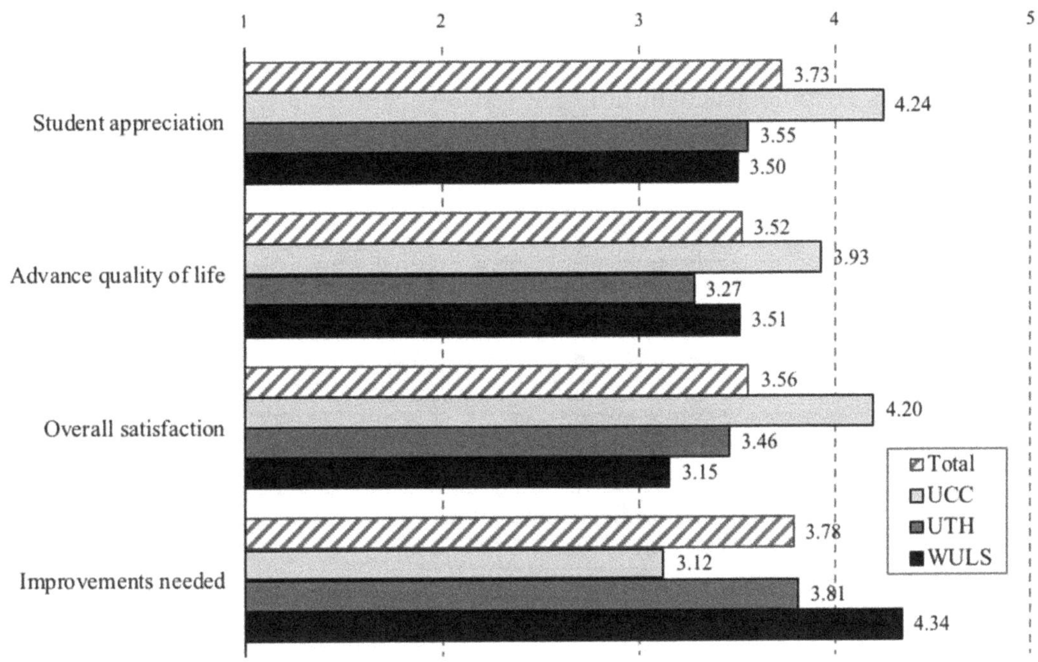

Fig. 11. Evaluation of UPS

A set of questions explored how students actually use the UPS. Firstly, we examined how often students visit the UPS they use most. Figure 12 portrays these patterns. We see that of the three cases under study, UCC students are those who visit UPS more intensively; the majority (31.1%) use UPS multiple times a day. Polish and Greek students, in contrast, are less frequent users, the majority of which (33.3% and 45.7%, respectively) uses UPS more than three times a week (but not every day).

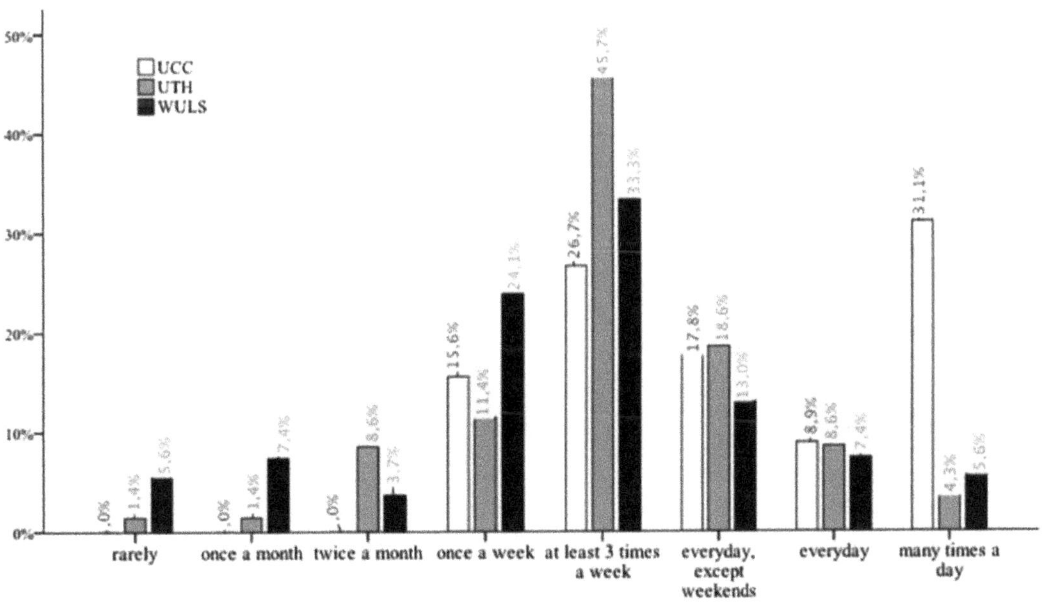

Fig. 12. Intensity of UPS use

With regard to the activities undertaken when in UPS, as expected, most students go there to work/study and to socialize with their fellow students (Fig. 13). This for the Polish students is combined with drinking (coffees, soft drinks, etc.), eating (snacks, sandwiches, etc.), relaxing and strolling, whereas Greek students spend more time on

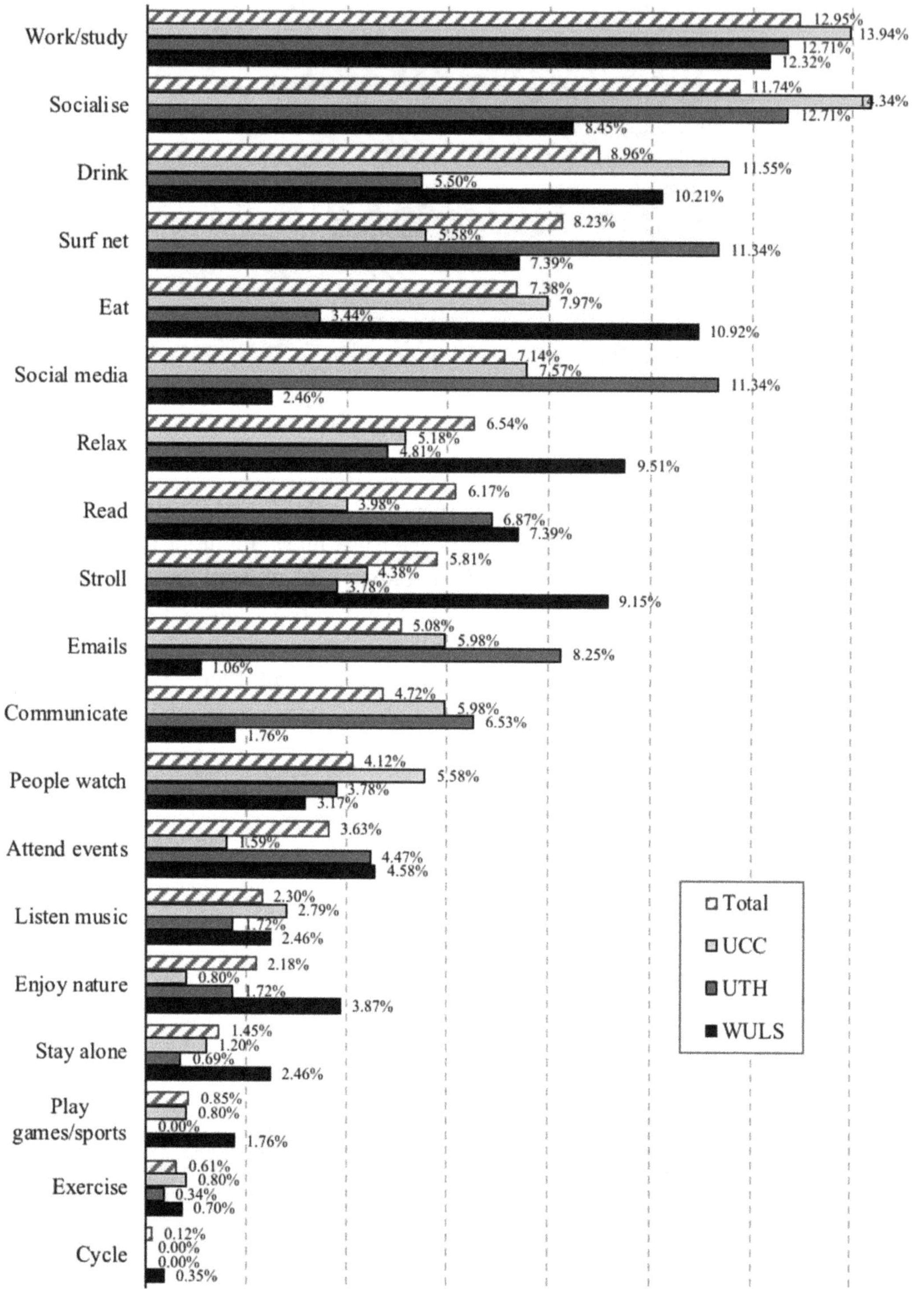

Fig. 13. Activities undertaken in UPS

rather private activities, such as surfing the internet, catching up on social media and checking the emails. Interestingly, spending time alone is not a favourable option for all three student groups examined.

A number of subsequent questions explored how university students use ICTs, both in general and when they are in UPS. Figures 14 and 15 respectively present data on which personal devices respondents use and the intensity of their employment in the course of a single day, whereas Fig. 16 shows where people access the internet the most. As expected, smartphones, followed by laptops, are the devices used the most by all students; tablets are the least used technological devices. Desktop computers are not very popular in all cases examined, but students of UCC seems to use them at a higher degree as compared to students of UTH and WULS. Respondents access the internet mainly at home and on campus, both of which are places where students naturally spend most of their time. Irish and Polish students, as compared to Greeks, are more connected in every place (always connected), whereas Greeks seems to use the internet higher, compared to others, when they are at shops and retail outlets. As expected, all students use the internet in their daily life; since none of the respondents selected the option "I never use the internet".

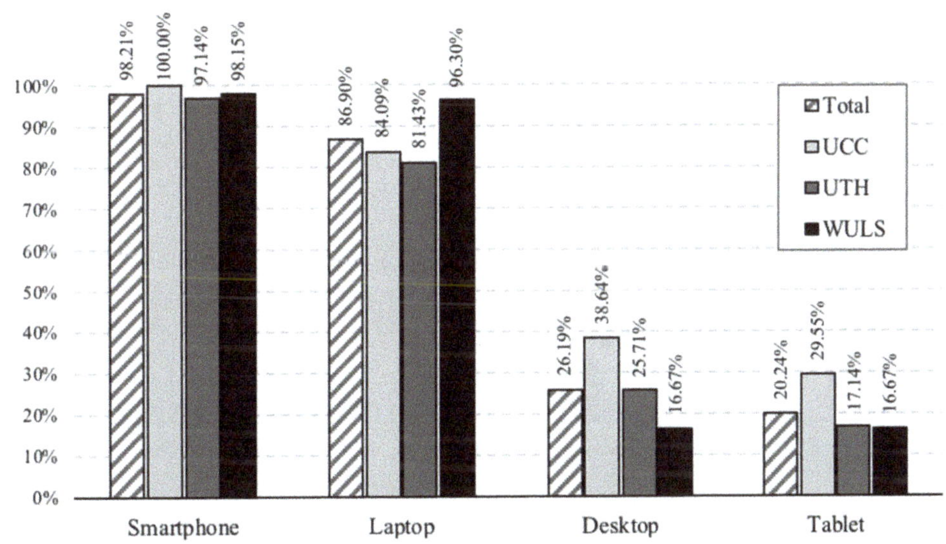

Fig. 14. ICTs used in everyday life

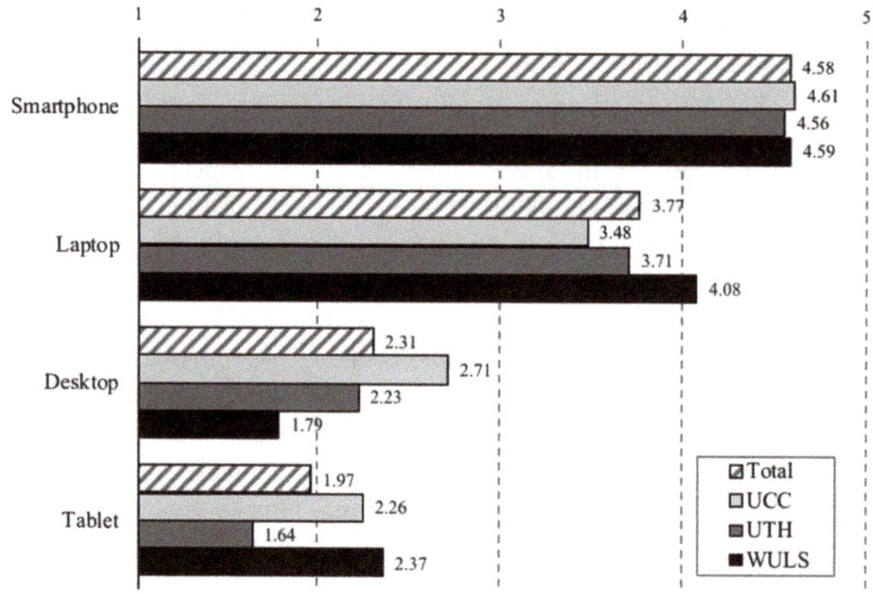

Fig. 15. Intensity of ICTs use in everyday life

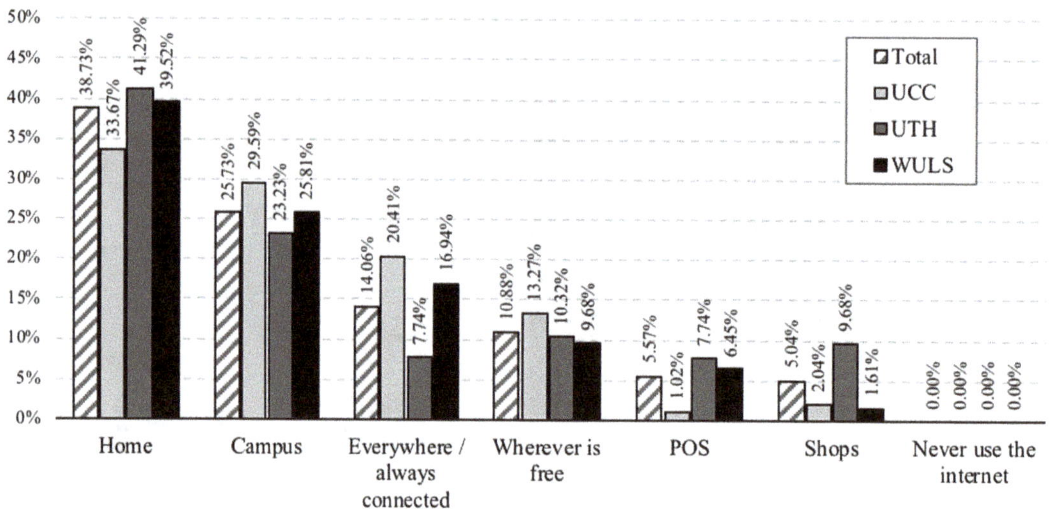

Fig. 16. Internet use in everyday life

Turning to technologies usage in UPS, Fig. 17 depicts how often personal mobile devices are used by the students. As before, smartphones are the principal instrument used, followed by laptops. Greeks, as compared to Irish and Polish students seem to use, at a lesser extent, both laptops and tables when they are in UPS. Polish students, in turn, use their tablets to a higher degree, in comparison to the other two groups. Internet use in UPS is quite popular (Fig. 18); the majority of UCC students are always connected (53.5%), whereas both WULS and UTH students use it quite a lot (50% and 38.6% of them respectively). Interestingly, of the three groups examined, Greek students seems to be those that use the internet the least when they are in UPS, as one out of three (that is about 30%) reports that they use it only occasionally.

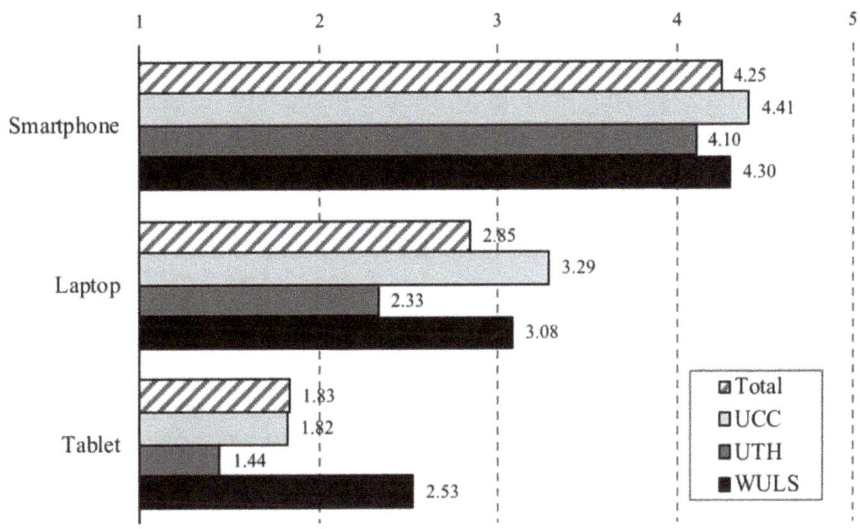

Fig. 17. Intensity of ICT use in UPS

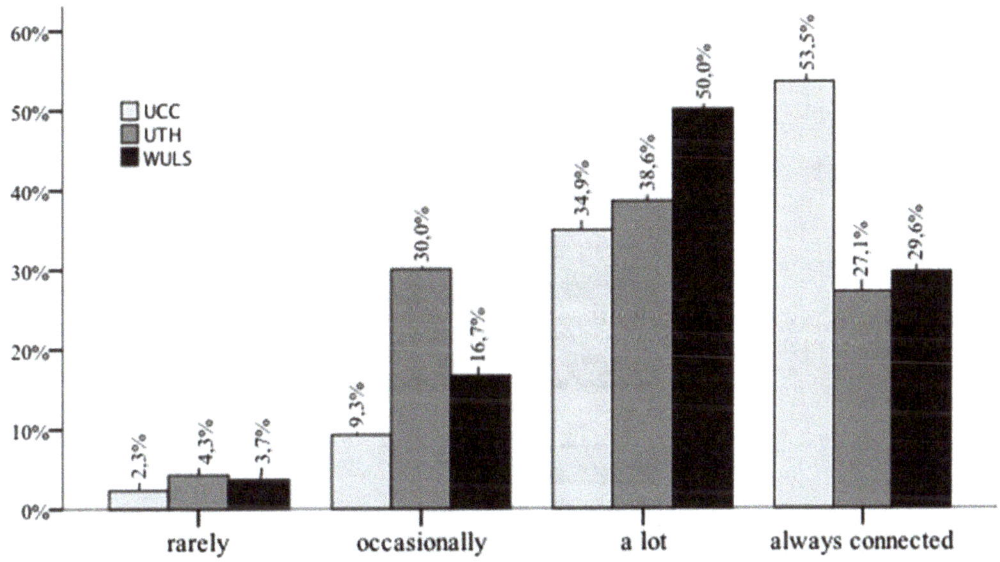

Fig. 18. Internet use in UPS

The questions that follow focus on management issues concerning UPS. First, we examine students' perceptions and attitudes towards ICTs and UPS and their maintenance (Figs. 19 and 20), then we move to assessments of stakeholders' capability to efficiently manage the UPS (Fig. 20), and finally we explore students' willingness to contribute to the provision, maintenance and improvement of the UPS by volunteering personal time (Figs. 22 and 23) or offering a small part of their income (Figs. 24 and 25).

To shed light on views and stances towards UPS and ICTs we asked students to evaluate (on a scale of 1: strongly disagree, to 5: strongly agree) the following statements: (1) UPS are absolutely essential to the university campus, (2) internet and Wi-Fi provision is absolutely essential to UPS, (3) students (i.e. users) should be heavily involved in UPS design, (4) students (users) should be heavily involved in UPS management, (5) security cameras should be applied in UPS, (6) controlled access should be applied in UPS, and (7) people should contribute financially to the creation and maintenance of UPS. As Fig. 19 reveals, all students believe that both UPS is necessary to the university campus and that Wi-Fi provision is essential to UPS. Turning to issues of user involvement in UPS design and management, students are rather neutral. In comparative terms, more prone to get involved are those of WULS and the least those of UTH. This might be related to the educational background of both; the former are studying (in majority) landscape architecture (so UPS design presents a challenge), whereas the latter are mainly students of economics. In regard to the issue of controlling access in UPS, students seem rather negative. Free UPS access for everybody is certainly what they prefer (though Greeks to a lesser degree), whereas students appear less negative (as compared to the controlled access) to the question of applying security cameras in UPS, with the Irish being more tolerant (in relation to Greeks and Polish) to such a development. Moving to the matter of financial contribution for the creation and maintenance of UPS, students are unanimously opposed to it.

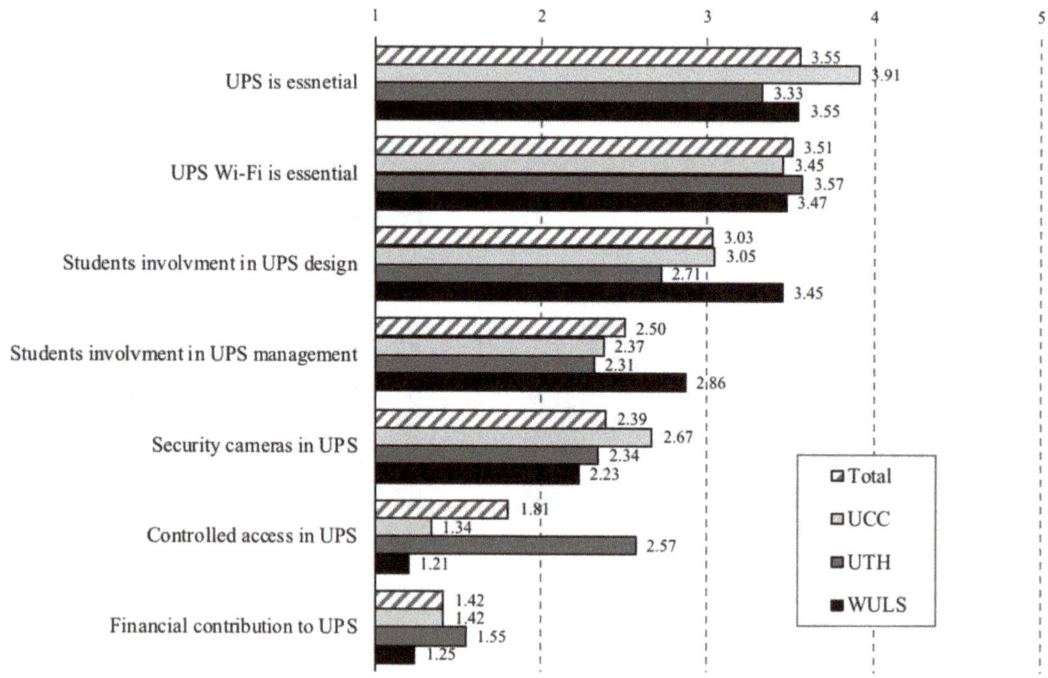

Fig. 19. Attitudes towards UPS and ICTs

This brings us to the question of who should pay for the costs of UPS. Figure 20 depicts the answers given by our sample. Clearly, the university is held responsible for the provision of this service and to a lesser degree the city and its administration; certainly such costs should be not born by the students.

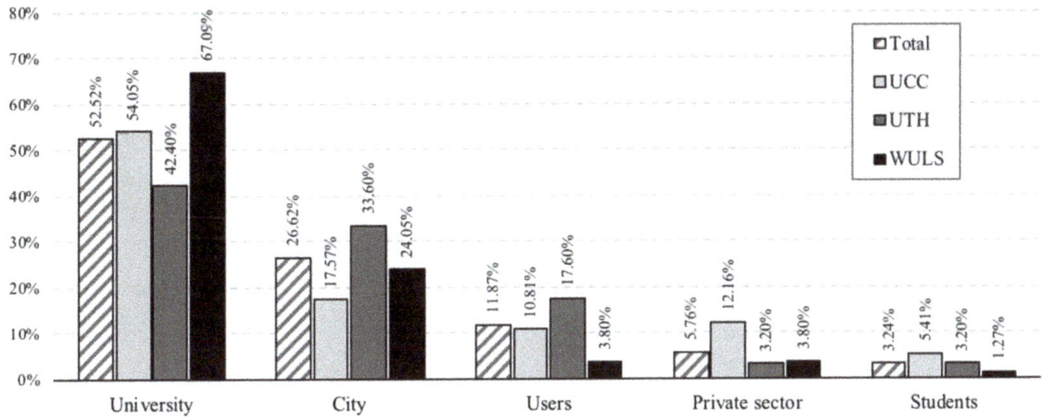

Fig. 20. Paying the costs of UPS

Moving to assessments of stakeholders' capacity to manage UPS, Fig. 21 shows that respondents believe that the university is the most capable of doing so. Provocatively, Polish students value very high student clubs and associations for their ability to perform the task (actually higher than the University). A special body created for this job is assessed relatively higher in Ireland, and the city authorities score relatively higher in Greece. Interestingly, the private sector scores last in all cases examined.

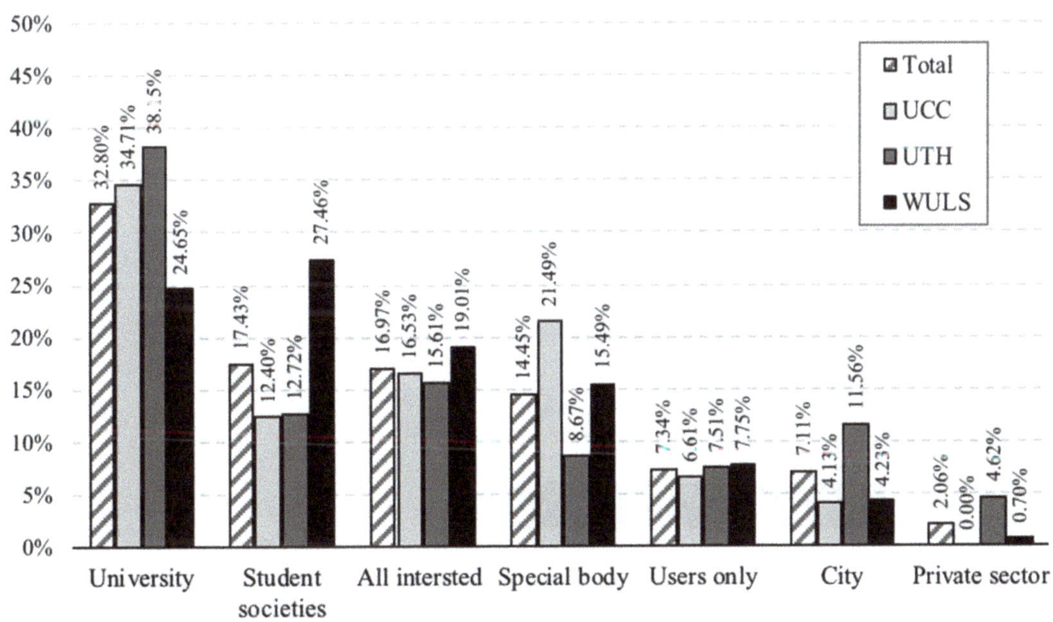

Fig. 21. Capability for UPS management

Finally, we examine the willingness of students to contribute in the provision and maintenance of UPS, by either donating money or volunteering some of their spare time to help look after the resource. Figures 22 and 24, corroborating our previous findings, reveal that students are reserved (to a degree) to help look after UPS and rather unwilling to offer money towards their improvement and maintenance. Of those willing to contribute, Greeks seem a bit more keen (compared to others) on providing both time (on average 3.96 h) and money for UPS management, and Polish are more reserved to both options (on average the hours that are willing to volunteer are 2.22).

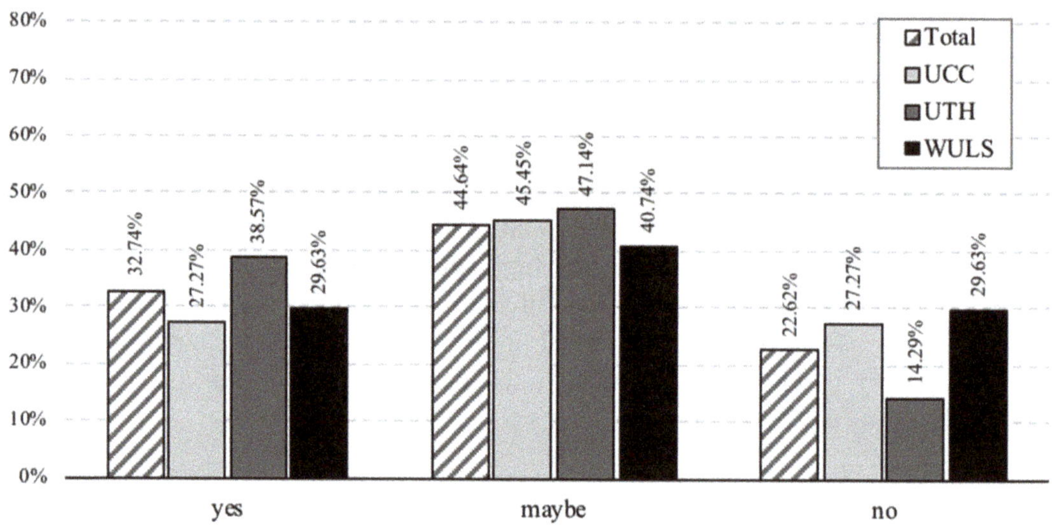

Fig. 22. Willingness to help look after UPS

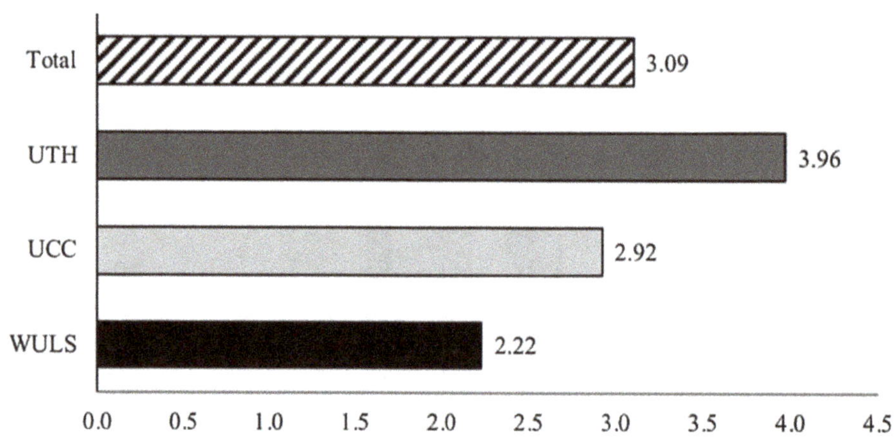

Fig. 23. Willingness to help look after UPS – hours volunteered

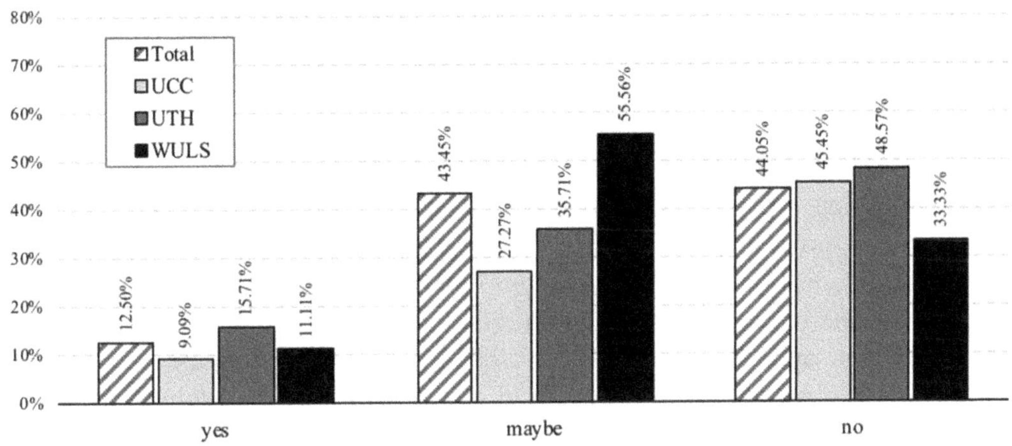

Fig. 24. Willingness to contribute financially for UPS

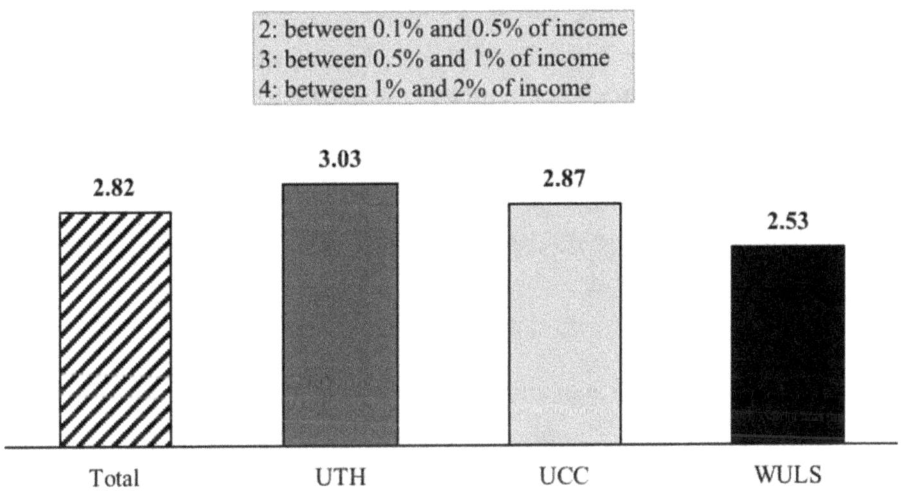

Fig. 25. Willingness to contribute financially to UPS – percentage of income offered

4 Conclusions

This chapter has explored how university students perceive and use UPS and ICTs in three cases across Europe: The University College Cork in Cork (Ireland), the University of Thessaly in Volos (Greece) and the Warsaw University of Life Sciences in Warsaw (Poland). Data were collected through an online questionnaire survey that explored students' self-reported views, attitudes, stances and behaviours towards UPS and ICTs, examining a number of issues, including the qualities of and facilities available in UPS, the frequency of UPS use and the activities performed, the kind of technological devices and services employed and the intensity of such usage, as well as student's willingness to participate in UPS maintenance and provision. This allows to identify practices of UPS usage and emerging patterns of engagement with people and space, along with preferable designs and ways of management. Moreover, the three case studies examined enable us to spot similarities and differences in the above trends, i.e. between North Europe (Ireland) vs. South Europe (Greece) vs. Central/East Europe (Poland), that should be attributed to culture and local socio-economic conditions and lifestyles.

The analysis we conducted, though preliminary and descriptive in nature, revealed a number of points which we highlight thereafter. First, *mutatis mutandis*, all universities examined provide good quality UPS, with adequate facilities, that advance contemporary student life. An issue perhaps exists in Warsaw, where students report problems with the internet facilities and a relative shortage of places to sit and work. Second, students appreciate the UPS available and use them quite a lot in their everyday life as places to meet, interact and collaborate with their fellow students, as well as spaces where, taking advantage of the Wi-Fi facilities available, they can resort to study and work, to search for information and to communicate with the rest of the world. As such UPS play a key role in strengthening students' interaction and socialisation and reinforcing their technological acquaintance and literacy. Third, smartphones constitute the principal ICTs device that students use, both outside university and when they are in UPS, satisfying their needs for wireless connection at any time and place. Fourth, despite the importance of good-quality 'wified' UPS in contemporary life, students seem rather reluctant to take part in their improvement and management, approaching it as a kind of public good which the University is obliged to provide at no (extra) cost to the user. This explains, in part, why they are also unwilling to accept measures of UPS surveillance and controlled access, which though they will increase security and protection of property and life, they would presumably jeopardise their freedom of expression and movement.

References

Arvanitidis, P., Nasioka, F.: Urban open greenspace as a commons: an exploratory case study in Greece. Öffentl. Sekt. **43**(1), 19–32 (2017)

Aurigi, A., De Cindio, F.: Augmented Urban Spaces: Articulating the Physical and Electronic City. Ashgate, Aldershot (2008)

Boren, Z.D.: There are officially more mobile devices than people in the world. The Independent, Tuesday 7 October 2014. http://www.independent.co.uk/life-style/gadgets-and-tech/news/there-are-officially-more-mobile-devices-than-people-in-the-world-9780518.html. Accessed 7 Oct 2015

Graham, S.: Bridging urban digital divides? Urban polarisation and information and communications technologies (ICTs). Urban Stud. **39**(1), 33–56 (2002)

Griffith, J.C.: Open space preservation: an imperative for quality campus environments. J. High. Educ. **65**(6), 645–669 (1994)

Gumprecht, B.: The campus as a public space in the American college town. J. Hist. Geogr. **33**(1), 72–103 (2007)

Hampton, K.N., Gupta, N.: Community and social interaction in the wireless city: wi-fi use in public and semi-public spaces. New Media Soc. **10**(6), 831–850 (2008)

Hampton, K.N., Livio, O., Sessions, G.L.: The social life of wireless urban spaces: internet use, social networks, and the public realm. J. Commun. **60**(4), 701–722 (2010)

Hatuka, T., Toch, E.: The emergence of portable private-personal territory: smartphones, social conduct and public spaces. Urban Stud. (2014). https://doi.org/10.1177/0042098014524608

Leyshon, M., DiGiovanna, S., Holcomb, B.: Mobile technologies and youthful exploration: stimulus or inhibitor? Urban Stud. **50**(3), 587–605 (2013)

McFarland, A.L., Waliczek, T.M., Zajicek, J.M.: The relationship between student use of campus green spaces and perceptions of quality of life. Hortic. Technol. **18**(2), 196–319 (2008)

Speake, J., Edmondson, S., Nawaz, H.: Everyday encounters with nature: students' perceptions and use of university campus green spaces. Hum. Geogr. **7**(1), 21–31 (2013)

Valentine, G.: Living with difference: reflections on geographies of encounter. Prog. Hum. Geogr. **32**(3), 323–337 (2008)

2.4

Teenagers' Perception of Public Spaces and Their Practices in ICTs Uses

Marluci Menezes[1(✉)], Paschalis Arvanitidis[2], Carlos Smaniotto Costa[3], and Zvi Weinstein[4]

[1] National Laboratory for Civil Engineering – LNEC, Lisbon, Portugal
marluci@lnec.pt
[2] Department of Economics, University of Thessaly, Volos, Greece
parvanit@uth.gr
[3] CeiED Interdisciplinary Research Centre for Education and Development, Universidade Lusófona, Lisbon, Portugal
smaniotto.costa@ulusofona.pt
[4] Israel Smart Cities Institute, Tel Aviv, Israel
zviw@nonstop.net.il

Abstract. The new information and communications technologies are expanding human connectivity, reconfiguring urban spatialities and generating a kind of social space that spans real and virtual, personal and impersonal, private and public. As a result, the space and time boundaries become blurred, giving rise to novel needs for, and practices of, public space usage. However, the ways in which these new practices affect public space engagement and public life in general, remain yet unclear. In addition, variations might exist due to differences in local culture and conditions, or due to specific lifestyles and behaviours favouring isolation and privatism or, at best, interaction only with close friends and kin. The above issues become even more critical for young people, who born in a digital era are able to handle new technologies with utmost ease. This chapter sheds light on the related perceptions and practices of adolescents. Structured interviews were applied to eight teenagers living in Hannover (Germany), Lisbon (Portugal), Tel Aviv (Israel) and Volos (Greece) to gather focused, qualitative and textual data. It examines how young people of distinct sociocultural contexts perceive and use both public spaces and digital technologies. This enables to identify emergent logics, needs and patterns of socialization and public space engagement placing specific emphasis on the role information technologies can play in them.

Keywords: Spatial practices of teenagers · Teenagers and public spaces · Use of digital technologies · Methodological contribution

1 Introduction

The term "adolescent" is used in this work to mean anyone between the age of 14 and 16 years, and is used interchangeably with other terms "teenager" and "young people". Adolescence, marking the passage from childhood to adulthood, is a crucial stage of human development. It is a period of life with substantial changes on the biological,

C. Smaniotto Costa et al. (Eds.): CyberParks, LNCS 11380, pp. 109–119, 2019.
https://doi.org/10.1007/978-3-030-13417-4_9

physical, cognitive, emotional and social fronts, that move teenagers towards a more mature sense of self and purpose. Adolescents learn how to develop and manage healthy relationships with their peers, family and other members of their social sphere, to fully understand abstract ideas and to develop their own opinions, beliefs and viewpoints along with an increasing ability to understand their environment. This personality and identity development is accompanied by a call for independence and privacy, along with establishment of close relationships with peers and other people beyond family (ACS 2013). Thus, parent attachment and adult supervision decrease and gradually teenagers come to expand their social circle of friends and acquaintance, being free to decide on their own, how, with who and where to spend their time. However, unlike adults, teens have limited control of private space, both in their homes and schools, making them to resort to public space or to cyberspace both for their isolation and social interactions (Childress 2004). Yet, little research has explored how these young people approach and use both public space and the new technologies that enable them to enter the virtual space, let alone the links between the two.

With the broad penetration of digital technologies and new media devices the world has increasingly become hyper-connected, melting together the real and virtual worlds and this makes the call to identity and address the complex, multi-causal, and even sometimes contradictory, relation of social life and spaces, termed here as urban spatialities (Menezes and Smaniotto 2017). Teenagers of the 21st Century are born in a cybernetic era and are able to handle new technologies with utmost ease (Boyd 2014). Moreover, they are not only highly digital-literate people, but also constitute the citizens, users and policy makers of tomorrow. It is therefore important to explore their perceptions, preferences, behaviours, practices and needs of both public spaces and technology. Such knowledge is expected to shed light on how ("smart") cities would, or should be developed in the near future, taken under proper consideration the views of teenagers.

On these grounds, this chapter comes to elucidate the aforementioned issues, examining the perceptions and practices of teenagers (14–16 years of age), using informal interviews structured in the form of a questionnaire with eight adolescents living in Hannover (Germany), Lisbon (Portugal), Tel Aviv (Israel) and Volos (Greece). It examines how teenagers of different sociocultural contexts perceive and use public spaces and ICTs, in an attempt to identify emergent logics (and needs) of socialization and public space engagement. This enables also to explore, in a preliminary manner, the links between public space and the use of ICTs. Obviously, a study of eight people does not intend to obtain a statistical representation; it simply aims to identify specific aspects and patterns of teen behaviour to guide future research on related issues.

2 Teenagers, Information Technologies and Public Space

ICTs have greatly changed society and how people work, learn, communicate and interact, and increasingly the way they spent leisure time. This trend will continue to proliferate, as the digital realm is getting more and more ubiquitous in our lives (Bahillo et al. 2015). Computers, internet and mobile devices became ordinary part of life, even stronger in teens' lives. They use ICT devices to communicate, for social interaction and learning, and increasingly for entertainment. RSPH (2017) notes that 91% of teens use internet mainly for social media and acknowledges a causal link between, and a negative impact of, internet intensive use and the physical and psychological health of young people, especially of females, causing anxiety, depression and the like. While teens are quite confident with ICT use (digital literate), very little is known about their behaviour and needs on public places and the role technology can play in this relationship.

For many readers it may come to a surprise that young people are among the most frequent users of public space (Travlou et al. 2008). This is partly due to the fact that, as minors, they have no formal (legal) rights to spaces of their own (Childress 2004), something that makes them to depend on public space both for their isolation and social interactions (Lieberg 1995; Worpole 2005). Thus, parks, squares, alleyways, sidewalks, and the like, become the appropriated places whereby adolescents resort to stay private, as well as to meet and to interact with their friends and peers (Matthews 1995; Depeau 2001). As a result, these places are imbued with their own cultural values and meanings. This suggests, at least, the need to examine public space in the way young people understand, approach and appropriate it.

Despite the fact that public space plays an important role for adolescents physical, mental, emotional and social development and well-being (Robinson 2000), teenagers' appropriation of public space is usually seen in particularly charged ways, attributing these public spaces a sense of "difference" in relation to adults' space (Jupp 2007; Lieberg 1995). Thus, young people are seemingly invisible in the urban landscape (Travlou et al. 2008); they are excluded from the dominant "adult" public space through controls and rules, afforded only with "leftover" or "token" spaces (Matthews 1995; Childress 2004), which are usually not sufficient to their needs (Lieberg 1995). In their attempts to contest adults' spatial domination and to declare their independence, adolescents develop their own "micro-geographies" in space (Matthews et al. 1998). That is, they resort to alternative patterns of public space usage and leave their own markers (e.g. graffiti) as symbolic gestures of resistance to adult hegemony (Bell et al. 2003; Valentine 1996; Matthews 1995). These actions are sometimes seen as threats to the safety of other user groups (ACS, 2013), giving rise to conflicts and generating stricter controls on the part of the adults (Livingstone et al. 2015; Bell et al. 2003). At least partly, due to these restrictions, young people's spatial freedom and mobility appears to be decreasing, and teenagers retreat to virtual space (through mobile phones and the internet) and/or to semi-public spaces (such as, the indoor space of shopping/leisure centres, libraries, churches, etc.) as a new experiential place for isolation and interaction (Childress 2004). The latter study highlights an increase in the sedentary lifestyle, raising further concerns about youngster's obesity and related health risks, let alone the devastating effects on their personality and well-being due to disconnection from the natural environment and from nature in general (Louv 2008).

The way cities, the build environment and open spaces are designed, and function affect people's life. There is a growing body of evidence illustrating how spatial planning and urban design impact on public health, sociability and well-being. An environment that encourage people to walk, cycle, move physically and exercise leads to increased social interactions and healthy relations with one other (Smaniotto Costa

2016). This highlights that urban planning decisions have a key role to play in combating growing levels of obesity and helping prevent lifestyle related diseases, through facilitating physical activity and social interaction (COB 2011). ICTs' place in these processes is also significant. As scholars (e.g. Hampton and Gupta 2008; Hampton et al. 2010; Hatuka and Toch 2014) have pointed out, ICTs affect public space use and design enabling involvement in outdoor social practices, and public participation and empowerment. Thus, a vast spectrum of innovative ways of public space engagement becomes a possibility, where ICTs constitute a resource to be used in the production of more responsive, liveable and inclusive urban environment (Smaniotto et al. 2017). On these grounds, it is paramount to explore the role and impact of ICTs on public spaces from a teenagers' point of view.

All the above, and especially the apparent invisibility or, perhaps, disappearance of teens from public spaces and their alleged antisocial behaviour, make a call for an intergenerational dialogue and further study on the issues (Lieberg 1995). With a view to initiate such a forum where adolescents can articulate their needs, preferences, views, concerns, etc. regarding urban public spaces, the present exploratory study aims to introduce some aspects that stand out from the perspective of eight adolescents living in different sociocultural contexts of four distinct cities.

3 ICTs and Public Space: The View of Teenagers

3.1 Study Methodology

The questionnaire used was composed of two main blocks of questions: The first block concerns the interviewees' profile, containing 34 (mostly closed) questions, which collected socio-demographic data, information on the different ways' ICTs are employed, how free time is spent, and public spaces are used, in addition to other aspects of interviewees' social life. The second set of questions, all open, gathered opinions on public spaces (quality, frequency of use, etc.) and how the ICTs could increase their use by the respondent and their friends and peers. The last question of this block asked for additional comments regarding all aspects of the issues raised. The initial idea of this question was to initiate further discussion in the form of informal conversation within the topics of study.

In order to implement the process of inquiry, each one of the authors identified (and then interviewed) two adolescents who were, somehow, part of the interviewer's wider social network in the cities they live. This choice enabled to speed up the process of inquiry and fostered the establishment of more relaxed conversations-interviews, that made the collection of information not only easier but also oriented it towards more in-depth and qualitative kind of data. The process of inquiry took place between May and June 2017.

3.2 General Information About Interviewees and Their Families

The following information presents key demographic characteristics, composing the profile of the eight adolescents participated in the study:

- The majority of interviewees (six in number) are female, the only two boys are each from Hannover and Tel Aviv.
- The interviewees are between 14 and 16 years old (two girls of 14, one boy and two girls aged 15, and one boy plus two girls are 16 years old).
- Seven of them are in the secondary school (five attend the 9th grade and two in 10th grade, one in 8th grade).
- Six of the interviewees live in a household composed of three to four people, one respondent, from Lisbon, lives in a household of five, and one from Tel Aviv in a household of six persons.
- Except for a single case (Tel Aviv), whose mother completed only primary education, all other parents have a university degree; out of these seven, four have completed postgraduate studies (two mothers from Lisbon and Volos, and two fathers from Hannover and Volos).
- Except for one parent who is retired (Lisbon), all other parents are currently employed. In terms of professional occupation, there are six people who are highly educated professionals, e.g. doctors, engineers, etc. (three parents from Lisbon and three parents from Hannover), two mothers working in service and sales sector (respectively in Hannover and Tel Aviv), five people are employed in education (one mother from Tel Aviv and four parents from Volos), one is a businessman (from Hannover); and for the remaining two people (from Lisbon and Tel Aviv) such information have not been provided.
- Five of the adolescents identified themselves as belonging to a household with moderate to high income, and the other three indicated their family income to be moderate to low (one from Tel Aviv and two from Volos).

3.3 Study Results

Regarding how the eight interviewees use ICTs and related devices, as expected, all adolescents have some kind of digital devices at home and, in particular, some of them are for their personal use. The following information presents synoptically our findings:

- Smartphones: all household members of respondents from Hannover and Tel Aviv and one from Lisbon have own personal smartphones. In the other families some members do not own a smartphone, presumably the too young ones, these are one family member in Lisbon and two family members in Volos.
- Desktop computer: with the exception of two cases, one in Lisbon and in Hannover, all families had at least one desktop computer. Notably, a respondent from Tel Aviv reported of having two desktops at home.
- Tablets: four of the cases reported of not having a tablet at home (Hannover, Lisbon, Tel Aviv and Volos). One case (Hannover) reported having four tablets in the household, one for each member of the family. Interesting is also the case of a Lisbon family mentioning that there is a tablet in the household, but it is not working. The last case, a Volos family of four people counts on two tablets.
- Laptop/Notebook: all households report that there is at least one laptop/notebook available. In two families (one from Hanover and one from Lisbon), all members

have for their own such a device. The second family from Lisbon reported four notebooks for five people.

- Other technological equipment: with the exception of one case from Lisbon and the two cases of Tel Aviv, all other families stated that there is at least one such device in the household, namely: N2DS and Kindle (in one case from Hannover), iPod, SmartWatch and mp3 (one case from Lisbon), and mp3 player (one case from Volos).

Teenagers were also asked about the use of GPS through the ICT devices they own. Three of the interviewees (one from Tel Aviv, Volos and Hannover) replied that they did not make such use. All others reported that they use this function mainly for locating and consulting transport services. All teens have reported they have internet access at their homes and at school (both Wi-Fi and cable connection), and they use it for research purposes and for obtaining all kind of information.

Adolescents were asked to identify from a list of seven places (home, school, other family members' home, friends' home, shopping centres, public spaces, and public transport) where they access the internet most. Unfortunately, only in Lisbon the question was answered as expected; in all other cases this question was unsatisfactory answered, preventing us from drawing comprehensive conclusions on the issue. For example, the respondents from Hannover marked the places where the internet are accessed (with no identification of relative importance between the places), whereas the respondents from Tel Aviv and Volos indicated the importance of some, but not all of the places (presumably only those used). In any case, the answers indicate the following:

- Home: Except for one case (Tel Aviv), all other interviewees have selected this option. Moreover, the two cases of both Lisbon and Volos, reported "home" to be the most frequent place for accessing the internet.
- School: The two interviewees from Hannover marked this as a place of frequent internet access, whereas all responders from Lisbon identified "school" as the second place of importance. The other cases, i.e. in Tel Aviv and Volos, teenagers reported that they use the internet for research, without however providing further information on where they access to it.
- Other family members' home: Only the cases of Lisbon and Volos have place identified as important; in Lisbon it came as second, while in Volos it was classified fourth and fifth most frequent way to access to internet. One of Hannover's respondents selected this option (but without ranking its importance); and for the cases of Tel Aviv no answers were delivered.
- Friends' home: This place was selected by two interviewees, one from Hannover and from Tel Aviv. This option was select as first and second place in Volos, and the fourth and the fifth in Lisbon.
- Shopping centre: This place was marked by one case in Hannover and by another in Tel Aviv. In Lisbon, it was marked as the third and last rank.
- Public spaces: It was ranked second and third in Volos, fifth and fourth in Lisbon. It was marked as important by one of the Hannover teenagers.
- Public transport: This place was ranked as last and third in importance by teenagers of Lisbon and fourth of Volos. One interviewee from Hannover ranked it too.

The frequency of internet connection was explored in the next question, revealing that teenagers have access to Wi-Fi internet services to a great extent. Both respondents from Volos, one from Lisbon and one from Tel Aviv reported that they are always connected, whereas the other two respondents from Lisbon and Tel Aviv and the one from Hannover, indicated that they stay connected several times during a day. Notably, only one interviewee (from Hannover) replied to have internet access only a few times a day. Turning to the question of how many hours the internet is used every day by the teenagers, the majority of interviewees mentioned to use it between four to seven hours, and only two of the respondents (from Tel Aviv and Volos) use it about one to two hours per day. Moreover, these answers allow us to spot the following findings:

- Girls specify that they spend more time using the internet than boys (to note, however, that only two boys participated in the study);
- Internet time used for email communication seems to be quite lower relative to time spent in other activities, especially those related to social network/media;
- Regarding the time teenagers spend connected to the internet for recreational activities has been mentioned most often.

The next set of questions explored how teenagers spent their free time. First, on a given list of activities (watch TV, go for a walk, stay at home with friends, play computer games, listen to music, study, read books, access social networks, other) the teenagers are asked to rate on a scale of 1 (low) to 7 (high) what they usually do in their free time during the week. The results show that the majority of the adolescents spend most of their free time in playing computer games and in studying (both answers scored equally high), and in listening to music (scored third). Apart from these, other preferred activities that are high scored are: watching TV (indicated by one respondent from Hannover and one from Tel Aviv), book reading (mentioned by the other respondent from Hannover), accessing social network (selected by one teenager from Tel Aviv and one from Volos) and walking (indicated by the same respondent from Volos).

The second question explored which places from a given list (shopping centre, cinema, theatre, museum, concert/festival, club/association, urban park, square, garden, or other) teenagers visit most during their free time. It becomes evident that semi-public places and, in particular malls, cinemas, museums and theatres, score top in the preferences of respondents. Interestingly, public open spaces, such as squares and parks, score lower, but above other places of social gathering such as festivals, clubs or associations. These findings corroborate the arguments raised in the literature that adolescents tend to withdraw from public spaces and to resort to semi-public spaces as the new rhetorical and experiential landscape. Regarding the individual responses, teens from Hannover are more into spending time in festivals and clubs, Lisbon's teenagers are more into theatres and museums, Tel Aviv respondents spend time in parks and shopping centres and in Volos in cinemas and squares.

Teenagers were also questioned about their practices and behaviour in public spaces. They have been asked on the frequency they go to a public space, how much time they usually spend there, what they do there, and with who they go. As regards the first question, the answers show that four out of eight teenagers visit public spaces every day (the two teens from Lisbon, one from Hannover and one from Tel Aviv); others mentioned to go only on weekends (both from Volos) or sporadically (one respondent from Hannover and one from Tel Aviv). With regard to the time spent in public spaces, three respondents (the two from Tel Aviv and the one from Hannover) replied that they go to the public spaces for an hour or less per day, others that they stay between two to four hours a day (two from Lisbon, one from Hannover and one from Volos). One adolescent (from Volos) replied that during the summer she stays in parks and squares about six hours per day. The interviewed teens expressed to go to the public spaces mainly to meet with friends (seven out of eight), to walk (six respondents), to relax and rest (five respondents), to picnic (three respondents), to read and study (three respondents), to practise sports and exercise (two respondents) and to attend events and play games (two people in each category, respectively). All teenagers mentioned to go to public spaces with their friends and some with family members (the two from Lisbon, one from Hannover and one from Tel Aviv).

Finally, a number of questions explored what teenagers think of public spaces and the role ICTs can play in increasing their use. The first question is about the teens' judgment upon the public space suitability for the needs of adolescents. Respondents were generally positive; the two teens from Tel Aviv answered with "definitely yes", highlighting the fact that the parks they use have sections that enable privacy and isolation. This approval was also shared by the teenagers from Hannover and Lisbon, as they answered with "rather yes". On the other hand, adolescents from Volos were not satisfied with the public spaces, reporting a number of problems and deficiencies they see in these places. This builds the bridge to the next question: what teenagers do think is missing in these places and what should be done to increase the usability for young people. The teens from Tel Aviv reported no problems, as they are satisfied with the public spaces they have. Furthermore, three teenagers highlighted problems of dog fouling (one each from Hannover, Lisbon and Volos), others pointed out issues of maintenance and cleanliness (one each from Lisbon and Hannover, and the two from Volos), two have highlighted the need of more natural elements and pleasant environment (one each from Lisbon and Hannover), the girl from Hannover brought out the need of coffee shops nearby green spaces, one of the Lisbon girls stressed the absence of drinking water in parks, and the one from Volos asked for more events and cultural activities in public spaces. Remarkably, three of the interviewees (two from Volos and one from Hannover) highlighted the lack for privacy for teenagers and emphasised the need for special places within parks, where adolescents (as well as other people with special interests and needs, as children) can claim for themselves, places where they can loiter, hang out and interact with their friends and peers. The third question of this block asked if ICTs can improve public space usage, and if so, what kind of ICTs would be most supportive. Six adolescents, out of eight, replied to this question (the two who did not are from Hannover), all in a positive manner. Three teens highlighted the need of providing online information (the girl from Lisbon and two from Tel Aviv) related to public-space facilities and functions (such as, the available public-space qualities and the activities that can be performed in them, and the availability and frequency of public transport). The two teens from Volos stated that high quality Wi-Fi would be very helpful, it would improve communication and coordination between teenagers, and eventually attracting more young people, making "these spaces more fashionable". They also suggested the development of special apps attached to public spaces (like Pokémon-go).

4 The Lessons Learnt: Discussion and Conclusions

This small-scale study outlines the view of eight teenagers living in different cities: Hannover, Lisbon, Volos and Tel Aviv, to provide some insights on teenager's perspectives and on their ICT practices in relation to public open spaces. Teenagers as Digital Natives belong to the "Z" generation, a generation born completely within the technological age having a true global culture with quite uniform characteristics.

That said, it is almost natural that ICTs are scored very high in the preferences of teenagers interviewed. If there are any differences among them, these should be attributed to the local conditions in each country, the standards of living, differences in education, culture, degree of ICTs penetration and provision of quality public spaces. Even so the results let us to draw the following conclusions:

- Teenagers are using intensively the most advanced tools and particularly smartphones, which become a very common device among more and more youngers of any gender.
- Differences in socio-economic status do not matter, both lower and higher economic levels use ICTs to a similar degree. Of course, some parents are more cautious (and protective) with regard to how their children should engage with technology, and in these cases, teens have to negotiate the access to digital media and technology.
- ICTs devices are acquiring the status of "humanized friend" among the adolescents. ICTs become not only the everyday companion of teenagers but in some cases their 'best friend', substituting other friends and peers.
- Possession of smartphones and other mobile devices gives teenagers a kind of social status, prestige and acceptance by their peers. It is also a medium for showing off, or, as Veblen (1899) terms it, for "conspicuous consumption".
- Internet, especially wi-fi, is a companion of teens and they use it in diversified situations, needs and contexts, and through different devices. This means that providing wi-fi in public spaces can be a way to lead more young people to get outside and maybe engage with the city and nature.
- Equipped with advanced ICT services, public spaces would attract teenagers, but yet this requires the provision of "private" and retreat places they need for doing a number of activities, e.g. getting together, for entertaining themselves and for practicing sports, etc.
- This reinforces the need to better prepare public spaces to meet the needs and preferences of teenagers. Their activities in public spaces, as reported, are common across to all four cities examined.
- "Good" public spaces can play an important role in teens' socialisation. As Childress (2004) has shown, teens need to mark "their" places (with graffiti, skateboarding or even loitering). This calls for providing teenagers a legitimate and unchaperoned public space, designed in such a way as to make them feel welcomed.
- Teenagers do miss useful information regarding amenities in open spaces and especially about facilities aimed at young people. This becomes an opportunity for technologies to provide such information, motivating teenagers to be more outdoors and forget for a while the gaming indoors.

This small study, due to its limited sampling and resources did not address risks of a digital technology addiction by teenagers, this is an issue that has been increasing being investigated. However, an aspect that becomes clear in the relationship of adolescents with technology, is the speed of the changes in a teenagers' life, be them physical, mental, sentimental and social. These continuous and accelerated changes provoke also changes in their perspectives. The same adolescent interviewed in May might manifest him/herself in a different manner compared to, say, six months later. This goes also in line from a technology perspective, the rapid and continuous digital development poses a continuous challenge for those interested in the nexus people, places and technologies. We cannot stop changes, but we can try to understand these and inform and educate teenagers, and especially in a co-creation process engage young people in the production of more inclusive and responsive public open spaces.

Acknowledgement. This work has been supported by the Cost Action TU1306 – CYBER-PARKS (www.cyberparks-project.eu) and by C3Places – Using ICT for Co-creation of Inclusive Public Places (European Union's Horizon 2020 research and innovation programme under grant agreement No 693443) – www.c3places.eu.

References

ACS, Australian Computer Society Inc: Digital Technology and Australian Teenagers: Consumption, Study and Careers (2013). www.acs.org.au

Bahillo, A., Goličnik Marušić, B., Perallos, A.: A mobile application as an unobtrusive tool for behavioural mapping in public spaces. In: García-Chamizo, J.M., Fortino, G., Ochoa, S.F. (eds.) UCAmI 2015. LNCS, vol. 9454, pp. 13–25. Springer, Cham (2015). https://doi.org/10.1007/978-3-319-26401-1_2

Bell, S., Ward Thompson, C., Travlou, P.: Contested views of freedom and control: children, teenagers and urban fringe woodlands in central Scotland. Urban Forest. Urban Green. **2**, 87–100 (2003)

Boyd, D.: It's Complicated: The Social Lives of Networked Teens. Yale University Press, New Haven (2014)

Childress, H.: Teenagers, territory and the appropriation of space. Childhood **11**(2), 195–205 (2004)

COB, Childhood Obesity Prevention: Growing up healthy - discussion framework for a childhood obesity prevention strategy. Nova Scotia, Ca (2011)

Depeau, S.: Urban identities and social interaction: a cross-cultural analysis of young people's spatial mobility in Paris, France, and Frankston Australia. Local Environ. **6**(1), 81–86 (2001)

Hampton, K.N., Gupta, N.: Community and social interaction in the wireless city: Wi-Fi use in public and semi-public spaces. New Media Soc. **10**(6), 831–850 (2008)

Hampton, K.N., Livio, O., Sessions Goulet, L.: The social life of wireless urban spaces: Internet use, social networks, and the public realm. J. Commun. **60**(4), 701–722 (2010)

Hatuka, T., Toch, E.: The emergence of portable private-personal territory: Smartphones, social conduct and public spaces. Urban Stud. **53**(10), 2192–2208 (2014). https://doi.org/10.1177/0042098014524608

Jupp, E.: Participation, local knowledge and empowerment: researching public space with young people. Environ. Plann. A **39**(12), 2832–2844 (2007)

Lieberg, M.: Teenagers and public space. Commun. Res. **22**(6), 720–744 (1995)

Livingstone, S., Cagiltay, K., Ólafsso, K.: EU kids online II dataset: a cross-national study of children's use of the Internet and its associated opportunities and risks. Br. J. Educ. Technol. **46**(5), 988–992 (2015). https://doi.org/10.1111/bjet.12317

Louv, R.: Last Child in the Woods: Saving Our Children from Nature deficit Disorder. Algonquin, Chapel Hill (2008)

Matthews, H.: Living on the edge: children as outsiders. Tijdschr. voor Econ. en Soc. Geogr. **86** (5), 456–466 (1995)

Matthews, H., Limb, M., Percy-Smith, B.: Changing worlds: the microgeographies of young teenagers. Tijdschr. voor Econ. en Soc. Geogr. **89**(2), 193–202 (1998)

Menezes, M., Smaniotto Costa, C.: People, public space, digital technology and social practice: an ethnographic approach. In: Zammit, A., Kenna, T. (eds.) Enhancing Places Through Technology, pp. 167–180. Edições Universitárias Lusófonas, Lisbon (2017). ISBN 978-989-757-055-1. http://cyberparks-project.eu/sites/default/files/publications/cyberparks_enhancing placestechnology.pdf

Robinson, C.: Creating space, creating self: street-frequenting youth in the city and suburbs. J. Youth Stud. **3**(4), 429–443 (2000)

RSPH, Royal Society for Public Health: Status of Mind - Social media and young people's mental health and wellbeing. London (2017). https://www.rsph.org.uk/our-work/policy/social-media-and-young-people-s-mental-health-and-wellbeing.html

Smaniotto Costa, C.: A framework for guiding the management of low-impact mobility towards making room for sustainable urban green infrastructure. J. Traffic Logist. Eng. **1**(4), 74–82 (2016). https://doi.org/10.18178/jtle.4.1.74-82

Smaniotto Costa, C., Bahillo Martínez, A., Álvarez, F.J., Šuklje Erjavec, I., Menezes, M., Pallares-Barbera, M.: Digital tools for capturing user's needs on urban open spaces: drawing lessons from cyberparks project. In: Certomà, C., Dyer, M., Pocatilu, L., Rizzi, F. (eds.) Citizen empowerment and innovation in the data-rich city. STCE, pp. 177–193. Springer, Cham (2017). https://doi.org/10.1007/978-3-319-47904-0_11

Travlou, P., Owens, P.E., Thompson, C.W., Maxwell, L.: Place mapping with teenagers: locating their territories and documenting their experience of the public realm. Child. Geogr. **6**(3), 309–326 (2008)

Valentine, G.: Children should be seen and not heard: the production and transgression of adults' public space. Hum. Geogr. **17**(3), 205–220 (1996)

Veblen, T.: The Theory of the Leisure Class: An Economic Study of Institutions. Random House, New York (1899)

Worpole, K.: No Particular Place to Go? Children, Young People and Public Space. Groundwork UK, London (2005)

2.5

Challenging Methods and Results Obtained from User-Generated Content in Barcelona's Public Open Spaces

Montserrat Pallares-Barbera[1](✉), Elena Masala[2], Jugoslav Jokovic[3], Aleksandra Djukic[4], and Xavier Albacete[5]

[1] Universitat Autònoma de Barcelona, Bellaterra, Spain
montserrat.pallares@uab.cat
[2] SiTI - Higher Institute on Territorial Systems for Innovation, Turin, Italy
elena.masala@polito.it
[3] University of Nis, Niš, Serbia
Jugoslav.Jokovic@elfak.ni.ac.rs
[4] University of Belgrade, Belgrade, Serbia
adjukic@afrodita.rcub.bg.ac.rs
[5] University of Eastern Finland, Kuopio, Finland
xavialmar@gmail.com

Abstract. User-generated content (UGC) provides useful resources for academics, technicians and policymakers to obtain and analyse results in order to improve lives of individuals in urban settings. User-generated content comes from people who voluntarily contribute data, information, or media that then appears in a way which can be viewed by others; usually on the Web. However, to date little is known about how complex methodologies for getting results are subject to methodology-formation errors, personal data protection, and reliability of outcomes. Different researches have been approaching to inquire big data methods for a better understanding of social groups for planners and economic needs. In this chapter, through UGC from Tweets of users located in Barcelona, we present different research experiments. Data collection is based on the use of REST API; while analysis and representation of UGC follow different ways of processing and providing a plurality of information. The first objective is to study the results at a different geographical scale, Barcelona's Metropolitan Area and at two Public Open Spaces (POS) in Barcelona, Enric Granados Street and the area around the Fòrum de les Cultures; during similar days in two periods of time - in January of 2015 and 2017. The second objective is intended to better understand how different types of POS' Twitter-users draw urban patterns. The Origin-Destination patterns generated illustrate new social behaviours, addressed to multifunctional uses. This chapter aims to be influential in the use of UGC analysis for planning purposes and to increase quality of life.

Keywords: User-generated content · Big data · Twitter · Public open spaces · Spatial analysis

C. Smaniotto Costa et al. (Eds.): CyberParks, LNCS 11380, pp. 120–136, 2019.
https://doi.org/10.1007/978-3-030-13417-4_10

1 Introduction

The implications of User Generated Content are changing the daily life of people. Everyone is involved, but some institutions have stored the data and the power to exploit them. We can contribute to make this power more democratic and available to improve the life of people. This chapter has the goal to do it. The objective of this chapter is to deepen the study on user-generated data (UGD, User Generated Content, UGC) for exploring new methodologies that could support and improve the understanding of spatial patterns for urban planning and design of open spaces in urban areas. This chapter aims at taking a step forward form current literature. It provides, on the one hand, three methods for social science analysis using Big Data; and, on the other hand, it expects to motivate the possible outcomes of UGD coming from three Information and Communication Technologies (ICT) platforms into policy driving strategies, where results can be used to improve quality of life. This chapter examines the spatial pattern of UGD in three public open spaces in Barcelona: Enric Granados Street (Carrer Enric Granados), Forum (Fòrum de les Cultures) and Barcelona Metropolitan Area; and the spatial patterns generated by weekday and by hourly interval in order to study the further insides of how users construct different configuration in visiting a city. Methodologically, we have used two different platforms (Twitter and WAY app). Twitter, the web social network is currently used by 284 million of monthly active users (Twitter Inc. 2015). Twitter provides large amounts of data georeferenced. Although only a part of the entire urban population uses Twitter, the remaining data are a useful source to analyse the location of people in the city are and why there is more activity-clustering in places vs. others. The second platform is the app WAY Cyberparks, an application developed by DeustoTech Mobility within the COST Action TU1306 – CyberParks (Bahillo et al. 2016, 2015; Masegosa et al. 2015). This GPS-based platform focuses on the use of ICT for understanding and collecting data on the use of urban open spaces.

The possibility to communicate worldwide through common smartphones opened up new perspectives and interaction pathways to individuals, who very quickly responded with a massive use of social network platforms and applications. Since most smartphones include Global Positioning System (GPS), if activated, outgoing data from each device can be geo-referenced. Thus, the large amount of data can be geo-located with a time reference. The consequence is the constant production of "Big Data" (Targio et al. 2015; Snijders et al. 2012) which can be overlaid on maps and analysed by mathematical, semantic techniques (Language detection API 2016), and by means of spatial analysis methods. Substantial works on the nature of geography have discussed the spatial pattern formed by many purposes of analysis, since the classical works of Hartshorne (1939), Harvey (1963), Friedman and Alonso (1964), Berry (1973), and Chorley and Haggett (1965) among many others till nowadays. Their relevant research on the organization and settlement of people and activities in the human world, the regularity of distribution brought significant and worthy results which made huge advancements in Geographical Thought and society. In 2018, UGC brought a new paradigm in the study and analysis of spatial patterns in Human Geography. Related problems are more associated to find appropriate models and methodologies to draw a good statistical sample from the population, to depurate the data, to discriminate the data size and to analyse consistently the results.

Case studies are very specific and different POS in Barcelona. Enric Granados is located at the urban centre, in the "Cerdà's Eixample" (Cerdà enlargement) of Barcelona (Pallares-Barbera, Badia and Duch 2011). It is a residential lively, dense street with services and amenities; Forum is located at the end of the Diagonal, very close to the 22@Barcelona neighbourhood (Casellas and Pallares-Barbera 2009). It is mainly a complex of buildings and cement plazas built for the 2004 Forum of Cultures exhibition. For the most part, locals use Enric Granados Street, while Forum's facilities are used for large meetings, conventions and festivals; otherwise it is an unoccupied space.

This chapter is formulated in different sections. Section 2 analyses the state of the art regarding uses and applications of UGC by different institutions, firms and policy makers. Section 3 describes the case studies. Section 4 focusses on data and methodology, while Sect. 5 is about results and discussion of them. Conclusions, provided in Sect. 6, aim to offer insides of expected future developments for the integration of UGC with new methodologies within contemporary spatial planning processes.

2 Background and Related Work

The availability of big and open data is nowadays offering new opportunities for rethinking the human behaviour and its impact on Earth. Since these data is often georeferenced, its overlaying on maps provides useful information on particular organization and structure of spatial systems. Therefore, urban planning, and design, transport planning, social sciences and human geography can benefit from their use.

Although a large number of applications and experiments constellates the landscape of research, the academic research has barely yet found a specific own pathway within these huge opportunities. However, relevant academic work is coming out as well as public and private bodies have begun to use big data for their own development; for example, NOAA Big Data Project, or DataKind for the treatment of trees in NYC. A concise overview on the state of the art on the use of geolocated user-generated contents in spatial planning is meant to show analysis, applications and uses.

Cities have the pressure of millions of inhabitants to increase their quality of life. Through the introduction of ICT, cities try to cope population needs with strategies based on an integrative framework, including management, technology, governance and policy; a reunion of factors which some call smart city (Chourabi et al. 2012). The concept of smart city has not a clear consensus and nor a consistent understanding among academia and practitioners, but in this chapter, it will be used to refer to a city with massive implications of ICT. City information is collected by sensors, tools and applications and used on the city policy. Data-information relies on the diffuse use of devices for quantifying movements, environment quality and healthiness, and energy consumption. Private enterprises, such as the biggest technological companies like IBM, Cisco or Siemens are also interested on data collection and analysis for their own objectives and strategies.

Local institutions such as governments or urban planning firms use big data to organize exhibitions with different goals. Some of them are under the idea of crowd-sourcing, in which citizens' digital footprint such as tweets or use of online municipal services help city planners improve city's design and functionality. For instance, the Chicago Architecture Foundation (CAF) partnering with IBM (Chicago Architecture Foundation 2014; IBM 2014; Snodgrass 2014) launched "Chicago: City of Big Data." Its goal was to open up a dialogue on the connection between big data and human lives and to show how spatial systems are impacted by this information, and how relevant each individual was to the design of their environment. The exhibition's dashboards were built with IBM's City Forward platform, a free web-based "civic resource that enables people to visualize and interact with city data" (Kokalitcheva 2014). The methodological basis for selecting data sources used two central criteria: the data's availability at a large enough scale; and its capability to communicate valuable insights about the city's needs and flows. Then, they used complex geographic information systems (GIS) and web-based tools to compile and visualize the data in effective ways. Data sources consisted of over 18 million Twitter data points, with only timestamp and location attributes, which turned into dynamic and "interactive models of city's human activity." (Kokalitcheva 2014). On the broad objective of "explor(ing) the emergence of the database as a framework for cultural and political thinking and the effects of datafication of the world.", the Big Bang Data exhibition (Spain) (organised by the Centre de Cultura Contemporània de Barcelona (CCCB) and Fundación Telefónica 2015) took under consideration different topics about city' shape and layout on the basis of different kind of data.

Academic literature based on Twitter-use patterns has developed at different geographical scales. The spatial pattern of social networks and the threshold of their activities have been analysed at urban scale across three cities in order to produce an inter-urban analysis (Bawa-Cavia 2010). Diverse methods, such as attempts to aggregate the activity on the network onto a grid (400 × 400 m) of dots representing the 'walkable' cells showed the threshold walking distances in urban areas (O'Sullivan and Morral 1996). At wider scale, human flows are gathered, extracted and analysed in geolocated social media data through different instruments. An example is FlowSampler, an interactive interface for visual analysis of flows in geolocated social media data. It adopts a graph-based approach to infer movement pathways from spatial point type data and expresses the resulting information through multiple linked visualizations to support data exploration (Chua et al. 2014). Additionally, it allows characterizing places in base the "density" of arc traces and keywords within the local groups. Big data also helps to study prescription planning such as to plan routes of buses and subways to satisfy public demand in several cities around the world (Fisher 2012).

Through the spatial analysis of UGD, we come to understand that some cities are far more active early in the morning, while others show higher activity at night or on weekends (Neuhaus 2011). The Centre for Advanced Spatial Analysis (CASA) at University College London (UCL) Twitter-use monitored several cities over a week to determine patterns in temporal activities and learn about spatial networks. Other analyses on UGD and available data from social networks - Twitter, Facebook, Flickr and Instagram - captured information about citizens' feelings, citizens' uses, citizens' comfortability and conditions of problematic situations. Funded by the German Research Foundation, the "Urban Emotions" project (Heidelberg and Kaiserslautern Universities) tested UGD by checking whether the emotions measured correlate with the subjective assessments in the social media. "People as Sensors" used measures emotions and stress levels, such as "unsafe bike paths, traffic jam stress, frightening underpasses" (Heidelberg University 2014). Therefore, measurements of citizens' emotional responses to their environment were made with by the use of sensors, similar to a wristwatch "that allows us to measure skin conductance, body temperature and variations in heart rate that change, for instance, when someone is startled" (Resch et al. 2015). Differently, but also tracing emotions, the exploration of how people express excitement online show a regular pattern; in which as much higher levels of excitement and more intense the flurry of messages in the collective, the shorter the messages become (Senseable City Lab and Ericsson 2015; Szell et al. 2014). Emotional bursts become faster and more impulsive online than offline. Many associated questions and outcomes become still unanswered, such as: "Are people doing this independently, or in response to seeing other short messages? Are we following the herd? Could we use these insights to learn more about financial bubbles by measuring more impulsive, less rational responses? And can we design better communication services?" (Lanzerotti et al. 2013).

Nevertheless, cautions have to be taken in considering the use of big data. There are many positive aspects on big data analysis, but many fears can be raised too. The obvious one is the intrusion on in the private sphere of our lives. In addition, putting data culture at the centre of decision-making and on the way of interpreting the world opens up many possibilities and involves numerous risks. The main danger of data-centrism is that it encourages the idea that whatever the problem, the answer lays in data. This important discussion escapes the goal of this chapter.

3 Case Studies

The several big data methodologies presented in this chapter are better understood if different geographical scales are used for analysis. Besides the metropolitan area of Barcelona, two very diverse morphological and social POS are chosen: Enric Granados and Forum (Fig. 1).

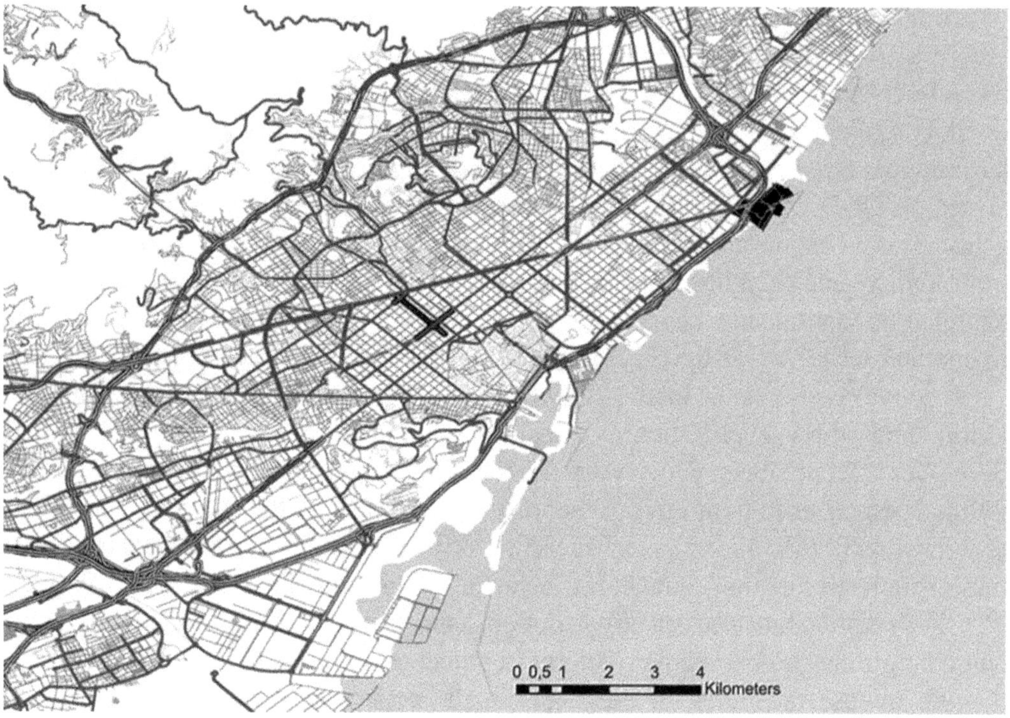

Fig. 1. Location of two case study areas in Barcelona

Enric Granados is within the consolidated historical city; and connects the Diagonal Avenue with a foundational building of the University of Barcelona. Differently from Rambla de Catalunya and Passeig de Gràcia, which are parallel to it, the Enric Granados width is slightly more than 20 m and hosts several leisure activities mostly for neighbours and local people. The urban transformations that followed the Olympic Games in 1992 changed the role of this street in the urban hierarchy. From a traditional car-oriented road, it became a pedestrian that is a user-oriented space. This was made possible by modifying the car mobility of the street.

The Forum rises on the old industrial Poblenou, an urban district that was renewed during the end of the twentieth, beginning of the twenty-one century; and hosted the Universal Forum of Cultures (2004) (Casellas, Dot-Jutgla and Pallares-Barbera 2012). Forum is where the Diagonal Avenue meets the Mediterranean Sea. The new character of the area is pointed by a number of new architectures, with building, skyscrapers designed by very famous architects. Nevertheless, the functional connectedness of the whole area is inexistent. The large paved esplanade provides a sense of incompleteness with no seats, nor trees, nor shadows.

4 Data and Methodology

The several methods used in this chapter are based on geo mapping. Focus is placed on intensity and concentration of users in open public spaces. Data was collected using 3 different ICT methodologies in 3 periods of time in Barcelona. First, Twitter data was collected by SiTI (Higher Institute on Territorial Systems for Innovation, Torino) during the period between January the 12th and 18th, 2015. Second, Twitter data was compiled using TSE (Tweeter Search Engine) application in January from the 13th to the 20th, 2017. Third, WAY app gathered data in November 27, 2014 (COST Action 1306 2014), with a selected group of users moving in and between the two case study areas.

4.1 Twitter Data Information

Twitter is used by only 23% of the total population in the U.S.A. Its data-base is open for free use and can provide very large amount of records and information, including attributes on time and location of each single tweet (geo-referenced points and the given radius are settled only when sender is geotagged (Poblete et al. 2011; Krumm, Davis and Narayanaswami 2008; Haining 2003)). Each message can be downloaded and stored on a personal database through Twitter REST API (Twitter REST API 2016). Some of the characteristics of the database include: the text, time and date, the nick-name of the sender, the eventual name of the receiver, and the latitude and longitude from sender (Table 1).

Table 1. Data records of a single tweet

D	Message	User from	User to	Date	Lat	Lon
	🌄❄□ @ Outside - Calvin Harris http://t.co/14oG7mPxwE	albasancho95	fjdh	Wed Jan 07 08:55:20 +0000 2015	41.47267	2.27114
	Nos aventuramos a las rebajas... Tengo micdo xD	zaidas-phyxiated		Wed Jan 07 08:55:18 +0000 2015	41.52691	2.229489
	#cyberparks #TU1306	e_frola		Fri Jan 09 10:29:08 +0000 2015	41.50982	2.229217
	....	.....	.....	.....	.....	....

For each single user, it is possible to collect other specific data, which can be joined to previous one. This data is listed below.

- User ID
- Name
- Location
- Info given by the user
- Following
- Creation data
- Time zone
- Language
- Status message and date
- Follower ID.

4.2 Methodology for Data Mining for Twitter by SiTI, January 12–18, 2015

The total amount of records was 72,257 Tweets, of which 67,251 (93.07%) were georeferenced. Among these, only 2,802 (4.17%) records were from users who passed across one or both of the two case study areas within the city. The following six steps were used: first, we elaborated Twitter data in Excel; second, we imported Twitter data in ESRI Arc Map; third, we used information about time and coordinates of data from Cyberparks App to trace plausible paths of single users (or group of users); fourth, we worked the information about time and coordinates of tweets to trace plausible paths of single users (or group of users) within specific areas; fifth, we used information about time and coordinates of tweets to trace plausible paths of single users (or group of users) who pass through specific areas; and sixth, we used tweets information about languages, presence of tweets for large periods (to differentiate local users from tourists or visitors), keywords, to identify different kinds of densities within specific areas.

4.3 Methodology for Data Mining for Twitter Using Twitter Search Engine (TSE), January 13–20, 2017

To collect, storage, process and analyse Twitter data in January 13–20, 2017 (15–17000 tweets per day), we employed Twitter Search Engine (TSE) (Dinkic, Jokovic and Stoimenov, 2016). It is a micro-blogging platform that provides a rich collection of real-time commentaries which are on the Twitter REST API, which storage tweets sent the previous week within a given radius. TSE allows collection and storage of data for unlimited periods of time; it offers a display, analysis and execution of complex geospatial queries of the data stored in the database. These queries are executed with the help of relational geospatial functions offered by MySQL database. TSE functions are correlated in terms of interrelationship between two objects determined with geo-referenced points. TSE has the option of drawing a polygon on the map of Google by using Google Maps JavaScript API. This polygon site must be within the area for which information was collected. TSE also has the ability to detect the language using web service Language Detection API (Language detection API, 2016). This API has the capacity to detect 160 different languages and to offer 5.000 requests for free on daily basis[1]. Each request must contain text and API key. The request example can be found at the link[2]. Language Detection API produces results in *.json format. Response contains array of language candidates. Each object contains language code, confidence score and is reliable - true/false (Table 2).

---

[1] To use this API, one has to register on their website using a valid email address. Then, the user receives an API key; which can be used for client application and depending on the needs sends GET or POST requests to server.

[2] http://ws.detectlanguage.com/0.2/detect?q=buenos+dias+señor&key=demo.

Table 2. Language Detection API - Response example


```
{
  "data":
  {
    "detections":
    [{
      "isReliable":false,
      "confidence":0.45171339563862928,
      "language":"es"
    }]
  }
}
```


4.4 Methodology for Data Mining for WAY App, November 27, 2014

The WAY app (Deusto Tech Mobility 2014) is a GPS-based platform that, differently from Twitter data, registers the users' movements twice a second. The result is a point database which allows building up a timeline with the full path travelled by users, with continuity and precision. The app is conceived as a Volunteered Geographic Information (VGI) platform where users collaborate for producing information. In particular, it collects data for better understanding the use of public open spaces in order to improve their production and their relevance to sustainable urban development. It collects also data on the user such as age, sex, education, job, the distance from home and from working place, and the reason of being in a public space, such as walking, running, reading, kids or pets. The main limit of WAY data is given by the fact that the person who generates the data, the user, is conscious that he/she is producing data for some specific analyst task. Therefore, it is necessary to consider that this awareness can alter the veracity of the data. Geovisualization of these data is done by importing data from WAY and converting the *.json file into a readable file for ESRI ArcMap.

5 Results and Discussion - Maps and Visualizations

Several spatial patterns have arisen from the planned methods analysing the use of Twitter and WAY app. Although these initial analyses can be developed further, their opportunities for specific additional improvements are open in future research; where data comparisons, fitness of the methodology and so on are to be implemented to meet diverse research structural questions.

5.1 Tweet Patterns in Barcelona Metropolitan Area, January 12–18, 2015 and January 13–20, 2017

The Origin/Destination (O/D) matrix and the points of twitter messages show the centrality of the city, respect to its hinterland (Fig. 2a, b). City diversity is perceived by the number of user languages (22 (2015) and 120 (2017)) (Table 3).

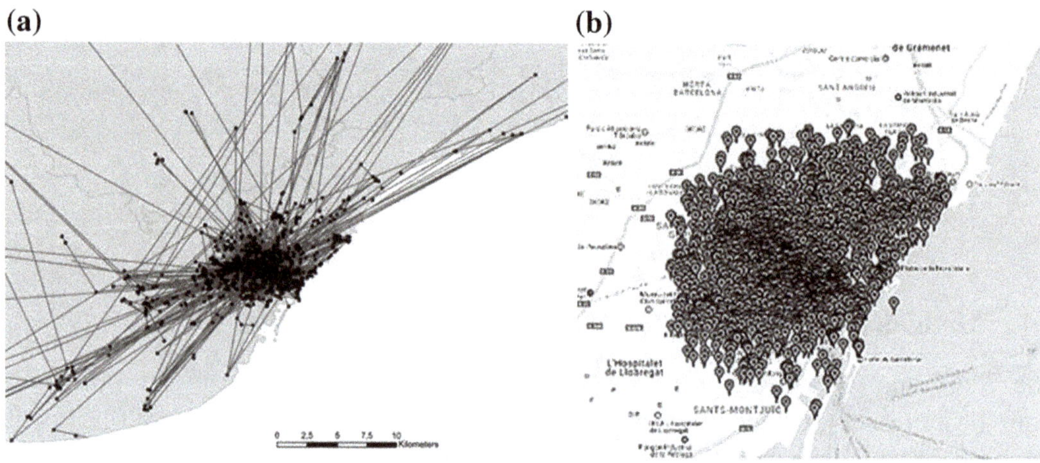

Fig. 2. Twitter messages. Barcelona Metropolitan Area (BMA) (a), and Barcelona City (BCN) (b)

Table 3. Data collected for Barcelona

Type of analysis	January 12–18, 2015	January 13–20, 2017
Number of tweets	67251	117017
Number of users	9823	10412
Number of retweets	–	20208
Number of likes	–	51989
Number of applications	–	45
Number of languages	22	120

5.2 Tweets by Weekdays in Barcelona Metropolitan Area, January 12–18, 2015, January 13–20, 2017

There are variations in the use of the space by weekdays, and between years 2015 and 2017. 2017 has almost doubled the number of tweets of 2015; it might correspond to the increase of tweeter users globally (Table 4, Fig. 3). In 2015, the day with less number of tweets is Thursday, while Monday is the day with more activity. On 2017, on Friday 17 there are fewer tweets than the rest of days. It is obvious that for statistics analysis testing more data values would be required; these two weeks are not representative of others.

Table 4. Tweets by day

Day	January 12–18, 2015		January 13–20, 2017	
	Number of tweets	% of tweets	Number of tweets	% of tweets
Monday	10535	15.67	17295	15.00
Tuesday	9500	14.13	17122	15.00
Wednesday	9410	13.99	16542	14.00
Thursday	8649	12.86	16927	14.50
Friday	9464	14.07	15681	13.00
Saturday	10474	15.57	16533	14.00
Sunday	9219	13.71	16917	14.50
Total	67251	100	117017	100
Mean	9607		16717	

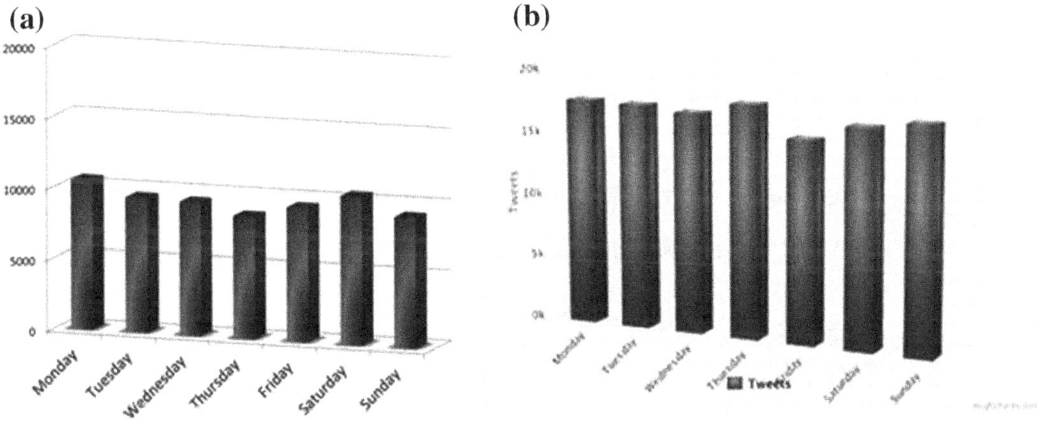

Fig. 3. Tweets by days in the period January 12–18, 2015 (a), and January 13–20, 2017 (b)

Further visualization for the period in 2015 shows subsequent tweets connected by semi-circular arches, whose radius is proportional to the spatial distance which separates each couple of tweets (3D arches) (Fig. 4). On Wednesday 14, 2015 arches are shorter than other days, then activities are concentrated in a smaller space within the city centre; or Sunday 18, the activity around Plaça de Catalunya is comparatively less, shops are closed.

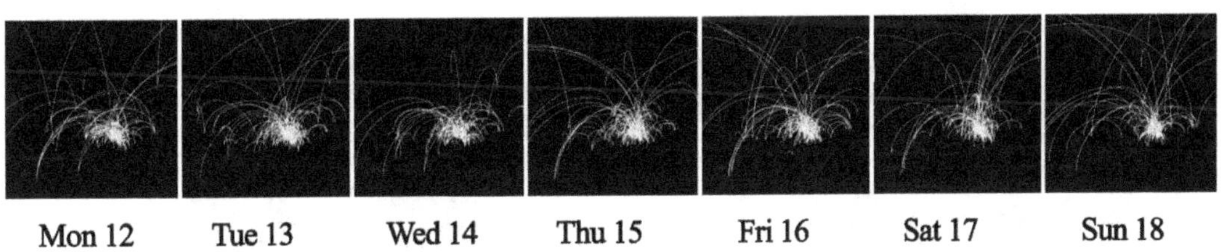

Fig. 4. Distribution of subsequent tweets by each same user, January 12–18, 2015, Barcelona

5.3 Tweets Per Hour, January 12–18, 2015, January 13–20, 2017

City life changes during the day. Seen by number of tweets, the tendency is to increase during the evening, decreases at night, and start increasing in the morning (Table 5 and Fig. 5). Tweets are concentrated around axes that pass Rambla; and most of tweets (75% in 2017) have been sent from 12.00 until 24.00, which relates to working time and street activity (Table 5).

Table 5. Percentage of tweets by time interval

Interval	January 12–18, 2015	January 13–20, 2017
0–3	6.54%	4.28%
3–6	2.52%	1.71%
6–9	8.85%	7.95%
9–12	12.77%	13.85%
12–15	15.42%	17.64%
15–18	15.05%	18.05%
18–21	19.68%	20.38%
21–24	19.17%	16.14%

5.4 Results Provided by WAY App During November 27, 2014

The results of the WAY app provide more detailed perception by users at a micro-scale level. In one sense, WAY data is continuous and is following users' path; while tweets are diffuse in space and time dimensions (Figs. 6 and 7). In another sense, WAY data is concentrated only in the two case studies, whereas Twitter data is sparsely located around the city (Fig. 8). Finally, WAY offers very detailed information on places and on single user's movements, while Tweets provide general information about hierarchical functions in places.

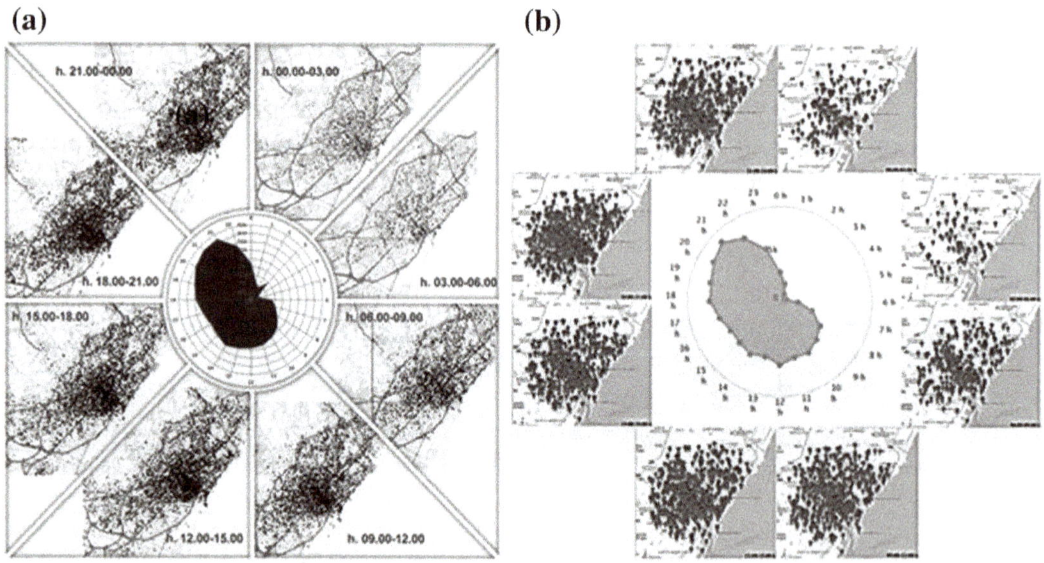

Fig. 5. Tweets by time interval, in the period January 12–18, 2015 (a) and January 13–20, 2017 (b)

Fig. 6. Visualisation of data gathered in Forum through WAY app

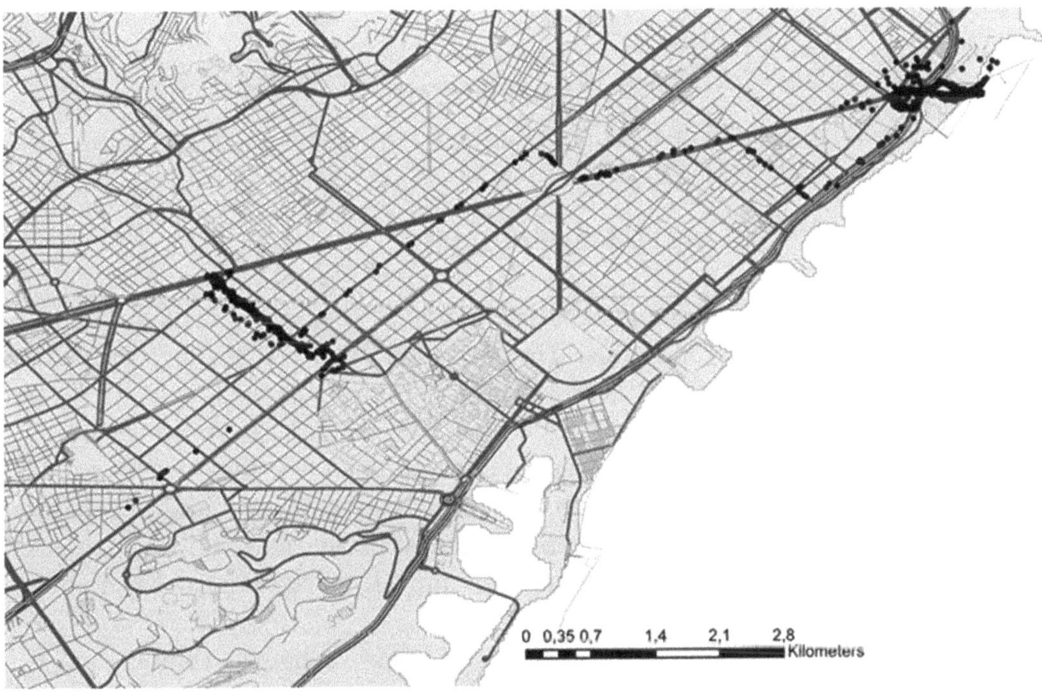

Fig. 7. Data collected by the WAY app in Enric Granados, Forum and in the way between both areas

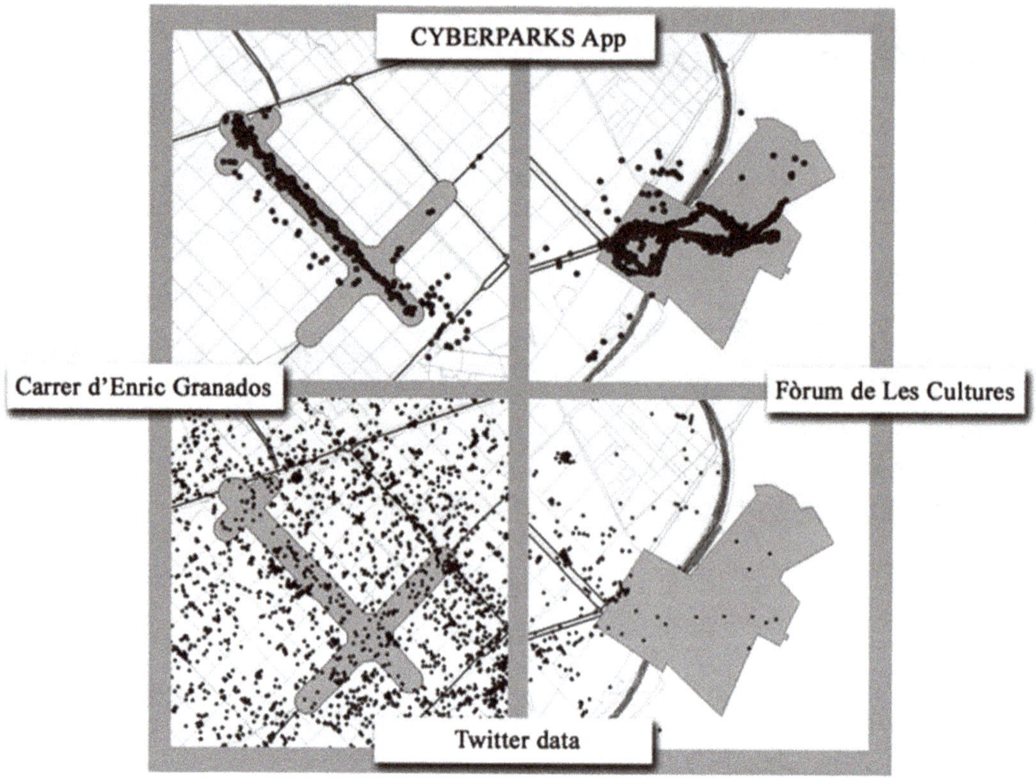

Fig. 8. WAY and Twitter data compared, November 24, 2014

6 Conclusions and Future Developments

The overview on the state of the art shows how spatial planning is facing a transition presenting new challenging scenarios. The trend led by the smart city opened the spatial planning to logic of numbers and data. City-sensors as well as UGC systems constantly provide huge amounts of data which can be used to supply the citizens' demands. In this context, two main branches are emerging. The first branch is a data-oriented and technology-driven approach, which makes use of quantities for assessing and justifying decisions. Eye-catching visualizations are the most evident outputs of such an approach, where analysts and statistics prevail on the human experience of professionals and experts.

The second branch uses new technologies to improve human abilities and it is mostly used to support the decision and policy-making processes. Particular efforts are spent in understanding how data can support can be complementary to the traditional approach, providing new insights on spatial issues. The debate on the use of big data is nowadays shifting from a technology-driven vision towards a more human dimension, introducing the concepts of people friendliness and a human-to-human approach (Melis et al. 2014). To achieve this social vision, the collaboration between different experts such as urban planners and data analysts and designers appears essential in order to guide them towards relevant questions and policy issues (Goodspeed 2012). Simple visualizations offer opportunity for both horizontal and vertical communication.

From a technical point of view, some considerations are necessary for improving future map production. First of all, paths created using subsequent tweets are just possible routes and probably not the real ones covered by users. A method for dealing with this issue is necessary, and different research is being undertaking. Secondly, the use of Twitter data is most suitable for larger scale than the micro-urban areas. However, the continuity along space and over time provide important element for considering their hierarchical position.

In this chapter, the analysis was limited to visualisation and maps; it did not considered semantics, the written content of the tweets (however, a method for experiencing has been suggested); statistical testing has not been performed. Nevertheless, the humble objectives have been stated and proved. We know that integration of new methodologies within spatial planning processes are very relevant, such as in the data collecting and information; defining goals, objectives and strategies and implementation of users' participation through crowdsourcing.

References

Bahillo, A., Aguilera, T., Álvarez, F.J., Perallos, A.: WAY: seamless positioning using a smart device. Wirel. Pers. Commun. **94**(4), 2949–2967 (2016)

Bahillo A, Diez, L.E., Perallos, A., Falcone, F.: Enabling seamless positioning for smartphones. In: Proceedings of Conference XXX Simposium Nacional de la Unión Científica Internacional de Radio (URSI), Pamplona, Spain (2015)

Berry, B.J.L.: The human consequences of urbanisation: divergent paths in the urban experience of the twentieth century, vol. 3, Macmillan, Basingstoke (1973)

Bawa-Cavia, A.: Sensing the urban: using location-based social network data in urban analysis. Presented at 1st Workshop on Pervasive Urban Applications PURBA 2011, San Francisco, USA (2010)

Casellas, A., Dot-Jutgla, E., Pallares-Barbera, M.: Artists, cultural gentrification and public policy. Urbani izziv **23**(Suppl. 1), S104–S114 (2012)

Casellas, A., Pallares-Barbera, M.: Public sector intervention in embodying new economy in inner urban areas: the Barcelona experience. Urban Stud. **46**(5–6), 1137–1155 (2009)

Centre de Cultura Contemporània de Barcelona, CCCB & Fundación Telefónica (2015). http://bigbangdata.cccb.org/en/sec-exhibition/. Accessed 12 Jan 2015

Chicago Architecture Foundation (CAF) (2014). http://bigdata.architecture.org/. Accessed 12 Jan 2015

Chorley, R.J., Haggett, P.: Trend-surface mapping in geographical research. Trans. Inst. Br. Geogr. **37**(4), 47–67 (1965)

Chourabi, H., et al.: Understanding smart cities: an integrative framework. system science (HICSS). In: 45th Hawaii International Conference on Hawaii, USA, pp. 2289–2297. IEEE (2012)

Chua, A., Marcheggiani, E., Servillo, L., Vande Moere, A.: FlowSampler: visual analysis of urban flows in geolocated social media data. Presented at: International Conference on Social Informatics, Barcelona, Spain (2014)

COST Action 1306: First working meeting at the geography department (Universitat Autònoma de Barcelona), Cerdanyola, Spain (2014)

Deusto Tech Mobility: Public open spaces monitoring tool (2014). http://www.costcyberparks.eu/. Accessed 12 Jan 2015

Dinkic, N., Jokovic, J., Stoimenov, L.: Software application: Twitter search engine, developed at the University of Nis, Faculty of Electronic Engineering, during the Ph.D. course "Advanced topics in data and knowledge engineering", Nis, Serbia (2016)

Fisher, E.: Paths through cities (2012). www.flickr.com/photos/walkingsf/sets/72157629014750905/detail/. Accessed 11 Feb 2015

Friedman, J., Alonso, W.: Regional Planning and Development. The MIT Press, Cambridge (1964)

Goodspeed, R.: The democratization of big data. 27 February (2012). http://www.planetizen.com/node/54832. Accessed 2 Jan 2015

Haining, R.: Spatial Data Analysis: Theory and Practice. Cambridge University Press, Cambridge (2003)

Hartshorne, R.: The nature of geography: a critical survey of current thought in the light of the past (conclusion). Ann. Assoc. Am. Geogr. **29**(4):413–658 (1939). www.jstor.org/stable/2561166. Accessed 2 Mar 2016

Harvey, D.W.: Locational change in the kentish hop industry and the analysis of land use patterns. Trans. Papers (Inst. Br. Geogr.) **33**, 123–144 (1963). https://doi.org/10.2307/621004

Heidelberg University: Urban design with emotions. Press Release No. 166/2014 (2014). www.uni-heidelberg.de/presse/news2014/pm20140911_urban-design-with-emotions.html. Accessed 9 Jan 2015

IBM: A new blueprint: how chicago is building a better city with big data (2014). http://people4smartercities.com/series/new-blueprint-how-chicago-building-better-city-big-data. Accessed 12 Jan 2015

Kokalitcheva, K.: How a swarm of data is helping Chicago re-map urban life (2014). http://venturebeat.com/2014/05/14/how-a-swarm-of-data-is-helping-chicago-re-map-urban-life. Accessed 12 Jan 2015

Krumm, J., Davies, N., Narayanaswami, C.: User-generated content. IEEE Pervasive Comput. **7**(4), 10–11 (2008)

Language detection API (2016). https://detectlanguage.com/. Accessed 15 Apr 2016

Lanzerotti, L., Bradach, J., Sud, S., Barmeier, H.: Geek cities: how smarter use of data and evidence can improve lives (2013). www.bridgespan.org/Publications-and-Tools/Performance-Measurement/Geek-Cities-Data-Improves-Lives.aspx#.VLZ9BSvF9Ks. Accessed 13 Jan 2015

Masegosa, A., Bahillo, A., Onieva, E., López, P., Perallos, A.: A new optimization approach for indoor location based on differential evolution. In: Proceedings of Conference International Fuzzy Systems Association (IFSA), Gijón, Spain (2015)

Melis, G., Masala, E., Tabasso, M.: From the smart city to the people-friendly city: usability of tools and data in urban planning. In: Vesco, A., Ferrero, F., (eds) Social, Economic, And Environmental Sustainability In The Development Of Smart Cities, IGI global, pp. 363–381 (2014)

Neuhaus, F.: Twitter data - seeking spatial pattern (2011). http://urbantick.blogspot.it/2011/03/twitter-data-seeking-spatial-pattern.html. Accessed 9 Jan 2015

Open street map community (2004). www.openstreetmap.org. Accessed 29 Dec 2014

O'Sullivan, S., Morral, J.: Walking distances to and from light-rail transit stations. Trans. Res. Rec. **1538**, 19–26 (1996)

Pallares-Barbera, M., Badia, A., Duch, J.: Cerdà and Barcelona: the need for a new city and service provision. Urbani izziv **22**(2), 122–136 (2011)

Poblete, B., Garcia, R., Mendoza, M., Jaimes, A.: Do all birds tweet the same? characterizing Twitter around the world. Presented at CIKM 2011 20th ACM Conference on Information and Knowledge Management (2011). www.ruthygarcia.com/papers/cikm2011.pdf

Resch, B., Summa, A., Sagl, G., Zeile, P., Exner, J.-P.: Urban emotions—geo-semantic emotion extraction from technical sensors, human sensors and crowdsourced data. In: Gartner, G., Huang, H. (eds.) Progress in Location-Based Services 2014. LNGC, pp. 199–212. Springer, Cham (2015). https://doi.org/10.1007/978-3-319-11879-6_14

Senseable City Lab & Ericsson (2015). http://senseable.mit.edu/tweetbursts/. Accessed 12 Jan 2015

Snijders, C., Matzat, U., Reips, U.D.: Big data: big gaps of knowledge in the field of internet science. Int. J. Internet Sci. **7**(1), 1–5 (2012)

Snodgrass, N.: Chicago: city of big data. exhibition explores the digital age of urban design (2014). www.architecture.org/document.doc?id=1074. Accessed 12 Jan 2015

Szell, M., Grauwin, S., Ratti, C.: Contraction of online response to major events. PLoS one, 2(26) (2014)

Takhteyev, Y., Gruzd, A., Wellman, B.: Geography of Twitter networks. Soc. Netw. **34**(1), 1–25 (2011)

Targio, I.A.H., Yaqoob, I., Anuar, N.B., Mokhtar, S., Gani, A., Khan, S.U.: The rise of big data on cloud computing: review and open research issues. Inf. Syst. **47**, 98–115 (2015)

Twitter Inc. About Twitter, Inc. (2015). https://about.twitter.com/company. Accessed 4 Feb 2015

Twitter REST API (2016). https://dev.Twitter.com/rest/public. Accessed 15 Jan 2016

2.6

Social Implications of New Mediated Spaces: The Need for a Rethought Design Approach

Antoine Zammit[1(✉)], Therese Kenna[2], and Gabriela Maksymiuk[3]

[1] Department of Spatial Planning and Infrastructure, Faculty for the Built Environment, University of Malta, Msida, Malta
antoine.zammit@um.edu.mt

[2] Department of Geography, University College Cork, Cork, Ireland
t.kenna@ucc.ie

[3] Department of Landscape Architecture, University of Life Sciences, SGGW, Warsaw, Poland
gabriela_maksymiuk@sggw.pl

Abstract. Departing from the traditional understanding of the social implications of urban design and the underlying notion of 'place', the chapter first questions its current relevance vis-à-vis the mediated city. It examines whether ICT has given rise to the establishment of new notions of space and place, identifying new design challenges for cities and rethought approaches to the production of space. In view of the latter, the chapter subsequently questions the manner with which digital media may facilitate inclusive design of public spaces. In order to address this objective, the chapter illustrates some interesting empirical data emanating from literature and research projects based in the UK, Poland and Malta. The case studies in the literature illustrate how ICTs are being used as tools within participatory processes for the inclusive design of urban public and recreational spaces and in order to gauge citizen/user expectations towards urban space. The chapter finally attempts to redefine public participation through ICT and to frame the above discussion within the potentially newly redefined role of urban designers involved in such processes. The underlying question to be addressed in this chapter, therefore, has to deal with the manner with which urban professionals may effectively achieve inclusive participatory design, particularly in light of new phenomena brought about by the mediated city and with the potential of this newly obtained and enriched data.

Keywords: Mediated open spaces · Participatory planning processes · Inclusive design · Place · P-GIS · SoftGIS · PPGIS

1 Introduction

Urban design theories that flourished between the 1960s and 1980s were particularly concerned with the social dimension of urban design – some born through the necessity of addressing social and economic inequalities in cities (Jacobs 1961), others seeking to

C. Smaniotto Costa et al. (Eds.): CyberParks, LNCS 11380, pp. 137–150, 2019.
https://doi.org/10.1007/978-3-030-13417-4_11

understand the social life of urban spaces (Whyte 1980) and others still seeking to redefine and reconceptualise the notion of space in social terms (Lefebvre 1991). The discussion is still central to the urban design agenda today. Numerous authors discuss the social processes, both "formal and informal […] that shape the urban environment" (Tonkiss 2013: 1) and, therefore, the indelible relationship between the physical urban space and social practices. This relates to the deeper understanding of place making and its significance in creating quality urban environments that relate to broader quality of life considerations.

2 Changing Notions of Space and Place Within the Mediated City

The reshaping of public spaces by mass media goes back to the early 19th century. The introduction of newspapers activated public spaces in new ways, and cafés became hubs for community building by providing a space for information exchange and dialogue. With the rise of the consumer culture, new public spaces were created that were linked with shopping and entertainment (Riether 2010) and with an increasing role for media therein. As ICTs continue to change our social dynamics, they simultaneously modify the space that we use daily.

Aurigi (2005b) argues that new virtual spaces brought about by ICT may indeed possibly replace human interaction as traditionally occurring within urban spaces, in turn generating a new form of urbanism. Other authors, such as Graham and Marvin (1999, in Carmona et al. 2008), contend quite the opposite – arguing that in actual fact the traditional city is being reinforced even more as people working in IT increasingly opt to live in urban areas in order to maintain important human contact. Carmona et al. (2008) further argue that the need for face-to-face communication remains, reinforced by the increasing role of 'third place spaces'. At the same time, such face-to-face interaction within physical places occurs in tandem with so-called "'distant proximities' of socialities that are mediated by ICTs" (Waltz, 2002 in Graham 2004: 241), which are not necessarily less rich or meaningful than physical encounters. These issues are heightened when one considers the new design challenges brought about by ICT.

2.1 The New Design Challenges

The intensive use of Internet and other digital technologies over the last two decades has caused urban public space to transition from its (traditional) dual social role as instrumental (providing a physical link between architecture and land-uses) and expressive (facilitating a link between people, thus serving as places for social interaction) (Stadler 2013). ICT is today deeply rooted in the urban fabric of contemporary cities worldwide (Bibri and Krogstie 2017).

Modern cities face a number of challenges including population growth, environmental pressures, socio-economic and socio-cultural changes and unpredictable phenomena. As more people move towards urban cities, there is increasing pressure on resources and capacity. ICTs can allow for more innovative ways to make better use of existing space, thus help manage resources more efficiently. Cities must be dynamic in their conception, flexibly planned, scalable in their design and efficient in their operations, and all these actions rely to a large extent on ICT and its presence in urban systems (Bibri and Krogstie 2017). Undoubtedly, at the strategic scale of the city, ICT has had major spatial implications. Research on the development of ICT in urban contexts and on the 'cyber' dimension of cities reveals that, today, major urban functions and activities have been blurred into almost any place in the city (Malecki 2017).

A number of spatial scientists (including Aurigi 2005a; Stadler 2013; and Malecki 2017) concur that the key design challenges for urban public spaces that must be addressed include:

1. a problem of 'scale' (as with ubiquitous ICT usage the city is more than a physical space);
2. public spaces' accessibility issues (as the contribution of ICTs to counteract social inclusion in public spaces is highly controversial);
3. issues of visibility vs. invisibility (as display technologies scatter urban landscape, while ICTs are believed to be largely invisible); and
4. issues of physical vs. virtual (as online delivery of certain urban services is held responsible for interrupting the spirit of public spaces, especially streets).

ICT has the potential to convert public space into a highly interactive environment wherein the observer is also the participant in the collection and distribution of information. In turn, this may produce a new type of public space that is characterised by an active interchange between virtual and real spaces (Riether 2010). This necessitates a deeper understanding of the process that is leading to the production of physical space.

2.2 The Production of Space

Authors concur that 'social space' forms with each societal member's specific relationship to the physical space (Lefebvre 1991). Its shaping requires, therefore, the input of each citizen within the process leading to the physical product that is urban space. Indeed, implicit to the discussion of public space and place making is the notion of inclusive urban spaces.

A number of social movements have also spurred a newly found attitude towards citizen empowerment and bottom-up participatory planning – issues that have become more pronounced with privatisation (and neoliberal urban policy) that has changed the nature of urban public space over the past decades. Some readers may consider the above themes to be overly debated; nevertheless, they provide an important prelude to a deeper discussion as they have taken on a new dimension in the face of the mediated city. ICTs may provide an added value to design and planning processes – today's technologies may aid researchers in their study of people interacting with urban spaces, through the application of important digital tools that collect and analyse data.

At the same time, research has also drawn attention to the fact that ICTs may be enhancing or widening already-existing social and economic inequalities in the city, due to the digital divide or the lack of access to technology (Kruger 1997; Graham 2004). This may have a detrimental effect on individuals, instilling a feeling of disempowerment and alienation from the rest of society, which in turn would reinforce existing exclusionary patterns. Kruger (1997) illustrates this through a discussion of the electronic business culture and its tendency to be targeted towards specific sectors of the population on the basis of affluence and social status. Graham (2004) further argues that, particularly through sorting software techniques, specific users are identified, targeted and marginalised as attractive or risky, profitable or not.

The other important aspect is that the more traditional understanding of 'community' and 'place' merits considerable rethinking, as these terms are not solely territorially defined. This, therefore, requires an acknowledgement that moves beyond a (limited) physical understanding of these terms.

The transformation of urban space is challenging new forms of interaction between different social actors and digital media. The new urban setting encompasses the widespread availability of data and, as discussed above, the opportunities for citizens to be the leaders, as well as the objective, of urban innovation (Cook et al. 2015). Clearly, new strategies for citizen engagement and bottom-up planning and design practices, themselves redefined through the possibilities offered by ICT, need to increasingly develop sensitivities to any possible inequalities to be accessible to all. It is to this important theme that our attention now turns.

3 Inclusive Approaches in the Mediated City

Over the past two decades, urban designers, together with other urban professionals such as urban planners, have paid increasing attention to the issues of participation and inclusion in their professional practice after calls to move away from top-down urban design and planning, towards more bottom-up approaches (Watson 2014). Indeed, how the state, and the various professional organisations involved in urban design and development, relate to society and the public has been one of the more prominent themes in the academic literature (Watson 2014). These recent calls were not just for a more inclusive or participatory design process; they were also aimed at encouraging greater focus on the people who use the city – a people-centred approach (Gehl 2010).

As a result of these calls, over the last few decades, urban designers have sought to closely align themselves with the future users of the urban spaces and products they design. This alignment, or relationship with the users, has occurred in differing ways (Sanders and Stappers 2008). The first was a user-centred design approach, with the user seen as a subject. Here, design occurs from the perspective of an expert whereby "trained researchers observe and/or interview largely passive users, whose contribution is to perform instructed tasks and/or to give their opinions about product concepts that were generated by others" (Sanders and Stappers 2008: 5). Under this style of urban design, users are included, but are generally passive participants, offering their thoughts or opinions on already-formed ideas. Secondly, and mostly in European circles, the participatory approach (user as partner) became increasingly prominent in urban design during the 1970s. Under this model of urban design, people – the users – were "given more influence and room for initiative in roles where they provide expertise and participate in the informing, ideating, and conceptualising activities in the early design phases" (Sanders and Stappers 2008: 5). The participatory approach allows for the users of the future urban spaces to be included in the design process, especially in relation to the final product. However, the user-centred design approach began to lose appeal as it was deemed that the approach could not "address the scale or the complexity of the challenges we face today" (Sanders and Stappers 2008: 10) and this is where more rounded participatory approaches, such as co-design began to fill the void, defined as:

[…] any act of collective creativity, i.e. creativity that is shared by two or more people. By co-design we indicate collective creativity as it is applied across the whole span of a design process […] a specific instance of co-creation. (Sanders and Stappers 2008: 6)

This shift in discourse and terminology to 'co-creation' and 'co-design' within the urban design profession is to ensure that the application of participatory design practices occurs "both at the moment of idea generation and continuing throughout the design process at all key moments of decision" (Sanders and Stappers 2008: 9). It is believed that this will ultimately reflect a 'true' participation by users and all relevant stakeholder groups.

While the approaches of co-creation and co-design have gained considerable support and traction over the last two decades, they are not without flaws. As Sanders and Stappers (2008) highlight, some co-design approaches can be highly selective in terms of the inclusion of users.

With the rapid infusion of ICTs in our personal and professional lives, ICTs present a possible new method for enhancing co-design of urban spaces and for creating wider participation from users. Lim et al. (2016) argue that "the innovations of the twenty-first century in digital technology and media have had major influences in the way young urbanites and future city designers think as well as experience places" (Lim et al. 2016: 638).

A range of new digital and information communication technologies are entering the field of urban design and planning, creating new possibilities for inclusion and co-creation in the urban design process. Fredericks and Foth (2013) note that social media sites such as Twitter and Facebook have "grown beyond the purely 'social' realm and [are] now increasingly used to cause real impact, in terms of community activism, civic engagement, cultural citizenship and user-led innovation" (Fredericks and Foth 2013: 245). Furthermore, Evans-Cowley and Hollander (2010) suggest that research on online citizen participation has demonstrated that ICT tools can work to enhance public participation, so much so that in certain neighbourhoods or communities, "there is a growing expectation on the part of citizens that there will be online participation opportunities" (Evans-Cowley and Hollander 2010: 399). ICT-mediated participation is therefore not something that is solely seen to be desirable; rather, it seen to be essential by certain sections of the community.

In recent years, planning practitioners have begun to comprehend the importance of incorporating more inclusive methods into their work. The most commonly used method is participatory mapping with a physical map and space for discussion. Now ICTs are used to facilitate and advance the process. Most notably, there is a growing interest in using participatory geographic information systems (P-GIS) to engage the public. Numerous international examples show that GIS can be used not only for planning and managing the city, but also for including the residents in these processes

(Goodchild and Glennon 2010; Haklay 2010). The objective is to integrate bottom-up processes in the domain of urban planning, using the full potential of citizens by sharing ideas in the co-production of decision making. Therefore, the relationship between decision-makers and their respective communities is continuously evolving from closed, top-down approaches into a more interactive exchange.

The following sections discuss three examples from the UK, Poland and Malta illustrating the implementation of digital tools that seek to enhance ICT-mediated participation.

3.1 Participatory GIS in UK Cities: Improving Participation in Urban Design

Recent work from three cities in the UK by Cinderby (2010) sought to understand how Participatory Geographic Information Systems (P-GIS) could be used for more inclusive urban design. A particular focus of the research was on whether or not these new ICT tools could improve the participation of 'hard-to-reach' communities, which includes (though not limited to) people from Black Minority Ethnic communities, asylum seekers, people with disabilities, young people, older people and people living in deprivation or on low incomes. Part of the rationale for this focus was that the use of traditional methods of participation (such as open public meetings) "fail to reach significant segments of communities" (Cinderby 2010: 239). The study sought to examine whether P-GIS was an efficient tool to overcome the barriers to engagement experienced by the aforementioned groups with the more traditional methods of participation. Three case studies were used: a health walk development in the inner city of Salford, UK; public perceptions of streets and squares in the city centre of York, UK; and the development of transport options for one of the suburbs of Blackpool, UK (Cinderby 2010).

The research identified a range of problems that might be causing a lack of engagement from certain groups, including: "language barriers, cultural differences, time and ability to attend public meetings even if they were interested in the issue" (Cinderby 2010: 240). P-GIS was explored as a way of overcoming barriers and challenges such as these. Cinderby (2010) discusses the utility of P-GIS "to capture local stakeholder knowledge" (Cinderby 2010: 240), arguing that "[t]he visual nature of participatory mapping removes, to some extent, the barriers of literacy and, to a degree, language […] that other forms of engagement, such as focus groups or questionnaires, require" (Cinderby 2010: 240). In this manner, importantly, maps become the central element, transcending issues such as the presence of specific individuals who might take over during public debates and meetings.

From the outset, this form of participatory engagement with mapping is viewed to overcome barriers to engagement for a range of social groups. In the case study areas, the researchers were involved in on-street engagement with participants. They used a series of on-street events to take the mapping exercise to their participants, so as to overcome issues of access to digital technologies such as computers and the Internet.

For example, in the Salford case study, the on-street events were held at “a health centre, alongside a parade of local shops and at a community fun-day event” (Cinderby 2010: 240). In this manner, “these venues allowed pensioners, children, teenagers and young adults from a low-income community to communicate their local knowledge and preferences for the proposed walking route to the research team” (Cinderby 2010: 241). From these on-street events, there were 120 participants and 200 comments, a quarter of which were from hard-to-reach groups, particularly children and teenagers.

The team identified a number of advantages to the on-street approach: participants did not need to make special arrangements for childcare, transport, and the like; the time involved was less than 15 min; the one-on-one conversations between the researcher and the participant meant that participants did not have to justify their comments to their peers (as might be the case in open public meetings); and “the use of in-situ on-street mapping allowed people to physically engage with the area in a way that would be impossible using conventional approaches” (Cinderby 2010: 241–242). In all, this brief discussion illustrates that in certain circumstances, the use of technologies and participatory approaches can work to overcome some of the challenges relating to the inclusion of ‘hard-to-reach’ groups and thus widen participation in urban planning and design processes.

3.2 SoftGIS in Participatory Management of Natural Areas in Polish Cities

Poland’s political and economic transformation in the 1990s, which was characterised by a shift from a centrally planned economy into a market economy, and the introduction of democracy, resulted in many achievements including a more bottom-up approach in governance. At the city level this process is actualised through engaging citizens to be involved in planning and management of public spaces and the introduction of participatory budgets allowing residents to propose projects and later on nominate those for realisation through official voting. Many of those projects deal with green urban spaces and public spaces. However, a civic awareness and sense of shared responsibility for urban space is still not fully developed, and there are certain groups of citizens that are not interested in participation at all (Maksymiuk and Kimic 2016) – a ‘non-engagement’ attitude that is deeply rooted in the history of a post-Soviet society. At the same time, in most Polish cities, the local authorities strive to involve dwellers in local affairs; however, the traditional methods of participation seem to be insufficient. The question, therefore, is whether the application of new technologies may enhance the level of residents’ involvement in issues related to the co-design of public spaces.

Since most decisions on nature in cities have a spatial dimension, the application of GIS offers a notable potential for public participation (Czepkiewicz 2013). Recent research in three Polish cities carried out by the Sendzimir Foundation (2015), similar to Cinderby’s (2010) work in the UK discussed previously, dealt with the applicability of the SoftGIS methodology to study residents’ perception of urban green spaces and to crowdsource their ideas and opinions on public spaces in their cities or neighbourhoods.

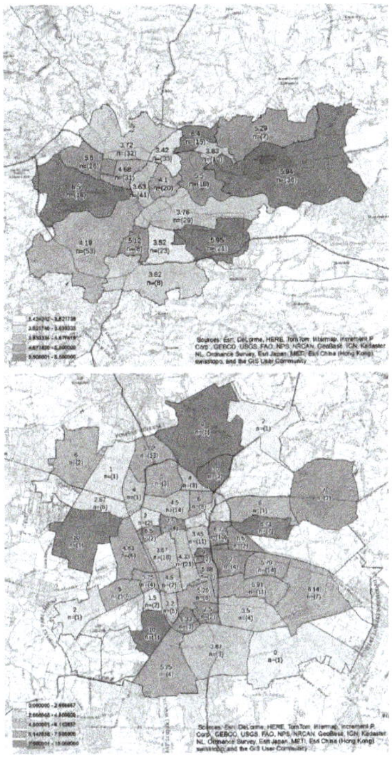

Fig. 1. Example of geo-questionnaire applied in the "Count on green" project. Results for assessment of green spaces in regards to their potential for recreational and social integration (Cracow - upper image, Lodz - bottom image). Source: Data derived from Fundacja Sendzimira is licensed under a Creative Commons Attribution 4.0 International License.

The SoftGIS methodology enables a researcher to conduct a quantitative social research, using geo questionnaires (linking internet maps and questionnaires), followed by spatial and statistical analysis, and communicating the outcomes to planners and officials. In this way, the SoftGIS allows the everyday knowledge and point of views of residents, soft data, to be added to hard data about infrastructure (Report from the Project 'Count On Green' 2015). The 'Count On Green' project resulted in around 12,500 spatial indications emanating from more than 1,600 filled questionnaires that appeared on interactive maps of greenery in three Polish cities – Cracov, Łódź and Poznań (Fig. 1).

The main research focus was to collect data that could be useful for the management of green areas in each city, but also to test the SoftGIS methodology. The residents supplied information on their favourite urban green spaces, preferred walking routes, areas requiring better maintenance, top city districts (in term of liveability) and they indicated the most neglected neighbourhoods. The project was advertised online through social media channels and was also promoted alongside open cultural and recreational events in the three cities under study. The residents could share their opinions via an online platform. In addition, 50 volunteers gathered data about greenery using tablets during various events for a total of 480 h. In general, the participation of younger adults was much wider and, while it was observed that older residents rejected the active use of new technologies on their own, they were nevertheless very receptive towards volunteers with tablets, who approached the residents individually and who helped to add the data to the maps. The local authorities of all three cities eagerly accepted the results of the project. The above example illustrates how research methods using digital tools such as SoftGIS may be utilised in different ways – to first generate data on a specific topic, but also to encourage public participation among the younger generation who would otherwise avoid traditional ways of public participation, such as public meetings or having to send written comments by mail.

3.3 Public Participation GIS in Valletta, Malta: Hybridity in Citizen Participation

Public Participation GIS (PPGIS) was used in Valletta to assess the impact of cultural infrastructure generated by the European Capital of Culture 2018, as seen through the eyes of its citizens and visitors. This research stage is part of a larger five-year study that investigates the socio-spatial impacts of culture-led regeneration through the inclusion of new cultural infrastructure. Understanding the relationship between physical interventions and social changes enables researchers to examine different dimensions that concern broader liveability and quality of life considerations (Zammit 2018).

The research centres on four pre-selected sites in the Capital chosen as pilot regeneration projects, geographically spread around Valletta's territory and led by different public and private stakeholders. In particular, the study centres on the analysis of impact due to change of uses on the surrounding neighbourhoods, with an interest in the commercialisation of buildings and urban spaces that in turn has strong implications for residential amenity. For this reason, it was imperative to obtain an in-depth understanding of participants' views, concerns and future aspirations for each of the four neighbourhoods. PPGIS may provide a potentially rich dataset in this regard (Zammit 2018).

In collaboration with Mapping for Change – a social enterprise within University College London – a 'communitymaps' interface was adapted for use in the Maltese Islands. The PPGIS was first piloted in a workshop held in December 2016. A few months earlier, another residents workshop (Design4DCity), had been held in Valletta that yielded key themes, which were chosen for the streamlined digital online interface. The latter was tested with the participating residents through their personal devices, followed by a physical mapping session. Participants remarked that the digital mapping was more useful when it was preceded by a face-to-face communal discussion whilst mapping elements of the discussion on a physical map.

A participatory mapping walkabout around the sites was subsequently held in November 2017. The objective was to integrate the participatory mapping system to the Design4DCity themes. Participants were presented with a paper map showing both the site to be mapped, spaces within which to jot down comments and details of how to use the online platform (Fig. 2).

Fig. 2. Sample of paper map used by PPGIS participants during the mapping exercise carried out in one of the four Valletta neighbourhoods, the Biccerija. Source: studjurban.

The participants were broadly briefed on these themes as well as the importance of their open-ended participation in data gathering. Limiting the themes to be observed by the participants provided more definitive responses that could be free of any influence and bias from the project coordinators. Following the PPGIS walkabout the hundreds of collected responses were digitised and mapped (Fig. 3). Around a third of the participants were able to map their observations during the walkabout immediately onto the online platform and most of them also used the paper mapping method; thereby combining both physical and digital participatory mapping. The session ran for around an hour and enabled the participants to engage with the coordinators and fellow participants, as well as with members of the public. It was observed that although the physical map provides a context for discussion, participants are not always easily adapted to the technology. Those who faced challenges with Internet access carried out the mapping manually on paper.

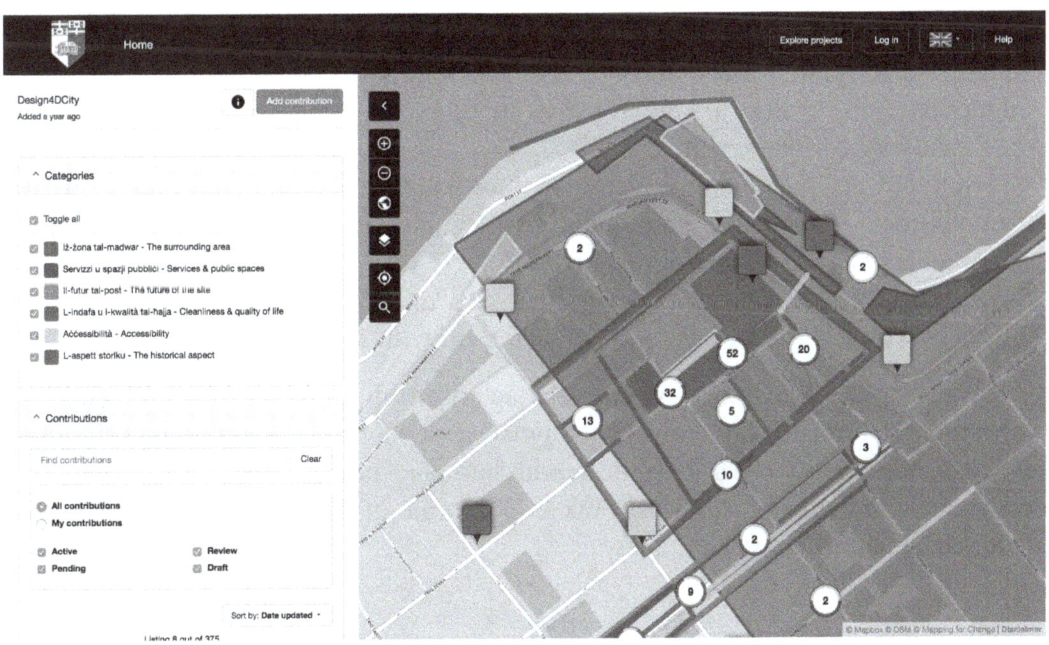

Fig. 3. Digital mapping of PPGIS responses. Source: https://uom.communitymaps.org.uk/project/design4dcity

Key repeated observations were extracted for the four sites, which consequently permitted further extraction of themes from participant responses to create specific categories for numerical evaluation. The data for the four sites was subsequently overlaid for comparative analysis and results from previous stages of the research, based on an analytical framework using criteria for the same themes, were compared to those extracted from the PPGIS.

3.4 Concluding Thoughts from the Three Examples

The awareness of communities' conflicting interests is important for all policy areas to be able to find common understanding and solutions to all needs. In the case of urban planning, there are additional challenges since participants, whether urban planners or citizens, need to comprehend and envision undeveloped urban spaces. Participants thus need to analyse the primary values and needs of a community, and in addition translate abstract ideas about physical space into specific proposals (Gordon and Manosevitch 2011). The introduction of powerful new ICT tools has made this visualisation possible and easily accessible to the public. It has also opened communication within the public and private sector, therefore changing the conventional systems and relations of governance and citizenship. ICTs have enabled citizens to have a more active role in public service. Consequently, public participation has become vital to the land use planning processes.

From the three examples discussed above we may extract the following salient points:

- The importance of the visual nature of participatory mapping that offsets literacy and language barriers.
- The map as the central participatory element, and the possibility of everyone equally accessing such map rather than select individuals, thus overcoming possible barriers to engagement.
- The need for participatory planning to happen close to home – either in the areas under analysis, or next to known places that the community may relate to and that are easily accessible for all.
- Technology is a much more effective tool for youths than public meetings or written submissions, while older participants still require face-to-face interaction which may nonetheless co-exist with technology.
- The utility of physical mapping and the need to complement the digital mapping process with a physical one, and following up with face-to-face discussions.

The examples discussed above are characterised by a combination of formal and informal social structures in terms of the power and control in institutional settings: in each case, there are the participants, researchers and policy makers. Involving non-professionals in mapping should not exclude the role of professionals, as it is needed for guidance and to assist with analysis.

4 Concluding Thoughts

4.1 Redefining Public Participation Through ICT

Public participation may be achieved through different levels of public engagement. Digital tools, including GIS, may be applied at any level of the participation spectrum, from informing, through consulting, engagement, cooperation, up to empowerment (International Association for Public Participation, 2007). Similarly, Nobre (1999, cited in Laurini 2001) outlines four levels of community participation that represent the different scales of involving the public in the planning process: to inform, to consult, to discuss and to share. The higher levels of participation require two-way interaction as the public's feedback plays a role in the decision-making process. Sharing power decision-making, that is empowering communities, is the highest level of community participation.

It is at this level that ICT really becomes a game-changer. Gordon and Manosevitch (2011) introduce augmented deliberation as a "possible design solution that addresses uniquely difficult contexts where deliberation is complicated by external factors" (Gordon and Manosevitch 2011: 80). In addition, augmented deliberation can potentially transcend other critical challenges that are normally commonplace and that hinder the achievement of these higher levels of participation, including language barriers, power differentials, and other communication challenges. It is here that ICTs seem to present one of the greatest opportunities for urban planning and design – the inclusion of social groups that would otherwise not engage in planning and design processes and decision making. The use of ICTs, such as in participatory GIS, can ensure that urban professionals are not simply producing urban spaces (in historically top-down ways) but rather they are more effectively co-producing and co-designing urban space, which will ultimately ensure that urban public spaces are designed for diverse users and diverse needs.

4.2 A Redefined Role for Urban Designers

ICTs are becoming more and more integrated with our daily lives. They are bringing about new social behaviours that directly impact the way users interact with their physical surroundings, including how people interact in public spaces. Alongside diminishing the usual interaction between people, technology has introduced a new type of public life. Social media has allowed short term and temporary public life with its instant messages to large audiences, drawing a mass of people to use an urban private or public space for a short period of time. Simultaneously, traditional spaces are being challenged to rethink the desire for new social interaction, as discussed above. This is redefining the roles of design professionals, which requires them to think more comprehensively and inclusively.

These continuous trend changes have challenged the conventional role of urban designers. They can no longer deal with urban fabric as static systems but instead need to adapt a multidisciplinary way of planning that combines traditional design skills with a modern understanding of society's current behaviour (Southworth 2014). Creative rethinking has become a crucial design tool, as cities must become experiment grounds to improve the residents' wellbeing as they continue to expand and grow. The need to merge conventional problem-solving planning tactics with ICTs is becoming a necessity.

It is evident that the opportunities and challenges brought about by ICT demand the engagement of multiple actors in the creation and activation of mediated urban spaces. In between the top-down approaches (needed for structural changes and planning of future investment in ICT) and bottom-up, participatory and inclusive initiatives, the urban designer has the potential to become a central figure, enabling and empowering communities using digital tools to overcome traditional barriers and ensuring the inclusion of this invaluable input in the preparation of strategies, objectives and tangible design outcomes for the mediated city.

References

Aurigi, A.: Tensions in the digital city. Town Country Plan. J. **74**, 143–145 (2005a)

Aurigi, A.: Making the Digital City: The Early Shaping of Urban Internet Space. Ashgate, London (2005b)

Bibri, S.E., Krogstie, J.: Smart sustainable cities of the future: an extensive interdisciplinary literature review. Sustain. Cities Soc. **31**, 183–212 (2017)

Carmona, M., de Magalhães, C., Hammond, L.: Public Space: The Management Dimension. Routledge, Oxon (2008)

Cinderby, S.: How to reach the 'hard-to-reach': the development of Participatory Geographic Information Systems (P-GIS) for inclusive urban design in UK cities. Area **42**(2), 239–251 (2010)

Cook, J., Lander, R., Flaxton, T.: The zone of possibility in citizen led hybrid cities. In: Workshop on Smart Learning Ecosystems in Smart Regions and Cities, 15 September 2015, Toledo, Spain (2015)

Czepkiewicz, M.: Systemy informacji geograficznej w partycypacyjnym zarządzaniu przyrodą w mieście. In: Zrównoważony rozwój - Zastosowania nr 4 (2013)

Evans-Cowley, J., Hollander, J.: The new generation of public participation: internet-based participation tools. Plan. Pract. Res. **25**(3), 397–408 (2010)

Fredericks, J., Foth, M.: Augmenting public participation: enhancing planning outcomes through the use of social media and web 2.0. Aust. Plan. **50**(3), 244–256 (2013)

Gehl, J.: Cities for People. Island Press, Washington, DC (2010)

Goodchild, M.F., Glennon, J.A.: Crowdsourcing geographic information for disaster response: a research frontier. Int. J. Digit. Earth **3**(3), 231–241 (2010)

Gordon, E., Manosevitch, E.: Augmented deliberation: merging physical and virtual interaction to engage communities in urban planning. New Media Soc. **13**(1), 75–95 (2011)

Graham, S.: The software-sorted city: rethinking the "digital divide". In: Graham, S. (ed.) The Cybercities Reader, pp. 324–331. Routledge, Oxon (2004)

Haklay, M.: How good is volunteered geographical information? A comparative study of OpenStreetMap and Ordnance Survey datasets. Environ. Plan. B: Plan. Des. **37**(4), 682–703 (2010)

International Association for Public Participation: Spectrum of Public Participation (2007). http://www.iap2.org/associations/4748/files/spectrum.pdf. Accessed 5 July 2017

Jacobs, J.: The Death and Life of Great American Cities. Vintage Books, London (1961)

Kruger, D.: Access denied. In: Graham, S. (ed.) The Cybercities Reader, pp. 320–323. Routledge, Oxon (1997, 2004)

Laurini, R.: Information Systems for Urban Planning: A Hypermedia Cooperative Approach. Taylor & Francis, London (2001)

Lefebvre, H.: The Production of Space. Blackwell Publishing, Malden (1991). English translation/version (Translated by Donald Nicholson-Smith)

Lim, R.M., Azevedo, L.N., Cooper, J.: Embracing the conceptual shift on new ways of experiencing the city and learning urban design: pedagogical methods and digital technologies. J. Urban Des. **21**(5), 638–660 (2016)

Maksymiuk, G., Kimic, K.: Green projects' in participatory budgets inclusive initiatives for creating city's top quality public spaces. Warsaw case study. In: Marina, O., Armando, A. (eds.) Inclusive/ Exclusive Cities, Skopje (2016)

Malecki, E.: Real people, virtual places, and the spaces in between. Socio-Econ. Plan. Sci. **58** (2017), 3–12 (2017)

Report From the Project 'Count On Green': A fresh look at greenery. Geo-questionnaires: a new source of information about a city, Sendzimir Foundation, p. 11 (2015)

Riether, G.: Digital phantasmagoria: an urban space of intensified interaction. In: SIGRID 2010, Bogota (2010)

Sanders, E.B.-N., Stappers, P.J.: Co-creation and the new landscapes of design. Co-Design **4**(1), 5–18 (2008)

Southworth, M.: Public life, public space, and the changing art of city design. J. Urban Des. **19** (1), 37–40 (2014)

Stadler, R.L.: ICTS as a tool to increase the attractiveness of public spaces, K. Šešelgis' Readings – 2013. **5**(3), 216–228 (2013). https://doi.org/10.3846/mla.2013.39

Tonkiss, F.: Cities By Design: The Social Life of Urban Form. Polity Press, Cambridge (2013)

Watson, V.: Co-production and collaboration in planning – the difference. Plan. Theory Pract. **15** (1), 62–76 (2014)

Whyte, W.H.: The Social Life of Small Urban Spaces. Project for Public Spaces, New York (1980)

Zammit, A.: Assessing the relationship between community inclusion and space through Valletta 2018 cultural infrastructural projects. In: Valletta 2018 Foundation Evaluation and Monitoring. Research Findings 2017 – Theme 3: Community Inclusion and Space, Malta, pp. 21–35 (2018)

Part III Programming and Activating Cyberparks

Edited by Michiel de Lange and Martijn de Waal

3.1

Programming and Activating Cyberparks: An Introduction and Overview

Michiel de Lange[1(✉)] and Martijn de Waal[2]

[1] Utrecht University, Utrecht, The Netherlands
m.l.delange@uu.nl
[2] Amsterdam University of Applied Sciences, Amsterdam, The Netherlands
b.g.m.de.waal@hva.nl

1 Introduction: Programming and Activating Cyberparks

Part 3 Programming and Activating Cyberparks deals with the variety of ways in which urban public spaces can be reinvigorated through the use of digital media technologies. As is outlined in the introduction to this volume, digital media technologies profoundly shape the use and perception of urban public spaces. Critical observers have noted that digital media may threaten the public nature of our cities and civic spaces. For instance, elsewhere we have described these threats in terms of three Cs: commercialisation, control, and capsularisation (de Lange and de Waal 2013). First, the combination of digital media technologies and consumer culture overlays everyday urban life with a market logic of pervasive customer tracing, quantification, and a vying for attention. Datafication and personalized recommendation services capitalise on our habitual everyday movements in the city, turning them into an ever-expanding string of (potential) customer 'touchpoints'. This affects the spatial, social and cultural dimensions of almost every realm of urban life, from work to meeting to leisure to travel to home. Visible illustrations include the rapidly changing appearance of high streets in most cities, or the nature and quality of inner-city neighbourhoods coinciding with the popularity of platforms like Airbnb (for more on platforms, see van Dijck et al. 2018). As a result, our polyvocal and frictional public open spaces are being transformed into silent and seamless marketplaces, where public interactions are reduced to commercial transactions.

Second, cities are being equipped with a range of technologies pervasive control. Governments in the post-9/11 landscape have sought ways to monitor, react and increasingly often also pre-emptively act to calamities in order to secure urban life (Crang and Graham 2007; Crandall 2010). New technologies of control include crime maps, CCTV surveillance, urban dashboards based on real-time data, and smart algorithms and AI that can detect out-of-the-ordinary signals (e.g. loud impact noises) and behaviour (e.g. outdoor group gatherings). Crang and Graham (2007) paint a bleak scenario in which these technologies have turned our cities into quasi-militarised zones aimed at maximising transparency where nothing out of the ordinary is allowed.

Third, interactions in public open spaces are increasingly characterised by the widespread availability of personal and portable media technologies like mobile

C. Smaniotto Costa et al. (Eds.): CyberParks, LNCS 11380, pp. 153–156, 2019.
https://doi.org/10.1007/978-3-030-13417-4_12

phones, tablets, laptops, portable audio devices, smart watches, and so on, plus ubiquitous access to networked content (e.g. Netflix, Spotify), and networked social relations through social media. This drives a tendency towards retreating in one's personal media bubble, which some have described as capsularisation (De Cauter 2004) or cocooning (Ito et al. 2009).

How can we wrest public open spaces from these developments? The chapters in part 3 suggest a range of possible approaches to this challenge. Some of the key words in this part include playfulness, hackability, the commons, resilience, placemaking, civic participation, local knowledge and cultural heritage. The series of chapters taken together form a variegated and incomplete mosaic of possible entry points to engage with this question. They are not so much answers as much as suggested venues for further exploration and experimentation. In a sense, what connects these interventions is an underlying drive towards making the city 'hackable', that is, open to interventions and systemic forms of city-making by non-experts (de Lange and de Waal 2019).

2 Overview of Chapters

The chapter **Smart Citizens in the Hackable City: On the Datafication, Playfulness, and Making of Urban Public Spaces through Digital Art** (3.2) by **Michiel de Lange, Kåre Synnes, Gerald Leindecker** explores a variety of people-centric narratives as corollaries to the dominance of technologically driven smart city visions. They argue that smart city visions can be criticized for lacking a perspective on the inclusion of citizens in city-making, for emphasizing efficiency at the expense of urban public life, and for its technology-centeredness in which technological fixes for complex societal issues are suggested. To counterbalance this dominant narrative, the authors forward a range of alternative options. People-centric strategies include playfulness, collaborative forms of datafication and visualization, the use of interactive (media) art and public installations, and new types of making and hacking in the city. While none of these narratives provide the same attractive promise of solving urban woes through technology, they do have the advantage of placing people at the forefront rather than an afterthought. They emphasize the capacity for change that city inhabitants have.

In their chapter **Using ICT in the Management of Public Open Space as a Commons** (3.3) **Georgios Artopoulos, Paschalis Arvanitidis and Sari Suomalainen** argue that public open spaces (POS) are not just simply physical spaces, but should be understood as a commons, or common pool resource. Narratives play an important role in the formation of public open spaces as assemblages. These narratives include cultural codings of a place, and the practices, users and uses that are understood as belonging to particular places. In contemporary cities, ICT use becomes part of these assemblages. Particular technologies and services may open up the construction of narratives around places or provide new means through which POS can be managed. This means that process of appropriation of public open spaces can become more open, and pluralistic. And in turn, this could contribute to a process in which, as the authors write, stakeholders "collectively develop institutional arrangements [..], which enable them to ensure proper use and longevity of the common pool resource." In the development of that argument, the chapter contributes to the discussion of Public Open Spaces by showing how new mobile ICT could help communities to collectively appropriate POS and bring out an understanding of these public open spaces as common pool resources that can be managed by local communities.

In their contribution **Revealing the Potential of Public Places: Adding a New Digital Layer to The Existing Thematic Gardens in Thessaloniki Waterfront** (3.4) **Tatiana Ruchinskaya, Konstantinos Ioannidis and Kinga Kimic** argue for the inclusion of ICT in place making strategies to activate public spaces. They base their study on an analysis of the thematic gardens developed at the Thessaloniki waterfront. These open urban public spaces were to revive the gardens existing in Thessaloniki in the 19th and 20th century that had been demolished in the urban expansions of the 1960s and 1970s. The new gardens were laid out as a string of fifteen sites at the seafront, expressing the relationship between the city and the sea. Each garden has its own theme. Walking through them can be experienced as a spatial narrative in which various symbolic meanings unfold. An analysis and survey of the site found that visitors highly appreciate this thematization. However, many users note that the gardens were often empty and lacked a number of facilities to make them truly attractive. While the original design didn't include any digital amenities, the authors lay out a range of options for the application of site-specific digital layers that could enhance the experience and usefulness of the Gardens. They see potential in combining the themed design of the gardens with digital narrative experiences and adding digital platforms that could be used to share knowledge or personal experiences. Digital media thus might be used to add new symbolic layers, turning the gardens in an example of hybrid read-write publishing surfaces. Hence, the chapter gives an overview of various strategies for the hybridization of Public Open spaces that could be beneficial for designers and policy makers.

Konstantinos Lalenis, Balkiz Yapicioglou and Petja Ivanova-Radovanova, in their chapter **Cyberpark, a New Medium of Human Associations, a Component of Urban Resilience** (3.5), analyse how the resilience of public open spaces can be increased by integrating cyberparks into its spatial planning and policies. Urban resilience is understood in two ways. First, as the capacity to absorb a sudden crisis or disaster in the short run, and second as the capacity of cities to integrate this robustness into infrastructures and governance in the long run. The authors underline that 'resilient thinking' has become an increasingly imported concept in urban planning to update important physical and societal systems for future adaptations. Cyberparks, as digital-physical hybrids of public open spaces, are significant resources in urban resilience, as they combine physical infrastructure and digitally mediated information that may aid in disaster management. In a case study of the refugee crisis is Greece, the chapter shows how this works in practice.

In the contribution **A Spotlight of Co-Creation and Inclusiveness of Public Open Spaces** (3.6), **Ina Šuklje Erjavec and Tatiana Ruchinskaya** focus on co-creation to engage a variety of stakeholders with everyday urban environments based on equality, diversity and social cohesion. Different from public participation and citizen engagement, co-creation as a method entails a special type of collaboration, an act of collective creativity where people are working or acting together with others to create something that is not known in advance. The authors then proceed to connect this notion of co-creation to the 'Four-D Model', which highlights four types of civic engagement: discover, debate, decide and do. The authors analyse the potential strengths of digital media technologies for fostering these four aspects of civic engagement with public open spaces in co-creation processes. The chapter also gives an overview of a large number of digital tools available for these purposes.

The last contribution to part 3 is the chapter **CyberParks Songs and Stories - Enriching Public Spaces with Localized Culture Heritage Material such as Digitized Songs and Stories (3.7)** by **Kåre Synnes, Georgios Artopoulos, Carlos Smaniotto Costa, Marluci Menezes, and Gaia Redaelli**. The chapter looks at the ways in which technologies can contribute to archiving and accessing intangible cultural heritage. It does so by examining a concept for a heritage app called CyberParks Songs and Stories. This app aims to increase the understanding of European cultures through localized storytelling. By analysing three cases that are listed as Intangible Cultural Heritage by UNESCOs Intergovernmental Committee for the Safeguarding of the Intangible Cultural Heritage, the authors highlight how users can contribute their own narratives and insights to the platform. In doing so, the concept addresses the next big challenge in cultural heritage after the digitisation phase, which is how to manage and opening up the vast troves of data in meaningful ways and involve people in contributing content.

References

Crandall, J.: The geospatialization of calculative operations: tracking, sensing and megacities. Theor. Cult. Soc. **27**(6), 68–90 (2010)

Crang, M., Graham, S.: Sentient cities: ambient intelligence and the politics of urban space. Inf. Commun. Soc. **10**(6), 789–817 (2007)

De Cauter, L.: The Capsular Civilization: On the City in the Age of Fear. NAi Publishers, Rotterdam (2004)

Dijck, J., Poell, T., Waal, M.: The Platform Society. Oxford University Press, New York (2018)

Ito, M., Okabe, D., Anderson, K.: Portable objects in three global cities: the personalization of urban places. In: Ling, R.S., Campbell, S.W. (eds.) The Reconstruction of Space and Time: Mobile Communication Practices, pp. 67–87. Transaction Publishers, New Brunswick. (2009)

de Lange, M., de Waal, M.: Owning the city: new media and citizen engagement in urban design. First Monday, **18**(11) (2013)

de Lange, M., de Waal, M. (eds.): The Hackable City: Digital Media and Collaborative City-making in the Network Society. Springer, London (2019). https://doi.org/10.1007/978-981-13-2694-3

3.2

Smart Citizens in the Hackable City: On the Datafication, Playfulness, and Making of Urban Public Spaces Through Digital Art

Michiel de Lange[1](✉), Kåre Synnes[2], and Gerald Leindecker[3]

[1] Utrecht University, Utrecht, The Netherlands
m.l.delange@uu.nl
[2] Luleå University of Technology, Luleå, Sweden
Kare.Synnes@ltu.se
[3] Institut für Strukturentwicklungsplanung, Wels, Austria
office@iapl.eu

Abstract. This contribution explores concepts, approaches and technologies used to make urban public spaces more playful and artful. Through a variety of compelling narratives involving play and art it assists in the design of new cyberparks, public spaces where digitally mediated interactions are an inherent part. How can play and interactive art be used to strengthen urban public spaces by fostering citizen engagement and participation? We propose to not only utilise interactive media for designing urban (public) spaces, but also for social innovation for the benefit of citizens. in cyberparks. The contribution connects urbanity, play and games, as well as concepts of active and passive interactive digital art as part of trends towards pervasive urban interaction, gameful design and artification. We position this as an important part of developing human-centred smart cities where social capital is central, and where citizens engaging in play and art are prerequisites for sustainable communities. Using art, play and games to foster citizen engagement and collaboration is a means to develop social technologies and support the development of collective intelligence in cyberparks. This is studied in concrete cases, such as the Ice Castle in Luleå, Sweden and the Ars Electronica in Linz, from a multi-disciplinary stance involving interaction design, digital art, landscape design, architecture, and health proficiencies. We will analyse two cases of gameful design and one case of digital interactive art being used to address urban issues. Rezone the game is an interactive multimedia game developed to tackle vacancy in the city of Den Bosch in the Netherlands. The Neighbourhood is a board game developed to involve various stakeholders in making their neighbourhood using water as a collective resource.

Keywords: Playful city · Games · Interactive art · Civic participation · Smart city

---

Parts of this chapter were drawn from de Lange (2015).

C. Smaniotto Costa et al. (Eds.): CyberParks, LNCS 11380, pp. 157–166, 2019.
https://doi.org/10.1007/978-3-030-13417-4_13

1 Introduction

This contribution addresses the question of how urban media digital media technologies can help citizens to gain more ownership of their environment. How can digital data, game and new forms of creativity and art make the city hackable, that is, open to systemic changes by 'smart' city-makers?

Digital media technologies have become increasingly intertwined with everyday urban life. One only has to think of mobile interfaces, wireless networks and protocols, GPS navigation, smart cards, camera surveillance, sensors, a large number of large and small screens, big data and smart algorithms present in today's cities. Such digital media technologies affect the spatial use and design, social situations and behaviour in our everyday urban life, and affect how we work, travel, live, spend our free time and meet each other. This interweaving of digital and physical worlds is the starting point for so-called 'smart city' policy and design agendas (see for example Hollands 2015). Municipalities, technology companies and knowledge institutions use smart technologies to try to more efficiently organize urban processes and solve problems such as energy and water supply, transport and logistics, health, safety and well-being, air and environmental quality. The hope is that this improves the quality of life of people and city governance. This is a commendable endeavour. However, there are a number of more critical aspects about such visions.

In the first place, the term smart lacks definition and precision. Who or what are actually 'smart' in smart cities? Often it isn't the people for whom all those high-tech solutions are being devised. Take, for example, emblematic greenfield developments like Masdar City in the Arab Emirates and New Songdo in South Korea, smart cities planned on the drawing board in the first decade of the 21st century. In these visions, smart citizens do not have an active role in shaping their living environment. They are allowed to live in an envisioned high-tech utopia designed by companies and city governments for them, not with or by them. By contrast, already existing cities such as Rio de Janeiro, Barcelona or Amsterdam tend to take care of this differently. Here, the role of the municipal government is much more pronounced, and attempts are made to allow people to play a much more active role. Still, the question remains: smart city, for and by whom?

A second point of criticism is the underlying idea of cityness. The emphasis on efficiency is rather unilateral. The smart city conjures up modernist images of control, efficiency and control. As a vision on urban future it is rather totalizing and offers a generic template with little space for local and cultural differences. Similar to the 'creative city' visions popular two decades ago, as a type of city marketing the smart city offers quite a superficial narrative. Which city does not want to be creative or smart? The smart city denies the messy and unpredictable improvisation character make cities charming and exciting places. This messiness fosters creativity and innovation and is the pedagogical foundation for learning to coexist with others in increasingly super-diverse urban society.

Thirdly, the vision of technology as a solution machine is problematic. Many issues in this complex world are extremely complex, challenging and 'wicked' (Rittel and Webber 1973). It is naive to think that solutions come from purely technological interventions. What's more, technologically driven solutions may have side-effects that counteract initial aims or produce perverse effects. For example, smart parking apps that show free parking places in real-time makes car mobility as a system more attractive. The more complex underlying issue of how urban societies can deal with questions of traffic and mobility remains untouched. This example shows how technological solutions may in effect undermine the public debate about what kind of city we actually want with each other. In addition, the question arises what role we think commercial platforms should play in the current reshuffling of individual, collective and public interests. How desirable is outsourcing decision-making power to computerized systems in which algorithms make the decisions? 'Smart' urban technologies reinforce trends that can be labelled as the logics of the three C's logic: consumption (commercialization of urban public space), control (increased surveillance in public spaces), and capsularisation (retreat in secure private spaces while being in public) (de Lange and de Waal 2013).

In this light, it is hopeful that a growing number of cities look for future scenarios that do not focus so much on smart technologies but on smart urban residents. In this contribution, we look for these human-centred stories about the smart city. These stories are variegated but all entail people-centric perspectives on what makes a city 'smart' as well as 'just'. This way, we can find answers to the question of how we can provide more humane directions to the future of the city under the influence of digital technologies and media culture.

2 The Data City

There is great enthusiasm about the potential to deploy big data urban for monitoring and controlling a range of urban processes (see for example Goldsmith and Crawford 2014). Predominantly, it is companies and governments that use data to this end. In addition, data also represent potential social value. Opening up datasets and doing useful things with these data can be a way to make this value publicly available. Meanwhile, urban residents too are currently measuring, quantifying and visualizing all kinds of aspects of everyday life thanks to the emergence of mobile media and sensors such as the Fitbit and iWatch, and popular mobile apps like Runkeeper and Strava.

Somewhere in between institutional data and personal quantified self-data, we can discern collective data initiatives. In many places all over the world, urban residents with sensors and networked technologies are busy generating data about, for example, air quality. People thus form a public that works in a networked way on issues that are of common interest to them (Gabrys 2014). Examples of this from the Netherlands are Sensornet, a noise pollution project around Schiphol Airport (http://geluidsnet.nl), and Urban AirQ, a project involving urban residents in measuring air quality (https://waag.org/en/project/urban-airq). Remarkable in the Dutch context is that oftentimes civil society organizations take the initiative to act as a link between the so-called triple helix of citizens, companies and governments.

The role of data in the smart city is often presented as a government management tool and business intelligence tool for companies. Governments and companies are using data and dashboards to make decisions. The municipality of Amsterdam for instance works with various data sources and dashboards in areas such as housing, public health, tourist flows and energy consumption (https://data.amsterdam.nl). Important questions include: What do we get to know about the city, and what not? What translations will take place when data are linked together? And how does that direct decisions in, and about, policy and management?

The data city suggests that cities can be approached as complex systems that can be known and managed based on data and rules for rational decision making. We may wonder to what extent data represent or construct reality? For example, crime maps can affect our perceptions of certain neighbourhoods, and strengthen self-fulfilling tendencies. It is likely that people, as well as law-enforcement, will experience and behave differently in neighbourhoods known as dangerous. An exciting question is how data and dashboards, in addition to rationalized control and transparency, can also contribute to affective experiences of the city, serendipity, creative expressions, and collective interventions. Can we use data to tell other appealing stories about (the future of) the city?

3 The Playful City

Another narrative is that of the playful city. The relationship between cities and play goes a long way back. The city has traditionally been a centre for entertainment, a stage for everyday role play and drama, a place for playful learning and for subversive ludic actions. Moreover, city simulations have been around for decades. The rise of mobile technologies in the city combined with game culture offers opportunities to involve people in playful ways with the city. Play and games can be used to involve people in the planning process, with specific urban issues, to encourage meeting with strangers and other ways of urban space use, or to allow people to temporarily allow urban space. A Dutch example is Play the City, which offers a playful method to allow various stakeholders to discuss the future of the city in a game setting and through game dynamics (http://playthecity.eu). Indeed, architects and urban planners are turning to games and play to shift the way they work on designing cities.

Play and games appeal to different audiences, like young people, who do not come to town hall discussion evenings. Play and games offer horizons for action. In safe environments players can experiment and practice without serious consequences. Some game types provide insight into rules, procedures and parameters; others encourage players to develop team-based strategies and build trust. Ranging from competition, strategy, role play to agility games, play and games appeal to creativity, innovation capacity, learning ability and social self-organization of people. This seems a promising way to address and further strengthen citizen smartness. In free spaces, new imaginaries of the future city are created.

Nevertheless, the scenario of the playful city also raises more critical questions about, among other things, the exploitation of free labour under the guise of play, known under the portmanteau 'playbour' (Kücklich 2005). Players are usually not paid but they do provide valuable input. Other thorny issues concern the 'spectacularisation' of the urban public realm in the current experience economy, and the extent to which governments and other institutional parties take seriously the outcomes of playful interventions and commit themselves to firmly and sustainably anchor this in policy. Moreover, simplistic 'gamification' of urban public space through external reward mechanisms itself undercuts the autotelic quality of play itself and risks instrumentalising social interactions (Alfrink 2015).

4 Case Rezone the Game, Playing Against Vacancy[1]

At this point we take a look at a concrete case, in order to see how participatory smart citizenship may work in practice. Rezone the Game is a project to help address the complex urban issue of vacancy[2]. Two cultural organizations from Den Bosch in the Netherlands, the Bosch Architecture Initiative and art organization Wave of Tomorrow, collaborated with a game design school to create Rezone the Game (www.rezone.eu), challenging players to 'fight blight'. In the game, players work together to keep the city safe from deterioration by salvaging real estate from decline. There are four player roles: the proprietor (owner of real estate), mayor (representing the municipality), engineer (urban designer) and citizen (neighbours). Rezone the Game is composed of a physical board game with a number of 3D printed iconic buildings that represent the neighbourhood, an augmented reality layer of real-time information about these buildings projected on a screen, and a computer algorithm programmed to let buildings descend into vacancy like a wildfire. A camera above registers the players' moves by scanning QR codes on pawns. The game engine continually adapts to changes. To beat the system players must strategically collaborate instead of pursuing self-interests. The game was tested during a series of events like The Playful Arts Festival (2013), and Rezone Playful Interventions (2014), with among others the mayor of Den Bosch playing. Major Dutch construction company Heijmans became interested. Their involvement started a new collaboration and lead to a follow-up game concept. Part of the motivation for the development of Rezone the Game was that it is hard to address complex questions like vacancy through conventional means. Traditional parties involved in urban development are not inclined to invest in initiatives with uncertain outcomes and wait for others to take the first step. In a game, it was believed, stakeholders would feel freer to experiment without immediate (financial) consequences.

This game informs the three elements for a human-centred smart city that have been mentioned in the introduction: smartness, the role of technologies in civic participation, and the notion of cityness. A 'playful civic smartness' is strengthened in various ways. Players have to manage their different stakeholder roles, they must forge coalitions with other players and quickly negotiate, they must unpack the underlying mechanisms of vacancy and think of ways to address this issue. Rezone the Game involves all of the play types identified by French philosopher Roger Caillois: competition, role-playing, chance, and even dizzying speedy interactions with the computer system. The competitive element exists not between players but between players and the system (Caillois 2001). Playing together forges trust and connections between players.

[1] This case description is based on de Lange (2019).

[2] De Lange has been involved in this project as a paid advisor and researcher.

Real world stakeholders can meet each other in a playful atmosphere instead of at the negotiation table. The game is fun and acts as a catalyst for ensuing discussions and reflections among players (a crucial part of the play sessions), and even potential follow-ups. It is a deliberately simplified artificial safe setting where real emotions and preferences emerge. It invites people to temporarily stand in adversaries' shoes. This could lead to better understanding of mutual standpoints through embodied experience and affect, instead of mere argumentation and deliberation. No longer passive users of the city players temporarily become smart planners.

Rezone the Game helps to foster citizen engagement with the issue of vacancy. The game was used to invite real world stakeholders around the table. This happened during special play sessions and events such as the Playful Arts Festival (2012) and Rezone Playful Interventions event (2013). Stakeholders met in a joyous atmosphere instead of tense town hall meetings or around the negotiation table. Playing together allowed relationships to form based on trust. Importantly, Rezone the Game is not a 'solutionist' attempt to solve a complex urban problem via technology. Playing the game helps people to become incentivized and take ownership for an otherwise abstract issue like vacancy. Playing makes the issue tangible through personal lived experience and provides possible horizons for action. The game mechanics and dynamics are deliberately aimed at stimulating social interactions and experimentation with collective action. Hence, we can conclude that this playful intervention strengthens a new hybrid liberal/communal type of citizenship: people's individual rights to the city are extended into a collective right to the smart city.

Furthermore, Rezone the Game represents a particular take on the notion of cityness. A superficial reading might suggest that it is a game that helps to solve the issue of vacancy. The underlying notion of cityness in such a view, would be one of a playable system with citizens as productive problem-solvers. In this view, a complex urban problem can have an optimal solution, which leads the city into a state of equilibrium. By contrast I understand the game to actually have a deeper narrative, which tells that urban issues like vacancy are far too complex to model, let alone solve, by simple technological means. We suggest that the special quality of playful urban interventions like Rezone the Game is that they act on a meta-level. Gregory Bateson famously theorized that play always consists of a level of meta-communication. When monkeys in the zoo engage in play-fighting they exchange signals that say that it is not actually to be understood as fighting. In his words, we face "two peculiarities of play: (a) that the messages or signals exchanged in play are in a certain sense untrue or not meant; and (b) that that which is denoted by these signals is nonexistent" (Bateson 1972/1987: 141). This is precisely the strength of playful city interventions like Rezone the Game: it questions its own solutionist promise by signalling to not actually do what it purports to do (solving vacancy). Instead, the game impels players to stake claims about what kind of city they actually want, to negotiate the underlying issue, and to agree on how to address it collectively. This involves a view of the city as a commons, a space of perpetual tension and conflict and at the same time a space that allows for negotiation and collaboration (Foster and Iaione 2016: 288).

Understanding city life in terms of play and games stands in a long tradition (de Lange 2015). Arguably, this connection is becoming even more important today. An increasing number of people grow up playing games as part of their cultural repertoire.

They are 'ludo-literate': knowledgeable about how games work and what you can do with them. We live in a playful media culture in which we are continuously surrounded by a plethora of technologies that offer spaces for playful experimentation and shape our understanding of the world as playful (Frissen et al. 2015). Playing means acquiring knowledge about the world and the capacity to act in it. Therefore, truly human centred smart cities should be playful cities.

5 The Interactive Art City

The narrative of interactive art in the city looks at urban life from the perspective of art and culture. While the city of art has a long history - ranging from urban design-shape masterpieces like the city of Palmanova or Brasilia to the support of public spaces and squares by artefacts of art like the Capitol square in Rome as well as symbols (Leindecker and Duschlbauer 2003) and the intellectual concept of the city of art (Calvino 1972) - the new layer of interactive digital media art in urban public space is only recently evolving.

Digital Media Art in public space has started with small interventions, and the domain was mainly initiated from computer science. It is understood as the cross-section of interaction with the spectators and auditors with new concepts of multimedia art. This mandate attracted the art scene as a whole, since it is part of the concept of art to reflect on society and how to deal with the technology challenge. A fine example of this movement can be demonstrated by the Ars Electronica in Linz (Austria). The yearly festival along the river Danube and the park along the classical music hall using digital information to create a new form of space in relation with contemporary art including music, light, digital information and live performance. The highlight of the event, that is organised similar to a fair with a Prix Ars Electronica competition, lectures and interactive digital art, is a public event, first held in 1979, where there is a free public performance using various media disciplines to perform. This single event attracts yearly up to 50.000 spectators, that become also parameters for the interaction and can partly interfere with the performance on predefined parameters. In 2016 it was the flight of coordinated 100 drones in direct relation and interaction with the visual sound- cloud of the concert.

6 The Maker City

Another narrative looks at urban dwellers as creative makers of their own life world. In order to understand this urban 'maker culture', we must look not only at the technology but also at associated cultural practices and institutional arrangements. People today use a wide variety of digital tools, like computers, semi-professional software, and 3D printers, to design and develop new products and services. In addition, there exists a cultural norm and practice to share this work online with others. Open standards, licenses and platforms allow people to exchange and edit home-made files and offer their own work. According to some therefore, we are living in the era of a 'third industrial revolution' (Anderson 2012). After the mechanization and automated mass production, the time supposedly has come in which consumers are producers and everyone is a maker.

Many cities harbour so-called fablabs, hackerspaces, repair cafes, and hackathons: indoor places where people 'do it themselves', often with the help of others. In addition to these so-called maker spaces, there is a rich set of urban interventionist practices, mostly outdoors on the streets. Often these interventions are organized through social media, with catchy labels like urban acupuncture and tactical urbanism. Characteristic is their temporary nature and sometimes subversive appropriation of public urban space, often stemming from the desire to counter dominant discourses and practices of commercialization, control, and cocooning in urban spaces.

Here too we see an interesting semi-institutionalized intermediate form in the so-called 'urban labs', or 'living labs'. These are designated innovation spaces for creative experimentation, with less rules and more open frameworks. An example of such an urban laboratory is the Buiksloterham district in Amsterdam North, where home buyers could purchase their own lots and develop their own sustainable living space.

The maker city draws our attention to shared 'ownership' issues in processes of urbanization, participation culture, and "the right to the city". However, this narrative also has a downside. Some people argue that digital work in a platform economy leads to a downward spiral, a race to the bottom of precarious labour where people tend to outcompete each other for ever cheaper rates. Others point to the underlying neo-liberal ethics that formulates citizenship increasingly in terms of entrepreneurship and productivity. The good citizen in the participation society manages her own business, takes care of her neighbour, and thus generates savings and social profits.

7 Conclusion: Towards a Hackable City?

A common line in the different stories discussed above is the capacity for change that city inhabitants have. Smart citizens take care of the future of their city. Seen in this light, we can speak of the city that is 'hackable' (de Waal, et al. 2017; de Lange and de Waal 2019). This term refers to the many similarities between original hackers (computer hobbyists who wrote their own software for existing machines and shared code with each other and the world) and contemporary do-it-yourself city makers, who also provide incremental and open innovations for the city using limited resources. With digital media they can bend, circumvent, or initiate all kinds of urban infrastructures, systems and services. We can see this cooperative way of city making at work in a range of domains. For instance, in self-building, joint sensing of air quality, and the organization of collective services from insurance to energy generation to healthcare. The hackable city is the nexus where the production and management of valuable resources in the data city joins the personal imagination and social drive of the playful city and the creative do-it-yourself character of the maker city (Fig. 1).

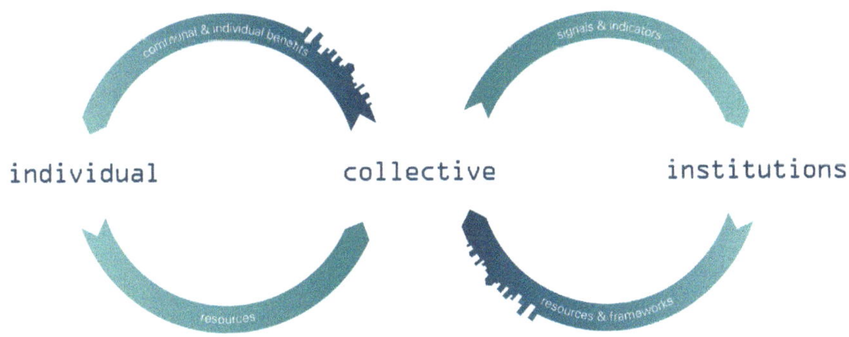

Fig. 1. The hackable city model, source: www.thehackablecity.nl

The figure above provides insight into the dynamics between individual attitude and drive, collective practice and exchange, and the system world of rules and infrastructures. It shows how an individual ethics of self-reliance can be connected to collective practices of knowledge sharing and exchange of resources. Reciprocity is crucial here. The model also shows how collective interests relate to institutional frameworks. For example, self-building groups should make plausible arguments for their approach, which can convince institutional stakeholders to change their frameworks. The notion of 'hacking' is provocative. For some, it evokes associations with computer criminality, but its productive value lies in providing possible answers to questions about the use of digital media for issues of public interest and for empowering smart citizens to become involved in their cities. The truly smart city is a hackable city.

References

Alfrink, K.: The Gameful City. In: Walz, S.P., Deterding, S. (eds.) The Gameful World: Approaches, Issues, Applications, pp. 527–560. The MIT Press, Cambridge (2015)

Ampatzidou, C., Bouw, M., van de Klundert, F., de Lange, M., de Waal, M.: The Hackable City: A Research Manifesto and Design Toolkit. Amsterdam Creative Industries Publishing, Amsterdam (2015)

Anderson, C.: Makers: The New Industrial Revolution, 1st edn. Crown Business, New York (2012)

Bateson, G.: Steps to an Ecology of Mind; Collected Essays in Anthropology, Psychiatry, Evolution, and Epistemology, 1987th edn. Chandler Pub. Co., San Francisco (1972)

Bogost, I.: Persuasive Games: The Expressive Power of Videogames. The MIT Press, Cambridge (2007)

Caillois, R.: Man, Play, and Games. University of Illinois Press, Urbana/Chicago (2001)

Calvino, I.: The Invisible City, 1st edn. Giulio Einaudi Editor, Italy (1972)

van Dijck, J., Poell, T., de Waal, M.: The Platform Society: Battle for Public Values in an Online World. University Press, Amsterdam (2016)

Foster, S.R., Iaione, C.: The City as a Commons. Yale Law Policy Rev. **34**(2), 280–349 (2016)

Frissen, V., Lammes, S., de Lange, M., de Mul, J., Raessens, J. (eds.): Playful Identities: The Ludification of Digital Media Cultures. Amsterdam University Press, Amsterdam (2015)

Gabrys, J.: Programming environments: environmentality and citizen sensing in the smart city. Environ. Plan. D: Soc. Space **32**(1), 30–48 (2014)

Goldsmith, S., Crawford, S.: The Responsive City: Engaging Communities Through Data-Smart Governance. Jossey-Bass, San Francisco (2014)

Hollands, R.G.: Critical interventions into the corporate smart city. Camb. J. Reg. Econ. Soc. **8**(1), 61–77 (2015)

Kücklich, J.: Precarious playbour: modders and the digital games industry. Fibrecult. J. **5** (2005). http://fijive.fijibreculturejournal.org/fcj-025-precarious-playbour-modders-and-the-digital-games-industry

de Lange, M.: The playful city: citizens making the smart city. In: Glas, R., Lammes, S., de Lange, M., Raessens, J. (eds.) The Playful Citizen: Power, Creativity, Knowledge. Amsterdam University Press, Amsterdam (2019)

de Lange, M.: The playful city: using play and games to foster citizen participation. In: Skaržauskienė, A. (ed.) Social Technologies and Collective Intelligence, pp. 426–434. Mykolas Romeris University, Vilnius (2015)

de Lange, M., de Waal, M. (eds.): The Hackable City: Digital Media and Collaborative City-Making in the Network Society. Springer, London (2019)

de Lange, M., de Waal, M.: Owning the city: new media and citizen engagement in urban design, waves, bits & bricks: media and the social production of urban space. First Monday **18** (2013)

de Waal, M., de Lange, M., Bouw, M.: The hackable city: citymaking in a platform society. Arch. Des. **87**(1), 50–57 (2017)

Leindecker, G., Duschlbauer, T.: The tower and the evil - a cultural retrospective of a symbol. In: Clavaron, Y., Dieterle, B. (eds.) La Memoire des villes, pp. 323–334. Universität Saint Etienne, Saint Etienne (2003)

Rittel, H.W.J., Webber, M.M.: Dilemmas in a general theory of planning. Policy Sci. **4**, 155–169 (1973)

Schouten, B., Ferri, G., de Lange, M., Millenaar, K.: Games as strong concepts for city-making. In: Nijholt, A. (ed.) Playable Cities: The City as a Digital Playground, pp. 23–45. Springer, London (2016). https://doi.org/10.1007/978-981-10-1962-3_2

Sicart, M.: Playin' the city: artistic and scientific approaches to playful urban arts. Navig. J. Media Cult. Stud. **16**(1), 25-40 (2016)

3.3

Using ICT in the Management of Public Open Space as a Commons

Georgios Artopoulos[1(✉)], Paschalis Arvanitidis[2], and Sari Suomalainen[3]

[1] The Cyprus Institute, Nicosia, Cyprus
g.artopoulos@cyi.ac.cy
[2] University of Thessaly, Volos, Greece
parvanit@uth.gr
[3] Häme University of Applied Sciences, Hämeenlinna, Finland
sari.suomalainen@hamk.fi

Abstract. The chapter defines public open space as a commons and explores innovative ways for its management and sustainable development through the use of new information and communication technologies. It argues that hybrid conglomerates of space and technological interfaces provide this possibility. Section 2 defines common pool resources and discusses issues of its management, before it moves to identify public open space as a commons and to outline key directives for governance. Section 3 outlines the new ICT and considers practices and technologies that can be used in order to enhance community identity, social interaction and user engagement in the governance of the public open space as a commons. Finally, the last section concludes this chapter with some remarks on the conditions under which the hybrid of a public open space with ICT features could be approached as yet another kind of 'soft' type of common pool resource.

Keywords: Public open space · Common pool resource · Spatialised cultural interaction · Open data · User engagement

1 Introduction

Public Open Space (POS) is a key element of our cities. It can be defined as outdoor urban spaces of any size, design or physical features, which are readily and freely available to the public for amenity, recreation, and socialisation purposes (Lemonides and Young 1978). POS affords many benefits to urban dwellers, and provides opportunities for relaxation, association and social interaction, which help communities to shape their identity and to strengthen their social fabric (CABE space 2004). Yet, most writers on public space issues acknowledge a general decline in the quality and quantity of POS worldwide, attributing this to the lack of resources and/or vision, to outdated working practices, and to fragmented organisational structures on the part of the local authorities (Carmona and De Magalhaes 2006; Arvanitidis and Nasioka 2017). Along these lines, a number of scholars, policy makers and international

C. Smaniotto Costa et al. (Eds.): CyberParks, LNCS 11380, pp. 167–180, 2019.
https://doi.org/10.1007/978-3-030-13417-4_14

organizations have placed emphasis on bottom-up approaches, acknowledging (at least implicitly) that POS is, in essence, a common pool resource (CPR) and as such users, and the public in general, together with the local authorities and other stakeholders, should collectively engage in its management, planning and protection (Fraser et al. 2006; Ernstson et al. 2008).

Contemporary approaches to landscape architecture make an argument for inclusive strategies in urban design placing emphasis on the use of event spaces (Shinew et al. 2004). Recent research in psychology of space reveals how event spaces that are incorporated in natural landscapes and ecosystems create vivid experiences and offer the conditions necessary for creative learning and participatory action. Importantly, these spaces should be seen as parts of, and convergent locales within, an extended network of POS. This network is not fixed, like a snapshot of space at a specific point in time, but rather in a process of continuous development and transformation that is associated with the human activities that it hosts and is contextualised in space. New information and communications technologies (ICT) and the development of visualisation techniques expand human experience to enrich interaction with both people and space (De Souza e Silva and Frith 2012).

This chapter acknowledges that most discussions in the field approach the analysis of common resources with economic terms. The chapter expands its scope beyond urban economics in order to engage in the discourse a more diverse approach to considering POS as CPR. It does so by arguing that spatialised (inter)cultural exchanges of views, habits, occupation patterns and everyday activities can be studied as yet another set of performative capacities of the space as CPR (Gidwani and Baviskar 2011) to be facilitated by ICT. ICT can potentially play an important role in activating POS because the latter is characterised as being more uncertain in valuation than exemplar cases of CPR – and therefore more difficult to be measurable or defined by the tools and theories mentioned below. Based on this approach, the chapter defines POS as a commons and explores innovative ways for its management and sustainable development through the use of new ICT. By augmenting the lived experiences of a place, they create a feeling of 'belonging' and 'togetherness' supporting the emergence of common identities (Low et al. 2005) between users. This chapter offers some remarks on the conditions under which the hybrid of a POS with ICT features could be approached as yet another kind of 'soft' type of CPR.

2 Public Open Space as a Commons

2.1 The Common Pool Resources and the Commons

In economics, CPRs refer to goods that at one and the same time, are not amenable to exclusion, but are subject to rivalry; the first signifying the excessive difficulty or cost in excluding people from their appropriation, and the second that use by some compromises the quality and availability of the resource to other potential users. Due to these attributes CPRs are susceptible to overuse, leading to congestion and engendering the progressive depletion, degradation and eventual destruction of the resource; something Hardin (1968) terms "the tragedy of the commons".

In the quest to resolve the quandary and avoid the inevitable tragedy, scholars have suggested the idea of promoting the ethics of stewardship among users in an attempt to encourage more moral and altruistic behaviour patterns that would improve prospects of sustainability (Barclay 2004). Others (e.g. Libecap 2009), in line with Hardin (1968), have emphasized the necessity of designating such resources with clearly defined property rights; thus, endowing the putative 'owners' with the incentive and ability to safeguard the future of these resources in their own interests. Two prospective governance regimes have been proposed to achieve this: the first is privatisation, allowing the attribution of all property rights to individuals (Smith 1981), and the second, nationalisation, involving an empowered regulator (primarily the state) to acquire and enforce all rights regarding the resource (Heilbroner 1974).

However, approaching the problem of governance binarily has attracted significant criticism on the grounds that both proposed solutions (privatization vs. nationalization) result in restricting the rights and actions of the actual users so as to destroy the social relationships and values which characterize a local community (i.e. the social capital), compromising both the long-term sustainability of the community and the effectiveness of the use of the resource. The best-known exponent of this perspective is Elinor Ostrom, the 2009 Nobel laureate in economics, who cites a series of empirical studies from across the world to show how communities are able to manage CPR for themselves, even without the existence of individual property rights (privatization) or an empowered regulatory authority (nationalization) (Ostrom 1990, 1992, 1999). This view raises the possibility of an alternative and more socially acceptable governance regime, the commons, enabling the end users to surmount the problems of collective-action to create strong and stable institutions capable of appropriating and managing their CPR in a sustainable manner. These institutions comprise specific social/informal arrangements (rules, norms, practices etc.), which define and allocate rights and obligations among the parties involved within an appropriate framework of legislation that involves mechanisms allowing for effective policing, enforcement and conflict resolution.

Furthermore, this literature (inter alia: Ostrom et al. 1999; Agrawal 2003; Arvanitidis et al. 2015) defines a series of factors shared by all successful collective governance regimes. These elements are categorized under five headings: the first of these concerns the resource itself; the second category delineates the particular characteristics of users: the third focuses on the nature of the relationship existing between the resource itself and its users; the fourth category is concerned with the specifics of the arrangements for governance and the institutional structures created to manage the CPR; and the last of the categories takes into account the external environment and the role of local and central authorities.

Put succinctly, the success of a collective governance regime is enhanced with the collective management of the resource by a clearly identifiable community involving interlinked stakeholders able to control the utilization of the CPR in compliance with local needs, preferences, practices and modes of collective action (formal and informal). The essence of this perspective is instrumental approaching the commons from an institutional or economic standpoint by concentrating on the internal nature and structures of governance regimes and emphasizing the primacy of practical issues in long-term CPR management and maintenance (Huron 2015).

2.2 The Governance of Public Open Space as a Commons

'Public open space' connotes an all-embracing concept to encompass the various public spaces existing within the urban frame, that are, in general, open, freely accessible and available for use by the population for purposes of recreation, amenity and socialisation. Thus, POS can include such spaces as parks, sports fields, playgrounds, urban squares, plazas, the property of land trusts (school and church yards, vacant plots etc.), the normal roads, pavements, walkways, sidewalks and the whole slew of other public urban spaces. Access to POS is crucial for the well-being of the community by providing a variety of aesthetic, ecological, physical, psychological, and social benefits to residents (CABE space 2004).

POS constitutes a special category of CPR, since excluding the general population is not possible, (non-excludability), but use by some people can diminish the quantity or quality of space available to the rest (rivalry), including non-local visitors and tourists. This degradation of quality and/or quantity for others is a result of the 'saturated nature of cities'; the tendency to house ever larger numbers of people in relatively constricted areas of the urban fabric (Huron 2015). This engenders sufficient pressure on urban land use to force the residents into competing for the resource. Moreover, this situation is exacerbated by a lack of investment in providing and maintaining existing POS by local authorities (because of economic constraints, insufficient political will or administrative problems) thus leading to the deterioration and decline of these spaces. Avoidance of the impending 'tragedy' presaged by this decline necessitates the adoption of new and imaginative solutions for managing this developing situation. The option of a model of collective governance offers a solution.

To facilitate the collective governance of POS as a commons requires an institution of specific arrangements (rules, norms, mechanisms etc.) to control and regulate the use, appropriation and sustainable management of these spaces. To be effective, this would necessitate the joint evolution and development of such arrangements by the local community of users in conjunction with other stakeholders relying on these resources for their well-being. Qualifying for membership in these communities could be formally defined, or, perhaps more convivially, negotiated using ex post criteria, including residence or the agreement of the existing membership. The spectrum of interest groups involved in such a governance regime perform differing roles and have different rights (defined de jure or de facto) without these being either transferable or exclusive. Here, it is of crucial importance to underline that the practicalities of managing such resources is a critical element predicating the success of such governance regimes, with this more dependent on providing a framework for the allocation and enforcement of these diverse rights to the involved parties rather than on land ownership per se (Colding et al. 2013). The manner of structuring and implementing these rights has a crucial impact on the quality and quantity of the resulting benefits, and thus on the incentives to sustain the arrangements for the resource (Colding and Barthel 2013).

Our ability, as a community, for communication, becoming involved, entertaining ourselves, even for working have been, potentially at least, enormously enhanced over the last decade or so by innovations in ICT (McCullough 2007). The advent of wireless networks, smart devices, on line apps, services and cloud technology have provided previously undreamt-of facilities for becoming informed and acting and engaging with other people and space. The new possibilities for social interaction, networking, and collaboration, offering, at least in theory, the formation and function of new communities of shared interest. This constitutes something with major implications for new means of public participation and collective action (Sheller 2004; Hampton et al. 2010). In sum, such new ICT opportunities enable a whole new gamut of innovative means for the management of public spaces and the sustainability of collective governance. The following section is an attempt to chart these technologies and explore the potential of their relevance to the management of POS as a commons.

3 Public Open Space, Humans and Information and Communication Technologies

POS is not simply physical space (Carr et al. 1993); it is rather an assemblage, a synthesis, of space and narratives (stories) (DeLanda 2006). These narratives (Miles 2016) are mechanisms that enable indeterminate interactions between users (citizens) and resources (space). This scheme applies to complex urban environments where layers of human activity and the everyday life contribute to the experience of organically associated urban palimpsests. The affordances of this symbiosis, of plural narratives and spaces, contribute to the sustainable management of the city as a whole due to their impact on the social sustainability of the communities that inhabit the city.

Social sustainability and resilience can be explored through socio-ecological systems (SES) that offer a base to analyse interaction between humans and nature in different scales. Knowledge between social and environmental dynamics is essential for the development of SES (Cote and Nightingale 2011). Ongoing symbiosis between citizens and physical environment contributes narratives. Opportunities to utilize them in dynamic management is a vehicle to develop the cyberpark concept. Firstly, artful inquiries are used to recognize and communicate citizens′ experiences and narratives associated to specific spaces, secondly this process offers the grounds for critical co-reflection, through which key implications are identified and the initial conceptualization if ICT tools is constructed. This process is a driver to support citizens' agency in social sustainability contributing also to the ecological and economical sustainability of the space. Human adaptation to SES is continuously promoted by sharing knowledge and cultural exchange whilst the dialogue with POS management creates novel and resilient management (Suomalainen et al. 2017).

Arguably there is evidence of user segmentation of POS (Heritage Lottery Fund 2016), and in principle ICT add a new layer of interface – and therefore, ICT represent yet another mediation between space and its users - but this chapter argues for the conditions under which ICT can be used productively for enhancing a POS. These include mostly the parameters of a new way of asynchronous dialogue and information transmission that is performed not only between users, i.e., social aspects of spatial occupancy (Marušić 2010) but also between the POS and its users. Ward (2014) highlights that the "regulation of access and use of resources are of central concern to the maintenance and sustainability of the commons", suggesting that the latter involve conflict between individuals, social classes and communities. Collective uses of CPR are considered as an added value of a common 'stage' that hosts dialogue, communication and shared activities. In our case ICT render the access to the resources associated with a POS even more sensitive to regulation. This chapter though is occupied with this kind of POS that is characterised as open, inclusive, unplanned, of uncertain function, or lightly regulated (Sennett 2006). Williams et al. (2009) suggest that ICT can promote and facilitate these collective uses through digital media and platforms (such as wikis) that enable collective management and valuation of planning solutions. The chapter argues that in addition to interference between users of POS and physical access to its resources by means of promoting and managing activities that are typically highlighted by the conviviality of POS, such as leisure, sports, contemplation, meeting and co-presence, as well as open air museum, cinema, street theatre and other performances (Low et al. 2005), ICT could potentially contribute greatly to interpretation and inference of meanings through space occupancy. These data when managed openly, freely and creatively can facilitate engagement of users with the management of the resources of the space, and by doing so to add value to the POS towards its integration into a larger network of CPR (Taplin et al. 2002).

The appropriate use of ICT reintroduces physical space into the digital stage of the contemporary technologically-enabled social network of the cities (Graham 2005). This hybrid of spaces brings back to the cityscapes the micro- and nano-scales of relations that enable place-making and promote social interaction and belonging. Specifically, the framework of this approach involves the enabling of smart citizenship initiatives by means of:

- Citizen engagement in POS management through participatory design practices and ICT, since a sense of common purpose is induced typically by opportunities of or threats to change things (Schmelzkopf 1995) and this commoning is a meaningful performance of a POS;
- Citizen participation in urban monitoring and observation (congestion, noise, pollution);
- Exploitation of ICT and geo-referenced data for urban reactivation planning and policy making concerning important sites that have been neglected; cultural promotion and give prominence to less popular tourist destinations (Dodge and Kitchin 2007).

The above areas of contribution are empowered by the capacity of said tools and technological solutions to facilitate, and sometimes accelerate, the self-organisation of thematic communities that form groups around topics and sites of interest, and actively contribute relevant knowledge to the associated network. In this context the exploitation of ICT can disrupt typical considerations regarding accessibility of urban commons and equality of usage. As presented in Chapter 5.5, ICT integration can be expanded in order to reach larger audiences than the stakeholders of a POS, and enable even remote users to contribute knowledge. These crowdsourcing platforms can provide a stage for intercultural dialogue and informal contributions without the direct control/regulation of information exchange by intermediate stakeholders (Paulos et al. 2008).

Using the capacity of ICT tools in data transfer and communication of information of technologies such as GPS, RFID, Bluetooth, wireless beacons, surround sound, augmented reality and mixed reality, can enrich user experience of POS as urban commons, by means of interaction. This becomes possible by the likes of blogs, mobile apps for video and photo sharing, and other Web 2.0 applications (O'Reilly and Battelle 2009) that can enhance the degree of personalisation, openness and participation of users and citizens in the management of the POS (Rheingold 2001). Their engagement through activism, participation and smart citizenship is further facilitated not only by the operation of large-scale screens and projections in space that are open to everyone (Brignull and Rogers 2003) but mostly by developing virtual communities, which can be established by the technological interfaces above (Boyer 1996).

4 Open-Ended Creative Practices of Accessing Public Data

Digital technologies stage an interface that conditionally facilitates engagement between individuals and space (Calabrese 2009; Artopoulos 2012). This approach to technology as an interface between individuals (urban citizens) that are strangers (Jacobs 1961) and spaces that are occupied in habitual ways is based on the premise that rites and habits generate feelings of familiarity and in doing so contribute to the establishment of a sense of connection and belonging. Relevant discourse has been largely occupied for decades with the impact of ICT on both the erosion of social relationships and the capacity for intervention on inclusivity of POS, as well as on intensifying the disengagement of users that are already excluded (Barlas and Çalişkan 2006; Graham and Marvin 2001; Servon and Nelson 2001).

Nevertheless, there are many examples that showcase the contrary, with the recent cases of using social media for the communication of virtual communities of not only activists, but also of producers, sellers etc., and socially responsible practices such as carrotmob.org (2010), or the so-called 'civic hacking' (mySociety.org, 2010). Distinct from their exploitation as a tool for social segregation, there are opportunities for ICT to be used in a more inclusive way (Horelli and Kaaja 2002), and this chapter aspires to contribute to this end. This section suggests that the following steps of user engagement in co-management and co-creation (Figs. 1 and 2) could benefit from the use of ICT:

- Mapping of assets by means of spatially-distributed individual narratives, collective meanings and geo-location of stories;
- Visualisation of real-time (observation) data, and tools for user co-development of visualisation workflows that would be meaningful to them;
- Open-ended practices of data interpretation and enabling users to have meaningful access to real-time data.

These parameters and aspects of ICT are necessary for software and digital platforms to be explored as inclusive mechanisms for users to access POS in positive ways, e.g., in order to increase the openness of POS to variation and multiplicity (Stavrides 2016). This understanding of ICT-enabled POS builds on the use of a cybernetic electronic infrastructure (Batty 2013) that facilitates the engagement of the users in new idiomatic and localized conditions of urban commons (Artopoulos and Charalambous 2017). 'Devices' of engagement sourced from narrative-based cultural and creative industries, such as an 'exploration for learning' incentive, when integrated in

Fig. 1. The post-excavation management of the archaeological site of Paphos Gate in the historic core of the last divided capital of Europe, Nicosia, has been developed in line with the concept of cyberpark. It integrated spatially-distributed narratives and exposed users to interpretations of these data (as shown by Fig. 2). The research team devised a real-time interaction platform that aimed at the reintroduction of the archaeological site in the everyday life of the neighbourhood. Expected completion of construction works: February 2018 (© Cyprus Institute; AVL, NSCA, University of Illinois at Urbana-Champaign; Cyprus Department of Antiquities; Municipality of Nicosia).

communication interfaces, can serve as a vehicle to empower users. In this approach visitors and citizens of the city, as well individuals and communities that may be excluded could be enabled to raise their voice and participate in the future development of the POS (Páez and Darren 2005). These technological solutions are built on conceptual devices for individuals' entanglement with space through goal-oriented activities, such as gamification (Atkinson and Willis 2009), playful engagement and serendipity (Wetzel et al. 2011).

Contextualised in societal challenges for the social resilience of urban space, these approaches differ from typical, corporate visions of smart cities. The former differs from the latter, as it interprets the user of ICT-networked information as a consumer. Current corporate visions of smart cities focus on data-consumption and the commodification of access to the big-data of the city (Schnitzer 2013), and value the citizens' well-being by the ease of access to such resources as public transport, infrastructure and digital media (Peugeot 2013). These visions of smart cities produce a

Fig. 2. Using mobile ICT is a low-budget solution of user engagement in meaningful interpretations of real-time data associated with a POS. Paphos Gate cyberpark was exhibited at the Seoul Biennale of Architecture and Urbanism 2017, titled "Imminent Commons", convened on the thematic of nine Commons in 50 cities.

false sense of accessibility to what is actually a representation of the city as a (cybernetic) machine, and the notion of acquiring a lightweight control over the city's non-interpretable complexity.

Alternatively, the approaches to ICT-augmented POS presented in the chapter are concerned with issues of equal opportunities in accessing 'other' types of urban commons (Bollier and Helfrich 2015), such as urban agriculture and community gardens, timebanks and telecommunications infrastructures (e.g., Guifi.net), which are self-regulated via collectives, fabrication labs and hackathons (Rodotá 2012). Annotating physical space with digital representations of ideas, feelings, thoughts, memories and informal narratives enables the observation, communication and visualisation of individual tolerance, contested realities and exchange of insights through space (i.e., resource) exploration.

In the context of this chapter, CPR are understood in a more open definition that is inclusive of interwoven networks of natural and social resources as well as of inhabitant's cultural production mechanisms (Patterson 2010), such as ecological zones and public spaces, air, water and infrastructure management systems, odours, and built heritage. The latter is here defined as anything that helps us collectively understand our present and speculate about our future conditions (http://www.heritageexchange.co.uk/, 2014). These opportunities for habitual interaction and familiar encounters are arguably limited in contemporary urban everyday life (Gilroy 2004). The ICT solutions presented are facing exactly this challenge as they aim to augment and multiply, in a pluralistic way, these opportunities for interaction across space and time, in the virtual projection of plural conditions and times (e.g., historical events) on the physical space of POS.

Finally, another important aspect of the presented approach regards the capacity of said ICT tools in offering to citizens new opportunities for temporal personalisation of POS. This chapter suggests that the use of ICT on POS should allow for the interpretation of observation data by their users themselves, through the appropriate visualisation interfaces. The chapter argues that associating activities that are typically hosted by POS with individual narratives and meanings introduces additional values to a POS which increase civic participation and could potentially benefit the function of the larger network of POS in the city.

5 Overview and Conclusions

POS constitutes an urban commons that faces serious risk of decline (both in terms of quality and quantity), and even destruction (the so-called "tragedy of the commons"). This eventually leads to a degraded urban environment and a disadvantaged urban community. The conventional CPR literature prescribes as appropriate solutions to the problem either privatization or nationalization of the resource. However, many countries exhibit a number of characteristics (e.g., not clearly defined private property rights on specific resources, rigid and bureaucratic institutions with deficient policing and enforcement mechanisms, limited financial capability of local authorities, etc.), which preclude successful implementation of such governance structures. On the other hand, as Elinor Ostrom and other scholars have established, the stakeholders themselves can collectively develop institutional arrangements (more socially acceptable and with lower implementation costs), which enable them to ensure proper use and longevity of the common pool resource. The new mobile ICT, by enhancing human connectivity and enriching interaction, enable the reconfiguration of urban spatiality and of public spaces, and as a consequence allow for greater degree of creativity and freedom in the management, interpretation and valuation of the POS by its users through participation and engagement.

Contributing to this literature, the chapter has explored issues of data accessibility, data sharing, interoperability and mostly interpretation – and to this end data visualisation – that are now deemed prerequisites for the inclusive operation of ICT in POS, in order for the latter to be considered part of the network of CPR. Given that technological platforms and ICT are open to, and accessible by, all users, their exploitation through accessing content and exchanging information could expand the capacity of those areas in staging intercultural dialogue. This dynamic operation contextualises the use of ICT in a broader effort that attempts to bridge the gap between ecological and civic commons (Gidwani and Baviskar 2011). All these are aspects of interacting with a POS that can be valued for its conditionally positive impact to the space by tacitly promoting exchanges that grow new relations with the space and its users. In this context the chapter approached the hybrid of the POS and embedded ICT solutions as a seemingly indivisible new condition of urban commons in contemporary cities that is capable of contributing, under the right circumstances, to the resilience of the urban environment.

References

Agrawal, A.: Sustainable governance of common-pool resources: context, methods, and politics. Ann. Rev. Anthropol. **32**, 243–262 (2003)

Artopoulos, G.: Prototype spatial models of interaction. Int. J. Vis. Des. **6**(3), 39–56 (2012)

Artopoulos, G., Charalambous, P.: Virtual environments as a technological interface between built heritage and the sustainable development of the city. Int. J. E-Plan. Res. (IJEPR) **8**(1) (2019). ISSN: 2160-9918

Arvanitidis, P., Nasioka, F.: Urban open greenspace as a commons: an exploratory case study in Greece. Public Sect. **43**(1), 19–32 (2017)

Arvanitidis, P., Nasioka, F., Dimogianni, S.: Water resource management in larisa: a 'tragedy of the commons?'. In: Filho, L.W., Sumer, V. (eds.) Sustainable Water Use and Management: Examples of New Approaches and Perspectives, pp. 65–89. Springer, Heidelberg (2015). https://doi.org/10.1007/978-3-319-12394-3_4

Atkinson, R., Willis, P.: Transparent cities: re-shaping the urban experience through interactive video game simulation. City **13**(4), 403–417 (2009)

Barclay, P.: Trustworthiness and competitive altruism can also solve the "tragedy of the commons". Evol. Hum. Behav. **25**, 209–220 (2004)

Barlas, A., Çalişkan, O.: Virtual space as a public sphere: rethinking the political and professional agenda of spatial planning and design. METU J. Fac. Archit. **23**, 1–20 (2006)

Batty, M.: Big data, smart cities and city planning. Dialogues Hum. Geogr. **3**(3), 274–279 (2013)

Bollier, D., Helfrich, S. (eds.): Patterns of Commoning. Commons Strategy Group, Amherst (2015)

Boyer, C.: CyberCities: Visual Perception in the Age of Electronic Communication. Princeton Architectural Press, New York (1996)

Brignull, H., Rogers, Y.: Enticing people to interact with large public displays in public spaces. In: Human-Computer Interaction INTERACT 2003: IFIP TC13 International Conference on Human-Computer Interaction, Zurich, Switzerland (2003)

CABE Space: The value of public space: how high quality parks and public spaces create economic, social and environmental value. CABE Space, London (2004)

Calabrese, F.: WikiCity: real-time location-sensitive tools for the city. In: Foth, M. (ed.) Handbook of Research on Urban Informatics: The Practice and Promise of the Real-Time City, pp. 390–413. Information Science Reference, Hershey (2009)

Carmona, M., De Magalhaes, C.: Public space management: present and potential. J. Environ. Plan. Manag. **49**(1), 75–99 (2006)

Carr, S., Francis, M., Rivlin, L., Stone, A.M.: Public Space. Cambridge University Press, Cambridge (1993)

Colding, J., Barthel, S.: The potential of 'Urban Green Commons' in the resilience building of cities. Ecol. Econ. **86**, 156–166 (2013)

Colding, J., Barthel, S., Bendt, P., Snep, R., van der Knaap, W., Ernstson, H.: Urban green commons: insights on urban common property systems. Glob. Environ. Change **23**(5), 1039–1051 (2013)

DeLanda, M.: A New Philosophy of Society: Assemblage Theory and Social Complexity. Continuum, London (2006)

De Souza e Silva, A., Frith, J.: Mobile Interfaces in Public Spaces: Locational Privacy, Control, and Urban Sociability. Routledge, New York (2012)

Dodge, M., Kitchin, R.: 'Outlines of a world coming into existence': pervasive computing and the ethics of forgetting. Environ. Plan. B: Plan. Des. **34**(3), 431–445 (2007)

Ernstson, H., Sorlin, S., Elmqvist, T.: Social movements and ecosystem services - the role of social network structure in protecting and managing urban green areas in Stockholm. Ecol. Soc. **13**(2), 39 (2008). http://www.ecologyandsociety.org/vol13/iss2/art39/

Fraser, E.D.G., Dougill, A.J., Mabee, W.E., Reed, M., McAlpine, P.: Bottom up and top down: analysis of participatory processes for sustainability indicator identification as a pathway to community empowerment and sustainable environmental management. J. Environ. Manag. **78** (2), 114–127 (2006)

Gidwani, V., Baviskar, A.: Urban commons review of urban affairs. Econ. Polit. Wkly, **66**, 50, 10 December 2011. http://www.epw.in/journal/2011/50/review-urban-affairs-review-issues-specials/urban-commons.html

Gilroy, P.: After Empire: Melancholia or Convivial Culture?. Routledge, London (2004)

Graham, S.: Software-sorted geographies. Prog. Hum. Geogr. **29**(5), 1–19 (2005)

Graham, S., Marvin, S.: Splintering Urbanism: Networked Infrastructures, Technological Mobilities and the Urban Condition. Routledge, London (2001)

Hampton, K.N., Livio, O., Sessions Goulet, L.: The social life of wireless urban spaces: Internet use, social networks, and the public realm. J. Commun. **60**(4), 701–722 (2010)

Hardin, G.: The tragedy of the commons. Science **162**, 1243–1248 (1968)

Heilbroner, R.L.: An Inquiry into the Human Prospect. W.W. Norton, New York (1974)

Heritage Lottery Fund: State of the UK public parks II: Public survey. Report prepared by Britain Thinks. Heritage Lottery Fund, London (2016)

Horelli, L., Kaaja, M.: Opportunities and constraints of "internet assisted urban planning" with young people. J. Environ. Psychol. **22**(1), 191–200 (2002)

Huron, A.: Working with strangers in saturated space: reclaiming and maintaining the urban commons. Antipode **47**(4), 963–979 (2015)

Jacobs, J.: The Death and Life of Great American Cities. Random House, New York City (1961, 2002)

Lemonides, J.S., Young, A.L.: Provision of public open space in urban areas: determinants, obstacles, and incentives. J. Am. Inst. Plan. **44**(3), 286–296 (1978)

Libecap, G.: The tragedy of the commons: property rights and markets as solutions to resource and environmental problems. Aust. J. Agric. Resour. Econ. **53**(1), 129–144 (2009)

Low, S., Taplin, D., Scheld, S.: Rethinking Urban Parks, Public Space and Cultural Diversity. University of Texas Press, Austin (2005)

Marušić, B.: Analysis of patterns of spatial occupancy in urban open space using behaviour maps and GIS. Urban Des. Int. **16**, 36–50 (2010)

McCullough, M.: New media urbanism: grounding ambient information technology. Environ. Plan. B: Plan. Des. **34**, 383–395 (2007)

Miles, A.: Telling tales of participation: exploring the interplay of time and territory in cultural boundary work using participation narratives. Cult. Trends **5**, 182–193 (2016)

Cote, M., Nightingale, A.J.: Resilience thinking meets social theory: situating social change in socio-ecological systems (SES) research. Prog. Hum. Geogr. **36**(4), 475–489 (2011)

O'Reilly, T., Battelle, J.: What's next for web 2.0? In: Web Squared: Web 2.0 Five Years On (2009)

Ostrom, E.: Governing the commons: the evolution of institutions for collective action. Cambridge University Press, New York (1990)

Ostrom, E.: Community and the endogenous solution of commons problems. J. Theor. Polit. **4** (3), 343–351 (1992)

Ostrom, E.: Coping with tragedies of the commons. Ann. Rev. Polit. Sci. **2**, 493–535 (1999)

Ostrom, E., Burger, J., Field, C., Norgaard, R., Policansky, D.: Revisiting the commons: local lessons, global challenges. Science **284**, 278–282 (1999)

Patterson, O.: The mechanisms of cultural reproduction: explaining the puzzle of persistence. In: Hall, J.R., Grindstaff, L., Lo, M.C. (eds.) Handbook of Cultural Sociology, pp. 139–151. Routledge, Abingdon (2010)

Paulos, E., Honicky, R., Hooker, B.: Citizen science: enabling participatory urbanism. In: Foth, M. (ed.) Handbook of Research on Urban Informatics: The Practice and Promise of the Real-Time City, pp. 414–436. Information Science Reference, Hershey (2008)

Páez, A., Darren, M.S.: Spatial statistics for urban analysis: a review of techniques with examples. Geo J. **61**(1), 53–67 (2005)

Peugeot, V.: Collaborative ou intelligente? La ville entre deux imaginaires. In: Carmes, M., Noyer, J.M. (eds.) Devenirs Urbains. Mines Paristech, Paris (2013)

Rheingold, H.: Rethinking virtual communities. In: Rheingold, H. (ed.) 2001 Edition of The Virtual Community, pp. 323–327. MIT Press, Cambridge (2001)

Rodotà, S.: Il valore dei beni communi, intervention Teatro Valle (2012). http://www.teatrovalleoccupato.it/il-valore-dei-beni-comuni-di-stefano-rodota. Accessed 6 Jan 2012

Sennett, R.: The open city. In: Urban Age. Cities Programme, London School of Economics and Political Science, London (2006)

Servon, L.J., Nelson, M.K.: Community technology centres: narrowing the digital divide in low-income urban communities. J. Urban Aff. **23**(3&4), 279–290 (2001)

Schmelzkopf, K.: Urban community gardens as contested space. Geogr. Rev. **85**(3), 364–381 (1995)

Schnitzer, M.: Herbert Reid, Betsy Taylor. Recovering the commons: democracy, place, and global Justice. Urbana and Chicago: University of Illinois Press 2010. Peace Change **38**, 366–368 (2013)

Sheller, M.: Mobile publics: beyond the network perspective. Environ. Plan. D **22**(1), 39–52 (2004)

Shinew, K., Glover, T., Parry, D.: Leisure spaces as potential sites for interracial interaction: community gardens in urban areas. J. Leis. Res. **36**(3), 336–355 (2004)

Smith, R.J.: Resolving the tragedy of the commons by creating private property rights in wildlife. Cato J. **1**(2), 456–457 (1981)

Stavrides, S.: Common Space: The City as Commons. Zed Books, London (2016)

Suomalainen, S., Pässilä, A., Owens. A., Holtham, C.: Facilitating sustainable development through artful inquiries. In: 2nd Artem Organizational Creativity and Sustainability Conference Artem OCC 2017. Nancy School of art and design, ICN Business School and Mines Nancy (2017, forthcoming)

Taplin, D., Scheld, S., Low, S.: Rapid ethnographic assessment in urban parks: a case study of independence national historical park. Hum. Organ. **61**(1), 80–93 (2002)

Ward, D.: The Commons in History: Culture, Conflict, and Ecology. The MIT Press, Cambridge (2014)

Wetzel, R., Blum, L., Feng, F., Oppermann, L., Straeubig, M.: Tidy city: a location-based game for city exploration based on user-created content. In: Mensch and Computer 2011: überMEDIEN|ÜBERmorgen. Universitätsverlag der TU Chemnitz, Munich (2011)

Williams, A., Robles, E., Dourish, P.: Urbane-ing the city: examining and refining the assumptions behind urban informatics. In: Foth, M. (ed.) Handbook of Research on Urban Informatics: The Practice and Promise of the Real-Time City, pp. 1–20. IGI Global, Hershey (2009)

3.4

Revealing the Potential of Public Places: Adding a New Digital Layer to the Existing Thematic Gardens in Thessaloniki Waterfront

Tatiana Ruchinskaya[1(✉)], Konstantinos Ioannidis[2], and Kinga Kimic[3]

[1] JT Environmental Consultants Ltd., TVR Design, Cambridge, UK
tvr281@hotmail.co.uk

[2] aaiko arkitekter, Oslo, Norway
konionn@aaiko.no

[3] Department of Landscape Architecture, Warsaw University of Life Science, Warsaw, Poland
kinga_kimic@sggw.pl

Abstract. In recent years, mobile devices have become very popular communication tools that provide access to information and communication, influence people's social behaviour and change patterns of their everyday activities. The use of communication technologies in public open spaces has become significant for the outdoor experiences of people and the relationship between users and technologically mediated outdoor activities. More specifically, wireless digital cultures not only influence spatial layout, infrastructure systems and moving patterns, but also require ICT-based placemaking strategies. This is often not considered sufficiently during the physical design stage. It is important to consider a space appropriation approach to the use of digital technologies in public spaces, based on user requirements and the local context. This is demonstrated with a case study of the Gardens at new waterfront of Thessaloniki, Greece. In this project space analysis and users' questionnaires were applied to relate digital space to the reality of the physical landscape as a first stage in the design process. This approach has wider implications for successful place making strategies. This chapter considers the possibilities of extensive outdoor use of digital media technologies in traditional forms of spatial experiences. It proposes that the new digital layer overlaying the physical space should first be methodologically explored in a way that could advance understanding of the extent to which immaterial networks and relationships can affect material planning and design dimensions.

Keywords: Added value · Mediated public spaces · Successful placemaking · Thessaloniki's waterfront · Users

C. Smaniotto Costa et al. (Eds.): CyberParks, LNCS 11380, pp. 181–195, 2019.
https://doi.org/10.1007/978-3-030-13417-4_15

1 Introduction

In recent years digital cultures have not only influenced the spatial layout of public spaces, infrastructure systems and moving patterns, but also facilitated place making strategies, based on the local context. However, the question of the relation between human activity, public open space and new media technology finds its significance within the broader context that defines the social and experiential potential of emerging forms of hybrid outdoor spaces (Ioannidis et al. 2015). Can we consider technologically mediated spaces as places which accommodate users' preferences, activities and behaviours? How can the user-orientated spatial requirements be addressed by the digital overlay? Do these spaces have a structural relation with the immaterial volume of data offered within them, a relation that can possibly transform the mediating tool into a mechanism for shaping their content? The two-way communication between space and people has been revealed in the work of scholars like Appleyard (1969, 1972, 1977); Lefebvre (1991) and Banerjee (1971, 2001). The social and experiential potential of places supports possibilities for social interaction, long-lasting activities and changes in behaviour patterns. They are products of the active relationship between users and a place's locale. This chapter relates to users' appropriation and engagement with public open spaces in the post digital age.

This hybrid landscape of physical and digital relations is investigated through the case study of the New Waterfront of Thessaloniki, Greece. The chapter develops a space analysis, employing a methodology based on both empirical-analytical approaches (users' questionnaires, data statistics) and focusing on explaining and understanding this emerging phenomenon, which relates digital space to the reality of the physical landscape as a first stage in the design process. This methodology has wider implications for successful place making strategies. Three thematic gardens along Thessaloniki's Waterfront are critically assessed for how digital enhancements can foster future user needs, place appropriation, new experiences and added values. Finally, the chapter proposes that the new digital layers, which are overlaying the physical space and exceeding the physical limits of the gardens, should be methodologically explored in a way that could advance understanding of the extent to which immaterial networks and relationships can affect material planning and design dimensions.

2 Literature Overview

Place making is a multi-dimensional approach to the planning, design and management of public spaces, which allows people to make public places more attractive and meaningful for their lives (Anderson 2013). The place making process capitalizes on social interactions in public places, a local community capacity to participate and results in the creation of quality public spaces that reflect community aspirations and contribute to people's' wellbeing (New Castle City Council 2012; PPS 2015). Therefore, social construction of public places refers to the active process of connecting communities, relating them to locations and making them meaningful for their lives (Holland et al. 2007).

Intangible values, embedded in the public places, and sometimes referred as a "spirit of the place", are layers of meanings by different communities under different contexts (Garagnani et al. 2016). The intangible and tangible (physical) elements of public places contribute to a community's sense of belonging and cultural identity (García 2013). Therefore, valorisation of public spaces should be based on their appropriation and identification by different users and communities (CEM 2011). That is why successful places promote sociability, things to do, they are safe, comfortable and attractive (Gehl 2011).

There is evidence that in the age of digitalisation while people are connected in virtual spaces, their activities in the public places are reduced (Gumpert and Drucker 2004). Therefore, digital technologies should be provided in the public spaces together with other physical design features (for example trees, water, or other amenities), aiming to encourage people to spend more time in public places facilitating private time, providing flexibility of choices, promoting communications, activities, collaborative practices, collective empowerment and creating experiences (Abdel-Aziz et al. 2016; Bhalla 2016; Janner-Klausner 2017; PPS 2014).

A local sense of place can be facilitated by digital tools through complex links and interconnections between the tangible and intangible layers created in the public places, encouraging people to personalise public places, and engage with them and with each other (Harrison and Dourish 1996; Nisi et al. 2008). Personal meanings of public places can be created by digital adjustment of physical surroundings, digital storytelling, personal photos, and annotations, contextualizing in virtual space and relating to past experiences. This approach uncovers social values of public places and allows people to have physical and virtual possession of places.

By introducing new digital layers, public spaces are turned into "hybrid geographies", which consist of layers of interpretations of the place, where people can re-programme their surroundings, reflect on experiences, and redefine possibilities to relate to objects and processes (Berry and Hamiton 2010; Morley 2003; Sappleton 2013). The interaction between these layers results in changing private and public boundaries of people and places (Ampanavos and Markaki 2014). In other words, digital tools capture a "cognitive landscape" of people's perceptions about places and provide a combined creative and combined knowledge about the place and people (Farina et al. 2005). This knowledge overrides any time references (for example historical references) of the place and allows movement through different layers of space (Van Assche et al. 2012).

Digital tools can help to overcome distances and create sites of fantasy and memory, turning the place into a read/write, publishing surface (Iaconesi and Persico 2011; Lughi 2013). In this context public places can be turned into "a time/space continuum for multiple, stratified layers of information and opportunities" related to specific place (Fattahi and Kobayashi 2009; Iaconesi and Persico 2013; Markaki 2014; Zook and Graham 2007).

It is argued that people and places "influence each other by being part of actor networks" and the concept of place can be framed as "an entanglement of people and things associated by meanings and memories" (Dork and Monteyne 2011).

This mutuality of new media and urban environments is why cities are being referred to as interfaces. For example, with no physical signs in sight, spaces can be a meeting place, a co-working space, a weekly market, etc., which can be only discovered by accessing digital information (Avram 2014; De Waal 2014).

A range of targeted projects have been conducted to add social values to public spaces. For example, the Visualizing Venice project aimed to enhance the understanding of the city "as an on-going process of change and transformation over time" and to communicate new knowledge about place and space to the public through portable devices and on the Visualizing Venice website (Visualising Venice 2017). The European Street Design Challenge project created a new urban identity for Seine-Saint-Denis La Plaine in Paris, aiming to propose digital opportunities to support a design idea. (ESDC European Street Design Challenge (ESDC) 2013). The Play the City project is using game mechanics as a model for engaging stakeholders to have fun and participate in co-creation process (Play the city 2017). The POBLEJOC installation was a site-specific public art installation, supported by digital platforms developed in Barcelona for San Marti district to create new pedestrian areas and public spaces (Active Public Space 2016). The collaborative project Big Screens between the BBC, LOCOG and UK local authorities used multimedia screens as a socialising platform (Thomson 2012). 3D digital water curtains were instated in major cities in Spain for public entertainment and community building (Digital Water Curtain 2017).

These projects attempted to improve individual and collective appropriation of public places where collective appropriation aims to strengthen community's sense of belonging, empowerment, collaboration, public participation, community engagement and connectivity of the people involved (de Hann 2005). The social activities that were used in the projects included activities connected with:

- Understanding urban reality.
- Creating new and preserving old identities.
- Co-creation, including public engagement and participatory activities.
- Educational activities.
- Public entertainments.

The existing projects developed frameworks for successful placemaking by proposing 'hybrid geographies', composed of layers of interpretations of the place in digital form and perceptions of the place that digital tools can record, visualize, reshape and share and physical features. The following digital layers were added to the existing urban fabric to address site-specific requirements:

- Mobile applications including applications for digital place-based storytelling, geo-tagging, location specific digital annotations (Nisi et al. 2008).
- Urban art games (Lughi 2017).
- Co-creation platforms used for community engagement, participation and joint activities.
- Monitoring platforms.
- Navigation platforms.
- Platforms for access to information.
- Sharing and checking in platforms.

- Announcing & directing platforms.
- Urban media art including digital site-specific art installations.
- Multimedia experiences with participatory functions. Interactive screens for community engagement, interactive arts and play.
- Animated architecture, combining landmarks and digital platforms.
- NFC (Near-field communication) and QR (Quick Response) touchpoints (Connecthings 2017).

It is notable that despite different urban realities, these mediated experiences proved to be successful because they delivered a set of urban planning objectives, encouraged interactions between people, reinforced existing urban features, and created novel urban experiences (Han et al. 2014).

In the current study we are going to explore possibilities to adopt the framework of adding additional digital layers to the existing urban fabric of public open spaces (Gardens) along the waterfront of Thessaloniki.

3 Study of Gardens of New Waterfront of Thessaloniki, Greece

Addressing the current upswing of digital solutions available to facilitate the use and attractiveness of public open spaces in relation to the new mediated reality of wireless connectivity, data access and retrieval "on the go" (Ioannidis 2017), this chapter explores the possibility of user centred improvements for existing public open spaces (Gardens) along the waterfront of Thessaloniki. It analyses its physical and design characteristics—spatial layout, greenery, landscape formations, materials - to consider how its thematic organization can offer more than a reference device by implementing a digital layer to enhance its experiential content. The authors are not aiming to provide specific forms, types and techniques for human/machine interaction. However, a critical analysis of today's' requirements of the Gardens can provide a correlation between traditional landscape design and architectural features (sitting facilities, meeting points, gathering opportunities etc.) and user's quest towards a networked-like design where outdoor facilities and offered data can link not only people but also people with space.

3.1 Background and Original Design

In 2000, architects Prodromos Nikiforidis and Bernard Cuomo[1] attempted to construct a Garden-based narrative along Thessaloniki's edge in an attempt to return to the city its lost relationship with the sea. The adopted design strategy, apart from reviving the

[1] Project name: *Redevelopment of the New Waterfront of Thessaloniki* (European Architectural Competition, 2000. First prize. Architectural Prize 2005–2008 from the Greek Institute of Architecture, Client: Municipality of Thessaloniki, Greece. Study period: 2001–2005. Construction: (first phase) 2006–2008, (second phase) 2009–2013. Architectural and urban design proposal: Prodromos Nikiforidis, Bernard Cuomo, Atelier R. Castro – S. Denissof. Design team: Paraskevi Tarani, Efi Karioti. Cost: €18,000,000. Total surface: 74,000 m^2).

sense of the 19th and 20th century gardens found in the area but lost under the pressure of the massive urbanization process during the 1960's and 1970's, unfolds over space a set of principles emerging from a continuous plot – that is a story to be told to the visitors grounding meaningful concepts with the individual locality of space.

The constant earth fillings that occurred after the 1950s provided to the area its main visual characteristic - a dominant and undisturbed linearity. The strategy not only prioritizes and preserves this specificity but also elevates its experience into a new reality that challenges its conception as the dateless impermeable border between the city and the sea. Nikiforidis and Cuomo's winning proposal develops further the idea of a narrative, introverted spatial condition that runs parallel to the city's waterfront edge in a skilful and communicative way. They argued that their intention was indeed

> *the creation of a linear space with choices for entertainment, games, relaxation, education, and culture, the linkage of different spaces with various qualities that will cover a wide spectrum of human expression and mood, but will maintain the characteristics of unity and continuity imposed by the character of the urban frontage itself (Nikiforidis and Castro 2001:6).*

Above all, the project is lodged in a "collection of spectacles" (Loukaitou and Banerjee 1998), masterly inserted along the city's edge by the architects-as-tellers. The story is extracted by what scholars like Sternberg (2000) and Gottdiener (1997) define as "purposeful thematization" spatially manifested by the alignment of fifteen interrelated thematic events in which "introverted green spaces for leisure, a human-centred design, and water events, along with natural materials like wood, sand, and stone, construct an arranged set of allegorical representations of places whose meaning is gradually revealed, cultivated, and negotiated within the user's mind" (Ioannidis 2011:223).

In the proposed set of purposeful thematization the formulation of the so-called 'episodes' is a central methodological approach and enhances, in a way, the means to tell the story. The architects argue that:

> *The intention to maintain the linearity of the coastal frontage, its unity and continuity, and leave the horizon of water along with the main promenade uninterrupted by any sort of seaside construction, is a central one. However, the need to find meaningful points of interest during unfolding this coastal track led to the decision to create specific interventions, like "episodes" that thematically are always related to the notion of water. The episodes "lower" the scale of the urban fabric creating points of rest and places to play; they signal specific points without destroying the linear unity of the track (Nikiforidis and Castro 2001:9) [the translation from Greek by Konstantinos Ioannidis].*

The narrative sequence behind the spatial events of the fifteen Gardens is, namely, a set of memory-recalling notions: the Garden of the White Tower, the Garden of Alexander, the Garden of the Evening Sun, the Garden of Sand, the Garden of Shade, the Garden of Seasons, the Garden of Odysseus Foka, the Mediterranean Garden, the Garden of Roses, the Garden of Sculptures, the Garden of Friends, the Garden of Sound, the Garden of Memory, the Garden of Water, and the Garden of Music. Initially, the original design proposal of the competition submission included even more gardens, but some of them were not eventually materialised due to economic or legislation reasons.

What is rather remarkable is that, out of these themes, the architects managed, first, to let the story make the activity patterns alongside the edge challenging the public realm and, second, to let the users themselves make the story of the gardens told. Therefore, tellable green spaces offering moments of visual isolation and enclosure within various recreational uses and sport facilities narrate and connect the story of 'the city lost'. Their design proposal specifies adequately the ontological status of those thematic areas, framing specific concepts behind lost images and atmospheres. By doing this, it reconstructs the lost identity of Thessaloniki's waterfront in a modern and communicative way, rendering the above-mentioned notions either as real, like those of the sand, the evening sun and the water, or as fictitious like the notions of the friend and the music.

3.2 The Survey of the Current Use of the Waterfront Gardens and Its Findings

In order to explore the possibility of user-centered improvements for existing public open spaces an online Survey of the current use of the Waterfront Gardens was conducted. The survey measured users' preferences, and strengths and weaknesses of the whole area with a focus on three of the fifteen Gardens – the Gardens of Sculptures and of Sound and the Mediterranean Garden. The questionnaire presented 15 questions with multiple choices and ability for the user to record his/her individual statement on a specific topic in a narrative or descriptive format. People were allowed to express multiple preferences. The design and responses to the questionnaire are available online.[2]

The analysis of the Survey shows that the Garden of Sound was liked by 91.9% of respondents, the Garden of Sculptures by 73.8% and the Mediterranean Garden by 56.5% of responders. A total of 62 visitors to the Gardens participated in the web-based survey. People answering the questionnaire were mostly residents of Thessaloniki (85.2%) and 14.8% of them were living in nearby coastal neighbourhoods. The vast majority of respondents (61.3%) were between 15–24 years old, while 33.9% were between 25–44 years old. It is notable that people belonging to "digital native" generation of 24–44 years old (Prensky 2001) were the dominant age group, who said that they visit the Gardens and that the Gardens require various improvements. 37.1% Of the respondents visited the Gardens once a week and 33.9 once a month. 60% Of the respondents noted that the Gardens are empty for at least half of the time.

Respondents were asked to rate existing conditions of the Gardens. The connectivity of the Gardens to the other part of the city was considered important by 32.3% of respondents, ease of access to the Gardens by 27.3% of resonance and their identity by 37.1%. Specific design features of the Gardens were valued by 33.9% of respondents. 46.8% of respondents were attracted by the presence of sitting places, 33.9% liked shade in the Gardens and 33.9% valued its greenery.

[2] Survey on current use of Gardens in Thessaloniki New Waterfront (2017). https://docs.google.com/forms/d/1O0poG3li7DJRrvlmaltkEdBAa1Z6fWaYnthEBLfF2Xc/edit#responses.

Urban thematization of the studied Gardens in terms of added meaning, value and function were highly rated by the respondents. Natural landscapes, greenery, water features and light were considered as attractive features of the Mediterranean and Sound Gardens. The Garden of Sculptures attracted people by its design, though it was noted that there is no shade there and no greenery.

58.3% of the respondents requested improvements to communications and collaborative practices in the Gardens. The Garden's maintenance and landscape scored only 1.8% and 22.8% respectively which indicates that responders would like improvements in their management and more individual and collective empowerment over these activities. In addition, the security in the Gardens was given by the responders 16.1%.

The 46.3% of respondents commented on lack of provision of experiences, entertainment and spontaneous activities in the Gardens and 40.7% of the respondents requested day entertainment and 59.3% night entertainment. Furthermore, the 66.1% of users wanted to see "surprises" in the Gardens. Pop-up installations were requested by 67.2% of respondents. The requirement for shops and bars were important to only 26.2% of respondents.

The original design of the Gardens did not incorporate any digital layer, which can improve connectivity, accessibility and security as, requested by the respondents to support new activities in the Gardens. This could attract more people and make the Gardens more popular and successful. 39% of respondents wanted to have digital interactions in Gardens and 39.3% wanted to have Wi-Fi hot spots in the Gardens. Respondents pointed that they were using smartphones in the Gardens to take photos (79.7%), to get information about the place (40.7%) and to communicate with friends (37.3%). It is notable that 56.1% of the respondents noted that free Wi-Fi in the Gardens will not be a main reason to go there. The analysis of empirical data related to people's everyday experiences in the studied Gardens, shows that they are considered as memorable places, where local people like to return frequently. At the same time the majority of people noted that the Gardens are under-designed and inadequately adapted to their needs and contemporary lifestyle.

The findings of the survey on the experiences of users of the studied Gardens, validated the authors' initial assumptions made during their observation study held in the area during April 2016, particularly in relation to the emptiness of many spaces during the majority of weekdays. Therefore, the design tasks and solutions are pivotal for the introduction of new material/physical and immaterial/digital features. In order to enhance the Gardens' everyday use, we need to consider the technologically mediated approach which will support users' needs and develop creative design strategies that bridge the gap between the physical and digital landscape of the Gardens. Specific strategic solutions for effective urban improvements within the existing thematic strategy of Nikiforidis and Cuomo can be facilitated by digital solutions based on the local context.

4 The Proposal of the User-Centred Approach for Effective Urban Improvements, Facilitated by Digital Solutions in the Gardens of New Waterfront of Thessaloniki

Following analysis of the reasons for the current under use of the Gardens, we propose a user-centred approach for re-shaping and re-designing them to achieve a set of urban objectives that were identified in the survey. The methodological approach, the design tasks and proposed digital layers (solutions) to facilitate these objectives to improve the attractiveness of the Gardens of New Waterfront of Thessaloniki are summarized in Table 1.

Table 1. Table identifying the urban objectives required the design tasks and the digital solutions for improving the attractiveness of the Gardens of the New Waterfront of Thessaloniki.

Urban objectives required	Design tasks	Digital layers facilitating
Improvement to individual and collective empowerment	Joint decision-making and co creation	Digital tools supporting co-creation practices
Improvement to communications and collaborative practices	Joint decision-making and co creation: • Understanding urban reality & generation of ideas • Refinement of ideas • Creation • Delivery • Monitoring	• Dialogue incl. social networks, forum & social media • Engagement with locations • Sharing knowledge • Data collection • Community mapping • Making sense of data visualization & discussion • Personalising places (e.g. annotating places) • Storing information • Joint decision-making • Modelling concepts and virtual prototyping • Play a game and plan for your community • Showcase of results • Questionnaires & direct data-feedback from users

(*continued*)

Table 1. *(continued)*

Urban objectives required	Design tasks	Digital layers facilitating
Provision of experiences, entertainment and spontaneous activities including: • Day and night entertainment • Provision for sport activities • Entertainment for children	Organize events and entertainments	• Collaborative practices • Events • Smart& Interactive furniture • Access to information • Site-specific stories • Navigation • Modelling & prototyping • Site-specific media experiences • Social Inclusion & Accessibility
Increasing flexibility in use	Organize day & night events all year round and entertainments accessible for all users	• Events • Site-specific media experiences • Navigation • Collaborative and inclusive practices • Accessibility
Improvement personal security	• Organise events • Engage people • Give community powers • Manage boundaries • Improve site management	• Events • Site-specific media experiences • Navigation • User generated sense of place • Collaborative and inclusive practices • Community management
Design improvements to: • Shading, greenery & water features • Roads and paths • Attractiveness • Private & public spaces • Accommodate all users' needs in particular children & disabled people	• Physical solutions • Create additional routs and destinations • Introduce and manage new experiences with new boundaries • Mobilise community	• Smart & Interactive furniture • Pop up installations • Physical and virtual events • Navigation • Personalising places by user generated content • Site-specific media experiences • Collaborative practices and inclusive practices
Improve digital accessibility: • Improve wireless connectivity • Improve digital interaction	• Developing digital infrastructure & signals strengths • Digital skills • Digital solutions	• Digital infrastructure • Wi-Fi hotspots • Information • Site-specific media experiences • Physical and virtual events • Smart & Interactive furniture • Pop up installations

The urban objectives (Table 1), identified by users, are related to improving the inclusiveness of the Gardens including communications, collaborative practices, individual and collective empowerment, provision of experiences and spontaneous activities, flexibility in use, personal security and design improvements. All these objectives contribute to accessibility of the Gardens and closely relate to improving their inclusiveness, which is defined "as the process of improving the terms of participation in society, through enhancing opportunities, access to resources, voice and respect for rights" (UN 2016). It involves prioritising the needs of a community and providing opportunities for all to participate as full members of society.

The site-specific digital layers over the existing urban Gardens are proposed to exceed their physical limits. Types of digital layers were identified in Table 1. They are capable to facilitate Garden specific and user orientated urban objectives, which were identified in the Survey. These layers are contributing to creative knowledge about the Gardens, which is shared between the stakeholders. They are useful tools to enhance social capital and inclusiveness of Gardens, strengthen their original designed identity and foster digital skills of the community. Digital exclusion can create disadvantage and prevent access to proposed digital layers and social opportunities. Using digital solutions, urban places can be easily and effectively turned into more inclusive, attractive and alive settings. In particular the Gardens of the New Waterfront of Thessaloniki can be turned into an interface of new media and physical urban environment and the generators of new intelligence, which will satisfy user's needs and make the Gardens more attractive.

5 Conclusions

The designers Nikiforidis and Cuomo were successful in creating the linearity walk along the open horizon of Thessaloniki's waterfront creating a new identity of the place, where people have every day contact with the sea and shoreline. The Gardens were designed to provide secondary meaningful points of interest and additional functions. The original design of the Gardens has not incorporated any digital experiences overlaying the physical space.

The survey of the local users of the Gardens was a useful way of gaining a clear understanding of the existing conditions of the use and maintenance of the Gardens, strengths and weaknesses of the design and a variety of users' groups. The analysis of empirical data related to people's everyday experiences within three main Gardens, shows that the Gardens are considered to be memorable places, where local people like to go frequently. At the same time respondents noted that the Gardens are under designed and inadequately adapted to their needs and contemporary lifestyle.

Poor activities and attendance of the Gardens are influenced by a lack of diversity of opportunities that the Gardens can offer to the local community and closely related to improving the inclusiveness of the Gardens. The achievement of these urban objectives will strengthen the designed identity of the Gardens and add new social value to their existing features.

We propose site-specific digital layers to be applied over the Gardens to create digital site-specific urban spaces, which exceed the physical limits of the Gardens.

These layers of information create a creative intelligence shared between the stakeholders and enhance the collective creation and creativity. Digital urban thematization of the Gardens can be facilitated by digital tools, identified in the literature review and site-specific digital experiences, which combine digital content with physical places. The combination of digital narrative experiences and real time events uncovers social capital of the Gardens and their hidden meanings beyond the urban form, giving people new insights, increasing the significance of the Gardens and encouraging community participation. The new digital content will create digital personal stories about the Gardens, personal augmentation of the Gardens, providing knowledge sharing, visualizing and prototyping of user generated content, online sense of connection, memories and unique atmospheres in the Gardens. This approach improves the local sense of place and its attractiveness, increases the social interaction and people's attachments to the Gardens.

Integration of mediated experiences with physical design solutions and giving new media an important role in place-making, should be considered at the early stages of the design and retrofitting process. Exploiting digital solutions, the urban places can be easily and effectively turned into more inclusive, attractive and alive settings.

References

Abdel-Aziz, A.A., Abdel-Salam, H., El-Sayad, Z.: The role of ICTs in creating the new social public place of the digital era. Alexandria Eng. J. **55**, 487–493 (2016). https://doi.org/10.1016/j.aej.2015.12.019

Active Public Space: Barcelona Installation – Outcomes (2016). http://activepublicspace.org/

Ampanavos, S., Markaki, M.: Digital cities: towards a new identity of public place. In: The Mediated City Conference (2014). http://architecturemps.com/wp-content/uploads/2013/09/mc_conference_ampanavos_spyridon.pdf

Anderson, E.: Placemaking: a tool for rural and urban communities (2013). http://articles.extension.org/pages/67018/placemaking:-a-tool-for-rural-and-urban-communities

Appleyard, D.: Why buildings are known. Environ. Behav. **1**, 131–156 (1969)

Appleyard, D.: A planner's guide to environmental psychology: a review essay. J. Am. Inst. Plann. **43**(2), 184–189 (1977)

Appleyard, D., Lintell, M.: The environmental quality of city streets: the resident's viewpoint. J. Am. Inst. Plann. **38**, 84–104 (1972)

Architectural Themes: Architecture in Greece 37 Editions: Σύγχρονα Θέματα (2003)

Avram, G.: Turning spaces into places –weaving the digital double. In: NordiCHI 2014 (2014)

Banerjee, T.: Urban experience and the development of the city image. Ph.D. dissertation, Department of Urban Studies and Planning, MIT Press (1971)

Banerjee, T.: The future of public space: beyond invented streets and reinvented places. J. Am. Plann. Assoc. **67**, 9–24 (2001)

Berry, M., Hamiton, M.: Changing urban spaces: mobile phones on trains. Motilities **5**(1), 111–129 (2010)

Bhalla, G.: Collaboration and co-creation: the road to creating value. Mark. J. (2016). http://www.marketingjournal.org/collaboration-and-co-creation-the-road-to-creating-value/

CEM: Sustaining cultural identity and a sense of place – new wine in old bottles or old wine in new bottles? (2011). https://www.ucem.ac.uk/wp-content/uploads/2016/01/sustaining_cultural_identity.pdf

Connecthings: Solutions (2017). http://www.connecthings.com/solutions/#connected-city
de Hann, H.: Social and material appropriation of the neighbourhood space (2005). https://repository.tudelft.nl/islandora/object/uuid:436408d2-e9e3-42a6-80c5-6f9878cf1332/datastream/OBJ
de Waal, M.: The City as Interface: How New Media Are Changing the City. NAi010 Publishers, Rotterdam (2014)
Digital Water Curtain: Digital Water Curtain (2017). https://www.digitalwatercurtain.com/
Di Stasio, C.: Giant interactive wheels light up Montreal (2016). http://inhabitat.com/giant-interactive-wheels-light-up-montreal/
Dork, M., Monteyne, D.: Urban Co-Creation: Envisioning New Digital Tools for Activism and Experimentation in the City (2011). http://mariandoerk.de/urbancocreation/hpc2011.pdf
European Street Design Challenge (ESDC): ESDC 2013 (2013). http://streetchallenge.eu/?page_id=611
Farina, A., Bogaertb, J., Schipania, I.: Cognitive landscape and information: new perspectives to investigate the ecological complexity. BioSystems **79**, 235–240 (2005). http://citeseerx.ist.psu.edu/viewdoc/download?doi=10.1.1.601.9188&rep=rep1&type=pdf
Fattahi, K., Kobayashi, H.: New era, new criteria for city imaging. Theor. Empirical. Res. Urban Manag. **3**(12), 63–72 (2009)
Fredericks, J., Tomitsch, M., Hespanhol, L., Mcarthur, I.: Digital pop-up: investigating bespoke community engagement in public spaces (2015). https://www.researchgate.net/publication/285928221_Digital_Pop-Up_Investigating_Bespoke_Community_Engagement_in_Public_Spaces
Garagnani, S., Arteaga, J., Bravo, L.: Understanding intangible cultural landscapes. Digital tools as a medium to explore the complexity of the urban space (2016). http://papers.cumincad.org/data/works/att/ascaad2016_044.pdf
García, M.: Written at the place. The intangible values of the landscape (2013). https://www.researchgate.net/publication/282121024_Written_at_the_place_The_intangible_values_of_the_landscape
Gehl, J.: Life Between Buildings: Using Public Space. Island Press, Washington DC (2011)
Gumpert, G., Drucker, S.: Communication Landscapers (2004). http://citeseerx.ist.psu.edu/view-doc/download;jsessionid=13520C079130D5AADC7BEA1883ABD4FC?doi=10.1.1.596.7815&rep=rep1&type=pdf
Gottdiener, M.: The Theming of America: Dreams, Visions, and Commercial Spaces. Boulder, Westview (1997)
Han, K., Rosson, M.B., Shih, P.C., Carroll, J.M.: Enhancing community awareness of and participation in local heritage with a mobile application. In: Proceedings of the 17th ACM Conference on Computer Supported Cooperative Work & Social Computing, pp. 1144–1155 (2014). https://doi.org/10.1145/2531602.2531640. https://www.researchgate.net/publication/262165051_Enhancing_community_awareness_of_and_participation_in_local_heritage_with_a_mobile_application
Happich, J.: NFC concrete slabs for a smart city (2015). http://www.electronics-eetimes.com/news/nfc-concrete-slabs-smart-city
Harrison, S., Dourish, P.: Re-placing space: the roles of place and space in collaborative systems. In: CSCW 1996: Proceedings of the Conference on Computer Supported Cooperative Work. ACM Press (1996)
Holland, C., Clark, A., Katz, J., Peace, S.: Social interactions in urban public places (2007). https://www.jrf.org.uk/sites/default/files/jrf/migrated/files/2017-interactions-public-places.pdf
Iaconesi, S., Persico, O.: RWR Read/Write Reality. FakePress Publishing, Rome (2011)

Iaconesi, S., Persico, O.: The co-creation of the city. Re-programming cities using real-time user generated content (2013). http://www.academia.edu/3013140/The_Co-Creation_of_the_City

Ioannidis, K.: Designing the Edge: An Inquiry into the Psychospatial Nature of Meaning in the Architecture of the Urban Waterfront. KTH, Stockholm (2011)

Ioannidis, K.: Technologies of anthropogenic spaces: co-creation aspects in co-mediated landscapes. In: Smaniotto, C., Ioannidis, K. (eds.) The Making of Mediated Spaces, Edições Universitárias Lusófonas, Lisbon [on press, expected December 2017] (2017)

Ioannidis, K., Smaniotto, C., Suklje, I., Menezes, M., Martinez, A.B.: The lure of cyberpark: synergistic outdoor interactions between public spaces, users and locative technologies. In: Theona, I., Charitos, D. (eds.) Proceedings of the 3rd International Biennial Conference Hybrid City 2015: Data to the People, pp. 272–281. University Research Institute of Applied Communication, National and Kapodistrian University of Athens (2015)

Janner-Klausner, D.: Using online tools for community engagement and consultation (2017). http://www.commonplace.is/blog/using-online-tools-for-community-engagement-and-consultation

Lefebvre, H.: The Production of Space. Wiley-Blackwell (1991)

Jones, L., Wells, K.: Strategies for academic and clinician engagement in community-participatory partnered research. JAMA **297**(4), 407 (2007)

Loukaitou, A., Banerjee, T.: Urban Design Downtown: Poetics and Politics of Form. University of California Press, Berkeley (1998)

Lughi, G.: Text-space dynamics. The digital media in defining new urban languages. In: NUL - New Urban Languages. Conference Proceedings. J. Urbanism **28**(2), 1–5 (2013)

Lughi, G.: Interactive Media in Urban Space. Screencity Lab. 3 (2017)

Markaki, M.: Digital cities: towards a new identity of public space. In: The Mediated City Conference, London, UK (2014)

Morley, D.: What's "home" got to do with it? Contradictory dynamics in the domestication of technology and the dislocation of domesticity. Eur. J. Cult. Stud. **6**(4), 435–458 (2003)

Nikiforidis, P., Castro, R.: Redevelopment of new waterfront in Thessaloniki. Competition brief for initial study. Municipality of Thessaloniki, Thessaloniki (2001)

New Castle City Council: Place Makers Toolkit (2012). https://www.newcastle.nsw.gov.au/Newcastle/media/Documents/Community/Place-Making-Toolkit.pdf

Nisi, V., Oakley, I., Haahr, M.: Location-Aware Multimedia Stories: Turning Spaces into Places (2008). http://citeseerx.ist.psu.edu/viewdoc/summary?doi=10.1.1.451.9997

Play the city: City Gaming Method (2017). http://www.playthecity.eu/

PPS: Technology Brings People Together in Public Spaces After All (2014). https://www.pps.org/blog/technology-brings-people-together-in-public-spaces-after-all/

PPS: Placemaking and Place-Led Development: A New Paradigm for Cities of the Future (2015). https://www.pps.org/reference/placemaking-and-place-led-development-a-new-paradigm-for-cities-of-the-future/

Prensky, M.: Digital Natives, Digital Immigrants. On the Horizon, vol. 9, no. 5. MCB University Press (2001)

Sappleton, N. (eds.) Advancing Research Methods with New Technologies. Information Science Reference, Hershey (2013). https://books.google.ru/books?id = I_5kMPw3O-IC&pg=PA20&lpg=PA20&dq=Barry+%26+Hamilton+hybrid+geographies&source=bl&ots=zk7_iWSfOg&sig=UCo1fRDHP6LG2oDLPj91GtcgdPI&hl=en&sa=X&ved=0ahUKEwiFzemzo5LUAhWhJJoKHaL8Ay8Q6AEIPDAD#v=onepage&q=Barry%20%26%20Hamilton%20hybrid%20geographies&f=false

SEGD: Virtual Depictions: San Francisco (2016). https://segd.org/virtual-depictions-san-francisco

Sternberg, E.: An integrative theory of urban design. J. Am. Plann. Assoc. **66**, 265–278 (2000)

Thomson, C.: BBC and the Big Screens (2012). http://www.bbc.co.uk/blogs/aboutthebbc/entries/ea215929-b57e-3bb9-8d01-e0433f93fd62

UN: Identifying social inclusion and exclusion (2016). http://www.un.org/esa/socdev/rwss/2016/chapter1.pdf

Van Assche, K., Duineveld, M., De Jong, H., Van Zoest, A.: What place is this time? Semiotics and the analysis of historical reference. Landscape Archit. J. Urban Des. **17**(2), 233–254 (2012). https://doi.org/10.1080/13574809.2012.666207

Visualizing Venice: Visualizing Venice (2017). http://www.visualizingvenice.org/visu/

Zook, M., Graham, M.: Mapping digital space: Geocoded internet data and the representation of place. Environ. Plann. B: Plann. Des. **34**, 466–482 (2007)

Check for updates

3.5

Cyberpark, a New Medium of Human Associations, a Component of Urban Resilience

Konstantinos Lalenis[1(✉)], Balkiz Yapicioglou[2], and Petja Ivanova-Radovanova[3]

[1] DPRD, University of Thessaly, Volos, Greece
klalenis@prd.uth.gr
[2] Arkin University of Creative Arts and Design, Kyrenia, Cyprus
kaylabalkiz@yahoo.com
[3] Association for Integrated Development and Sustainability, Sofia, Bulgaria
petjaivanova@gmail.com

Abstract. The centre point of this chapter is how to increase the resilience of the urban environment by integrating the cyberpark in its spatial planning and policies. Disaster prevention and preparedness are a priority in resilience, and two major related sectors are infrastructure and information. Significant components of prevention infrastructure in cities are public/free spaces. Public spaces are used as refuge in cases of natural disasters (earthquakes, fires etc.), but also as spaces of physical contact, communication, community bonding, and provision of social services in cases of social crises (the cases of refugees). Information, as the other major sector of prevention, may vary from dissemination of information in an individual basis, to information exchange in a collective basis, the latter being of significant value in cases of prevention. The collective basis of information exchange is further expanded and technologically improved through Information and Communication Technologies (ICTs). This chapter focuses on the psychological and social roles of 'the cyberpark' in extraordinary events and illustrate the importance of its physical form and spatiality. Cyberparks combines and explores the relationship between Information and Communication Technologies (ICTs) and urban open/public spaces. In this sense, they combine elements of both, prevention infrastructure and information, and they constitute significant components of urban resilience.

Keywords: Urban resilience · Disaster prevention in planning · Planning for resilience · Social inclusion of refugees · Refugees and cyberparks

1 Introduction

The aim of this chapter is to discuss the necessity of cyberparks, as defined and developed by the COST TU1306, as redundant infrastructure in maintaining resilience of urban environment in times of crises. Resilience, for the purpose of this chapter, is the capacity of a system to cope with disturbances and safeguard overall system persistence. Disturbances are associated with disruption of the functioning of a community

C. Smaniotto Costa et al. (Eds.): CyberParks, LNCS 11380, pp. 196–208, 2019.
https://doi.org/10.1007/978-3-030-13417-4_16

due to events of natural, geophysical, technological, social, or human behavioural nature. Disaster prevention and preparedness is, thus, a priority, and can take the form of development of rapid response capacities, or of prevention through the formulation of a longer-range strategies and policies. Essential elements for disaster prevention and preparedness are infrastructure and information.

Public open spaces (POS) are significant components of both, prevention infrastructure and locations of information exchange and management. Being part of the urban fabric, besides their function as catalysts in the improvement of quality of life of city dwellers, they are also used as refuge spaces for local population in the event of disasters (earthquakes, fires, etc.). In such cases, as well as in cases of social or human behaviour events, they also function as spaces of physical contact, communication, community bonding, and provision of social services. The case of refugees gathering in POS, are indicative of the above. Information may vary from dissemination to exchange, on individual or collective basis, and it is further expanded and technologically improved through Information and Communication Technologies (ICTs).

In cyberparks, on the other hand, "POS characteristics and cyber technologies blend together to generate hybrid experiences and enhance quality of life" (Smaniotto Costa and Ioannidis 2017). ICT can be used in this context to give or gather information, to aid co-creation of space, to allow crowd sourcing of information and opinions, and to allow affective sharing or self-monitoring of activities. As such, they combine and explore the relationship between ICTs and urban open/public spaces. In this sense, they combine elements of both, prevention infrastructure and information and they constitute significant components of urban resilience. We presume cyberparks are able to support urban resilience faster and in a more efficient way than traditional POS.

The COST TU1306 mainly explores the relationship between ICT and POS and how this relationship can contribute, provide opportunities and support transforming cities into more social and inclusive environments. The above definition of cyberparks implies but does not adequately emphasize the resilience dimension of such urban landscapes. In fact, cyberparks might be also seen as places purposely used in cases of disturbances and disruption of the functioning of a community due to events of varying nature. Thus, the attempt of this chapter is to contribute to the definition of a role of ICT in planning and maintenance of the contemporary public open space in regard to risk prevention and maintaining resilience in the urban environment.

2 Concepts, Definitions, and Relationships

2.1 Research Concept and Methodology

Cyberparks combine and explore the relationship between ICTs and urban open/public spaces. In this sense, they combine elements of both, prevention infrastructure and information and they constitute significant components of urban resilience. However, firstly, there is a need to integrate the two meanings of resilience, that is, the short-term capacity of the 'Host City' to absorb the crisis of the sudden event by providing immediate safety and avoid panic by information and guidance, and the long-term capacity of the 'Host City' to develop structures facing this crisis by integrating cyberparks into spatial planning and related spatial policies. Illustrations of the above will be given by further analysis in case studies, covering aspects of cyberparks that increase urban resilience to physical disasters, as well as to disasters due to human behaviour (refugees). The latter will be given special emphasis, since it is a very recent, massive, unexplored, and with enormous humanitarian consequences phenomenon.

In analysing the potential of cyberparks to increase urban resilience to physical disasters the research will focus on particular sectors of Master Plans, where official guidelines prescribe the conditions and urban infrastructure for prevention and protection of natural disasters (earthquakes, fires, floods, etc.). (Ministerial Decision 9572/1845, FEK 209/7-4-2000). In the guidelines special emphasis is given to the uninhibited access to POS from the local population, and to the infrastructure of POS, which should facilitate information exchange between the responsible authorities and the population gathered in POS. The analysis will provide evidence for the adequacy of cyberparks to cover the above needs, and proceed a step further, in facilitating communication and contact between individuals, families, and groups of people in times of massive panic, and uncontrolled emotional reactions.

Cyberparks that increase urban resilience to human behaviour disturbances and disasters will be analysed within the frame of the refugee crisis, which "front line" European cities are forced to sustain. The need of refugees to gather in POS for contact and communication, and their –almost absolute- reliance in smartphones for information exchange with authorities, NGOs, friends, and family, are documented from various sources, these being articles in newspapers, the Internet, scientific publications, and related TV reporting. Verification for the above will also be sought from interviews taken in the course of research undergoing in the DPRD of the University of Thessaly (Pyrpiri 2017). The degree that the refugees cover basic, everyday needs by the above means indicates the state of resilience of the particular city, town, or neighbourhood. The appropriation of POS by the refugees, and their use of ICT for information exchange, proves the necessity of cyberparks for maintaining resilience in these cases, and even more since cyberparks can combine POS and ICT in the same place, at the same time.

Finally, the necessity of cyberparks as redundant infrastructure in maintaining resilience of urban environment will also be shown by investigating the "fitness" of cyberparks for accommodating the resilience indicators used in the Circle of 100 Resilient Cities, and more specifically, in its implementation in particular resilience studies.

2.2 Defining Urban Resilience

In the literature, the notion of resilience has been explained with reference to different perspectives from different fields and has attained multiple levels of meaning. However, even though resilience is defined differently according to these different research domains, a common factor underlying each definition is the notion of disturbance and adaptation in the context of a system, or, the ability or capacity to deal with disturbance. These disturbances might originate from variety of disasters and stresses (human made or natural) and might possess slightly different meanings, however, what they really point is some sort of internal or external change.

Resilience is not a new concept. However, it has evolved through its application in different disciplines with the majority of the work on resilience adapting the concept of ecological resilience. Within the notion of smart cities, for example, there is a shift in risk management on the city level in the sense that "resilient cities" are not in opposition to ecological modernisation, but rather a refinement. (Androbus 2011). In ecology, resilience is related to 'the ability to adapt to a change' (Holling 1973; Walker et al. 1981; Folke 2006), 'the capacity of a system to absorb disturbance' (Walker et al. 2004; Walker and Salt 2006), or "the capacity to change in order to maintain the same identity" (Folke et al. 2010). The theory of resilience has been influenced by general systems theory and complex adaptive systems (CAS), where a system is defined as complex interaction and relationships between different agents/elements, and can be anything that functions (Bertalanffy 1968; Holling 1973). This theory also posits that the relationships between the agents of the system are more important than the agents themselves. Resilience is also affiliated with other combinations of relationships, such as vulnerability, persistence, change and transformations.

The concept of resilience in urban studies has also evolved from the concept of ecological resilience where 'urban resilience' can be viewed as having the concept of resilience applied to that of cities. Using the perspective of ecological resilience, therefore, urban resilience is usually described as "the ability of a city or urban system to withstand a wide array of shocks and stresses". However, urban resilience is not only about surviving potential risks and threats and recovery, but rather about grasping the positive outcomes these changes and transformations might bring. Moreover, urban resilience requires us to think in an integrated way and should incorporate other important societal aspects. Like Folke et al. (2010) emphasize, a social perspective, especially regarding social change, is an essential part of resilience. We should also acknowledge the fact that creating resilient cities requires 'resilient thinking' to adapt to the outcome of change.

Urban spaces, from infrastructure to open spaces, are vital agents of the urban system and strengthened adaptable spaces can contribute to resiliency of a city. As a matter of fact, increased 'resilient thinking' is initiating urban adaptation planning within cities to update important physical and societal systems. As Montgomery (1998) posits, adaptable urban space can "accommodate complex patterns of diversity, mixture and economic grain".

2.3 Infrastructure and Information as Major Sectors of Disaster Prevention and Management. Public/Free Spaces as Important Component and Common Ground of Infrastructure and Information

Cities and infrastructure have always co-existed where their relation has been interdependent and co-evolutionary. Furthermore, along with social, political, administrative, and economic forces, the transformation of social space in general and urban space in particular is credited to the transformative power of infrastructure. As a matter of fact, cities owe their position on the global stage to the networking of the infrastructures, which have re-organized relations among peoples, institutions, and places (Neuman and Smith 2010).

The meaning of infrastructure has expanded over the years, whereas traditional meaning of infrastructure conjures up the notion of built facilities and networks made by humans for public consumption either above or below ground. Another important definition of infrastructure is that, as explained by Frischmann (2012), infrastructure is a 'resource' that should be "accessed and used concurrently by multiple users for multiple uses". This explanation combined with the traditional explanation of infrastructure then leads to categorize infrastructure as 'essential'. Essential resources are indispensable for survival; however, they are context specific and go beyond access to basic needs. Moreover, infrastructure resources conjure up the notion of a shared community resource claiming the identity of "commons" which take on a utilitarian character as open and accessible to life sustaining resources. Commons as a resource, on the other hand, include public spaces such as parks, streets, sidewalks and plazas and even extends to spaces where access by public is limited and regulated like schools, libraries, courthouses and even privately-owned shopping malls. Considering the above-mentioned combined definition of infrastructure as resources and commons then summons public spaces as essential elements of urban infrastructure.

Even though, the public spaces' spatial impact and transformative power that shape complex systems of human activity is well perceived "it does not receive the appreciation it deserves since its continuous availability is assumed and is just part of the background…however, the importance emerges when the disaster strikes" (Frischmann 2012). The essentiality of the infrastructures, herein the public spaces, should not only be considered for 'good' times, but 'bad' times as well. Cities are full of uncertainty and also face major disasters, shocks and disturbances (i.e. human crises, climate change or simply rapid demographic change). The pressure on public spaces increases during such events, especially with traumatic events like war, destruction and devastation with increased interest in public spaces. When we visit our recent history, we can observe this pressure from how public spaces are transformed into refuge spaces (from evacuation camps to places that serve basic human needs like temporary shelters) for disaster management to reduce vulnerability of cities, therefore contributors to city resilience (e.g., during the 2006 Lebanon war, Sanayeh Garden in Beirut acted as refugee camp for 450 people who lost their homes for months).

Considering importance of the public space during 'bad' times as a place of refuge, the connectivity to the rest of the world for exchange of information becomes another essentiality. When we define public spaces as essential urban infrastructure, therefore, we also have to take into account the deployment of information (ICT) in public spaces and their essentiality, and how ICT promotes efficiencies and functionalities in public spaces during crisis. As a matter of fact, public spaces are conceptualised as an opportunity for the exchange of messages with diverse others (Lofland 1985) and it is only natural that today cities incorporate ICT into planning of public spaces for creating more social and inclusive environments, not only for 'good' times but also for 'bad' times. In other words, public spaces as an infrastructure resources should be considered as spare capacity embedded in the city, or as a redundancy, which is one of the most important factors contributing for city resilience. As a matter of fact, according to 100RC (100 Resilient City) resilient cities demonstrate seven qualities; reflectiveness, resourcefulness, robustness, redundancy, flexibility, inclusiveness and integration.

2.4 Cyberparks as Significant Components of Urban Resilience. The Effective Combination of Infrastructure and Information in Cyberparks, for Disaster Prevention and Management

ICT (information), along with infrastructure, is another force that possesses the power to transformation in cities, or spatial impact. The power of information and its transformative power of public space is not a new concept (Hampton et al. 2015) but how this power can contribute to urban adaptation planning approaches for resilience is an area that needs attention. As Montgomery (1998) emphasizes, "the successful urban area-in this case public spaces- is one which offers in-built adaptability rather than in-built obsolescence". Increased resilient thinking is making urban planners within cities to update important physical and societal systems. Resilient thinking in urban adaptation planning requires new approaches to manage resources. With resilient thinking, however, we cannot expect to tailor a 'one size fits all' approach to city resilience because of the locality of the matter and different adaptability difficulties each city faces. The challenges of adaptation planning are quite diverse, nevertheless, the top three adaptation challenges identified are "(1) securing funding for adaptation; (2) communicating the need for adaptation to elected officials and local departments; and (3) gaining commitment and generating appreciation from national government for the realities of local adaptation challenges" (Carmin, Nadkarni and Rhie 2012). Considering the above-mentioned urban planning adaptation challenges, therefore, it is important we clearly communicate the multi-dimensional benefit of public space adaptation.

As per the objectives of COST TU1306, cyberparks are proposed as spaces with a power to transform cities into more social and inclusive environments (rather than just being parks equipped with high technology) and as spaces offering additional opportunities to people using these spaces. As a matter of fact, these objectives with the different approaches to manage urban resources suggested by resilient thinking lead this research to explore some other spill-over effects of cyberparks in cities specifically during a crisis.

When we look into the definition of resilience, especially city resilience, one of the most important components of resilience, is access to resources. Cyberparks, as public spaces, can be considered as a new resource within the urban adaptation planning where infrastructure and information are combined. Cyberparks may add different functions to public spaces (spill-overs as additional opportunities), which might also contribute as a redundant and flexible resource to city resilience in time of crisis. Therefore, respecting the objectives of the COST TU1306 project, public spaces incorporated with ICT, simply cyberparks, are proposed as part of city infrastructure resources and spaces of refuge for the people on the move (specifically for the refugees in receiving countries) contributing for city resilience. However, before we discuss how cyberpark can contribute to city resilience as a place of refuge, it is also critical that we further define the boundaries of public space within the context of this chapter. Therefore, for the purpose of this study, public spaces (cyberparks) will be defined as information landscapes, a new infrastructure resource, to which all members of public in a society have legal access, including people on the move, i.e. refugees, with no limitation and regulation. After all, as Carpenter et al. (2001) states we need to establish "of what, to what, and under what conditions" when considering resilience in a system.

3 Cases Studies

3.1 Cyberparks Increasing Urban Resilience to Physical Disasters. Provisions in Spatial Planning

Urban resilience, recently, has been an important element in planning, and has been included in Master Plans, Strategic Plans, and related sectoral studies of cities around the world. In most of these studies, public open spaces (POS), have been recognized as significant factors in almost all forms of urban resilience. In cases of natural hazards (earthquakes, fires), in particular, POS were treated in Master Plans as crucial elements of the city preparedness to reduce the magnitude of disasters, even before urban resilience was elaborated as a notion. They were organized as first stage refuge spaces, where local population should be gathered in order to escape from being trapped in buildings, to get first aid, water, food, temporary shelter, and try to get informed about friends and relatives. In these plans, prime emphasis was given to safeguarding safety and providing first aid. With the development and inclusion of urban resilience in planning, other forms of resilience were also examined, and disaster prevention and management were enriched with more elements than safety and first aid. Information and communication were quite important among them, which, if incorporated in POS, they are adequately covered by the definition of cyberparks, as provided by COST TU1306.

Cases from Germany and Greece illustrate how cyberparks may increase urban resilience to physical disasters. They are derived from families of nations in spatial planning with diverse traditions and practices, considered as occupying the two opposite ends in the spectrum of planning policies (ESPON 2.3.2): from the Comprehensive Integrated and the Regional Economic (Germany) and from the 'urbanism' tradition (Greece). In Germany, the cities of Bonn and Duisburg have been assessed in resilience concerning low carbon activities (Lindner et al. 2014:16). The importance of incorporating cyber technology in their green and open spaces is highlighted, mainly for raising public awareness in renewable energies through activities organized in POS, including the exhibition of a GIS heat map, where the information of a solar cadastre and the existing energy supply will be integrated, as a basis for strategic decisions. In Greece, on the other hand, the notion of resilience became apparent in most recent Master Plans, after 2010. The Masterplan of the city of Xanthi (47000 population, expected to be approved by the end of 2017), has a separate chapter concerning disasters and social crises. It was based on a sectoral plan, been provided by a national plan coded Xenocratis (2003), but besides referring and mapping the POS to be used as refuges of the affected population in earthquakes, floods, and fires, there was also specific focus on climate change and social crises (massive arrival of refugees). In that, special emphasis was given to the appropriate infrastructure of the above-mentioned POS, which would facilitate the multi-dimensional flow of information among the affected population and public and administrative bodies involved. It also prescribed for a special study of immediate priority, related to the resilience of the city.

The above examples illustrate the inclusion of the notion of urban resilience in European spatial planning, while giving special emphasis in importance of the role that POS equipped with ICT (i.e. cyberparks) may have for safeguarding and reinforcing resilience.

3.2 Cyberparks Increasing Urban Resilience to Disasters Due to Human Behaviour (Refugee Crisis in Europe)

The significance of cyberparks as a means for safeguarding and reinforcing urban resilience can also be exhibited in the case of social crises. The recent refugee crisis is on the forefront of international development, when the combination of natural disasters, and armed conflict have displaced millions of people in Europe and worldwide. Cyberparks are proposed as part of city infrastructure resources and spaces of refuge for the people on the move (specifically for the refugees in receiving countries) contributing for city resilience. Analysis of the relationships between a. refugees and POS, and b. refugees and information technology will test the validity of the above proposal. The interface between these two relationships is the relation between refugees and cyberparks and might be considered as a measure for urban resilience.

4 The Relationship Between Refugees and POS

Refugees arrive in high numbers, fighting with the waves of the Mediterranean Sea, in the Aegean islands and in the south of Italy. During their perilous journey, and upon their arrival in Europe, the needs for information and communication are of fundamental value to them. At the same time, various elements of their lives lose in individuality and become by need, increasingly collective. Accordingly, their needs and uses of space are transformed from individual to collective.

POS were usually among the first spaces to provide accommodation at the first waves of refugee arrivals, and some of them were since transformed in semi-permanent reception camps. Here, the phenomenon of appropriation of space appeared to take interesting dimensions, which, in turn, triggered rearrangements in the urban form, and readjusted social relations with the local communities. Examples in the main squares of Omonoia and Victoria in Athens (Greece), and Lavov Most and Maria Louiza Boulevard in Sofia (Bulgaria) are indicative examples of the above. The reverse phenomenon was later observed in the more organized reception camps, where new POS were co-created by refugees and the various social agents involved in the life in the camp.

The main needs of the refugees to use and often appropriate POS was analysed in various studies, and can be summarized in the following way: getting together, learning about family and friends, seeking to organize their lives in the immediate and midterm future, exchanging information, making new friends, and learning about their new environment and how they are expected to function in it. POS can be places that include rather than exclude. Refugees are not tucked away in a hall or community centre, but a visible and engaged presence within the diverse mix of local residents. (“Refugees welcome in parks” project, Sheffield University 2017).

However, there are challenges. The public realm can be a place where refugees feel uncertain about local norms, feel unwelcome, uncomfortable or are vulnerable to hate crime. Longstanding residents of a local area may react negatively to changing patterns of use of public spaces, especially when ‘hanging out’ is perceived as idle loitering, threatening, or fundamentally changing the ethos of a loved place. An increase in hostile architecture and management practice (implicitly acting against street sleeping) also impacts on combine and explore. («Refugees welcome in parks» project, Sheffield University 2017). In a series of face-to-face interviews of owners and/or shop-keepers of restaurants and coffee places in Lavov Most area in Sofia, carried out by Ivanova-Radovanova for the purpose of this chapter, it was found that the main concerns of the local shopkeepers were about security and safety issues, they attributed the causes of social disturbances to the massive arrivals of refugees, and they were asking for more police surveillance.

5 The Relationship Between Refugees and Information Technology

It has been observed that refugees very frequently carry smartphones, of quite advanced technology (Lloyd (2015:2). In fact, according to Middle East Online (19-8-2015), many migrants consider their smartphones to be more important than food. As Gillespie et al. (2016:2) state “For refugees seeking to reach Europe, the digital infrastructure is as important as the physical infrastructures of roads, railways, sea crossings and the borders controlling the free movement of people”. Current research and activities on refugee’s use of mobile technology focus largely on the following themes: connectivity, digital tools and platforms, family reconnection, education, and livelihoods and mobile money. In the above, one has to add that smartphones are also a means to document the tragedy through which these people have been through.

The multiple usage of smartphones by the refugees has been documented by many writers (Chib and Aricat 2016; Talhouk et al. 2016; Harney 2013, etc.). Gifford and Wilding (2013) argue that if refugees are able to maintain their connections to family and friends, which can be achieved through a variety of mobile-based apps and Social Media applications, they may experience a greater sense of “being at home” in a hosting country. Finally, the role of ICT in promoting social inclusion has been analyzed by AbuJarour and Krasnova (2017) in their research about Syrian refugees in Germany. In their analysis, they construct a context framework for refugees (home country, journey, hosting country) within which ICTs function. Three variables of this function are derived (ICT properties, capabilities enabled by ICT, and achievements in social inclusion) inter-influenced by indicators (immigration, family separation, new society, and also internet, smartphones, and social media).

Besides the above, though, the use of smartphones on a mostly individual basis suffers from significant disadvantages and shortcomings (Gillespie et al. 2016). Technical problems included frauds in buying SIM cards which did not provide the desired international communication, shortage of installations for charging batteries, instability of connections, Wi-Fi access not often available, affordability of SIM cards, profiteering of locals by selling phone charging services in extremely high prices, and/or information gap because of language barriers. Other problems are mostly related to gendered and generational differences in access and use, poverty, illiteracy, and inadequacies in provision of services such as education, physical and psychological health etc. Schmitt et al. (2016) detected and defined a «digital divide» among refugees in the Za’atari Syrian refugee camp in northern Jordan, creating, thus, social divisions among the refugees. In this way, the class structure of society was transformed in the refugee camps/communities in another class division, based on access and possession of means of connectivity and information. This social divide becomes highly striking considering that contrary to Syrians, Afghans and some Iraqis appear to be less well equipped with ICT. Furthermore, the divide gets deeper as it concerns specific subdivisions of the above groups. UNHCR found that women, the elderly, less educated and/or illiterate people are less likely to have access to technology, information, and devices, echoing the findings of other, non-refugee related studies of exclusion, such as GSMA's Connected Women (GSMA 2016).

6 Conclusions

This contribution has explored the inclusion of the notion of urban resilience in European spatial planning, while giving special emphasis to the role that POS equipped with ICT (i.e. cyberparks) may have for safeguarding and reinforcing resilience. Having also exhibited the strong relationships between a. refugees and POS, and b. refugees and information technology – mainly smartphones – and the accruing problems and shortcomings, we conclude with an equivalent relationship between refugees and cyberparks that can alleviate the above shortcomings and thus strengthen urban resilience.

ICT in cyberparks is not restricted to smartphones, but it includes multiple technologically advanced means for achieving the above objectives. Furthermore, they allow and encourage collective consumption and use of ICT, strengthening, thus, the internal bonds of the users as a social group. The organized provision of information and the multiple ICT tools in cyberpark infrastructures can tackle the technical problems incurred to refugees with smartphones, by guaranteeing usable means for desired international communication, availability and affordability of installations for charging batteries, stable and unlimited Wi-Fi access, affordability of SIM cards, and assistance in overcoming language barriers.

With education and language skills seen as being vital to successful integration and social inclusion, a shortage of teachers in refugee hosting places complicates current efforts towards this objective. Here, online modes of pedagogy can potentially fill the gap (AbuJarour and Krasnova 2017). It is argued, that this type of education is unlikely to be as effective as in-person education, and such education services towards social inclusion require particular infrastructures and process. Cyberparks may be equipped by this type of infrastructure and provide a collective environment for open air activities of educational nature for children and adults. This has been shown to be more productive than the equivalent isolated use of smartphones by individuals. In a similar collective vein, help for sometimes illiterate refugees could be offered by the use of video or sound resources. Important initiatives could be the provision of legal advice and information about language learning facilities in info kiosks, or similar information installations. These are key areas that cyberparks could focus on.

Finally, a means of social inclusion of great importance is supporting refugees in combining virtual and local communication. In cyberparks, it is feasible and desirable to bring both refugees and locals together to support the integration process. The need to feel connected to other people is one of the primary psychological concerns of refugees, while the stresses upon them can often lead to isolation. The design process of POS equipped with cyber technology can facilitate communal connections. Including local people and refugees in the design process and looking at desired ICT and other services, cyberparks can become more relevant to the populations that live there. ("Refugees welcome in parks" project 2017). A number of co-operative methods for understanding public needs, civic involvement in the development of urban policies, spatial planning, and design are essential. The improvement of urban resilience and quality of life requires participation of both, local population and refugees, their collaboration and citizen involvement, aiming at a shift in the relative power of actors involved. Common cultural activities with concurrent events transmitted from refugees homelands, games between groups located in different areas and brought together by ICT means, interaction in the common language of cyber matters between local and refugee youths, watching sports, concerts, and cultural and political events through big screens, ("Refugees welcome in parks" project 2017), and discussing and sharing experiences and knowledge from distant places through ICT, strengthen the community bonds between locals and the newcomers, and accelerate social inclusion.

BBC Media Action's Voices of Refugees project also finds a close relationship between resilience and the psychosocial capacity of refugees and their use of ICT. "The analysis showed that participants who stayed in regular contact with other refugees and who had wide communication networks were likely to be more resilient and feel less vulnerable than those who were not connected." (Bailey et al. 2016). Undoubtedly, there is a recognized need to keep POS as a neutral space for practice and learning. Further institutionalization and the development of cyberparks will support improvement of accessibility of information, and empowerment of different stakeholders, including refugees for spatial and social organization on both local level and city levels. In order to overcome problematic encounters between planning and society, the incorporation of a kind of self-organization in planning with support of ICTs might be a successful next step. If cyberparks, as shown above, can retain this psychological capacity and further enhance it by the provision of infrastructure of a more collective nature, and of a more global use of ICT technology, which surpasses individual phones, then cyberparks can safeguard and reinforce urban resilience in times of social crises.

References

AbuJarour, S., Krasnova, H.: Understanding the role of ICTS in promoting social inclusion: the case of syrian refugees in Germany. In: Twenty-Fifth European Conference on Information Systems (ECIS), Guimarães, Portugal, pp. 1790–1806 (2017)

Androbus, D.: Smart green cities: from modernization to resilience? Urban Res. Pract. **4**(2), 207–214 (2011)

Bailey, N., Hannides, T., Kaoukji, D.: Voices of refugees; information and communication needs of refugees in Greece and Germany. BBC Media Action (2016). https://downloads.bbc.co.uk/mediaaction/pdf/research/voices-of-refugees-research-report.pdf

Bertalanffy, L.V.: General systems theory: foundations, development, applications. New York (1968)

Carmin, J., Nadkarni, N., Rhie, C.: Progress and Challenges in Urban Climate Adaptation Planning: Results of a Global Survey. MIT, Cambridge (2012)

Carpenter, S., Walker, B., Anderies, J.M., Abel, N.: From metaphor to measurement: resilience of what to what? Ecosystems **4**(8), 765–781 (2001)

Chib, A., Aricat, R.G.: Belonging and communicating in a bounded cosmopolitanism: the role of mobile phones in the integration of transnational migrants in Singapore. Inf. Commun. Soc. **20**(3), 482–496 (2017)

Frischmann, B.M.: Infrastructure: The Social Value of Shared Resources. Oxford University Press, Oxford (2012)

Folke, C.: Resilience: The emergence of a perspective for social-ecological systems analyses. Glob. Environ. Change **16**, 253–267 (2006)

Gifford, S.M., Wilding, R.: Digital escapes? ICTs, settlement and belonging among Karen youth in Melbourne, Australia. J. Refug. Stud. **26**(4), 558–575 (2013)

Gillespie, M., et al.: Mapping Refugee Media Journeys Smartphones and Social Media Networks. Research Report, The Open University/France Medias Monde, 13 May 2016 (2016)

GSMA: Bridging the gender gap: mobile access and usage in low and middle-income countries, 2015 (2016). http://www.gsma.com/mobilefordevelopment/wp-ontent/uploads/2016/02/Connected-Women-Gender-Gap.pdf

Gunderson, L.H.: Ecological resilience in theory and application. Ann. Rev. Ecol. Syst. **31**, 425–439 (2000)

Gunderson, L.H., Holling, C.S.: Panarchy: understanding transformations in systems of humans and nature. Washington, Island (2002)

Hampton, K.N., Goulet, L.S., Albanesius, G.: Change in the social life of urban public spaces: the rise of mobile phones and women, and the decline of aloneness over 30 years. Urban Stud. **52**(8), 1489–1504 (2015)

Harney, N.: Precarity, affect and problem solving with mobile phones by asylum seekers, refugees and migrants in Naples. Italy. J. Refugee Stud. **26**(4), 541–557 (2013)

Holling, C.S.: Resilience and stability of ecological systems. Ann. Revi. Ecol. Syst. **4**, 1–23 (1973)

Montgomery, J.: Making a city: urbanity, vitality and urban design. J. Urban Des. **3**(1), 93–116 (1998)

Lindner, S., Li, L., Müller, A.: Chinese and German city policies - analysed in the cities of Chengdu, Bonn, Wuhan and Duisburg. Report, Ecofys, June 2014

Lloyd, A.: People are outraged to see refugees with smartphones. They shouldn't be. Mother Nature Network, 8 September 2015 (2015)

Lofland, L.: A World of Strangers. Prospect Heights, Waveland (1985). [1973]

Ministry of Internal Affairs of Greece: Xenocratis General Plan for Civic Protection. Ministerial Decision 1299, FEK 423 B, 10 April 2003 (2003)

Neuman, M., Smith, S.: City planning and infrastructure: once and future partners. J. Plann. Hist. **9**(1), 21–42 (2010)

Orum, A.M., Neal, Z.P. (eds.): Common Ground: Readings and Reflections on Public Space. Routledge, New York (2010)

Pyrpiri, L.: Spatial planning and management of refugee flows. Undergraduate thesis, DPRD, University of Thessaly (2017)

Schmitt, P., Iland, D., Belding, E., Tomaszewski, B., Xu, Y., Maitland, C.: Community-level access divides: a refugee camp case study (2016)

Sheffield University: Refugees welcome in parks project (2017). http://thebench-project.weebly.com/blog/research-assistant-positionrefugeewelcome-in-parks

Talhouk, R., et al.: Syrian refugees and digital health in Lebanon: Opportunities for improving antenatal health. In: Proceedings of the 2016 CHI Conference on Human Factors in Computing Systems. pp. 331–342. ACM, May 2016

Walker, B., Holling, C.S., Carpenter, S.R., Kinzig, A.: Resilience, adaptability and transformability in social-ecological systems. Ecol. Soc. 9(2) (2004)

Walker, B., Salt, D.: Resilience thinking: sustaining ecosystems and people in a changing world. Island Press, USA (2006)

Costa, C.S., Ioannidis, K. (eds.): The Making of the Mediated Public Space: Essays on Emerging Urban Phenomena. Lusófona University Press, Lisbon (2017)

3.6 A Spotlight of Co-creation and Inclusiveness of Public Open Spaces

Ina Šuklje Erjavec[1(✉)] and Tatiana Ruchinskaya[2]

[1] Urban Planning Institute of the Republic of Slovenia, Ljubljana, Slovenia
inas@uirs.si

[2] JT Environmental Consultants Ltd., TVR Design, Cambridge, UK
tvr281@hotmailco.uk

Abstract. This chapter focuses on co-creation as the way to engage different stakeholders with everyday urban environments based on equality, diversity and social cohesion. It presents the relationship of co-creation and inclusiveness of public open spaces together with different aspects of co-creation related to issues of publicness and space. It discusses why and how co-creation must take into consideration the characteristics of the comprehensive spatial development processes. It suggests that co-creation is a wider concept than co-design and is a multistage process that contributes to inclusive public spaces, providing measures for social sustainability of place. This chapter argues that digital tools may help to overcome challenges of co-creation and provide an opinion on the contribution of digital technologies to the co-creation process by engaging people in the design, use and management of public spaces, providing new resources for interaction and users' empowerment. For that it presents an overview of the possible contribution of digital technologies to support inclusiveness of the co-creation processes that is structured by typologies of digital tools and their possible interlinking with the steps of the co-creation process. To improve the understanding of such possibilities it critically addresses strengths and weaknesses of using digital tools for co-creation and inclusiveness and provides recommendations for their further development.

Keywords: Co-creation · Inclusiveness · Digital tool

1 Introduction

Public spaces are defined by UNESCO (2017) as "social space that is generally open and accessible to people". Public spaces are regarded as democratic if they are constituted with forms of participatory democracy, meaning a "variety of processes providing people's involvement in decision-making and the rights to participate in society" (Maduz 2010; Omtzigt 2009; Parkinson 2012).

Social inclusion contributes to provision of participatory democracy of the public places in design, use and their management and neglecting it can have detrimental consequences for a success of the public places (IGOP 2017). However even in the democratic societies the exclusion can be obvious, and in many cases, has to be

C. Smaniotto Costa et al. (Eds.): CyberParks, LNCS 11380, pp. 209–223, 2019.
https://doi.org/10.1007/978-3-030-13417-4_17

addressed between the lines. Social inclusion defined as "the process of improving the terms of participation in society, particularly for people who are disadvantaged, through enhancing opportunities, access to resources, voice and respect for rights" (UN 2016).

Active participation in design, use and management of public spaces can be facilitated by the following methods:

- Public participation, defined as a "two-way communication and collaborative problem solving with the goal of achieving better and more acceptable decisions" (Atkinson et al. 2003; Creighton & Creighton 2008).
- Community engagement is a dimension of public participation and "a process of inclusive participation which supports mutual respect of values, strategies, and actions for authentic partnership of people affiliated with or self-identified by geographic proximity, special interest or similar situations to address issues affecting the well-being of the community" (Jones and Wells 2007).
- Co-creation process as a special type of collaboration, where people are working or acting jointly with others to create something that is not known in advance. "Co-creation is an act of collective creativity" (Sanders and Stappers 2008).

It is notable that the co-creation method is fundamentally different from public participation and citizen engagement. It increases opportunities for achieving social inclusion in public places because it recognises the decision-making rights of people, produce a new public value, promote of community self-organisation and empowerment of the excluded. (Leading Cities 2014; Sanches and Frankel 2010). It has a potential for overcoming the limitations of time and geography and may allow a significant leap in the scale and influence of public involvement" (Leading Cities 2014).

Whereas public open spaces involve both spatial as well as social structures, their characteristics are as much formed by the activities, attitudes and perceptions of people as they are by physical setting, features and elements. Moreover, the presence or absence of people defines the character and spirit of public place, influences its attractiveness, and forms its visual appearance, extending the concept of co-creation beyond planning and design activities to the area of implementation, use and management of place as well. Being public, such places should also cater for diversity of population, allowing people of all ages, sizes, abilities and disabilities to use and enjoy public places. Providing facilities for one group of users should result in solutions that addresses the needs of many other groups. Aspects of equality and inclusion within processes of co-creation are challenging.

From here the co-creation process in design, use and management of public open spaces is investigated further as an advanced process of participative democracy and a necessary condition of a more inclusive society. Thus, inclusiveness is considered to underpin the philosophy of co-creation processes and is implemented through inclusive indicators, including collaboration of uses, empowerment of community, interactivity, connectivity, equality, accessibility, efficiency, convenience and flexibility (Design Council 2017; CABE 2006). However, in reality it is difficult to accomplish all of them. Thus, it is accepted that inclusiveness in co-creation process can be achieved on an offset basis, where the achievement of several inclusive indicators compensates for, or offsets, others.

The chapter studies co-creation processes in public spaces in its wider context and investigates advantages of using digital tools to support co-creation activities and facilitate inclusiveness of public places.

2 Co-creation Within the Context of Public Open Space

Initially, the term co-creation has been used as an innovation management term and a form of economic strategy. It was defined by Prahalad and Ramaswamy as part of a product development and business strategy as "the joint creation of value by the company and the customer; allowing the customer to co-construct the service experience to suit their context" (Prahalad and Ramaswamy 2004). Surprisingly, it is less common in 'creative' disciplines like architecture, urban planning and design. There collaborative approaches are defined as public participation, participatory design, cooperative design, co-design, hands-on urbanism and similar. However, such concepts are not covering all the important and relevant aspects of the co-creation related to comprehensive spatial development but represent its individual parts and units of the wider context.

Co-creation for spatial development means a joint development, generation, production and creation of new proposals of "contextual and unique solutions" that are based on specific, local and personal knowledge and skills, potentials and opportunities as well as problems, and obstacles of the community and place. In the Co-Creating Cities publication prepared by Leading Cities in 2014, the co-creative process is defined by nine key characteristics. These are: "systemic, innovative and productive, collaborative, diverse, hierarchy-flattening, bi-or multi-directional, repeated and intense, mutually beneficial and trusted and transparent" (Leading Cities 2014).

Co-creative techniques give communities and individuals more direct involvement in defining their needs and priorities, collaboratively finding solutions, influencing decisions and achieving better outcomes. This process requires a transparency of a co-creation process as well as good, supporting tools and methodologies for information and ideas flow among stakeholders, their interaction and mutual development of knowledge and skills. That produces significant challenges in terms of the time and costs required to effectively engage stakeholder groups and to create accessible representations that help citizens in their participation and engagement. The requirement to process a huge amount and complexity of information could create barriers for a successful co-creation process.

An even bigger challenge is to successfully address the aspect of "common benefits for the whole community," which is especially relevant in the context of public open space. To be "inclusive and collaborative" means to be a process accessible to all, involving and equally addressing different context-related stakeholders, from public authorities, experts, NGOs to entire publics, and foster cross-sectoral cooperation. Therefore, it should incorporate a variety of principles, methods and tools to encourage and support the participation and transforms stakeholders from "passive audiences" to "active players". Very important aspect for the long-term reliability and successfulness is 'credibility'. That means, that participants and all others concerned can trust and feel confident about the aims, issues and process development and see evidence that their views have been considered. This also means that all sources of information, creative process steps and decision-making elements are transparent and verifiable within the whole process.

To be "open and responsive" is not only sharing and deciding but also developing and doing things, which is flexible enough to respond and adapt to social and spatial context and change. And has no pre-defined optimum solutions or preferences. Such approach is neither top-down nor bottom-up but shares power between government, citizens and other stakeholders, and creates partnership for consensus.

Co-creation is also a co-learning process, in which stakeholders learn from one another and participants assist each other to develop better solutions and improve the quality of life and local environment of the whole community in the long-term. Creating new dimensions of collective creativity on each stage of co-creation from identification of the problem to implementation of results and managing outcomes, provide people an equal opportunity to engage in the decision making, where everyone can be creative and contribute to the place making. Integration of resources during co-creation improves the adaptability of co-creation process. The flexibility of the process achieved by integration of knowledge of different users and understanding that, what is being created can be changed by the community.

To effectively use all the potentials of the co-creation approach for the development of public open spaces, it is necessary to understand it in its broader sense. That means taking into consideration also aspects of spatial setting and social functioning of public open space. To achieve this, the concept of co-creating public open spaces must include all stages of the spatial development process and address all types of related collaboration activities. That is: involving end users (citizens) and other relevant stakeholders, sharing information and local knowledge, collaborating on data gathering, expressing opinions, needs, wishes and values, defining priorities visions and aims, decision making as well as the placemaking with different participatory planning and co-design activities, co-management.

When dealing with public spaces, the co-creation aspects of actual activities and creativity of users in real time and space, may be sometimes even more relevant for successful development of the place and its inclusiveness. Involving citizens into implementation and management of real public open space opens another dimension of co-creation, the dimension of actual 'doing'. It means co-producing, the physical, spatial solutions, interventions, values, identities, contents and messages thus co-forming and co-developing spatial and social characteristics of place.

This wider understanding of possible acts of co-creation for public open space development is in line with the Four-D Model for Civic Engagement, defining four important categories of engagement: "Discover, Debate, Decide and Do" (Digital Engagement Cookbook 2017). By the scheme bellow (Fig. 1), we present the interrelation between co-creation approach and open space development. It demonstrates how co-creation extends to the "DO category", thus the co-creating activities of implementation, use and management of place. To better explain how the co-creation could be applied into the comprehensive spatial development process, it presents different relations to some more often used aspects and methodologies.

With suitable design of place and its elements (especially when using opportunities of new technologies) such co-creation of real places could be extended in time as its

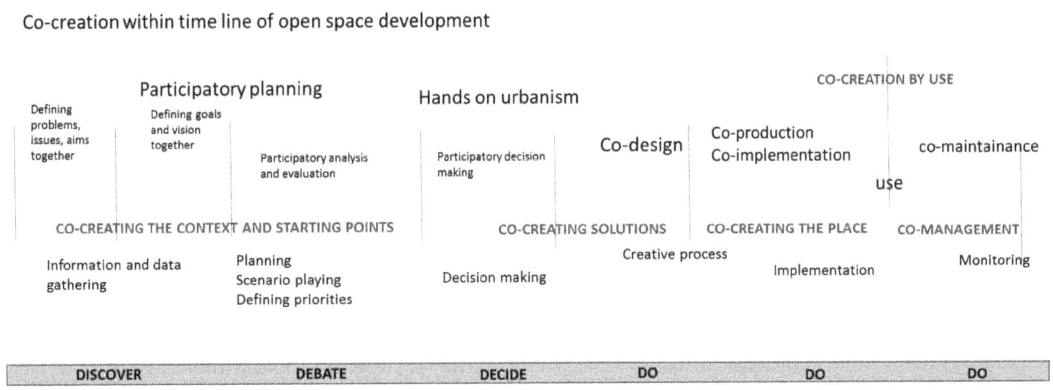

Fig. 1. Co-creation within the timeline of the public open space development

permanent adaptability and responsiveness to users' interventions and needs. Many new technologies such as touch screens, interactive surfaces and elements, smart furniture and other responsive environmental systems using sensors and actuators, embedded sound and video systems, microclimate control systems and similar, are offering a wide range of possibilities for users to temporarily or permanently change, adapt, personalise the place or respond to it by their activities and ways of use.

3 Using Digital Tools for Co-creation and Inclusiveness

The use of new technologies in our everyday life for work, education and leisure is becoming a reality as well as big challenge for urban development. Information and communications technologies (ICT) and digital literacy are increasingly necessary to engage in everyday social activities - to access public information, to bring together different kinds of knowledge, to facilitate communication and collaboration between a growing number of projects and initiatives, to communicate with social networks, to spread new skills and abilities, etc. Digital transition will not automatically provide us with inclusive society, but it can contribute to "building more equal, fairer and empowering society provided that there is a political will".

In the process of co-creation of public spaces, ICT can be a useful tool to overcome challenges and to achieve inclusiveness of public spaces, providing different types of assistance and contributing to equality and accessibility of co-creation process (Table 1). Digital tools are suitable for all age groups; they provide different forms of outreach to all, and an option of equal access to the internet and to important online resources.

The combination of offline and online tools is beneficial for changing the demographics of community engagement. Digital tools can assist in learning new skills and getting a new knowledge and sharing information. They can be especially supportive to particular groups of people (for example disabled users and young people) as may improve access and use of places for disabled people, encourage them to be socially active and increase opportunities that a place can offer to them.

Table 1. Using digital tools for supporting different actions and activities of the co-creation process.

Co-creation process actions	Co-creation activities	Examples of specific digital tools
PREPARATION Co-creating the context and starting points	Defining problems issues and aims, Defining goals and visions Public engagement Choosing priorities & Setting budgets	Better Reykjavik, CitizenLab, Engagement HQ, Front Porch Forum, Hy.OpenInnovation, i-Neighbors, MiMedellín (Colombia), NextDoor, Nexthamburg, Our Common Place, StickyRoom, Wheelmap (Germany); WayCyberparks; Budget Simulator, Citizen Budget, CrowdGauge, Wejit
DISCOVER for understanding urban reality Spatial and social analysis of the local context	Information, engagement, crowdsourcing	Better Reykjavik, CitizenLab, Engagement HQ, Front Porch Forum, Hy.OpenInnovation, i-Neighbors, MiMedellín (Colombia), NextDoor, Nexthamburg, Our Common Place, StickyRoom, Wheelmap (Germany); WayCyberparks;
	Engage with location, Community mapping, data collection	BlockPooling, Foursquare, Harvest Digital Planning, Madame Mayor I have an idea (France), Placecheck (UK), Social Pinpoint, Sparq® 3, Textizen Poll, YouCanPlan, Whrr
	Storing information	Cloud, harKopen, Social Pinpoint
	Making sense of data	CivicInsight, Many Eyes, FixMyStreet, VoiceYourView, Peckham Coal Line and Kirkwood green Space (UK)
DEBATE evaluation, refinement of ideas	Reporting	FixMyStreet, Public Stuff, SeeClickFix
	Brainstorming	Codigital, Ethel, e-deliberation, Loomio, Neighborland, Open Planet Ideas, Stickyworld
	Sharing knowledge	Community Almanac, Location-Aware Multimedia Stories, Neighborhow
	Annotating places	Placecheck app, Ushahidi
	Visualization & discussion	Lapse, Many Eyes, Spatial Media, StickyRoom
	Offline and online experiences	Consultation Manager, Quirky
	Offering rewards for ideas	Innocentive, OpenIdeo
DECIDE	Share ideas, joint decision-making	Civic Commons, Flemish Living Lab Platform, harKopen, Innocentive, Quirky, Loomio - Walk [Your City] (USA), Madame Mayor I have an idea (France), Many Eyes, M@nor Labs,

(*continued*)

Table 1. *(continued)*

Co-creation process actions	Co-creation activities	Examples of specific digital tools
		Minecraft (UN Programme), OpenIdeo, Open Planet Ideas, Sparq® 3, Wheelmap (Germany)
	Voting	Cityzen, Open IDEO,
	Raise awareness and lobby governments	Websites Walk Your City (USA)
	Budged voting	Citizen Budget
DO - design a solution	All in one	M@nor Labs, OpenIdeo, Open Planet Ideas
	Co-design	
	Modelling concepts and virtual prototypes	Connect to Life, Flux Space, Lapse, Many Eyes
	Site specific media experiences	Cityscape Digital, MetroQuest
	Play a game and plan for your community	Community PlanIt, CrowdGauge, Fold-it, Foursquare, M@nor Labs, Minecraft
DO - delivery & implementation	Execution of the project Showcase of results Physical co-implementation - public engagement	MetroQuest, Digital Planning
DO - use	Site specific (media) experiences Co-creation by use	Digital installations, media screens, The Intel Connect to Life Experience
MAINTAIN	Public engagement	
MONITOR	Questionnaires Direct data feedback from users	Ask Them PPF, All Our Ideas, Citizen Space, Google forms, Granicus SpeakUp, Wiki surveys

There is a big choice of digital tools available for the co-creation of public spaces. There are mobile applications, digital platforms, digital social networking websites, social media channels, blogs, site-specific media experiences, etc. These tools support either the whole process of co-creation of public spaces or its specific activities as presented in the overview table.

Examples of platforms that support the whole process of co-creation of public spaces include StickyWorld (StickyWorld 2017) and YouCanPlan (YouCanPlan 2017). There are also more general co-creation platforms, initiated by platform owners, or their partner organizations which could be used in any industry, for example Open-IDEO (OpenIDEO 2017) and Quirky (Quirky 2017), Idea Connection (Idea connection 2017), CitizenLab (CitizenLab 2017), Crowdbrite (Crowdbrite Solutions 2017) and

EveryAware (EveryAware 2016). They can me modified to customer requirements by their software providers. Webbased Networks (for example, Living Labs (ENoLL 2017) provide offline and online opportunities to participate in co-creation processes, which makes the process more attractive and accessible to certain groups of users. Digital platforms, where community members can initiate projects, connect community members around a shared interest, collect contributions and compile these contributions to a solution (HitRecord, Quirky).

There are city-specific co-creation projects, which use their own digital platforms with a strong local identity aiming to empower local communities to take ownership of changes in cities and combining online with offline approaches. OrganiCity is an EU-funded project, for co-creative practices in Aarhus, London and Santander, challenging mobility, air quality and urban regeneration. Zo! City was launched in 2010 in southeast Amsterdam (Netherlands) by TransformCity. It is based on storytelling to make the platform easy to engage with (Transform City 2015). Co-creation platforms Medellín (Medellín 2017) and Better Reykjavik (Citizens Foundation 2017) allow citizens to play a key part in the transformation of the city. They are designed for citizen solutions to these city's urban challenges. The Nooks and Crannies co-creation project and platform focused on local improvements in Bristol (UK) for the redesign of a link bridge and access lane (Hands on Bristol 2014). These platforms are "fragmented and uncertain on the demand-side and lacking common standards in the supply-side" and are not well-connected to "rapidly growing data" (European Innovation Partnership 2016). A common framework of co-creation process in cities should be established, so it can be applied to the needs of particular cities or places.

Platforms that support the whole process of co-creation are able to provide a high level of transparency of the process, activities and outcomes of co-creation, which motivates users to get engaged with the project (Nambisan and Nambisan 2013). It is argued that digital tools are successful in facilitating inclusiveness of co-creation process in public spaces and that they are good for supporting inclusive indicators (Table 2).

Table 2. Advantages and disadvantages of using digital tools for inclusive co-creation of public spaces.

Indicators of inclusion	Advantages of using digital tools for inclusive co-creation of public spaces	Disadvantages of using digital tools for inclusive co-creation of public spaces
Empowerment of community	• Assisting in giving people decision making powers, dialog and control • Personalize public spaces	• Requires a moderator, manager and facilitator. • Can be dominated by articulate and confident individuals if not carefully facilitated

(*continued*)

Table 2. (*continued*)

Indicators of inclusion	Advantages of using digital tools for inclusive co-creation of public spaces	Disadvantages of using digital tools for inclusive co-creation of public spaces
Collaboration	• Providing logistics to co-creation process, including understanding, improvement, and addressing urban issues • Provide an ability to communicate with social networks • Changing the demographics of co-creation process • Targeting at excluded or 'hard to reach groups' • Developing a common vision and assist to jointly create a product or service • Generating discussions • Assisting in handling conflicts • Building a sense of community ownership • Facilitating collaborating between projects and initiatives • Facilitating transparency of decision-making processes • Assisting in spreading of new skills and knowledge	• Requires a moderator, manager and facilitator • Workshops can be dominated by articulate and confident individuals if not carefully facilitated • Difference in participant confidence in their creative skills • Cybersecurity, targeted filtering, fake information, gender and racial bias embedded into various algorithms
Efficiency	• Cost & Time Effective • Robust data collection, its analysis, categorization, redistribution of information • Provide different forms of outreach to stakeholder groups • Efficient way of identifying and clarifying key issues • Bring together different kinds of knowledge • Easy evaluation of a results of co-creation	• Requires financial sustainability • Cybersecurity, targeted filtering, fake information
Interactivity	• Interactive and engaging • Creating debates and exchange of views • Assisting in decipher of urban information • Enabling participants to express their creativity	• Needs to be publicized to generate interest • Excludes those without access to the internet • Difference in participant's confidence in their creative skills • Difficult to interpret participant's ideas

(*continued*)

Table 2. (*continued*)

Indicators of inclusion	Advantages of using digital tools for inclusive co-creation of public spaces	Disadvantages of using digital tools for inclusive co-creation of public spaces
	• Facilitating transparency of decision-making processes • Adding variety to consultation • Engaging people who might not otherwise get involved	• Cybersecurity, targeted filtering, fake information
Connectivity	• Reaching a larger number of people • Spreading of new skills and knowledge	• Excludes those without access to the internet
Equality	• Suitable for all age groups • Providing different forms of outreach to stakeholder groups • Attractive to particular groups of people • Respecting people privacy • Providing an option of equal access to internet and important online resources • Spreading of new skills and knowledge	• Needs to be publicized to generate interest • Excludes those without access to the internet • Difficult to be sure that all stakeholders or interests are represented • Some people may feel intimidated • Cybersecurity, gender and racial bias embedded into various algorithms
Accessibility	• Accessible to people of all abilities and backgrounds	• Excludes those without access to the internet
Convenience	• Addressing the objectives of co-creation • Choosing a convenient time and place to participate • Providing different forms of outreach to stakeholder groups • Overcoming distances, • Moving through different layers of spaces and time • Creating boundaries and memory • Creating read/write publishing space • Respecting people privacy	• Cybersecurity
Flexibility	• Providing different forms of participation, connected to understanding, improvement, and subversion of urban issues • Providing different forms of outreach to different stakeholders • Designed for a specific purpose. • Choosing the most appropriate type and form of outreach	• Cybersecurity

Digital tools can be used to generate citizen empowerment by improving collaboration, dialog and control in co-creation process of public spaces and giving people decision making powers. At the same time, portable technologies have an ability to personalize public spaces through users' maps, photos, experiences, etc., which give people a feeling of personal belonging (Iaconesi and Persico 2013).

Digital tools can improve the efficiency of collaboration in co-creation process of public spaces. The support of digital tools in tasks that requires, scale, speed, interactivity, connectivity "is not a luxury, but a non-negotiable necessity" (Bhalla 2016). It makes the logistics simpler and brings a community into contact with the co- creation process. It provides more robust data collection and its analysis, categorization, redistribution of information and acquiring new skills. Online dialogues are less costly, quicker and easier to arrange, and can involve a much larger number of stakeholders and citizens (Viegas et al. 2007; Sinclair et al. 2007).

Digital tools can be applied in layers to address different objectives of co-creation in public spaces making the process more flexible and user orientated. For example, they can contribute to generation of ideas, which involves understanding, discussion of urban issues, refinement of features and co- creation (Janner-Klausner 2017; Bhalla 2016).

Technology-enabled approaches, providing different types of assistance, may contribute to equality and accessibility of co-creation process. They are suitable for all age groups; provide different forms of outreach to all, and an option of equal access to internet and to important online resources. Digital tools can be more attractive to particular groups of people (for example disabled users and young people) as they improve access and use of places for disabled people, encourage them to be socially active and increase opportunities that a place can offer to the users. They provide references to culture, heritage and public art in a digital format, which is very attractive to young people. Digital tools can assist in learning new skills and acquiring new knowledge. The combination of offline and online tools is beneficial for changing the demographics of community engagement.

Digital tools may encourage interactivity in co-creation of public spaces. They can support public debates, exchanging views, interpreting urban information, and enabling participants to express their creativity. They provide a variety of entry points to consultation and transparency around decision-making processes. The application of digital tools can provide a convenient and flexible way to co-create public spaces. These tools allow people to choose the appropriate methodology for the project that can be designed for a specific purpose at convenient time and place for participation, while at the same time respecting people's privacy. They assist in overcoming distance, to move through different layers of spaces and time. They can create boundaries, memories and read/write publishing spaces.

There are challenges of management, both personal and digital, in using IT tools for the co-creation of public places. Online co-creation processes require an experienced moderator as well as a manager and a facilitator. There are differences in participant confidence which should be considered when engaging different stakeholders in co-creation processes. Cybersecurity, targeted filtering, fake information, gender and racial bias embedded into various digital algorithms are challenges that should be addressed. Exclusion from communications and lack of ICT access, defined as service exclusion and considered as a dimension of social exclusion, are also known under the label 'digital divide' and should be resolved at the government level (Sinclair et al. 2007). There is evidence that lack of access to ICT can foster disadvantages "in a direct way, relating to access to services and opportunities or indirect way, relating to local relationships and social capital" (Servon and Nelson 2001; Pantazis et al. 2006). Unaffordable costs, lack of awareness and trust to go online, luck of digital skills and communications literacy can lead to self-exclusion (GOV. UK 2014). These individuals are unable to participate in normal social life are "condition of 'partial citizenship" (Sinclair et al. 2007).

4 Discussion and Conclusions

The co-creation of public open space is a way to engage different stakeholders with the everyday urban environment, based on equality, diversity and social cohesion. To appropriately address all the complexities of public space development, it should be considered a multi staged process, involving all phases of spatial development. That means addressing all types of related collaboration activities, including citizen engagement, sharing and interpreting information, co-learning, collaborating, expressing opinions, defining priorities, refining ideas, making decisions, creating common values, implementing solutions, monitoring, etc. In this way, positive outcomes of co-creation in public spaces exceed features of the final product, a spatial solution. It has a very strong potential to enrich the community life by creating interaction between the community members, to develop a local sense of place through active engagement with it, as well reducing vandalism and urban alienation.

However, it is difficult to involve diverse groups of people (e.g. academics, business people, non-profits, public servants, citizens) with different expectations regarding pace, style of work and timelines. The difference between experts and the general citizens, or between scholarly knowledge and informal knowledge, can also create conflicts and boundaries between stakeholders and undermine the legitimacy of the process. Any inequities that exist between groups of people involved should be balanced and effectively mitigated. Inclusive strategies for engaging hard-to-reach stakeholders, continuing dialogue, establishing partnerships and carrying out collaborative work should be introduced, while involving users in the process through workshops, user generated content, data collection, prototyping, or other activities, in order to get them engaged around the urban problem and suggest a solution.

This chapter argues that digital tools can be very useful to overcome different challenges of co-creation. They may provide different types of assistance for all age groups, contribute to equality and accessibility of co-creation process, enable learning new skills and promote healthier lifestyles. The overview of available digital tools proves there is a wide choice available for co-creation of public spaces, supporting either the whole process or its specific activities.

Many examples collected during the Cyberparks Project indicate that digital tools can contribute to a better understanding of public places, social networking, collaboration and community involvement (Cyberparks Project 2016). Introducing a digital layer to the existing public space for co-creation in real time and place may further improve an inclusive dimension of public place in physical and digital terms.

'Decoding', 'debugging', and 'hacking' in public space are forms of participation, connected to understanding, improvement, and subversion of urban issues, which follows the main objectives of co-creation (Dork and Monteyne 2011). They assign roles to citizens and propose a range of activities to change the perception and reality of urban relations. Decoding involves publishing of data and spatial knowledge and its interpretation. The digital tools that can help to "decipher urban code" and "make sense of urban information streams", focusing on specific aspects of urban life, and making the issues more accessible, interactive and visual. By filing 'bug reports', citizens can report on urban issues by web-based forms. 'Hacking' public place is another way to reach the public by creating prototypes of change and spreading them like computer viruses.

Surprisingly, the wide range of opportunities of the use of ICT is still poorly recognized and discussed among urban planners and designers (Houghton et al. 2014). There are many specific challenges related to the planning processes from the both perspectives, use of ICT and co-creation. To effectively use the co-creation approach for planning and design of public open spaces it is important to closely relate and adjust all different aspects as well as different types of ICT tools to the particular stages of the spatial development timeline. New projects, as for example C3Places (C3Places 2018), are turning the focus also on planning and development aspects of quality of place, exploring how different potentials of ICT could be better understood and integrated into the POS development practice.

Finally, it is important to point out, that digital tools may be used also as a part of the design of place and its elements to attract co-creation and enable permanent adaptability and responsiveness of public open space. Many new technologies such as touch screens, interactive surfaces and elements, smart furniture and other responsive environmental systems using sensors and actuators, embedded sound and video systems, microclimate control systems and similar, are offering a wide range of possibilities for users to temporarily or permanently change, adapt, personalize the place or respond to it by their activities and ways of use.

References

Atkinson, T., Cantillon, B., Marlier, E., Nolan, B.: Social Indicators: The EU and Social Inclusion. Oxford University Press, Oxford (2003). https://doi.org/10.1093/0199253498.001.0001

Bhalla, G.: Collaboration and co-creation: the road to creating value. Mark. J., 25 May 2016. http://www.marketingjournal.org/collaboration-and-co-creation-the-road-to-creating-value/

CABE. Principles of inclusive design (2006). http://www.cabe.org.uk/files/the-principles-of-inclusive-design.pdf

CITIZEN BUDGET. Features (2017). http://www.citizenbudget.com/

Citizens Foundation. Better Reykjavík – Connects citizens to city hall (2017). http://www.citizens.is/portfolio/better-reykjavik-connects-citizens-and-administration-all-year-round/, auge. CrowdGauge (2017). http://crowdgauge.org/

CitizenLab. Co-create our city (2017). https://www.citizenlab.co/product

Consultation Manager. Top 5 Online Engagement Tools, 17 September 2016. https://consultationmanager.com/top5-online-engagement-tools/

Creighton & Creighton, Inc. What is Public Participation? (2008). http://www.creightonandcreighton.com

Crowdbrite Solutions. Projects (2017). http://www.crowdbrite.net/

Design Council. Inclusive Environments (2017). http://www.designcouncil.org.uk/what-we-do/inclusive-environments

C3Places Using ICT for co-creation of inclusive public places, JPI Urban Europe, 2017–2020. https://c3places.eu/

Cyberparks Fostering knowledge about the relationship between Information and Communication Technologies and Public Spaces supported by strategies to improve their use and attractiveness, COST Action TU 1306, 2015–2018. http://cyberparks-project.eu/

Digital Engagement Cookbook. Digital Engagement Cookbook, Methods Directory (2017). http://engagementdb.org

Dork, M., Monteyne, D.: Urban Co-Creation: Envisioning New Digital Tools for Activism and Experimentation in the City (2011). http://mariandoerk.de/urbancocreation/hpc2011.pdf

ENoLL. Living Labs (2017). http://www.openlivinglabs.eu/node/1429

European Innovation Partnership on smart cities and communities (EIP). Towards Open Urban Platforms for Smart Cities and Communities (2016). https://eu-smartcities.eu/sites/all/files/MemorandumofUnderstandingonUrbanPlatforms.pdf

EveryAware. EveryAware Whitepaper, Enhancing Environmental Awareness through Social Information Technologies, November 2016. http://www.everyaware.eu/wp-content/uploads/2011/04/EveryAware.pdf

GOV.UK. Government Digital Inclusion Strategy, December 2014. https://www.gov.uk/government/publications/government-digital-inclusion-strategy/government-digital-inclusion-strategy

Hands on Bristol. Nooks and Crannies (2014). http://www.hands-on-bristol.co.uk/new-page-1/

Houghton, K., Miller, E., Foth, M.: Integrating ICT into the planning process: impacts, opportunities and challenges. Aust. Planner **51**(1), 24–33 (2014). https://doi.org/10.1080/07293682.2013.770771

Iaconesi, S., Persico, O.: The co- creation of the city. Re-programming cities using real-time user generated content (2013). http://www.academia.edu/3013140/The_Co-Creation_of_the_City

Idea connection (2017). https://www.ideaconnection.com/open-innovation-services.html

IGOP. Social Inclusion and Participatory Democracy (2017). https://www.uclg-cisdp.org/en/observatory/reports/social-inclusion-and-participatory-democracy-conceptual-discussion-local-action

Janner-Klausner, D.: Using online tools for community engagement and consultation (2017). http://www.commonplace.is/blog/using-online-tools-for-community-engagement-and-consultation

Jones, L., Wells, K.: Strategies for academic and clinician engagement in community-participatory partnered research. JAMA **297**, 407–410 (2007)

Leading Cities. Co-Creating Cities: Defining Co-Creation as a Means of Citizen Engagement, March 2014. http://leadingcities2014.files.wordpress.com/2014/02/co-creation-formatted-draft-6.pdf

Maduz, L.: Direct democracy. Living Reviews in Democracy, vol. 2, University of Zurich (2010). https://www.lrd.ethz.ch/index.php/lrd/article/viewArticle/lrd-2010-1/22

Medellín. ¡Perticipa Y Haz Parte de la Transformasion! (2017). http://www.mimedellin.org/

Nambisan, S., Nambisan, P.: Engaging Citizens in Co-Creation in Public Services: Lessons Learned and Best Practices. IBM Center for The Business of Government (2013). http://www.businessofgovernment.org/sites/default/files/Engaging Citizens in Co-Creation in Public Service.pdf

Omtzigt, D.J.: Survey on Social inclusion: Theory and Policy. Oxford University, Oxford Institute for Global Economic Development, January 2009. http://ec.europa.eu/regional_policy/archive/policy/future/pdf/1_omtzigt_final_formatted.pdf

OpenIDEO. Active challenges (2017). https://challenges.openideo.com

Pantazis, C., Gordon, D., Levitas, R.: Poverty and Social Exclusion in Britain. The Policy Press, Bristol (2006)

Parkinson, J.: Democracy and Public Place. Oxford University Press, Oxford (2012). https://chisineu.files.wordpress.com/2012/08/democracy-public-spaces.pdf

Prahalad, C.K., Ramaswamy, V.: Co-creation experiences: the next practice in value creation J. Interact. Mark. **18**(3) (2004). https://deepblue.lib.umich.edu/bitstream/handle/2027.42/35225/20015_ftp.pdf

Quirky. Start Inventing (2017). https://www.quirky.com/

Sanches, M.G., Frankel, L.: Co-design in public spaces: an interdisciplinary approach to street furniture development (2010). http://www.drs2010.umontreal.ca/data/PDF/105.pdf

Sanders, E.B.N., Stappers, P.J.: Co-creation and the new landscapes of design. CoDesign **4**(1), 5–18 (2008). https://doi.org/10.1080/15710880701875068

Servon, L.J., Nelson, M.K.: Community technology centres and the urban technology gap. Int. J. Urban Reg. Res. **25**(2), 419–426 (2001)

Sinclair, S., Bramley, G., Dobbie, L., Morag, G.: Social Inclusion and communication. Review of Literature, November 2007. http://www.communicationsconsumerpanel.org.uk/downloads/Research/LowIncomeConsumers_Research/Socialinclusionandcommunications/Socialinclusionandcommunications.pdf

StickyWorld. Ideas Matter (2017). http://info.stickyworld.com/

Transform City. TransformCity® is the most integral and actionable urban transformation platform (2015). http://www.transformcity.com/

UN. Identifying social inclusion and exclusion (2016). http://www.un.org/esa/socdev/rwss/2016/chapter1.pdf

Viegas, F.B., Wattenberg, M., van Ham, F., Kriss, J., McKeon, M.: Many eyes: a site for visualization at internet scale. TVCG: Trans. Vis. Comput. Graph. **13**(6), 1121–1128 (2007)

UNESCO: Inclusion Through Access to Public Space Social and Human Sciences (2017). http://www.unesco.org/new/en/social-and-human-sciences/themes/urban-development/migrants-inclusion-in-cities/good-practices/inclusion-through-access-to-public-space/

YouCanPlan. YouCanPlan (2017). http://www.participatedb.com/tools/193

3.7

CyberParks Songs and Stories - Enriching Public Spaces with Localized Culture Heritage Material such as Digitized Songs and Stories

Kåre Synnes[1(✉)], Georgios Artopoulos[2], Carlos Smaniotto Costa[3], Marluci Menezes[4], and Gaia Redaelli[5]

[1] Luleå University of Technology, Luleå, Sweden
Kare.Synnes@ltu.se
[2] The Cyprus Institute, Nicosia, Cyprus
g.artopoulos@cyi.ac.cy
[3] CeiED Interdisciplinary Research Centre for Education and Development, Universidade Lusófona, Lisbon, Portugal
smaniotto.costa@ulusofona.pt
[4] National Laboratory for Civil Engineering – LNEC, Lisbon, Portugal
marluci@lnec.pt
[5] Politecnico di Milano, Milan, Italy
gaiaangelica.redaelli@polimi.it

Abstract. This chapter offers theoretical considerations and reflections on technological solutions that contribute to digitally supported documentation, access and reuse of localised heritage content in public spaces. It addresses immaterial cultural heritage, including informal stories that could emerge and be communicated by drawing hyperlinks between digitised assets, such as songs, images, drawings, texts and more, and not yet documented metadata, as well as augmenting interaction opportunities with interactive elements that relate to multiple media stored in databases and archives across Europe. The aim is to enable cultural heritage to be experienced in novel ways, supported by the proliferation of smartphones and ubiquitous Internet access together with new technical means for user profiling, personalisation, localisation, context-awareness and gamification. The chapter considers cyberparks as digitally enhanced public spaces for accessing and analyzing European cultural heritage and for enriching the interpretation of the past, along with theoretical ramifications and technological limitations. It identifies the capacities of a proposed digital environment together with design guidelines for interaction with cultural heritage assets in public spaces. The chapter concludes with describing a taxonomy of digital content that can be used in order to enhance association and occupation conditions of public spaces, and with discussing technological challenges associated with enriching public spaces with localized cultural heritage material.

C. Smaniotto Costa et al. (Eds.): CyberParks, LNCS 11380, pp. 224–237, 2019.
https://doi.org/10.1007/978-3-030-13417-4_18

Keywords: Geotagged cultural expressions · Digital cultural heritage · Historic urban fabric · Immaterial heritage · Contextual cultures · Participatory design

1 Introduction

The purpose of this chapter is to discuss the theoretical and technological approach of the CyberParks Songs and Stories concept, which aims at increasing the understanding of European cultures and creating an intercultural bridge to respond to the need for reflective and creative societies. It envisions to provide plural meanings and interpretations of (and on) heritage to citizens through collective and collaborative methods for semantic classification, contextualisation and augmentation of digital assets and associated metadata by means of machine learning, social analysis, gamification and crowdsourcing. The proposed method has similarities to what Kontkanen et al. (2016) used for species identification in terms of collaborative mechanisms.

To understand and inform the present by richer interpretations of the past, three cases of socio-cultural environments are selected: Fado songs and the identity of Mouraria neighbourhood in Lisbon (PT), oral traditions and expressions of the Patios of Córdoba (ES) and Sami Yoiks and storytelling in Sápmi (Laponia region, SE). The three cases are listed as Intangible Cultural Heritage by the Intergovernmental Committee for the Safeguarding of the Intangible Cultural Heritage (ICH) of UNESCO since 1996 (Sami Yoiks), 2011 (Fado) and 2012 (Patios). The three cases are subject to the tension between continuity with the traditions and changes, in particular those that transform substantially the layout of the territories wherein the specific cases of ICH have emerged. This tension undermines safeguarding and may jeopardise the continuity of the ICH. The concept does not define ICH as something frozen and perpetuated, which contradict the procedural nature of the production of ICH, but as socio-cultural subjects consciously embodied in a process of enriching, enhancing and transmitting it. The intergenerational continuum, and the spatio-temporal context of social activity, further impact the fluidity of heritage and identity.

2 The Challenge of Accessing Intangible Cultural Heritage

The concept recognises the pressing need in contemporary societies for inclusion and integration of information stored in individuals' memories to the heritage archives. Specifically understanding information regarding ICH activities as embodied by people, communities and societies, is imperative for capturing non-institutional knowledge, as well as complex semantic and conceptual knowledge, often expressed as non-verbal practices, rites or social relations (Artopoulos and Bakirtzis 2016). In Stiegler's (2003) terms, humans leave traces of their histories, although not produced intending to immediate transmit memories, they do so, for example writing, photography, phonography and cinematography. This perspective addresses two critical challenges of contemporary approaches to ICH: (a) facilitating access to knowledge stored in archives, collections and digital assets; and (b) exploiting the capacity of digital tools for enabling users to better interpret and understand the big data of ICH.

The three scenarios demonstrate the way this concept will attempt to respond to these challenges:

Scenario – Fado songs | *Joaquim is a member of a parish council of Mouraria, which is responsible for the development of the district. He owns a small repair shop in the Mouraria and is very involved in sharing the Fado at local 'Tasca' - a typical café or restaurant - where his grandfather sometimes plays Fado songs on a Portuguese guitar. Today Joaquim is walking home from work and passes by a mural made with the traditional Azulejo tiles, when his smartphone starts to vibrate notifying him that a point of interest is nearby. He brings up his mobile phone and the vibration becomes more frequent as he walks closer to the mural.*

He stops in front of the mural and opens the mobile app to listen to the Fado song associated with it. Joaquim is reminiscent of his grandfather performing the song on his guitar, which awakes a lot of fond memories. He remembers in particular a narrative, a story that his grandfather tells at his favourite Tasca, which he decides to share with the community of Fado lovers connected through the app. Joaquim writes the short story and appends a photo of his grandfather performing the song in the Tasca. He makes a note of asking his grandfather to play it for him, so that the story can also be annotated with his performance.

Then the app suggests Joaquim to seek out similar murals associated with Fado songs located in the area. He accepts the suggestion and is presented with an annotated path along the way home. He stops at series of murals and associated places and is presented with not only other Fado songs but also with additional information such as ambient soundscapes, pictures, voice recordings and videos captured and uploaded by other users. Joaquim specifically is searching for additional information based on the Fado song played by his grandfather and when the app returns to him an image, he discovers that there are similar Fado songs, also related to the docks that were used in the past as harbours, located in the nearby neighbourhoods. Through the app he can add these locations on the map as points of interest for later, so that in his next walk around the city he can view the basins from specific vantage points that link back to his interests.

When Joaquim returns home, he uses the app to make a note on social media about his experience. Through multiple loops of this activity, shared by many, a community is formed about the docks and how to make their old uses and stories more visible to the public. Then more users of the app contribute content to this thematic group with additional narratives, effectively crowdsourcing a big amount of data related to the Fado and Mouraria. Eventually this common activity leads to the publication of articles by journalists that achieve to raise the interests of local policy makers, such as Joaquim himself, and to promote tacit arguments of the existing group of interest and researchers in the public. Finally, this action initiates social reporting activities that highlight everyday issues in Mouraria, such as destructive forms of graffiti, shortage of affordable housing and job opportunities, the degradation of built heritage, as well as the ever-growing gentrification of the area. In the appropriate context this community-building process can culminate in a process wherein people will be asking to their representatives for suitable solutions to these challenges and hence, to reviewing the existing urban policies.

Scenario – *The living patio* | *María is 92 years old and is living all her life in a patio in the district of Axerquía. There she spent her childhood, marriage and own family. She lived there with the extended family of other dwellings: they share the patio as a collective space, took care of it and in a time participated in the competition of patios. Maria's courtyard has not yet been bought by new owners, and now the houses are abandoned. Only María lives there, taking care of her plants and of the patio. María's daughter left the family home when she married in the 60's and went to live in a flat with her husband. Every year, in May, Maria's granddaughter Fuensanta returns to Córdoba to meet family and friends and "go to patios". Since Patios were declared by UNESCO ICH, the patios are attracting growing interest, in special during the Festival. This can affect the original way of living around most of the courtyards. Fuensanta arrived this year with a mobile app installed in smartphone. She uploaded some images of her grandmother's patio and other old images when they took part in the patio competition. She interviewed her grandmother about the patio, how the space was shared and the freshness of the summer thanks to shadow and vegetation. She uploaded this to the app to share it with the Patios' community. The app invites Fuensanta to explore the courtyard and to record other narratives related to her grandmother's and to her own life in the courtyard. They go to the laundry and she records her grandmother memoirs about when there was no washing machine and all the women used to wash by hand. María sings a song she used to sing while doing the laundry. Fuensanta uploads a photo of the current laundry and two sound records: the conversation with his grandmother and the song. Then they visit also the old communal kitchen and remember some of their favourite recipes. They look at a crockery hanging in the kitchen. They upload a photo of the crockery and hang some of the favourite recipes. The app offers diverse functions: A) to play songs uploaded by the community members; to localize in the map the sound records and the courtyards where they have been uploaded. Fuensanta discovers that there are other interviews of patio residents. B) to shows images and recipes uploaded by the community members and info about stores selling local and regional food products. Fuensanta and her sister "go to Patio" and visit some of patios, where some of their friends still live. One of them tells them that there is an association that is interested in creating in some patios of the Axerquía cooperative housing in right of use. Her friend shows her the drawing of a project for renovating the patio and Fuensanta uploads it to the application and shares it on social networks. Some people and associations interested in the patios, not as tourist product, get in contact with her. They organize a meeting inside the patio of their grandmother about how is living it, and upload photos, sound records and conclusions of the debate into the application. Many other members of the community join them, as the Instituto Andaluz del Patrimonio Histórico, which includes this new information in the Atlas of the Intangible Heritage of Andalucia. The municipality and the government of Andalucia add this action in Good Practices to Safeguard Intangible Cultural Heritage and to the reports for UNESCO. Some bio-construction cooperatives and the PAX strategy get in touch with the association and Fuensanta to participate in the patio's rehabilitation and select María's courtyard.*

Scenario – Sámi Yoiks | *Anna is 25 years old and of Sámi heritage, the only indigenous people of Scandinavia, but has as so many others of her generation left her ancestral region of Sápmi in the far north of Sweden, Norway, Finland and Russia. Anna is very aware of her Sámi heritage and wants to learn as much as possible of her heritage. She regularly visits Jokkmokk, a town above the arctic circle, which is famous for a traditional Sámi winter market and meeting place established early in the 17th century.*

This February winter day, Anna is visiting her aunt Marja in Jokkmokk, whom she will help sell handmade bracelets of pewter thread and reindeer skin at the market. This is an excellent occasion for Anna to learn Sámi stories and yoiks (songs), as Marja is known for her clear voice and keen memory. At the market, Anna notices a poster that describes the mobile app for collectively building annotated archives of songs and stories, such as yoiks. Anna asks Marja if she knows about it, which Marja says she does and that it is linked to the archives at Ajtte, the Sámi museum in Jokkmokk.

Anna downloads the app after the first market day and explores it. She adds yoiks as an interest and browses some of the publicly available yoiks. She listens to a few of them and are asked a few reflective questions by the app. When she arrives to the market in the morning, her smartphone vibrates, and she notices that the app has identified yoiks related to the Jokkmokk Winter Market. One of the yoiks is from the beginning of the 20th century. Anna is very intrigued and replays the yoik for Marja to learn more about the yoik and her heritage.

Marja laughs merrily and tells Anna that it is her grandmother's uncle PerAnte that sings the yoik about his visit at the market one exceptionally cold winter. Marja tells her that PerAnte was a bear hunter and that he was widely known for his bear hides at the market plus that his wife Sara also sang yoiks. To add information in the app about PerAnte's yoik becomes their joint task during the slower periods at the market, such as adding stories of PerAnte the bear hunter, his wife Sara and their life together. They use the app to also find images to associate with the yoik, such as of items exhibited at the Ajtte museum and a museum in Berlin. Marja has an old photograph at home of PerAnte, Sara and their children in front of a goathi (a traditional Sámi tent), which they later store using the app.

Marja has learnt PerAnte's yoik when Anna returns the following summer and they agree to use the app to capture and store a video of Marja singing the yoik in front of the remains of the goathi at the outskirts of Jokkmokk. When they store the yoik they are asked about the copyrights and Marja chooses to make it publically available, but not commercially free. Two years later, Marja is contacted by a producer that wants to use her yiok as a theme song for a film about the region, inspired by the story of PerAnte and Sara. The mobile platform marketplace, that is associated with the app, have made it simple to find and use the stored yioks while taking both private and commercial considerations into account. Marja accepts and are then also invited to play a role performing the yoik in the beginning of the film.

The story of PerAnte and Sara, through the efforts of Anna and Marja, first becomes known as a good example of documenting and promoting Sámi heritage. The story is then used by the Sámi community to show how hunting rights have belonged to the Sámi, and the value thereof for the heritage. The Sámi community is in minority in all four nations, but their joint Sámi council will be able to leverage of the press coverage and public opinion to improve the conditions for the Sámi community.

These three cases reflect a diversity of spaces, from the small scale of a historic city structures (Patios) to a medium scale of historic urban areas and riverside cities

(Lisbon), and the large scale of outdoors, green fields and forest landscapes (in the case of Sápmi). Further examples are discussed by Smaniotto et al. (2018).

3 Theoretical Framework and User Engagement

Cultural heritage is a key factor of European identity. Europe is a polyphonic society and its cultural wealth and advantage stem from the safeguarding and continuity of this diversity, which considers the pluralities of minorities (Pratt 2005). Societal changes affect the perception of cultural heritage by European citizens. Rapid urbanization, migration, wars and economic challenges impact European territories with ever-growing plurality of cultures and identities that must now adapt to a new concept of European citizenship. The importance of space for the preservation and communication of histories and identities has been long recognized. This understanding builds on the premise that space and landscapes contribute to the formation of local cultures and they are the framework of European natural and cultural heritage, contributing to human well-being and consolidating European identity (ELC). Co-safeguard, co-reflection on and transformation of these commons (e.g., heritage assets) can arguably contribute to the emergence of feelings of stability, continuity and belonging for people (i.e., new and existing inhabitants).

Manovich (2001: 193) argues that: "in the information age narration and description has changed roles. If traditional cultures provided people with well-defined narratives (myths, religion) and little 'stand-alone' information, today we have too much information and too few narratives which can tie it all together." The idea behind this concept is to utilise a framework of spatially - and contextually - organised narratives that relies on semantics and machine learning in order to facilitate the analysis and integration of everyday experiences, and the evolving memories of users into relevant digital cultural heritage assets. It envisions to achieve this by means of: (a) multi-user contributions, e.g., software that enables the following operations: mix, edit, reuse, enhance and enrich data features; and, (b) exchange of information, combined with expert input, guidance, reflection and discussion (Fig. 1). This data lifecycle in order to function requires the engagement of the three types of actors: (1) cultural operator, who will classify digital assets based on dedicated ontologies for each case, (2) expert users (cultural bearers), who will contextualize digital assets based on semantic models, and (3) common users, who will reflect on digital assets and add related meaning. This can be seen as an incremental and iterative process, where machine learning is applied for a high grade of automation and where these three main actors participate as part of a crowd-sourcing methodology spurred by gamification techniques. Additional actors will also be supported, such as the researcher (operating on the ontologies and algorithms) and the administrator (administrating and upgrading the platform).

The cellular structure illustrated in Fig. 2 is based on modules for Big Data Management (handling digital assets and associated metadata), the proposed platform (integrating and adapting existing tools), Machine Learning (techniques for reasoning on metadata through semantic analysis), and enabling techniques (gamification, crowdsourcing, Arianna, and social analysis), in order to facilitate the study of socio-cultural representations, and participant memories and interpretations that require the

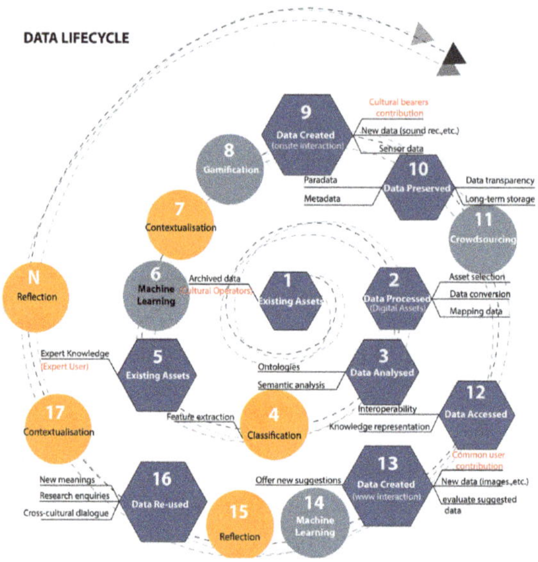

Fig. 1. Data Lifecycle. The exponentially iterative process of user engagement-collection-digestion-semantic classification-automated suggestion loops facilitates the enrichment of data collections and reflecting on them, and thus promotes dialogue between user communities.

various groups of actors to operate feed and steer them. The interaction between the supporting ICT and each group of actors (cultural operator, expert users and common users) is made possible through participatory development methods (e.g., FormIT methods[1]. The practical results of this interaction are illustrated in Fig. 1, in particular the iterative and incremental augmentation of digital assets with metadata in steps 1-5-9-13-16. Through the proposed technological and enabling solutions this iterative process is envisioned to become catalyst in the exponential engagement of ever larger groups of users. The use of state-of-the-art technologies, such as machine learning, and novel combination of participation and engagement methods, such as co-creation, crowdsourcing and gamification, not only responds to the needs of local communities, but also promotes formation of new communities, around special cross-thematic topics (e.g., semantics, metadata management, machine learning and gamification), and facilitates drawing links between digital assets of intangible heritage and their relevant tangible heritage.

The ICT platform should consider the following:

1. Digital assets, which describe an ICH (audio tracks, video clips, photos and text notes). These digital assets will be enhanced by the (1) quantitative metadata taken automatically from the smart device: location (where), timestamp (when), user profile (who), the info coming from the sensors integrated into the smart device such as the accelerometer, gyroscope, barometer, magnetometer or light intensity (how); and (2) Qualitative metadata inserted by different users' level such as key-words (what). The digital assets will be grouped, related within a hierarchy, and subdivided according to similarities and differences through a top-level ontology

[1] www.ltu.se/cms_fs/1.101555!/file/LivingLabsMethodologyBook_web.pdf.

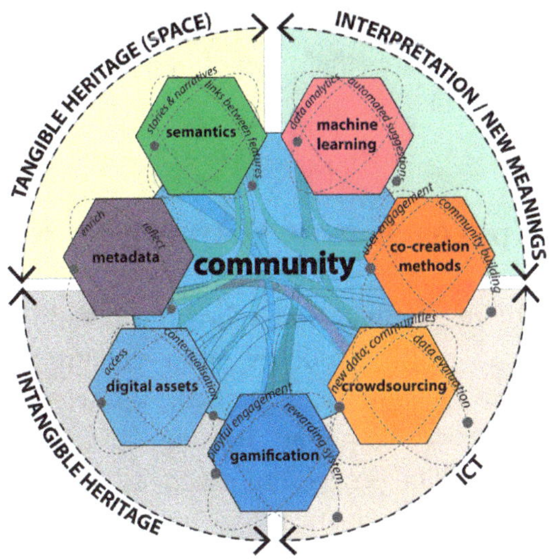

Fig. 2. Community building is the motive force of the research. By enabling this process, this platform exploits the capacity of disparate existing digital assets and local communities in order to document, collect, analyse and communicate users' interpretations of European heritage.

suitably expanded to cover the selected parts of the cases' domains. Note that localisation of ICH assets can be obtained by a number of many methods and techniques, such as automatically by Bluetooth (Nilsson et al. 2003) or user interaction with maps.

2. Users' level, each one playing different roles into the platform as explained above in data lifecycle: the cultural operator, who will provide the 1st metadata level, i.e., the museum that owns a fado song; the cultural bearer, who will provide the 2nd metadata level, i.e. a fado singer; the common, non-expert user, who will provide the 3rd metadata level, i.e., the visitor who will enrich the ICH with own narratives; the researcher who will interact with the ontology and machine learning; and the admin who will administrate and develop further the platform.

The ICT platform, available on cloud and accessible through computers and mobile applications, consists of the following main components:

1. A mobile application, as the main interface between the space and the application server. Through this mobile app a user can upload new digital assets, insert comments on previous uploaded digital assets, reproduce them, and map dynamic information on relevant site visual representations.
2. The website, as the main portal for crowdsourcing activities (Kontkanen et al. 2016) which integrates digital assets creation and visualisation tools. The web-based access GUI enables remote visitors to become users of data and metadata available for crowdsourcing applications that will drive not only dissemination policies of the cultural players involved (e.g., Museums, collections and archives) but will also empower the system's analytical capacity in research with the power of the many.
3. The machine learning algorithm which will produce suggestions and recommendations to the users based on different criteria according to the semantic structure of the digital assets.

4. The database, which deals with the development and execution of architectures, policies, practices and procedures that properly manage the full data lifecycle needs of the ICT platform (Fig. 1).

4 An Innovative Approach to ICH Interpretation

The most current need of researchers and scholars operating in the field of digital cultural heritage is how to produce quality from quantity, how to devise critical methodologies that produce meaning and generate knowledge out of big data. The process of interpretation is cross-disciplinary in nature and involves various faculties of human activity that rely on data processing, such as logical reasoning, associative analysis, descriptive capacity, linguistics and semiotic processes, decoding, and therefore cognition, abstraction and visualization, in order to reveal patterns and narratives, address the whole and provoke affection. After more than a decade of large-scale digitization processes spurring from most museum, libraries and archives, the next big challenge that all cultural heritage stakeholders are facing is to make sense, to add value and establish methods of interpretation that are common, comprehensive, sharable and easily applicable to the vast archives of data and complexity of digital assets in big data.

Existing digital platforms foster collaborations among specialists instead of promoting transdisciplinary research, e.g., researchers in museums, collections, cultural and social institutions and organizations are usually establishing intra-institutional collaborations, e.g. the H2020 e-Infrastructures Project Virtual research environment for regional interdisciplinary communities in Southeast Europe and the Eastern Mediterranean[2]. Even more so CH user communities point to the strong need for tools that will enrich the capacity of researchers to utilize technological advances to move beyond digitisation tools and storage of data, seeking for new tools that will enable them to address critical interpretation problems of ICH, an area of research that due to its context is highly transdisciplinary but has yet to invest in the digital in order to transform its models and practices. Mobile app platforms and services already available on the market include: Detour[3] is a GPS-enabled audio guide that contains audio clips for historical or pop culture spots around the globe. It can sync with other smartphones that run the application so that many people experience the same audio tour at the same time; Guidekick[4] is built for the San Francisco Bay Area's top historical destinations with fully interactive 3D maps, music, and narrative clips. Figure 3 illustrates a possible feature of the interface envisaged by the concept using the ICH Patios de Cordoba.

The CyberParks Songs and Stories concept builds on existing repositories (provided by the cultural operators of each case of ICH) to offer an innovative combination of automation (using machine learning methods) and crowd-sourcing (user

[2] www.vi-seem.eu.

[3] www.detour.com.

[4] www.guidekick.co.

Fig. 3. A possible interface for user interface with existing digital assets and user-input data, such as a voice-over describing aspects of the community about the Patios, and a sketch of a GUI for collecting experiential data by the users of the mobile app [right column].

contextualisation and reasoning), combining machine and human processing. This effort is innovative in several ways:

1. **Ensuring social inclusiveness to the data-knowledge-space continuum in heritage**. Through walking, individuals interfere with physical features and obstructions, disruptions of movement, points of stasis and unpredictable situations in space, moments that intensify lived experience. The platform captures and map users' interest in heritage, and through this process, enables in-depth analysis of heritage sites' management, everyday use and occupation along with its associated cultural identities. The Living Lab methodology (FormIT) and its co-creation tools, canvases and templates offer opportunities for knowledge transfer between disciplines and user communities (e.g., cultural institutions workers, academic researchers, the creative industry and social groups). The concept innovates in combining participatory techniques with advanced digital tools in order to promote social innovation and engage individuals and groups related with specific ICH in the development of these tools - contributing to local communities feeling ownership of the tools and therefore reaching better stakes in the sustainability of the platform. The experiences of similar projects have indicated that social innovation can benefit from the integration of local community knowledge, while participatory process can contribute to enhance the self-confidence and organisational structures of local communities. Sustaining and enhancing the impact of the approach in the long run requires developing or identifying institutions that will perform work after the completion of such project, actively engaging the community as a whole and particularly young people in managing the tool and working on the profitability of the use of the tool (Zoumides 2017).
2. **Crowd-sourcing for adding new meanings**. The added value of the proposed concept is that it will enable the analysis and comparison of informal narratives as

personalised interpretations (i.e., meanings). The experts' descriptions of those historical activities enriched by the (new) narratives will be expanded to include pluralities and variations that up until the present there were no tools to document and process. The enrichment of experts' knowledge with informal understandings and memories of cultural bearers who share a dual interest, not only in the specific cultural heritage but also in its associated space, can contribute to increase the understanding of European heritage.

3. **Gamification for collecting interpretations and meanings**. Gamification (through usage of badges, scoreboards, etc.) and playful engagement of users through storytelling, created by heritage experts rather than the entertainment industry, as in typical tourism-orientated mobile apps, and exploitation of collective intelligence through the introduction of a rewarding system for users that exploits the potential of gamification. The concept will have to give incentives to all types of users, those who add data (and metadata); who explore, assess data (and metadata) and offer suggestions to enrich them; and who exploit the platform. Playful user engagement can have multiple modes of interaction, described as they will be offered to common users inviting them to explore the associated knowledge or enrich it with their own experiences: Interactive stories, soundscapes, guided tours, audio adventure games, scavenger hunts, etc.
4. **Machine learning for knowledge sharing and advanced searching.** Automated semantic classification, machine learning for data analytics and personalized suggestions, and crowd-sourcing in service of heritage studies. A telling example of this innovative approach is the case of users searching in the proposed platform for a specific keyword related with a popular Fado song and being led by the automated suggestion feature of the platform to discover a relevant event to links behaviourally or thematically to the ICH of Patios – and this association facilitates the users to understand the topic they queried for from another point of view. Today changes in education and in society place new demands in learning process. Students are expected to become autonomous learners in order to self-discover knowledge rather than memorizing static information. They are asked to adopt more collaborative and critical approaches to learning than before. The discussed concept can function as a didactic platform addressed to the public that would make complex, otherwise unattainable, knowledge accessible by opening up the educational process to communities of the city that may be excluded, thus responding to the call for lifelong learning.

5 Discussion

The concept introduced is highly inter- and multi-disciplinary ranging from the consideration of social inclusion and gamification aspects to the application of crowd-sourcing and machine-learning techniques. The belief is that the societal impact would be large if such a system would be employed for enriching public spaces with localized culture heritage material. The impacts could be:

1. Widening the access to digitized songs and stories, to which today inherently limited to archives and museums. The potential of (mobile) Internet access to more effectively spread cultural content and knowledge is therefore huge.
2. The meta-data collected through multiple annotation processes (expert assessments, crowd-sourcing and machine learning) furthermore increase the searchability of the digitized songs and stories. Content will now be able to be match to users' context and situation as well as be possible to match with keywords expressed in an ontology structure.
3. Enriching the digitized songs and stories will furthermore add value to users. For example, digitized songs and stories can be provided with additional information and related content such as users' own versions based on the archived content.

All in all, ICH digital assets such as digitized songs and stories can thus reach a much wider audience and interest, promoting cultural heritage and its place in the modern European society. The connections between the ICH digital assets and public spaces are very important, as they provide an effective context for identifying and promoting cultural heritage. From a technical perspective, the most prominent novelties lye within the systemization of such a solution, but there are particular challenges identified:

4. The data management of the ICH digital assets is complex, as they can be stored in numerous types of archives and have various access rights. Creating one open and homogeneous system for access to the ICH digital assets are therefore a huge challenge.
5. In addition, user created content used to annotate ICH digital assets in archives are often of a more private nature, such that personal integrity issues need to be carefully considered. Users must be adequately informed; their consent retrieved and the access control for many types of applications must be provided (including social networks).
6. Perhaps the most challenging technical aspect is to jointly utilise expert knowledge, crowdsourcing and machine learning in conjunction with ontological frameworks to effectively link high quality metadata to ICH digital assets.
7. User involvement is key to the success along with applications and interfaces that support societal processes related to the use of cultural heritage. The creation of APIs for third party developers and the involvement of public organisations, such as related to public places, are therefore an important challenge.

The technologies utilised to expose cultural heritage through open access to ICH digital assets are expected to foster the development of a more inclusive and considering society that bring forth the strength of the multicultural Europe to challenge the trends of growing ultra-nationalism in many countries.

6 Conclusions

This chapter addresses a potential contribution of an innovative methodology for promoting intercultural dialogue beyond Euro-centred views and assumptions by enriching European cultural expressions by means of new knowledge on heritage. It is expected that this practice will create mechanisms that collect and diffuse the cultural assets, e.g. of those who are not established cultural authorities or even by marginalized categories. Through this process it is envisioned that it will safeguard European patrimonies through everyday use of ICH digital assets that offer new ways to enhance the understanding of cultural heritage. Concluding, this research aspires to build intercultural bridges, by offering tools to foster intercultural dialogue, focused on spatially-bound ICH, on immaterial heritage associated with specific locations, to construct an inviting idea of immaterial patrimony in Europe. The technological challenges include how to manage and provide (open) access to ICH digital assets, considering the rights associated to these, how to produce meta-data and annotations to increase quality and searchability, and how to engage users through third party applications.

References

Artopoulos, G., Bakirtzis, N.: Post-digital approaches to mapping memory, heritage and identity in the city. In: Caldwell, G. (ed.) Digital Futures and the City of Today, pp. 139–156. Intellect Books, UK (2016)

Artopoulos, G., Synnes, K., Bahillo, A., Smaniotto Costa, C., Rebernik, N.: Use of data analytics for enriching public spaces with unique experiences of localised cultural heritage content. In: Busch, C., Kassung, C., Sieck, J. (eds.) Kultur and Informatik: Hybrid Systems, pp. 99–112. VWG, Glückstadt (2018)

ELC-European Landscape Convention (preamble) - European Treaty Series - Doc. No. 176

Kontkanen, J., Kärkkäinen, S., Dillon, P., Hartikainen-Ahia, A., Åhlberg, M.: Collaborative processes in species identification using an internet-based taxonomic resource. Int. J. Sci. Educ. **38**, 96–115 (2016)

Manovich, L.: The Language of New Media. MIT Press, Cambridge (2001)

Pratt, M.L.: Arts of the Contact Zones, Profession 91. Modern Language Association, New York (1991, 2005)

Smaniotto Costa, C., Artopoulos, G., Djukic, A.: Reframing digital practices in mediated public open spaces associated with cultural heritage. J. Commun. Lang. **48**, 143–162 (2018)

Stiegler, B.: Our ailing educational institutions: the global mnemotechnical system. Cult. Mach. **5** (2003). http://www.culturemachine.net/index.php/cm/article/viewArticle/258/243

Zoumides, C.: Community-based rehabilitation of mountain terraces in Cyprus. Land Degrad. Develop. **28**, 95–105 (2017)

Nilsson, M., Hallberg, J., Synnes, K.: Positioning with bluetooth. In: 10th International Conference on Telecommunications, ICT2003, pp. 954–958 (2003)

Part IV Digital Hybrids - Between Tool and Methods

Edited by Konstantinos Ioannidis

and Carlos Smaniotto Costa

4.1
Digital Hybrids - Between Tool and Methods: An Introduction and Overview

Konstantinos Ioannidis[1(✉)] and Carlos Smaniotto Costa[2]

[1] aaiko arkitekter, Oslo, Norway
konionn@aaiko.no
[2] Universidade Lusófona, Interdisciplinary Research Centre for Education and Development CeiED, Lisbon, Portugal
smaniotto.costa@ulusofona.pt

Now, with new digital intersections, digital hybrids, digital combinations, the risk is that [space] is simply incapable of thinking of its entire repertoire ... This is the moment where elements [of space] that have never spoken or never listened are turning into communicating elements. Rem Koolhaas, quoted from Winston (2014).

1 Introduction: The Blur of the Physical Space

If last century's conception of open public space was understood as a performance stage where individuals could negotiate and establish relationships not only amongst them but also with elements of spatial manifestation demonstrating the significance of some visual, most times, qualities, a contemporary observer will probably not make this link. Today's conception of outdoor space cannot escape from being injected inside the relatively new scene of simulation which constantly changes the way people experience the given inputs. This scene has dramatically modified the series of our somehow culturally pre-structured views or habitual frames of reference about what is real, virtual, represented, perceived, fragmented or holistically experienced.

In the above introductory quote by Koolhaas, the provocation implied by the use of the words "incapability of thinking", as opposed to "turning into communicating elements", is largely related to the emerging conditions for the public open space in the contemporary post-digital era and the neo-analogue mode of outdoor lifestyle. However, in what follows in these chapters, our point is not just to stress a particular trend in the way ICT transform, rather inevitably, our outdoor living patterns, but to argue that such an incapability opens up the opportunity to challenge the human aspect beyond the digital, both spatially and conceptually. As of this writing, locomotional participation, agency and interactivity between the user and the digitally displayed material projected on a mobile device seem to appear more and more often as critical introductory elements of an evolved method of (re)connecting man, space and information. Mitchell (2004), in his influential Me ++: The Cyborg Self and the Networked City, argues that this is a method of completing "*a long project of seamlessly integrating our mobile biological bodies with globally extended systems of nodes and linkages*". For this session, these are not only simulation techniques that are called to somehow respond to the digital growth of our analogue surroundings. They also offer to a method

C. Smaniotto Costa et al. (Eds.): CyberParks, LNCS 11380, pp. 241–250, 2019.
https://doi.org/10.1007/978-3-030-13417-4_19

of decrypting that reassigns meanings and referents between man and space, between digital and physical landscapes. In this respect, the proposed method explores different mechanisms of awareness: tropes that manifest themselves as systems of hyperconnectivity in Mitchell's (2014:58) sense and as an arsenal of emerging concepts like those of blended spaces, digital hybrids, user empowerment or enhanced connectivism.

Some of the functional and methodological aspects out of these concepts are highlighted in the following chapters. Within them, the term digital hybrids makes it possible for the idea of enhancing places to detach from the "functional code" and refer to the process whereby research techniques and methodologies can standoff from the mute digitization of outdoor spatial experience. It could be argued that it is in book part thanks to multidisciplinary collaborative research, like the CyberParks TU1306 Project, that alternative forays for digitally mediated agency are currently explored. Moreover, we can argue that the detachment from the functionality of the code and the shift in thinking with the digital is somehow grounded upon Tomas Elsaesser's "cinema effect" and the "*cinematic perception* [that] *has become internalized as our mode of cognition and embodied experience*."[1] The necessity and abundancy of outdoor wireless hotspots and our perversely regulated culture by screen driven actions (walking in streets while watching a mobile device for example) validate this peculiar effect and perception.

Re-situating the argument of Elsaesser in our contemporary living patterns, we are at the threshold in which a broad range of disciplines – from architecture, design and the humanities to ICT and media. All call for acknowledge the limits of our ability to keep "thinking with thoughts" when there seems to be a pervasive replacement of our thoughts by digitally moving images. The German film theorist is thus suggesting tracing the multiple dynamics of this replacement and, in doing so, drawing on a range of new strategies and techniques. Indeed, during the 2010 s', new terms slip into the practice of enhancing places – digitization, multimedia, installation, interaction, interpretation, process-driven experiential strategies, and collective culture – to describe new abilities to steer pathways through open public space development and the individual participation to access, retrieve and interact with the wirelessly transmitted information which scarcely existed before the 1990 s.

Today, there is a considerable number of research initiatives with similar and even more interactive initiatives working with the making of mediated public spaces. Many of them depend on the locomotional position and the active participation of the user, making them promising examples for the neo-analog scene that this book prefigured at the beginning. By just reading and exploring further some of them presented within the previous sessions one can argue that the battle for humanizing the postdigital outdoor landscape is about to be won. While most of them deal with the interaction between real and virtual, arguably the epitome of the "simulation" heritage, it is no surprise that within them the issue of the mediated place keeps blending seamlessly with the question how the physical space can employ the digital component to motivate, engage and inject the user to the hyperconnectivity of the information.

[1] Here quoted from Reimer H. (2009). Awaiting the voice-over: the Øresund Film Commission location database and the mediatization of architectural landscape. In Chaplin and Stara (Eds.). Curating Architecture and the City. Taylor & Francis, p. 72.

This fourth session does not intent to equate the computational turn in placemaking as the possibility for hybrid outdoor experiences with digital platforms and applications per se. This has already been done by the endless online projects that everyone with a mobile "on the go" connection can access and retrieve in many parks and squares. The turn - heavily based on rapidly changing technologies - has already been shifted by time. The "cinema effect" is here understood as a critique to those digital modes of outdoor activities that revolve around the view that the offer of online information is the primary and user engagement with space is secondary. We can thus question the passivity of the search and retrieval powers of the "databases on the go", accepting a research into new dimensions formed from a neo-analog materiality. In this sense, the session attempts to inquire some creative ways in which the intellectual properties of the man - space relationship can reside within the structure of digitally enhanced experiences, even when traditional aspect of our outdoor living have been filtered and transferred to a projected immaterial state.

While outdoor human tasks are in a way even more pervasively regulated by machines, the humanistic content of the interaction often raises them in a more conceptual level. Cramer (2014), writing for A Peer Reviewed Journal About Post-Digital Research, described them as *"neo-analog do-it-yourself"* approaches that distant themselves from their "post-digital" predecessors that were simply referring "*to a state in which the disruption brought upon by digital information technology has already occurred*". Here, the term "neo-analog" doesn't refer to a chronological descendant of the post-digital, but to a shift that causes a new perspective to be emerged, one that expresses itself in complex patterns of user - machine interrelated activities, interlinked variables, and so forth. To some extent, we trace such intellectual/interactive tendencies in different neo-analogue methodologies and projects found around the web: from generative mindmaps, force-feedback algorithms to digital semantic relations, applications for visual music etc. Moving the issue of methodology to the foreground of a neo-analogue environment, offers us a great challenge to question the limits of hyperconnectivity in outdoor open public spaces.

This session situates the chapters within such a challenge and considers their innovative character to be a result not only of technological solutions but also of a humanistic re-orientation and re-focus. Having this in mind, it is rather critical to draw a distinction between two central aspects of our contemporary outdoor landscape given by man - machine convergence, a distinction according to which the digital can identify itself as a tool and as a of method.

The first aspect, in the sense of a "diagnostic" medium to access and investigate dimensions of the man/machine interaction, enables scholars to use the digital dimension in order to challenge the traditional boundaries that distinguish the spatial experience from the virtual one. Only the last decade, through transdisciplinary researches and explorations, we have come into possession of a challenging "functioning" tool with which places (and not only) have been enhanced and reactivated. From haptic or conversational interfaces of (some) embodied intelligence to platforms and networked systems of computers that capture and analyse inductive or deductive user responses, the idea of the digital as a medium tool to understand the importance of connectivity in different levels has significantly evolved the last decade. Yet it was only during the early-2010s that the idea of enhancing the already mediated public space received a distinctive typology: that of programming good public spaces by focusing "*on the ability of digital technology to enhance communication and interaction with (potential) users, as a way to transform the production and uses of public spaces into an interactive process, enabling creative community participation and empowerment*" (Smaniotto Costa 2017:19). To mention an example, the CyberParks Project (2014–2018) explored the typology of the mediated and hybrid outdoor place by investigating "*the shape and scope of ICT impacts and the opportunities opened to improve the legibility and liveability of urban spaces, as well as new forms of integrating people's needs into urban design processes*" (ibid:19). The second aspect of the method, in the sense of combining an intellectual inquiry into the digital landscape, refers to the cultivated logic beyond the tool and refers to user's agents of decision and choice.

2 Digital Methods and Tools onto Hybrid Space

The idea of the digital as a tool to increase the understanding of different levels of connectivity and to transform this knowledge into workings methods winged the discussions in Working Group 1 Digital Methods - of the CyberParks COST Action TU1306. The aim of this working group was to explore the digital as tool inserted into a research or methodology to increase the knowledge on people's use of public spaces (from current uses to future needs). This made the call to examine also user-behaviours and user's spatial needs. Within this working group scientific, technical and sociological information (or opportunities) were assessed, all relevant for understanding the interweaving of people in (and with) public spaces. Field experiments with new tools and methodologies were undertaken in several case studies.

The following chapters in Part IV, are based on the outcomes of the Working Group on Digital Methods. This working group had as main objectives: (1) to identify promising working approaches with ICT-tools and promote their use/test in different case studies; and (2) aggregate the experiences gained in the cases studies to a structure that help to better understand the ICT-tools available. For this an integrated framework could be useful, especially for aiding the development of people-friendly cities or the building of the communities' capacity to engage with their environment. The first step consisted on defining a classification rationale and a structure to specify the different uses and ways of penetration of technology into public spaces. This task was more easily said than done. First, the interactions between people and places were crucial for the CyberParks Project, and this interactions are per se a very large area of work, as demonstrated in the diversity of the topics tackled in this book. Second, this large area of work becomes even larger when the digital intertwines places and people relations. Fact is that there are several ways to tackle the pervasiveness of ICTs, which is intensified by the speed of technological development. Innovation is entering both the market and the city at an accelerated pace (Smaniotto Costa et al. 2017), challenging not only users but also those who want to understand their benefits in the medium and ling term. The Working Group on Digital Methods worked out three different frameworks – these are not mutually exclusive but can be used in complementary ways.

The first framework for an integrated approach resulted in a structure according to the degree of users' engagement along with the device/media/application used.

Thc framework is displayed in form of a tree-structure that groups the identified ICT-technologies into four main categories: Augmented Reality, Localization Technology, Wireless Network and Vision Technology. These four main dimensions are closely related to spatial quality, user needs, spatial attributes and added value delivered by the provision/implementation/availabily of ICT in public spaces. This framework backed the research design in the case studies developed within the Project. The results of case studies are described in several chapters of this book (Fig. 1).

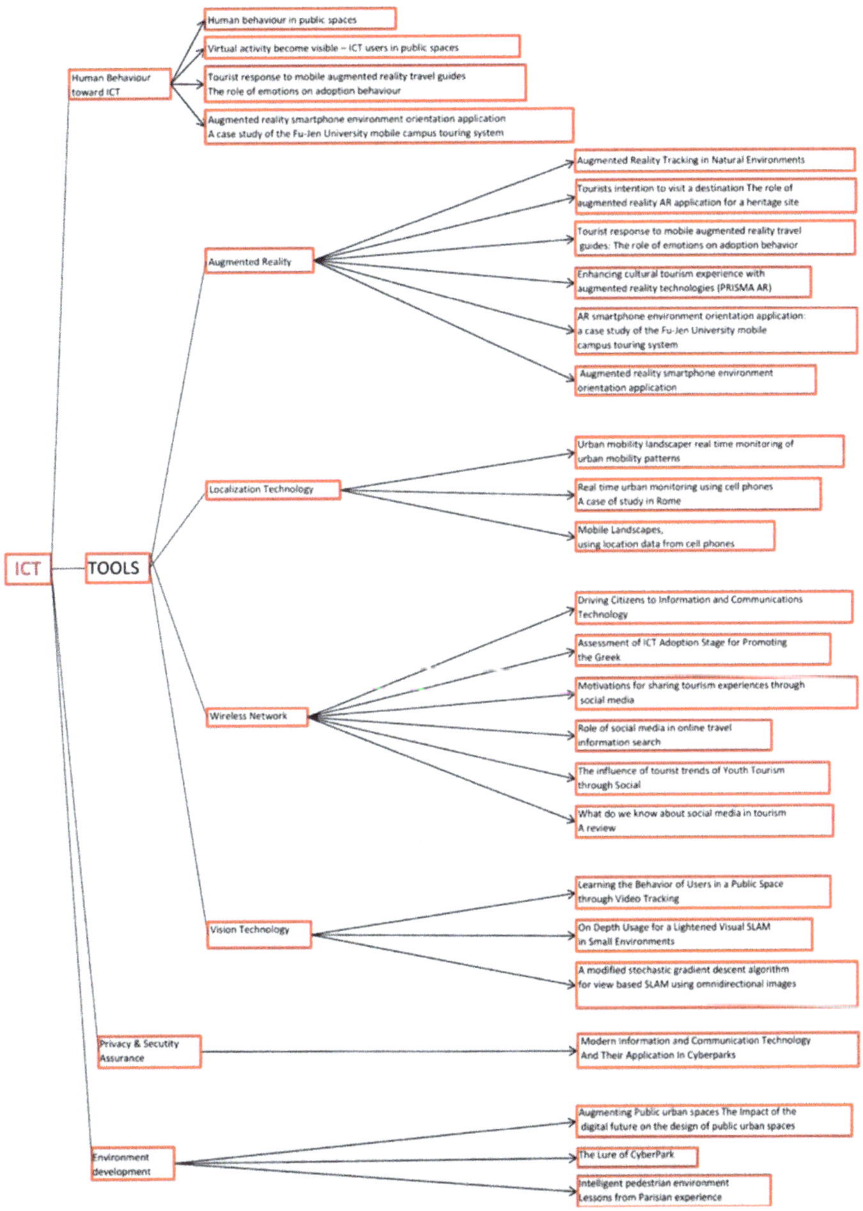

Fig. 1. Shows the main structure to understand the diffusion of the digital into public spaces

The second framework is based on the matrix of the applied technology and the added value this application results for users and uses of places. In this framework, the technology is understood in three categories: Position Informatics, Sensory informatics and Synergetic interfaces, when implemented in public spaces these technologies can result in several benefits (added values). The added values are listed as Enhance publicness, Increase the performance of public spaces, Increase the production and co-creation of public spaces, Increase the understanding on users, Increase the understanding on uses, Dissemination of information in/about public spaces, and the Use of ICT as a support and challenge for new outdoors activities. This framework is used in the POOL OF EXAMPLES[2] the Project CyberParks established. The Pool offers a wide range of examples of the penetration of technology into public spaces. Based on the available technology (selected into the three categories), a response matrix was built with the types of public spaces. With the Pool CyberParks seeks to increase the understanding of the benefits of technology to enhance places in order to achieve an added value (i.e. new outdoor experiences, innovative ways of using places).

The third framework is built according to the purposes of the ICT into spaces. This can be primarily structured in three major dimensions: (1) for research, i.e. as a way to produce, collect, manage, mediate and interpret data, (2) for design, i.e. as a range of possibilities for conceiving and/or creating public spaces, and (3) for implementation, i.e. by looking onto the transformations of the material production of space and and/or social interaction triggered by the continuous introduction of new hardware and software (Fig. 2). Further insights on this framework can be obtained at Smaniotto Costa et al. (2017).

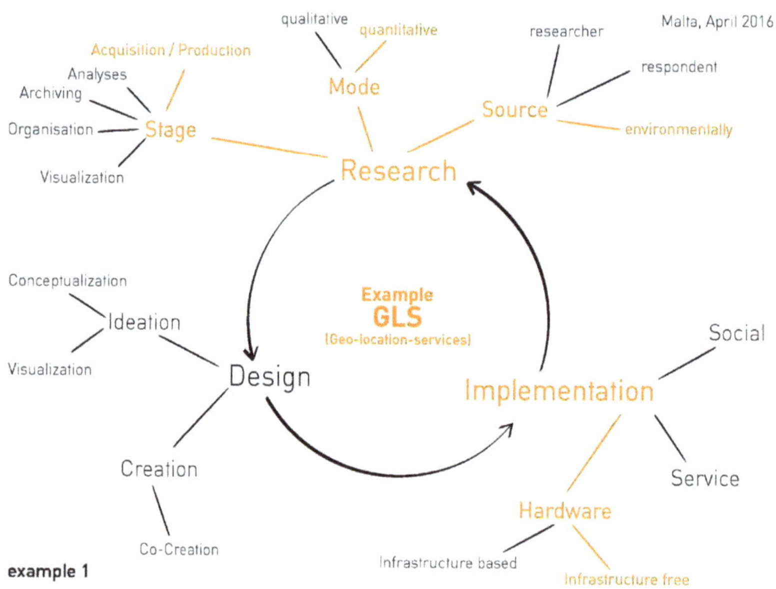

Fig. 2. Shows three modes of ICT use; highlighting the example of Geo-location services, it demonstrates the different subsystems or components, i.e. for research and implementation.

These three frameworks evidence the need to adopt integrated frameworks, those that enables a full overview on the benefits of technology advancements, and as noted above these are taking place at a rapid pace, challenging users, designers and

[2] The Pool is available at www.cyberparks-project.eu/examples, and enables the searching, navigating and adding new examples.

researchers. As highlighted in this introduction, public spaces remain a timeless patrimony and in Smaniotto Costa et al. (2017:172) about the quality of places, which [...] *remains a central issue, even in the digital era. No one will leave their home and use a public space, if it isn't safe or doesn't offer the requirements. Quality public spaces make up the richness of urban life.*"

3 Overview of Chapters

Acknowledging that digital hyperconnectivity usually offers the norms that affect people's behaviour and decisions, we can embark on a much larger investigation that touches fields that are heavily defined by humanities such as response, education or cognitive development. In this sense, and although interrelated, the "method" can be conceptually separated from the "tool" and it is in this sense that some chapters of this session present their working hypothesis.

In the first chapter (4.2) of part IV, **Barbora Čakovská, Mária Bihuňová, Preben Hansen, Ernesto Marcheggiani and Andrea Galli** in **Methodological Approaches to Reflect on the Relationships Between People, Spaces, Technologies** describe different methodologies, backed by their rationales. The authors are convinced that the ICT advancements can lead to increase in attractiveness of public spaces for both citizens and visitors. Moving in and through the space and understanding its features is still an important human activity, and as such it is susceptible to changes. In the blended space, so the authors, designers need to create and establish interfaces and systems that enable people to shape and achieve their goals and aspirations. These interfaces should include and inherit different physical, digital, perceptual, sensory and conceptual point of contact that are between people and the content that is contained and accessible by.

Following this, in chapter 4.3 **In Modelling co-creation ecosystem for public open spaces**, **Aelita Skarzauskiene, Monika Maciuliene and Petja Ivanova-Radovanova** argue that the logic of ecosystem presents a valid template for a tentative method toward the exploration of the new context and relationships between people, places and technology. The dynamics in the co-creative ecosystem propose an alternative reading of embedded networks based on the process of value creation. Inquiring the role (of actors) becomes a method by which to dislocate aspects of the network in a manner through which we can rethink "who can offer value in space". Their model suggests a method of approaching the value as emerging out of "*a number of entities* [that] *work collectively to create mutual benefits by granting access to one another's resources including people, technologies, organizations and information*".

In chapter 4.4 **Eneko Osaba, Roberto Pierdicca, Tiago Duarte, Alfonso Bahillo and Diogo Mateus** in the work entitled **Using ICTs for the Improvement of Public Open Spaces: The Opportunity offered by CyberParks Digital Tools**, introduce the three tools developed by the CyberParks teams: WAY CyberParks, CyberCardeto and EthnoAlly. The functionalities and features of each tool are described and discussed on the basis of different case studies. Backed by different technology and developed with different purposes, the three tools open for an interaction between researchers, city councils and users an innovative and wide range of possibilities. They offer valuable resources to make a significant contribution to the study of public spaces, enabling a quick and efficient collection of data, essential for a better understanding the interactions of people with the spaces. On the flip side, the tools allow users to get dynamic contextual information related to space, and therefore a better knowledge about their surroundings. The common feature of the three tools are free to use across the world.

To meet the posed challenge to better understand the benefits of mediated places, the chapter 4.5 by **Bonanno, Klichowski and Lister: A Pedagogical Model for CyberParks**, attempts to redefine the field of pedagogy as a composite neo-analogue experience involving intra-individual cognitive, affective and conative interactions together with inter-individual, networked, interactional processes. In their contribution, they theorise the "society of mediated learning" with digital tools while on the move and present a methodological insistence on *"learning by combining two types of cerebral operations: motor and cognitive control*". The authors further contend that the hybrid environments may trigger deep learning, this in turn changes one's competence profile and epistemological conception. Cyberpark, the mediated place, challenge people, so the authors: *to extend their learning boundaries through acquisition of new knowledge and skills, by sharing their understanding and by contributing to the distributed knowledge and networked experience.*

The final chapter 4.6 by **Jamal Raiyn and Jugoslav Jokovic**, entitled **The application of advanced IoT in public spaces towards promote their safer use**, examines how IoT can be used to manage the resources in hybrid places. The central issue of the authors is to clarify the opportunities of IoT tools in public spaces to prevent crime and to increase the safety of users. Their analysis contributes to a broader discussion towards their primarily interest: developing a new scheme for securing the privacy of users in a mediated public space.

Methodological aspects of digital mediacy in public open spaces have become part not only of our digital culture but also of our own evolved mechanisms of thinking and understanding space and place. The rising number of online cutting-edge technologies that undertake the task of dislocating outdoor experience from the analogue space of coordinate relations to the digital landscape and virtual reality of algorithmic relations is a testament to the distinction between using the digital as a "tool" and as a "method". Grasping the opportunities that the mediated space open is a central issue in the chapters of Čakovská et al. (4.2) and Osaba et al. (4.4), and Raiyn and Jokovic (4.6) to some extent. In their arguments the authors place emphasis on ICT as a tool and as method to increase knowledge through data analysis - with different tools and through different methods - the relational aspects between the physical places and users. Undoubtedly, the analogue space of urban squares and green parks remains a timeless patrimony, a constitutive dimension that deeply embeds itself to our cities as an engenderment of the materiality and physicality of urban form. It is also the traditional medium by which the logic of its symbolic systems and intellectual combinatory in the poetic world of Bachelard (1994) are transformed into material variations, allowing thus the reasoning human mind be attached to the sensible world. The analogue is the forefather; that necessary element which public space is tied up with in order to lend itself to further dialectical investigations that extend beyond the practical function of its forms. Čakovská et al. (Chapter 4.2) argue further that space is largely build by society and it makes no sense to conceive space without a social content, just as society does not exist without a spatial component. This interdependency, in a continuous process, creates and modifies spaces, while such transformed space at the same time influences the society. It is the common starting point from which we are infused in even more complex conceptions of either geometric or symbolic order - to mention one example, Arnheim's (2004) symbolic readings of forms seized upon the field of the analogue and its visual qualities as a way to project them "as images of the human condition" instead. The process and context dimensions of the network, as articulated in Skarzauskiene, Maciuliene and Ivanova-Radovanova's view (chapter 4.3), epitomize the heterogeneity of the co-creative dimension, essential for the understanding of the humanist content of the proposed ecosystem.

However, the chapters of this part argue that in the contemporary digitally mediated landscape in which the materiality and physicality of things give place to the impression drawn from protocol-based representations (computational images, animations or texts), we impose upon our conception of space a topological dislocation technique that has, quite literally, a reversible logic. In an interesting way, and from Arnheim's perception-and-response to the analogue stimuli evolving conception, the (post)digital dimension brings in a significant effect on this traditional process retaining at the same time its humanist condition - that is the active and personal aspects found within. The displacement, reacting to the withdrawal of the analogue materiality, seems to inaugurate a reversed method to understand man - machine interaction: from the observer's responses to data elements, the mind is challenged to construct an a posteriori perceptual content in the imaginary register, or better a trace to use a laconic term. This content is not as deterministic as its precedent analogous one, but can resurface in alternative versions based on an exchange of conscious and unconscious thought. However, is this trace enough to speak about a digitally-inspired method beyond the functioning tool and any technological underpinnings of the displacement? The chapters of this session suggest that the answer to this question is not an easy one while more complicated phenomena may appear. The digital mediacy doesn't only refer to "functional" aspects like information visualization and its presentation as a collection of online material. As argued by Bonanno, Klichowski and Lister (chapter 4.5), it goes into the transposition of deeper parts of the outdoor activity that take place in human mind, in desire, in mental patterns and conscious or unconscious organizational mechanisms. These are the deeper aspects that traditionally bound spatial experience with the subject/object relation. They are responsible for the possibility of the mind, by the use of the digital dimension, to implicate in transformational processes from abstract and intelligible thought to enhanced perceived relations. And in a sense, these are the main aspects from within mediated places enact as a dialectic activity between subject and object and begin to exist as a reflecting method outside the physical or Euclidean space.

The shift from Tool to Method is the departure point to discuss this apparent difficulty and the oxymoron that brings in: the digitalization and dislocation of experience that is meant to be analogue. This session is not at all about "mere digitization" and online dissemination of information. It is about how to turn, momentarily at least, a functional tool into a method by relating human mental activities like learning, desire, meaning and reason acquisition to an artificial intelligence.

In reading the following chapters, we have to say, the first reflex is to dismiss the concept of a "neo-age" from a nostalgic and mimetic revival of stereotyped ways of experiencing the contemporary public space, one that abolish space's valuable heritage from its injection with the digital technologies. It is an objective fact that the emerging methodologies discussed within the following chapters approach the space-related data as being "digital" almost by definition. Data to be collected, sorted, shared and reused across dynamically established links between analogue (human tasks) and digital (computational executions) methods of thinking and acting. In the age of the semiotic web and the web 3.0, these modes are nowadays beyond interactivity. They are intelligent forms of studying information based, for example, on users' personal desires and aspirations while utilising probabilistic parameters or algorithmic decision-making. As the chapters discuss later on, the neo-analogue methodologies presented from within the following pages propose a hybrid attitude preserving at the same time the analogue and symbolic value of open public space within digital actions.

References

Arnheim, R.: Art and Visual Perception: A Psychology of the Creative Eye. University of California Press, Berkeley (2004)

Bachelard, G.: The Poetics of Space. Beacon Press, Boston (1994)

Cramer, F.: What is 'Post-digital'? A Peer Reviewed Journal About Post-Digital Research (2014). http://www.aprja.net/?p=1318. Accessed 03 Sep 2014

Mitchell, W.: Me++: The Cyborg Self and the Networked City, p. 58. MIT Press, Cambridge (2004)

Smaniotto Costa, C.: A framework for defining principles for inclusive mediated public open spaces. In: Smaniotto Costa, C., Ioannidis, K. (eds.) The Making of the Mediated Public Space: Essays on Emerging Urban Phenomena, pp. 17–24. Lusófona University Press, Lisbon (2017)

Smaniotto Costa, C., Ioannidis, K. (eds.): The Making of the Mediated Public Space: Essays on Emerging Urban Phenomena. Lusófona University Press, Lisbon, Portugal (2017)

Winston, A.: "Scary" Venice Architecture Biennale show has "nothing to do with design" says Koolhaas (2014). www.dezeen.com/2014/06/05/rem-koolhaas-venice-architecture-biennale-2014. Accessed 22 Nov 2018

4.2

Methodological Approaches to Reflect on the Relationships Between People, Spaces, Technologies

Barbora Čakovská[1](✉), Mária Bihuňová[1], Preben Hansen[2], Ernesto Marcheggiani[3,4], and Andrea Galli[3]

[1] Horticulture and Landscape Engineering Faculty, Slovak University of Agriculture, Nitra, Slovakia
barboralipovska@gmail.com, bihunova.maria@gmail.com

[2] Department of Computer and Systems Sciences, Stockholm University, Stockholm, Sweden
preben@dsv.su.se

[3] Department of Agricultural, Food and Environmental Sciences, Università Politecnica delle Marche, Ancona, Italy
{e.marcheggiani,a.galli}@univpm.it

[4] Department of Forest, Nature and Landscapes, KU Leuven, Leuven, Belgium

Abstract. Social behaviour in public spaces has changed over the time and has become attractive to all those involved in designing people's spaces. Communities in different countries in Europe have shown more and more interest and various activities have started to shape the public spaces all round the world. The main objective of the chapter is to review development of the methodologies that have been used to analyse public spaces worldwide and to summarize their requirements and conditions to suggest how they can be applied in order to analyse the relationship between people and spaces, with the aim to boost the active participation of people in design process. The chapter describes the methodologies using ICTs, especially e-participation, mobile technologies, GIS systems, or on the methodologies increasing the attractiveness of the public open spaces for citizens and visitors (laser holograms, QR codes, interactive boards, online and interactive maps, questionnaires and social interaction, etc.). Information technology offers new potentials of citizen participation and provides a communication platform, which suppresses a barrier of non-professionalism, allowing for distant contacts and enabling participatory process management. Users, accustomed to communicating through ICT also in public spaces, feel by using this tool more anonymous and less harassed to express their opinion. Not only ICT are important in the 21st century society, but also new ways of social media, which are accessible/open to use for larger group of people. The institutions or municipalities could use them as semi-official information platform, public open discuss forums or resource of the public initiatives.

Keywords: Blended spaces · Public space users · E-participation · Playful tools · Top-down initiatives · Urban planning

C. Smaniotto Costa et al. (Eds.): CyberParks, LNCS 11380, pp. 251–261, 2019.
https://doi.org/10.1007/978-3-030-13417-4_20

1 Introduction

Carr et al. (1992) regard public space as "the common ground where people carry out the functional activities that bind a community, whether in the normal routines of daily life or in periodic festivities". It is the stage upon which the drama of communal life unfolds." For Madanipour (1996) public space is a space we share with strangers, people who aren't our relatives, friends, or work associates. It is space for politics, religion, commerce, sport; space for peaceful coexistence and impersonal encounter. Users are described by Lynch (1984) as all those who interact with the place in any way: live in it, work in it, pass through it, repair it, control it, profit from it, suffer from it, even dream about it.

Space and society are clearly related: it is difficult to conceive of 'space' without social content and, equally, to conceive of society without a spatial component. The relationship is best conceived as a continuous two-way process in which people (and societies) create and modify spaces while at the same time being influenced by them in various ways (Carmona 2003).

People's behaviour in public spaces has become attractive not only for psychologists, sociologists, interaction design or urban geographers but also for urban planners, architects, landscape architects and all those involved in designing people's spaces (Carr et al. 1992; Carmona 2003; Gehl 2011). Social behaviour in public spaces has changed over the time. Communities in different countries in Europe have shown more and more interest in these public spaces and various activities have started to shape these public spaces, or even the landscape where people live. Due to this development a new discipline of environmental participatory design emerged, devoted to researching how built environments work for people and how people affect the public space with their activities (Wheeler 2004).

2 People-Space Methods

The way the urban environment is designed and provides access to the natural environment and different types of activities reflects the current priorities of the society and its level of awareness. The assessments of the urban open spaces have been studied by scientist, architects, planners and sociologists. Several urban design guidelines have been published with the aim to respect the place, its functions, demands of the citizens, improving the quality of the life and environment, support the social contacts or include the minorities to the society and motivate and change social behaviour towards healthy living (Miková et al. 2010; Melková 2014).

It is well known as pollution affects human health and living organisms in general. Nevertheless, recent findings highlight that also the spatial topology and landscape arrangements - not limited to pollution - can lead to structural and functional human disorders. In particular, how brain neurotransmitters and limbic (emotional) systems changes during our life (Vanderhaeghen et al. 2010) as to register environmental inputs is being looked at by new branches of landscape ecology and neuroscience. First results of the so-called landscape Bionomy (Ingegnoli 2015) shows how a redundancy of neuronal connections during infancy is afterwards soon pruned around the age of 5.

This suggests that the environment in which man has to live form the wider part of the input modelling the brain concerns landscape conditions. It is inevitable that landscape structural alterations, could lead to human hilliness, even in absence of pollution. For the physical environment supports human behaviour, the bulk of human-space relationships are of extreme importance.

Researchers developed methods using behaviour observation, time-lapse photography, post-occupancy evaluation surveys, and cognitive mapping (in which people were asked to draw maps or images of how they perceived their urban environments) to provide factual information for improved urban design (Wheeler 2004). Cognitive mapping could be presented as mental maps or parish maps (in which people were asked to draw maps or images of how they perceived their urban environments as well as the open spaces (landscape in a wide sense) to provide factual information for improving the urban design. This method also enables local people and tourists to deeper discover the meaning of places while they enjoy all their attractiveness.

Beginning in the 1960s writers such as Jacobs, Lynch, William H. Whyte, Clare Cooper Marcus and Danish designer Jan Gehl emphasised the need to base urban design on study of how people actually experience and use urban environments. The American urbanist, organizational analyst, journalist and people-watcher William H. Whyte studied human behaviour in urban settings. He observed, and film analysed plazas, urban streets, parks and other open spaces in New York City. All told, Whyte walked the city streets for more than 16 years. As unobtrusively as possible, he watched people and used time-lapse photography to chart the meanderings of pedestrians. What emerged through his intuitive analysis is an extremely human, often amusing view of what is staggeringly obvious about people's behaviour in public spaces, but seemingly invisible to the inobservant (PPS 1999).

In 1980s Randolph Hester was a leader of planning process in Manteo town (North Carolina, USA). In this process residents identified what they valued about life and about their landscape. Hester comments that these important social patterns and places came to be called the „Sacred Structure "by locals and inspired a plan for community revitalization and development that was controlled by them. Planning focused on behaviour mapping that recorded what people did and where they did it - things that were not revealed in the standard surveys. Activities like the exchange of small talk at the post office, hanging out at the docks, checking out the water for the tides, the fishing, and the weather, happened in the same places every day. Daily rituals indicated a dependence on specific places that could be disrupted by changes in land use. A list of these was developed, and people were asked to rank them in order of their significance, and to indicate which ones could be sacrificed in the interest of tourist facilities. From these was published a map of places that people wanted protected from future development (Hough 1990).

Francis (1984) has presented in his method of downtown and neighbourhood planning the importance of traffic mapping, parking problems and pedestrian flow mapping. Activity mapping as a useful information for planning process was proved by Francis (1984), when he used the activity mapping in Davis town. Based on the activity analyses the design solution was made. The study and research of Danish architect Jan Gehl is worldwide known. In a book Life Between Buildings (2011) he has specified and described outdoor activities in public spaces into three categories, with special needs different demands on the design of the place. There are pointed activities: *necessary, optional and social.*

> *Necessary activities* are activities appeared almost every day, not depended on the weather conditions or willingness of the participants. These are activities as going to work, shopping, waiting for someone, standing on the bus stop.
> *Optional activities* represent voluntary activities, depended on the will of participants, good weather conditions and the suitable design of the outdoor open space. For example, playing games, meeting friends, doing sports or just sitting on the bench and relaxing.
> *Social activities* include active or passive social interaction. They can be seen between all age groups, between friends or people met randomly. Participants do not need to talk necessary, they could just watch or just listen to.

On the method of direct observation and comparison of results from studies that have been made in the urban environment, we can conclude that people in rural areas use public spaces, like in cities (Lipovská and Štěpánková 2013). Although most of these methods could be done in an unobtrusive way, there are time-consuming aspects, which the professionals might consider as inefficient and out-dated. The research published by Nassar (2015) in Egypt prove that is very important to understand human behaviour together with the social aspects of the local community in an urban space to create a design that increases residents' physical activity. He mentions that there is no perfect solution for the space: the goal is simply to create many opportunities by means of landscape features that allow residents to perform different types of physical activity (for different age groups).

Interesting phenomenon in Germany has been described by Schöbel (2006). While during the 20th century, open space planning was based mainly on quantitative arguments, the current change of attitudes and ideas in society has led to a discussion of 'quality of the open spaces instead of quantity'. Contemporary society is experiencing an economic change from an affluent and industrial society to a worldwide service-based society. Analyses of the spatial reality of urban society and urban space indicate that this change is being accompanied and increased by spatial polarisation within cities, which in the end affects the population's social chances. Different cultures and social backgrounds, which meet in the cities create challenges and those must be overcome in urban meta-cultures. Great examples are the Pallas-Park in Berlin's neighbourhood Schöneberg and the Park Spoor Noord in Antwerp's Seefhoek district, when the city councils decided to create urban parks, where the different cultures could meet each other. In England there are many state programmes that support the local communities and interaction with neighbourhood via community gardens and garden education. In the Northern countries (Norway, Sweden) the social policy and state support the residential equipment and qualitative design of open spaces with possibilities to play, practise sports, meet and interact with others. Schöbel (2006) has summarised five planning categories characterising the functions and qualities of the entire structure of urban green and open spaces according to the research done in Berlin. It could be applied in any other city.

The analysis of flows - such as human movements - can help spatial planners better understand territorial patterns in urban environments (Chua 2014; 2016). Nowadays interactive visual interfaces are designed to gather, extract and analyse human flows in geolocated social media data. Such a system adopts a graph-based approach to infer movement pathways from spatial point type data and expresses the resulting information through multiple linked multiple visualisations to support data exploration.

3 People-Space-Technology Methods

The World Economic Forum (2015) published the Top 10 Urban Innovations, which reflect the digital revolution and the best way to improve a city due to increasing number of population and more people living in urban than rural areas. The most interesting are:

1. **Re-programming the space** - Cities have started to look at reprogramming their space to get more from less: reduced its allowable urban footprint; changing the strategy of expansion to concentration; repurposing asphalt to expand footpaths and open space).
2. **Waternet: An Internet of Pipes -** Smart water management models use sensors in network pipes to monitor flows and manage the entire water cycle, providing sustainable water for human and ecological needs.
3. **Adopt a Tree through Your Social Network -** In a database trees could be named, its growth tracked and carbon offset, and data shared through social networks. Each tree could have its own email address which allows citizens to report problems and diseases and even send love letters.
4. **Augmented Humans: The Next Generation of Mobility -** Improved safety for pedestrians and non-motorized transportation leads to greater adoption of public transport, reduced congestion and pollution, better health and commutes that are quicker. Such relatively low-cost solutions include separate bike lanes, bike-sharing schemes, re-phasing traffic lights to fit the speed of bikes and planting trees along the side of roads to slow traffic.

4 How the ICTs Could Influence Public Open Spaces

Online interactive community mapping is the process by which individuals jointly create a community map using modern information and communication technologies (ICT). Such mapping is mostly done to identify the needs and concerns of a community living or brazen in a certain location.

Online interactive mapping is successful if at least some of the following conditions are fulfilled, ideally all. The local community is cardinal, because they are source of local experience and knowledge, they know best what they lack and what would contribute to a better quality of their lives. Second condition is ICT and sufficient e-skills. The local community must have sufficient motivation to participate in mapping. The entire process must have a coordinator and facilitator, best representative of the non-profit sector, scientific community or engaging civilian public. It is very important to collect the information only regarding to the aim of mapping. The final community map is created by locals and is great base for local authorities to solve problems and improve the quality of life.

Žufová (2015) presents on the example of Bratislava City when the citizens could participate at collection of information, pointing at the problems, control the environment. An interactive website for the citizens was established at www.odkazprestarostu.sk, with the mobile applications TrashOut and Park4disabled. Another possibility concerns the implementation of common ICT, e. g app's tools, to share the local knowledge and stories collected through the participatory process among all citizens that takes place when folk museums (or eco-museums) are in a building phase by a participative process involving a community. Actually, online ICT solutions, usually pieces of software broadcasted to public through the Web called applications or "apps" (Castells 2006; Lugano 2008) are easy to use and very popular. This is a very important prerequisite to the ultimate designing of a sound ICT tools, because a participative approach, traditionally build upon the delivering of a so called "parish maps", simply means "*… a dynamic way by which communities preserve, interpret, and manage their heritage for a sustainable development*" (Chart of Catania 2007). A key issue for this kind of projects is how to funnel considerable streams of information across and towards the local communities. Considering the widening on the Web mass communication media (GSM, smartphones, tablets, …), the idea of developing an ICT tools, tailored upon specific characteristics of a given public space or landscape, could represent a useful tool to design and manage these places taking in account all faces of sustainability (economic, ecological, social and cultural).

Nowadays, ICTs are part of everyday life and we still do not use their full potential. This potential could be understood in positive or negative usage. To create the New Social Place of the era of digitalisation, spaces must follow the concept of "human information interaction", which is a concept based on the relation between human, space, and information technologies. Aziz, et al. (2016) define four elements of ICT: Wi-Fi networks, digital interactive media façades, interactive public displays, and smartphones' applications in public spaces. These elements play major roles in the public space in terms of culture and art; education; planning and design; games and entertainment and information and communication. Clever use of ICTs helps to increase the attractiveness of the space, the interaction between people as well as between people and the space around them, which will foster the sense of place and the sense of belonging to the space.

To this purpose, the design of the logical model of an app/tool is the first and very crucial point to deal with. Referring to an experience led in Italy, Galli et al. (2014) were inspired at the contents of the "Parish Map of Montacuto, Paggese and other Acquasanta's villages" (Ascoli Piceno, Italy). The design of this mobile app aimed to provide "virtual scenarios" that reproduce, for example, thematic itineraries around characteristic areas represented in the "parish maps" with the aim to show the point of view (cultural, environmental, social) coming from communities living there. The app, to be used on mobile devices such as GSM, smartphones and tablets, has been engineered in order to offer thematic itineraries discovering the authentic local identity and sense of place. The routes are articulated in "role itineraries", each of them makes visitors to feel as visit-actors, playing roles as if they were a member of the local community, which are based on typical "local characters" of daily working activities in that territorial context. The "virtual scenarios" consist mainly of a map of the area, from which, some itineraries can be chosen by clicking on the icons representative of the of available "local characters". Moreover, users can upload and share new original contents, which the app makes visible to all the other members connected through social networks. In this way the "virtual scenarios" can be updated any time users upload new contents, bringing a continuous evolution to scenarios and a higher degree of vitality into social community. In few words, the app orients and encourages both local people and tourists to keep interactively a specific Parish Map alive. A similar approach could be effectively applied to tailor each app tool on the main characteristics of every public space, if the fundamental help of local people were actively favoured (Galli et al. 2015).

A key issue remains the development of innovative ways to manage the most remarkable comments coming from the users (insiders and outsiders) of the app; and how to foster the participation of administrators and land managers, in order to refuel the debate on the sustainable development of public spaces. Hampton (2014) compared the time-lapse photography of both William Holly Whyte and PPS to analyse human behaviour in the public space of Bryant Park in the early 1980s to contemporary observations by filming the same public space from similar angles. He is convinced that mobile device users provide a number of benefits to the social life of spaces, people are actually more likely to spend time in groups and there has been increase of women. Even if people are alone checking the news, reading blogs, or talking on the phone, still they are part of public space. He is convinced that design that takes technology into consideration is paramount for the future of cities.

MediaTeam Oulu (Ylipulli et al. 2013) has studied the appropriation process of two public computing infrastructures in the City of Oulu, Finland, a municipal WiFi network (pan OULU WLAN) and large interactive displays, which should provide novel applications and services to people. Some services enable the pairing of the mobile phone with the display by using Bluetooth, QR codes, and SMS. Municipal WiFi has been adopted very well and its usage is increasing rapidly. The adoption of the interactive public displays has been slow due to unfamiliarity of the technology and its questionable utility. Different demographic groups may experience these factors in differing ways; for example, for young people the creativity and playfulness of the applications was a more attractive feature than for elderly.

As the use of digital networks becomes an essential part of everyday life, a new digital layer is added on the existing urban landscape (Markaki 2014). This information age and the revolution have influenced the way people interact with each other and with their surrounded physical space. Information and communication are two essential factors of interest and attraction specific to urban environments and at the same time they represent key factors for the progress of the city, as bringing people together and supporting exchange of ideas generate development. Technology is only 10% of the problem. Ninety percent of it is about how it is used to connect and for a better quality of life. Technology is making it easier for people to connect to the places that they inhabit. The creation of hotspots providing wireless Internet access encouraged the return to the public, for both work and recreation. In addition, social media has a high potential for encouraging social interaction, in virtual as well as in real life public spaces, thus connecting them. The use of ICTs can significantly enhance public space, by creating access points to information and supporting education. In this sense, augmented reality can complete the toolbox, playing a significant role in engaging users and personalizing the urban experience.

The development of ICTs tools and the mobility of modern devices also bring new demands regarding urban design and the way public spaces are being planned. Namely, public spaces have to provide resources for proper functioning of gadgets (e.g., electricity, plugs). Street furniture should be able to satisfy the users' needs through its usage, comfort, quantity, accessibility, arrangement and aesthetics. They should be secured to avoid collapse by natural or human forces, and they should be regularly maintained by cleaning and repairing them. They have also to be easily adjustable in order to accommodate different activities, and have to encourage the shift of more and more activities from indoors to outdoors. Apart from the physical infrastructure, in order to successfully integrate ICTs in the urban life, the community has to be trained and prepared to embrace the change.

5 Blended Spaces – Spaces and Places for Human Interaction and Experiences

Human-Computer Interaction (HCI) is traditionally dealing with the design, evaluation and implementation of interactive computing systems for human use and the study of phenomena related to humans involved in these phenomena. As such, HCI has a more narrow approach than for example Interaction Design (ID). Interaction Design is concerned with the theory, research and practice of designing user experiences for all types of technologies, systems, objects and products. The process of interaction design involves basically four activities (Preece et al. 2011): Establishing requirements; Designing alternatives; Prototyping and Evaluation (ibid, 15). A similar, more recent approach has been mentioned as the Human-Centered Informatics (with the same abbreviation HCI). Human-Centered Informatics approach deals with the intersection of the cultural, the social, the cognitive, and the aesthetic with computing and information technology. Generally, Human-Centered Informatics deals with a more challenging area that includes the goals and activities of people, their values, and the tools and environments that help shape their everyday lives (Bannon 2011). HCI and Interaction Design (ID) are changing our ways of interacting and experiencing services and objects within our daily life and in our professional life as well. This involved designing for interaction on a broad macro-level as in our environmental surroundings to interaction on a micro-level. Today, when deigning, interaction is considered as a main component of the design process. Besides the focus on interaction design and HCI issues, user experience (UX) is also getting more and more attention and across different populations, devices and places/spaces. Thus, this means that we are moving around in different spaces and places inhabited with both physical objects and surroundings as well as interacting with digital objects and services. These spaces can be viewed as blended spaces (Benyon 2012). Furthermore, they are to be recognised as extended, but also as new social and cultural spaces. Finally, these blended spaces also constitute extended conceptual spaces.

User experience (UX) concerns the *navigation* of and within different spaces and how people experience this. Moving in and through the spaces and understanding spaces is an important human activity. Navigation is concerned with finding out about an environment. Three important activities are included (Benyon and Höök 1997):

- *Object identification*, (understanding and classifying the objects in an environment).
- *Exploration*, (exploring a local environment and how that environment relates to other environments).
- *Wayfinding*, (navigating toward a known destination).

6 Conclusions

Blended spaces applied in landscape design have close connection to user's experiences. As such, they can also constitute an environmental space and place that will affect humans and human activity (Parviainen, Lagerström and Hansen 2017). Design on a general level is very much about crafting your surroundings and often draws upon engineering, material and creative approaches. As Benyon (2014: 21) points out, design has been described by Donald Schön as a "conversation with materials". Schön means that in any type of design, designers must understand the nature of the materials that they are working with (Schön 1983). Thus, in landscape, environmental and urban design, knowledge and skills about both digital and physical material (Wang et al. 2017a, 2017b) is important since they surround us in our daily and everyday life. Blended spaces are spaces, or environments, where a physical space is explicitly integrated into a digital space. Blended spaces are conceptually close to tangible interactions (Wang et al. 2017a, 2017b) where the physical and digital are integrated. The purpose and understanding of designing a blended space are to enable people and groups of people to feel present in place, interacting with content and objects through senses and activities of the blended space (Benyon 2014).

Some challenges when designing for interaction are that designers need to think and elaborate beyond the immediate use of a place/space and consider wider physical, digital, cultural and social settings. Additional issues that are important is how interactions change over time and locations, as well as how content is experienced through different physical and digital objects and devices. People collaborating within physical and digital spaces and how information is created, shared and searched for is important (Hansen and Järvelin 2005). A further challenge is to deal with the human. People are flexible, dynamic, traditional, creative and resourceful. However, physical and digital 'systems' tend to be stable, static, with predefined goals, tasks and processes. This creates a challenge and a barrier that need to be focused on and dealt with. Since people's behaviour, language, feelings etc., that need to be recognized when designing for these spaces and places. As Benyon (2014: 22) points out, designers need to create and establish interfaces and systems that "enable people to shape and achieve their goals and aspirations. These interfaces should include and inherit different physical, digital, perceptual, sensory and conceptual point of contact that are between people and the content that is contained and accessible by.

References

Chua, A., Servillo, L., Marcheggiani, E., Moere, A.V.: Mapping cilento: using geotagged social media data to characterize tourist flows in Southern Italy. Tour. Manag. **57**, 295–310 (2016)

Abdel-Aziz, A.A., Abdel-Salam, H., El-Sayad, Z.: The role of ICTs in creating the new social public place of the digital era. Alex. Eng. J. **55**, 487–493 (2016)

Chua, A., Marcheggiani, E., Servillo, L., Vande Moere, A.: FlowSampler: visual analysis of urban flows in geolocated social media data. In: Aiello, L.M., McFarland, D. (eds.) SocInfo 2014. LNCS, vol. 8852, pp. 5–17. Springer, Cham (2015). https://doi.org/10.1007/978-3-319-15168-7_2

Bannon, L.: Reimagining HCI: toward a more human-centered perspective. Intersections **18**(4), 50–57 (2011)

Benyon, D., Höök, K.: Navigation in information spaces: supporting the individual. In: Proceedings of the Human-Computer Interaction INTERACT 1997, pp. 39–46 (1997)

Benyon, D.: Presence in blended spaces. J. Interact. Comput. **24**, 219–226 (2012)

Benyon, D.: Spaces of interaction, places for experience. Synthesis Lectures on Human-Centered Informatics, September 2014. https://doi.org/10.2200/s00595ed1v01y201409hci022)

Carmona, M.: Public Places, Urban Spaces. Architectural Press, Oxford (2003)

Carr, S.: Public space. Cambrige University Press, Cambrige (1992)

Castells, M., Fernández-Ardèvol, M., Linchuan Qiu, J., Sey, A.: Mobile Communication and Society: A Global Perspective. MIT Press, Cambridge (2006)

Francis, M.: Mapping downtown activity. J. Arch. Plan. Res. **1**(1), 21–35 (1984). http://lda.ucdavis.edu/people/websites/francis/Mapping%20Downtown%20Activity-Francis.pdf

Galli, A., Di Clemente, M.V., Marcheggiani, E., Scoppolini, F.M.: The design of ICT tools to strengthen the local identity in rural areas and to broaden the participation of large public to rural tourism experiences. In: The European Pilgrimage Routes for Promoting Sustainable and Quality Tourism in Rural Areas International Conference, 4–6 December 2014, Florence – Italy, Proceeding, pp. 871–880 (2015)

Gehl, J.: Life between Buildings: Using Public Space. Island Press, Washington, DC (2011)

Hampton, K.N.: Technology Brings People Together in Public Spaces After All, published on line By Project for Public Spaces on 17 July 2014 (2014)

Hansen, P., Järvelin, K.: Collaborative information retrieval in an information-intensive domain. Inf. Process. Manag. **41**(5), 1101–1119 (2005)

Lipovská, B., Štěpánková, R.: Assessing observation methods for landscape planning practice in rural villages. Curr. Urban Stud. **1**, 102–109 (2013). https://doi.org/10.4236/cus.2013.14011

Lugano, G.: Mobile social networking in theory and practice. First Monday, **13**(11), 3, November 2008. http://firstmonday.org/ojs/index.php/fm/article/view/2232/2050

Lynch, K.: Site Planning. MIT Press, Cambridge (1984)

Madanipour, A.: Design of Urban Space. Wiley, Chichester (1996)

Markaki, M.: Digital Cities: Towards a New Identity of Public Space. London (2014)

Miková, P.: Manuál tvorby veřejných prostranství hlavního města Prahy. Institut plánování a rozvoje hlavního města Prahy, 290 p. (2014). ISBN 978-80-87931-11-0

Miková, K., Paulíková, M., Pauliniova, Z.: Verejné priestory – ako tvoriť priestory s príbehom, pre ľudí a s ľuďmi. EKOPOLIS: Banská Bystrica, 2010, 135 p. (2010). ISBN 978-80-89505-00-5

Nassar, U.A.: Urban space design to enhance physical activities and motivate healthy social behaviour in Caro, Egypt. In: Proceedings of INTCESS15-2nd, International Conference on Education and Social Sciences, pp. 1137–1147 (2015)

Parviainen, E., Lagerström, E., Hansen, P.: Composting as interior design – encouraging sustainability throughout a participatory design process. In: DIS 2017 Companion Proceedings of the 2017 ACM Conference Companion Publication on Designing Interactive Systems, June 2017, Edinburgh, UK, pp. 167–171 (2017). https://doi.org/10.1145/3064857.3079139

Preece, J., Sharp, H., Rogers, Y.: Interaction Design: Beyond Human-Computer Interaction, 3rd edn. Wiley, Chichester (2011)

Project for Public Space (PPS): How to turn a Place Around: A Handbook for Creating Successful Public Spaces. Project for public spaces, New York (2001)

Schöbel, S.: Qualitative research as a perspective for urban open space planning. J. Landsc. Arch. **1**(1), 38–47 (2006)

Schön D.A.: The Reflective Practitioner. Basic Books. 2 Place; Publisher? (1983)

Thwaites, K., Simkins, I.: Experiential landscape: an approach to people, place, and space. Milton Park, Abingdon, New York (2007)

Ingegnoli, V.: Landscape Bionomics Biological-Integrated Landscape Ecology. Springer, Milano (2015). https://doi.org/10.1007/978-88-470-5226-0

Vanderhaeghen, P., Cheng, H.J.: Guidance molecules in axon pruning and cell death. Cold Spring Harb. Perspect. Biol. **2**(6), 1–18 (2010)

Wang, Y., Luo, S., Liu, S., Lu, Y., Hansen, P.: Crafting concrete as a material for enhancing meaningful interactions. In: Kurosu, M. (ed.) HCI 2017, Part I. LNCS, vol. 10271, pp. 634–644. Springer, Cham (2017). https://doi.org/10.1007/978-3-319-58071-5_48

Wang, Y., Lou, S., Lu, Y., Gong, H., Zhou, Y., Liu, S., Hansen, P.: AnimSkin: fabricating epidermis with interactive, functional and aesthetic color animation, June, 2017, Edinburgh, UK (2017b). http://dx.doi.org/10.1145/3064663.3064687

Wheeler, S.: The sustainable urban development reader. Routledge, London (2004)

Whyte, W.H.: The Social Life of Small Urban Spaces, The Conservation Foundation. Washington DC (1980)

Ylipulli, J., Suopajärvi, T., Ojala, T., Kostakos, V., Kukka, H.: Municipal WiFi and interactive displays: Appropriation of new technologies in public urban spaces. Technol. Forecast. Soc. Chang. **89**(2014), 145–160 (2013)

Žufová, M.: Lepšie data pre lepšiu Bratislavu. In: Public Spaces Bratislava. STU Bratislava, 28 p. (2015). ISBN: 978-80-227-4355-6

4.3

Modelling Co-creation Ecosystem for Public Open Spaces

Aelita Skarzauskiene[1(✉)], Monika Maciuliene[1], and Petja Ivanova-Radovanova[2]

[1] Mykolas Romeris University, Vilnius, Lithuania
{aelita,maciuliene}@mruni.eu
[2] Association for Integrated Development and Sustainability, Sofia, Bulgaria
petjaivanova@gmail.com

Abstract. Co-creation can be defined as the involvement of citizens in the initiation and/or the design process of public services in order to (co)create beneficial outcomes and value for society. Mediated public open spaces are ideal environments for co-creation to emerge due to the involvement of the community and ICT in the knowledge creation. The aims of the research presented in the chapter are two-fold: to conduct a mapping activity in order to collect the insights on civic technologies promoting the creation of open public spaces through the use of ICT and to define the critical dimensions in designing co-creative ecosystems. The mapping strategy was conducted by evaluating the civic technologies in Lithuania and Bulgaria. The insights from the empirical exercise allow to draw managerial and organizational recommendations for strengthening the collective efforts of citizens, IT developers, public and governmental institutions in creating open, inclusive and reflective open public spaces.

Keywords: Co-creation · Civic technologies · Community · Citizen empowerment

1 Introduction

In current societal settings influenced by globalization and ICT use, citizen engagement in development of public spaces should be approached holistically. Co-creation entails connections and collaboration in generation of added value for the involved actors (Alves 2013; Lönn and Uppström 2015). Mediated open spaces are ideal environments for the co-creation to emerge due to the involvement of entire community and information communication technologies in knowledge creation or aggregation. Co-creation offers an interesting perspective, as it enables the integration of a range of ICT-mediated and offline participatory methods and creates a shared domain between professionals and citizens. In its optimal form, co-creation has the dual benefit of reducing public sector costs and increasing stakeholder satisfaction (Gouillart and Hallett 2015). Co-creation of public services can lead amongst other to better allocation of resources (Cruickshank and Deakin 2011), enhance effectiveness (Jan et al. 2012),

C. Smaniotto Costa et al. (Eds.): CyberParks, LNCS 11380, pp. 262–277, 2019.
https://doi.org/10.1007/978-3-030-13417-4_21

reduce service quality gaps and planning mistakes (Linders 2012) and higher transparency (Bradwell and Marr 2008). Several authors (Cassia and Magno 2009; Skidmore et al. 2006) indicate that co-creative approaches increase the trust of citizens in public organizations. Recent literature within the co-creation of public spaces highlights the benefits collaboration brings by providing various examples of innovative projects and initiatives that have engaged citizens and had successful outcomes (Giest et al. 2016; Jacobsen 2016).

However, there is a relatively little research on the specific groups of activities that should be undertaken in order to enhance the co-creative capacity of various initiatives. Understanding what makes initiatives co-creative could lead to better design and management of projects. The aim of this chapter is to offer insights on the critical dimensions of co-creative ecosystems enhancing public open spaces based on the previous theoretical insights and empirical investigations. The ecosystem in this chapter refers to an interdependent social system of actors, organizations, material infrastructures, and symbolic resources that can be created in technology-enabled, information-intensive social systems. According to Harrison et al. (2012), "ecosystems are naturally occurring phenomena and the metaphor may be applied to any existing socio-technical domain, they can also be seeded, modelled, developed, managed, that is, intentionally cultivated for the purpose of achieving a managerial and policy vision."

The object of analysis in this framework are the civic technology platforms. It refers to the extendible platforms and applications that enable citizens to connect and collaborate with each other and with the government (Clarke 2014). The scope of the concept is wide and applicable in defining ICT-enabled technologies aimed at generation of value for the public ranging from online transparency and accountability initiatives to e-city applications. The rapid transformation of the society influenced by digital upheaval, budgetary pressures and evolving understanding of the citizen role in the workings of governments lead to a collaborative governance approach expressed in the literature on Open Government and Government 2.0 (e.g. Meijer et al. 2012; Uppström 2014). Such understanding is based on principles of collaboration, transparency and participation. Hence, in the context of proposed framework, the civic technologies are understood as the public services provided by non-governmental entities such as NGOs, educational organizations, individual citizens or grassroot movements.

Over the last decades, leading business and public management scholars and practitioners have highlighted the interactive and networked nature of the value creation both in business and in public sectors (Galvagno and Dalli 2014; Stembert and Mulder 2012). The new channels of communication and information flow enable the innovative involvement of the broader groups of society in collaborative activities in the shorter amounts of time. Hence, the authors develop a theoretically-oriented framework for conceptualizing co-creative ecosystems aimed at the enhancement of public spaces by evaluating civic technologies tackling issues related to public spaces in Lithuania and Bulgaria.

2 Co-creative Ecosystems: Theoretical Influences and Conceptual Analysis Framework

The section explores theoretical influences of the conceptual analysis framework and details the logics and elements of the model. The conceptual models help to clarify what is known and unknown about the system and are key in interpreting research results. The framework is built according to the guidelines put forward by Jabareen (2009) summarized in four main directions: (1) every concept has an irregular contour defined by its components; (2) every concept contains components originating from other concepts, (3) every concept is considered as the point of coincidence, condensation, or accumulation of its own components, and (4) every concept must be understood relative to its own components, to other concepts and to the problem it is supposed to resolve. In developing co-creative ecosystem framework, the authors have expanded on previous works of Service Science approach to co-creation and PPC analysis framework suggested by Warburton et al. (2010) aiming at evaluation of the success of various initiatives.

The Service Science theoretical approach provides the ecosystem logic for conceptual model and allows to understand the value co-creation processes in a holistic manner (Aladalah and Lee 2015; Lusch et al. 2008; Sterrenberg 2017). According to Meynhardt et al. (2016), most investigations on co-creation focus on micro and collective-macro levels. Systemic approach is often missing, and isolated investigations lead to incomplete research outcomes. Researchers at IBM and University of Cambridge suggest Service Science as an alternative method and research direction to discover underlying components of complex systems and the way they can be combined (IfM and IBM 2008). Hence, the it provides a much needed clarity and guidance for those wanting to apply principles of co-creation in managing organizations. The central concept of the Service Science as is a service ecosystem. It consists of several or many service systems connected by a network and Service Science focuses on value co-creation amongst them. Service system can be defined as dynamic configuration of people, technologies and organizations and their ecosystem can be defined as self-adjusting system of resource-integrating contributors connected by shared structures, social rules and mutual value creation (Akaka et al. 2013: 161).

In Service Science perspective, the value is created through three interrelated and cyclical processes in service systems (Goda and Kijima 2015: 85): resource integration, networking and service exchange. The Service Science suggests that value emerges when a number of entities work collectively to create mutual benefits by granting access to one another's resources including people, technologies, organizations and information. Interacting entities form service ecosystems consisting of several or many service systems connected by a network. The entities cannot create and deliver value alone; they can only propose value offerings to the other actors in the network and in this way co-create the value.

The elements of the framework are based on the model suggested by Warburton et al. (2010) who proposed that success of initiative depends on three elements – the process (how), the purpose (why) and the context (when, where) – the PPC framework. The PPC framework has been used in analysing open governance intelligence

(Krimmer et al. 2016), strategic change in governance systems (Hamann 2009), ICT-enabled social changes on community/societal level (Pozzebon and Diniz 2012), and organizational changes (Armenakis and Bedeian 1999). Figure 1 "Conceptual Analysis Framework for Co-Creative Ecosystems" illustrates the elements and the logics of the framework. Below detailed explanation of the framework elements is provided.

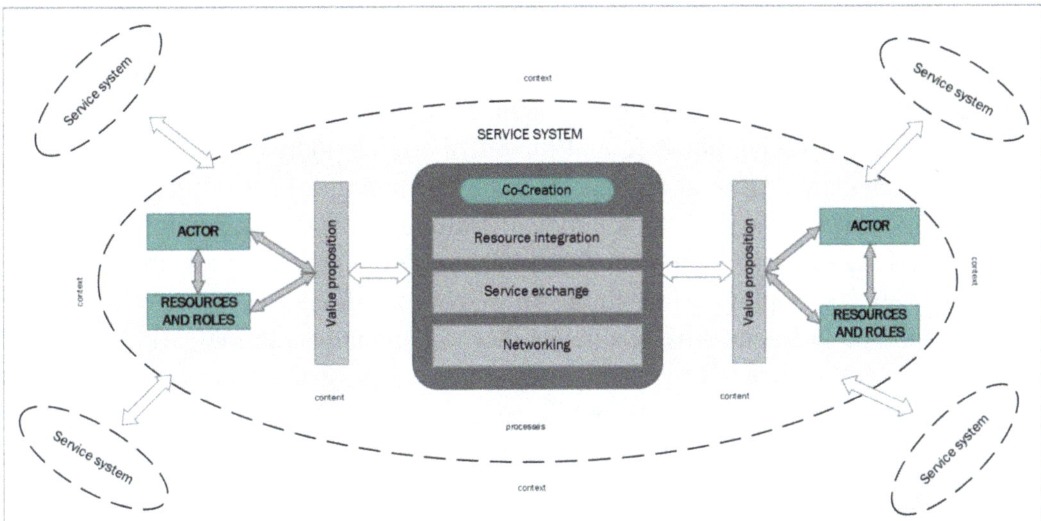

Fig. 1. Conceptual analysis framework for co-creative ecosystems. Source: developed by authors, 2017

The first, process, element is dedicated to analysis of the actors involved in co-creation processes – their roles and dynamics. (Voorberg et al. 2009) suggest that the success of co-creative initiatives depends highly on the position and interests of the involved stakeholders. Cobo (2012) states that "although collaboration has the potential to produce powerful results, not all collaborations realize this potential. Many collaborations fail to produce innovative solutions or balance stakeholder concerns, and some even fail to generate any collective action whatsoever". Brown and Osborne (2012) suggest that the collaboration efforts should be evaluated based on interests, goals and motivations of diverse actors involved. McNutt et al. (2016) suggests that the sustainability of co-creative initiatives in public sector depends on the networked relationships between the business entities, NGOs and more informal groups of citizens. The motivation to create partnerships comes from the recognition that collaborating organizations can accomplish what each partner cannot accomplish alone by maximizing the influence, creating collective resources and removing duplication of the efforts.

The purpose element examines reasons why the initiatives have been established. Earlier work by academics and practitioners (Emerson et al. 2011; Hepburn 2015) on evaluating the co-creative initiatives focused primarily on the process issues, largely ignoring the purpose of such projects. The predominant method was to examine best practice case studies based on a set of principles, and the process was often considered to be an end in itself rather than a means to an end. However, more attention needs to be paid to the content of the initiatives and contextual factors that can mitigate the effectiveness of co-creation and its outcomes in terms of the decision-makers or the participants. The design and structure of technological solutions can give impetus to the purposeful development towards common community good. On the other hand, if social values of the citizens acting in a collective environment are not aligned or coordinated and if technological decisions are implemented without scientific reasoning in an immature environment, these technological solutions can accelerate negative aspects of ICT and distance even more from the desirable goal of an inclusive community (Skaržauskienė et al., 2015). The context element refers to the contextual influences of the co-creative initiatives such as social context and the networks of collaboration and association, scale and type of the issue addressed.

The PPC elements allow to discuss the civic technologies in-depth and enables the comparison between varying technological solutions. The conceptual framework enhances existing research methods and models into the new context of people, places and technology by employing the logics of ecosystem. Identified dimensions should not be considered independently of one another. Such analysis framework will help to come to more comprehensive assessment of what makes such initiatives successful in engaging citizens and in enhancing public spaces.

3 Empirical Investigations on Co-creative Ecosystems and Civic Technologies in Lithuania and Bulgaria

The conceptual analysis framework was used to evaluate civic technologies (online platforms and applications) oriented towards enhancement of public spaces in Lithuania and Bulgaria with the task to provide managerial and organizational recommendations for strengthening the collective efforts of citizens, IT developers, public and governmental institutions in creating open, inclusive and reflective open public spaces. The methods of content mapping and analysis were applied. The mapping activity aimed at collection of data on the co-creative ecosystems in Lithuania and Bulgaria in order to develop insights on involved actors, type of co-creative activities and objectives and to determine the linkages and synergy between the actors. To achieve this goal, the method of online content analysis has been employed. The research process can be divided in to four stages: sample selection, design of the data collection template, data collection and evaluation of the results.

The platforms in the sample were selected according the selection criteria: (1) ICT-enabled and interactive. The platforms employ ICT solutions (i.e. online forums, ideation platforms) to be more open, inclusive and collaborative; (2) Based in Lithuania and Bulgaria. The platform activities aim to improve public spaces in Lithuania and Bulgaria; (3) Orientation. The platforms may be for non-profit as well as for profit; but their overall objectives should serve the community and improve the public spaces; (4) Contributors. Selected platforms have capabilities to involve a large number of members in making decisions or proposing ideas; (5) Duration. Projects with a minimum of 1 year of activity; (6) Data availability. Goals, metrics, initiators are listed on platform website; (7) Collective action. Projects allows collaboration between citizens and/or business and/or NGO's and/or governments. The sample was gathered through a review of the previous studies on civic technologies, European funding databases, municipal websites, popular blogs and through original Google searches on array of civic engagement related terms in Lithuanian and Bulgarian. Based on the listed criteria, the sample includes 13 civic tech initiatives oriented towards improvement of public spaces in Lithuania and Bulgaria. The sample and details of the initiatives are provided in the Table 1 below.

Table 1. Sample of civic tech initiatives

Name of the initiative	Code	Country of operation	URL address	Initiator
ABLE	P1	Bulgaria	www.ablebulgaria.org/en/	Community of entrepreneurial young people
Archmap.lt	P2	Lithuania	www.archmap.lt	"Architektūros centras", Lithuanian Architects' Association and "Architektūros fondas"
asLietuvai.lt	P3	Lithuania	www.asLietuvai.lt	Individual initiative
Cultural cosmos	P4	Bulgaria	https://culturalcosmos.com/cultural-cosmos/	Team of "Kosmos" cinema, the city of Plovdiv
Kelionės kultūros keliais	P5	Lithuania	http://idomiausiosvietos.lt/keliones	"Paveldo projektai"
Kurgyvenu.lt	P6	Lithuania	www.kurgyvenu.lt	"CodeIN"
mesDarom.lt	P7	Lithuania	www.mesdarom.lt	"Mes Darom"
Millenium	P8	Bulgaria	www.millennium.bg	Foundation Millenium
Nemasinis.lt	P9	Lithuania	www.nemasinis.lt	Individual initiative
pamatykLietuvoje.lt	P10	Lithuania	www.pamatykLietuvoje.lt	Individual initiative
Transformatory Association	P11	Bulgaria	www.transformatori.net/en	Group of young architects
Tuk Tam	P12	Bulgaria	https://tuk-tam.bg	8 young people used to live and study abroad together with Back2BG
Uspelite	P13	Bulgaria	http://uspelite.bg/	Superhosting.bg

Source: developed by authors, 2017

During the second stage, data collection template was designed based on the theoretical framework and publicly available data on selected platforms. The template is a necessary tool in order to make data collection process uniform across platforms and to enable patterning. The template is divided into 3 sections based on the elements in the theoretical framework: (1) purpose element (goals, operation type, context); (2) process element (users, initiators, funding, partners, developers, resources); (3) context element (networks of collaborators, dynamics of collaboration). The fieldwork was done during April–May 2017. Some categories were pre-defined based on previous chapters in order to help data structuration and evaluation. Third stage of the empirical study is data collection including systemic coding of textual content and semantic themes found on the platforms by reviewing uploaded documents, outgoing links, social media accounts, user activity and media mentions. The last stage involved evaluation and synthesis of the results. Comparison of the research data across the cases led to the generation of the insights on the co-creative ecosystems.

Described method has several limitations which need to be mentioned. The first limitation is the heterogeneity of Internet data which predetermined by the differences in content, user interfaces, semantics, structure, etc. The differences make it difficult for the researchers collecting online data (Bouchkhar 2013). Another limitation is the sample of platforms. It has to be mentioned that the sample is not representative of the universe of civic technologies. Moreover, due its limited size, it does not present statistical significance. However, as the first exercise in differentiating the building blocks of co-creative ecosystems, it can be considered as an effort of structuring the sample.

4 Analysis and Discussion of the Empirical Study Results

The analysis of the research outputs aimed at unfolding the purpose dimension (the goals, operation type) of civic technologies aimed at enhancement of public spaces in Lithuania and Bulgaria allowed to elaborate the types of value propositions offered for the actors in the ecosystem. Knowing why individuals and organizations build platforms, and why citizens participate in them, can guide the organizations and civic leaders in fostering ICT-enabled platforms. The findings of analysis are illustrated in Table 2 "The Results on Purpose Dimension".

The goals, orientation and operation type of the platforms analysed provide insights on the value the platforms aim to cumulate. The analysis allowed to cluster the Civic Technologies based on the changes they are seeking in the society expressed through the notion of value proposition. Six types of value propositions were identified in the sample: economic, self-expression, knowledge/information, status, functional and network. Economic value proposition refers to the pursuit of profit, savings, return of investments for the actors involved in service system. It was identified in four platforms. Self-expression value proposition was identified in all 13 platforms and deals with contribution to the society, expression of views by the actors of service system. Knowledge/information proposition was also observed in all the sample platforms and refers to the aim of information dissemination between the members of service system. The status value proposition refers to the pursuit of feeling more important by the actors in the system and is expressed in nine platforms. Ten platforms offer network value proposition expressed through the goals of closer partnerships, mutual benefits, increased impact, access to greater pool of partners and supporters. The last value proposition, functional, was identified in all of the sample platforms and refers to the core functional benefits the service provides to the members of society.

Table 2. The results on purpose dimension

Name of the platform	Goals of the platform	Value propositions identified
ABLE	"…The mission is to develop a civil society, inspire leadership, and spread entrepreneurial culture in Bulgaria; website, social network, offline events organization, project. Initiators met during participation in the Bulgarian Young Leaders Program (BYLP) and in 2011 decided to start a non-profit to serve as a platform for our ideas and for positive change in Bulgaria. Since then – with the proportional increase in our members – our projects, our influence, and their successes in Bulgarian society have been growing as well…"	Knowledge/information; functional; self-expression; network; status
Archmap.lt	"…To present Lithuanian architecture and public spaces to wider audiences in order to increase the public interest to get to know the architectural heritage. To represent Lithuanian architecture by expanding the scope from the cities to lesser explored regions…"	Knowledge/information; functional; self-expression; status
asLietuvai.lt	"…To achieve the breakthrough of Lithuanian thinking and mentality from destruction to flourishing…"	Knowledge/information; functional; self-expression; network
Cultural cosmos	"…Create platform for culture and society in partnership with Municipality of the city of Plovdiv; Enhancement civil society; Networking and partnership with cultural operators and institutions from BG and Europe…"	Knowledge/information; functional; self-expression; network; status
Kelionės kultūros keliais	"…To stimulate and motivate the need to travel in Lithuania, explore new regions and cultural objects…"	Knowledge/information; functional; self-expression
Kurgyvenu.lt	"…To help the owners, sellers, buyers, brokers, renters and other interest parties to make real-estate related decisions easier and more intelligent…"	Knowledge/information; functional; economic; self-expression; network; status
mesDarom.lt	"…Creation of sustainable society by uniting individuals, families, business, initiatives and other entities in order to preserve the country and public spaces for future generations…"	Knowledge/information; functional; self-expression; network; status

(*continued*)

Table 2. *(continued)*

Name of the platform	Goals of the platform	Value propositions identified
Millenium	"…Development of sustainable and balanced regions in Bulgaria and Europe; Enhancement of suitable conditions for economic development and employment in Support for economic development and social cooperation between regions in Bulgaria and Europe. Support and creation of suitable environment for decentralization of social services in Bulgaria…"	Knowledge/information; functional; self-expression; network
Nemasinis.lt	"…To collect and visualize interesting Lithuanian public objects that are outside the scope of traditional travellers and explorers due to the limited accessibility and bad conditions. It allows to expand the understanding about the surroundings…"	Knowledge/information; functional; self-expression
pamatykLietuvoje.lt	"…To motivate and stimulate internal tourism, find new interesting spaces and places, share the knowledge and experiences…"	Knowledge/information; functional; self-expression; network; status
Transformatory Association	"…The association aims to set good practice, realizing common initiatives with the specialized educational schools in the constructional and architectural field for improving the educational process…"	Knowledge/information; functional; self-expression; network; status
Tuk Tam	"…Community of knowledgeable, initiative and well educated Bulgarians from all over the world. We implement projects and organize events in the spheres of professional development, education and social economy in Bulgaria and abroad…"	Knowledge/information; functional; self-expression; network
Uspelite	"…Since 2015 it became the most popular positive media in Bulgaria…"	Knowledge/information; functional; self-expression; network

Source: developed by authors, 2017

The process dimension refers to the of individuals and organizations participating in the service ecosystem, their roles and resources. The mapping activity allowed to identify nine groups of actors involved in co-creative ecosystems–governmental entities, citizens, private organizations, NGOs, media, specialists, associations, public organizations and international organizations. The content analysis (see Table 3 below) of the user groups as defined by initiators showed that, in most cases, initiators define the user groups employing very abstract terms. Also, the 'official' focus is on the citizens (expressed variously e.g. young people, habitants, etc.). Non-citizen actor groups are mostly left out of the descriptions of the platform orientation. Hence, in-depth review of the platform content, the services they provide, funding sources and strategic documents was conducted and resulted in identification of eight actor groups – citizens, governmental organizations, NGOs, business organizations, media organizations, public organizations, associations, international organizations – which participate in the ecosystem directly and indirectly.

Table 3. The results on process dimension

Name of the platform	Types of initiators	Target groups identified by the initiators
ABLE	Individual citizens	"…Young people and urban development professionals…"
Archmap.lt	NGO and association	"…Professionals, amateurs, young and old, anyone interested in architecture…"
asLietuvai.lt	Individual citizens	"…Young and talented Lithuanian all around the world…"
Cultural cosmos	Individual citizens	"…Citizens of the city of Plovdiv, cultural industries with focus on young people and artists in the first stage of their development…"
Kelionės kultūros keliais	NGO	"…everyone interested…"
Kurgyvenu.lt	Business	"…travellers, teachers, lecturers, travel guides, families…"
mesDarom.lt	NGO	"…individuals, families, communities, governmental institutions, businesses, initiatives and other movement…"
Millenium	NGO	"…NGOs, local authorities, business, local people…"
Nemasinis.lt	Individual citizens	"…everyone…"
pamatykLietuvoje.lt	Individual citizens	"…everyone interested in travelling"
Transformatory Association	Individual citizens	"…Young people and urban development professionals…"
Tuk Tam	Individual citizens	"…Young and well educated people in Bulgaria and abroad…"
Uspelite	Individual citizens	"…Young people…"

Source: developed by authors, 2017

Six roles of the actors involved in the processes were identified – initiators, users, contributors, partners, sponsors and intermediaries. Figure 2 below illustrates the connections between the actors in the analyzed ecosystems. Initiators start the platforms by contributing their individual and organizational resources in terms of time, know-how, finances, etc. The roles identified can be filled by any of the actor groups identified. Meaning that the businesses can be initiators, users, contributors, initiators, partners and sponsors of the platforms. The same applies to the citizens and other actor groups. The role of the user refers to the actors using the platform and receiving ICT-enabled service. The role of the contributor is closely related to the role of user. However, it is more interactive and refers to more interactive collaboration efforts by means of suggesting ideas, voting, reporting issues, communicating with other contributors and other ways of creating content beneficial for the active processes of the platform. The role of partner is to share operant resources with platform initiators and managers. The role refers to mutually beneficial relationships which are developed without losing autonomy of individual actors. The Sponsors provide financial resources for enabling platform activities. The sponsoring can happen in number of ways through governmental, business funding or citizens backing up the platforms they find important.

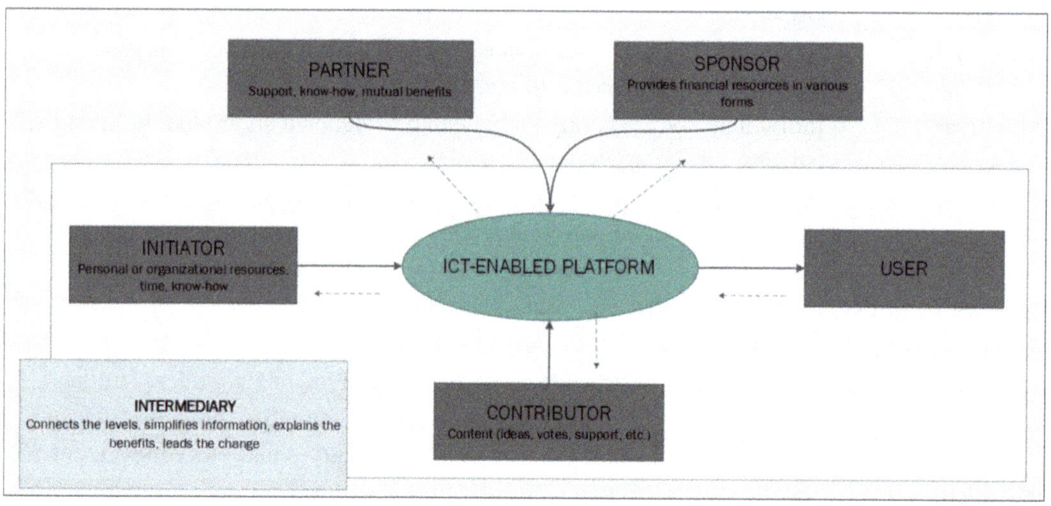

Fig. 2. Dynamics and roles of actors in the co-creative ecosystem. Source: developed by authors, 2017

The role of intermediary refers to actors connecting different actors in the ecosystem. For the society to evolve being more open and engaged, not all citizens have to be active, not all organizations have to be active – but there is need for intermediaries, civic leaders, active citizens who could translate the importance of active citizenship, transparency, translate the data and make it easier for citizens and governments to cooperate. The role of intermediary mostly refers to the individual actors, mostly specialists with the skills and knowledge in the fields of IT, open data, and governmental processes. The role of intermediary is especially relevant in the context of co-creating public value. Intermediaries translate the complex public sector information (i.e. legislation on the public spaces) and processes to the other groups in the system and allow connections to happen easier.

The context element refers to the settings the platforms operate within. In the digital economic era, resources and actors are embedded in networks. Therefore, the process of value creation is depending on the absorptive capacity and ability to operate in networks. The results of the empirical study on context dimension are illustrated in Table 4 below and discussed in the context of the framework below.

Table 4. Results of the context dimension

Name of the platform	Code	Number of partners identified	Type of partners
ABLE	P1	19 partners identified	International organizations, NGOs, associations
Archmap.lt	P2	5 partners identified	Governmental organizations, business, NGOs
asLietuvai.lt	P3	No partners identified	n/a
Cultural cosmos	P4	10 partners identified	Associations, municipalities, governmental organizations, business
Kelionės kultūros keliais	P5	5 partners identified	NGOs, governmental entities
Kurgyvenu.lt	P6	No partners identified	n/a
mesDarom.lt	P7	20 partners identified	Media organizations, NGOs, business organizations, public organizations
Millenium	P8	No partners identified	n/a
Nemasinis.lt	P9	No partners identified	n/a
pamatykLietuvoje.lt	P10	6 partners identified	Public organizations, NGOs, governmental organizations
Transformatory Association	P11	8 partners identified	International organizations, NGOs
Tuk Tam	P12	12 partners identified in the platform content	Business, NGOs, public organizations
Uspelite	P13	12 partners identified in the platform content	International organizations, business, NGOs, public organizations

Source: developed by authors, 2017

Although the majority of the platforms aim to increase citizen engagement, the role of citizens is often limited to being users and contributors rather than partners (i.e. collaborators, experts contributing operant resources) in creation and management of ICT-enabled initiatives. In addition, the analysis of the platform connections with the external partners shows that majority of the projects have no external partners (or they do not declare the affiliations publicly). The role of contributor in the context of civic technologies is especially important. The platform activities often depend on the active engagement by the end users in contributing the content in form of ideas, opinions, reactions and support. However, the prevalence of this role is limited in the sample platforms. In most cases, citizens are expected to contribute in co-creating public value through the platforms. Other types of actors are not invited to contribute a content with the few exceptions. The results correspond with the central ideas of the conceptual framework which suggests that organizations no longer depend on the internal capacities to satisfy external needs. The sustainable initiatives and organizations are required to maintain relationships with other actors in the ecosystem (e.g. partners, competitors, governments and end users).

5 Conclusions

While traditional approaches to public engagement and governmental reforms remain relevant, this chapter focuses towards the growing potential of networked society to solve their social problems. It expands co-creation field and provide innovative framework to the citizens co-initiated, heavily technology supported, and systems-oriented co-creation approaches. A critical reflection on the co-creation practices is relevant to evaluate how digital enabled managerial and organisational solutions influence the quality of co-creation results, to understand what works by implementing the co-creations methods and what doesn't work and why. The nature of all these problems is interdisciplinary and have to be solved under the complex manner.

The technological advancements, innovative managerial strategies, and new forms of interaction lead to the constantly changing roles of the organizations and their customers. The concept of co-creation is seen as an evolving framework describing the shift from considering organizations as the definers of value to a more inclusive and collaborative processes involving end-users and other external actors. The use of a theoretical study of the literature on co-creation and empirical analysis of civic tech platforms allowed to identify main building blocks and attributes of co-creative digital initiatives in Bulgaria and Lithuania. Understanding co-creation in the public sector through ecosystem perspective requires to rethink of who can offer value in this space. The model suggests that the value emerges when a number of entities work collectively to create mutual benefits by granting access to one another's resources including people, technologies, organizations and information. Initiatives based on collaboration can only flourish through networks by including residents, communities, business, governmental institutions and other actors in the act of value generation.

The co-creation of value for the public through technologies encompasses many different interpretations and views depending researchers, developers, users, research areas and disciplines. Therefore, various parties are likely to hold different views and perceptions on the concept. The proposed model sheds dynamic ideas for future researches to further identify, conceptualize and understand the underlying theories and perspectives which strongly influence the previous, current, and future concept of co-creation. The model needs to be tested in additional cases to further verify its validity and usefulness in diverse settings by producing detailed longitudinal case studies. Further research could elaborate on the applicability of the framework in diverse setting – different countries. The maturity model of the ecosystem could be designed in order to provide more detailed guidelines for the actor involved in how to achieve the value. Additional work is needed to formulate measures and indicators of successful initiatives.

References

Akaka, M.A., Vargo, S.L., Lusch, R.F.: The complexity of context: a service ecosystems approach for international marketing. J. Int. Mark. Am. Mark. Assoc. **21**(4), 1–20 (2013)

Aladalah, M., Lee, V.C.S.: Gov2.0: A Service Science Perspective. In Kankanhalli, A., Jones, A. B., Teo, T. (Eds.), PACIS 2015 Proceedings Atlanta, Georgia: Association for Information Systems (2015)

Alves, H.: Co-creation and innovation in public services. Serv. Ind. J. **33**(7–8), 671–682 (2013). https://doi.org/10.1080/02642069.2013.740468

Armenakis, A.A., Bedeian, A.G.: Organizational change: a review of theory and research in the 1990s. J. Manag. **25**(3), 293–315 (1999). https://doi.org/10.1177/014920639902500303

Bouchkhar, B.: Data sources on the Internet: towards a new and innovative solution. In: NTTS 2013, pp. 391–397 (2013)

Bradwell, P., Marr, S.: Making the Most of Collaboration: An International Survey of Public Service Co-design. Demos, London (2008)

Brown, L., Osborne, S.P.: Risk and innovation: public management review. Public Manag. Rev. **15**(2), 186–208 (2012)

Cassia, F., Magno, F.: Public services co-production: exploring the role of citizen orientation. Int. J. Qual. Serv. Sci. **1**(3), 334–343 (2009). https://doi.org/10.1108/17566690911004249

Clarke, R.Y.: Civic Tech Fuels U.S. State and Local Government Transformation. (2014). http://www.accela.com/images/resources/whitepaper/idc-civic-tech-report.pdf

Cobo, C.: Networks for citizen consultation and citizen sourcing of expertise. Contemp. Soc. Sci. **7**(3), 283–304 (2012). https://doi.org/10.1080/21582041.2012.683445

Cruickshank, P., Deakin, M.: Co-design in Smart Cities: a guide for municipalities from Smart Cities, 1–36 (2011). http://researchrepository.napier.ac.uk/5659/

Emerson, K., Nabatchi, T., Balogh, S.: An integrative framework for collaborative governance. J. Public Adm. Res. Theory **22**(1), 1–29 (2011). https://doi.org/10.1093/jopart/mur011

Galvagno, M., Dalli, D.: Theory of value co-creation: a systematic literature review. Manag. Serv. Qual. Int. J. **24**(6), 643–683 (2014). https://doi.org/10.1108/msq-09-2013-0187

Giest, S., Koene, A., Vallejos, E.P., Pitkänen, O., Fosci, M.: Online spaces for urban citizen engagement: a comparison of civic apps. In: Data for Policy Conference, pp. 1–6 (2016)

Goda, K., Kijima, K.: Modeling service ecosystems innovation. J. Bus. Manag. Sci. **3**(3), 85–91 (2015). https://doi.org/10.12691/jbms-3-3-1

Gouillart, F., Hallett, T.: Co-creation in Government. Stanford Social Innovation Review, pp. 1–16, Spring 2015

Hamann, R.: Strategic change in organisations and governance systems in response to complex socio-ecological problems in Southern Africa. Synoptic Strategy Outline, pp. 1–6, November 2009

Harrison, T.M., Pardo, T.A., Cook, M.: Creating open government ecosystems: a research and development agenda. Futur. Internet **4**(4), 900–928 (2012). https://doi.org/10.3390/fi4040900

Hepburn, P.: An evaluation of the "helping hands-co-creation of a digital application for elderly people" project, March 2015

IfM and IBM.: Succeeding through service innovation. Symposium A Quarterly Journal. In: Modern Foreign Literatures. Cambridge, United Kingdom: University of Cambridge Institute for Manufacturing (2008)

Jabareen, Y.: Building a conceptual framework: philosophy, definitions, and procedure. Int. J. Qual. Methods **8**, 49–62 (2009). https://doi.org/10.2522/ptj.20100192

Jacobsen, E.O.: Public spaces support social engagement and then provide the necessary buy-in to sustain moral engagement as well, 1–21 (2016)

Jan, P.T., Lu, H.P., Chou, T.C.: Measuring the perception discrepancy of the service quality between provider and customers in the Internet Protocol Television industry. Total Qual. Manag. Business Excel. **23**(7–8), 981–995 (2012)

Krimmer, R., Kalvet, T., Toots, M., McBride, K.: OpenGovIntelligence: Fostering Innovation and Creativity in Europe through Public Administration Modernization towards Supplying and Exploiting Linked Open Statistical Data (2016)

Linders, D.: From e-government to we-government: defining a typology for citizen coproduction in the age of social media. Gov. Inf. Q. **29**(4), 446–454 (2012)

Lönn, C.-M., Uppström, E.: Core aspects for value co-creation in public sector. In Americas Conference on Information Systems , Puerto Rico, pp. 1–12 (2015)

Lusch, R.F., Vargo, S.L., Wessels, G.: Toward a conceptual foundation for service science: contributions from service-dominant logic. IBM Syst. J. **47**, 5–14 (2008)

McNutt, J.G., et al.: The diffusion of civic technology and open government in the United States. Inf. Polity **21**(2), 153–170 (2016). https://doi.org/10.3233/ip-160385

Meijer, A.J., Koops, B.-J., Pieterson, W., Overman, S., Tije, S.T.: Government 2.0: key challenges to its realization. Electron. J. E-Gov. **10**(1), 59–69 (2012)

Meynhardt, T., Chandler, J.D., Strathoff, P.: Systemic principles of value co-creation: synergetics of value and service ecosystems. J. Bus. Res. **69**(8), 2981–2989 (2016). https://doi.org/10.1016/j.jbusres.2016.02.031

Pozzebon, M., Diniz, E.H.: Theorizing ICT and society in the Brazilian context: a multilevel, pluralistic and remixable framework. Braz. Adm. Rev. **9**(3), 287–307 (2012). https://doi.org/10.1590/s1807-76922012000300004

Skaržauskienė, A., et al.: Social Technologies and Collective Intelligence. Mykolas Romeris University, Vilnius (2015)

Skidmore, P., Bound, K., Lownsbrough, H.: Community Participation: Who Benefits?. Joseph Rowntree Foundation, York, UK (2006)

Stembert, N., Mulder, I.J.: Love your city! An interactive platform empowering citizens to turn the public domain into a participatory domain, (Section 4) (2012)

Sterrenberg, G.: A conceptual framework for evaluating e-government systems success: a service ecosystem approach. In: 50th Hawaii International Conference on System Sciences, pp. 2529–2538 (2017)

Uppström, E.: The Promise of Public Value Co-creation in Open Government. DSV Report Series. Stockholm. (2014). http://www.diva-portal.org/smash/get/diva2:697081/FULLTEXT03

Voorberg, W., Bekkers, V., Tummers, L.: The keys to successful co-creation: an explanation using causal proces tracing. EGPA Conference, 320090(320090), pp. 1–32 (2014). http://repub.eur.nl/pub/76034

Warburton, D., Wilson, R., Rainbow, E.: Making a Difference: A guide to Evaluating Public Participation in Central Government. London (2010). http://www.involve.org.uk/evaluation

4.4

Using ICTs for the Improvement of Public Open Spaces: The Opportunity Offered by CyberParks Digital Tools

Eneko Osaba[1,4], Roberto Pierdicca[2], Tiago Duarte[3], Alfonso Bahillo[1(✉)], and Diogo Mateus[3]

[1] Deusto Institute of Technology (DeustoTech), University of Deusto, Bilbao, Spain
{e.osaba,alfonso.bahillo}@deusto.es

[2] Dipartimento di Ingegneria Civile, Universtitá Politecnica delle Marché, Edile e dell' Architettura, Ancona, Italy
r.pierdicca@univpm.it

[3] Universidade Lusófona, Lisbon, Portugal
tiagoaduarte@gmail.com, p1710@ulusofona.pt

[4] TECNALIA Research & Innovation, Derio, Spain
eneko.osaba@tecnalia.com

Abstract. In the last decade, the potential of mobile devices for augmenting outdoor experience opened up new solutions, whose value is twofold. On one hand, users can experience new forms of interaction with space. On the other, stakeholders can have access to the so-called User Generated Data, that is different types of information related to public spaces that could be used to improve their conception of space. In line with this, several digital tools have been developed and tested within the framework of CyberParks COST Action TU-1306 with the intention of exploring how information and communication technologies (ICTs) can contribute to the improvement of Public Open Spaces (POS). In this way, this chapter aims to study the relationship between ICTs and POS, focused on the opportunities offered by three different digital tools: the WAY-CyberParks, the EthnoAlly, and the CyberCardeto. The main advantages of using these digital tools are: (1) the real-time data gathering, (2) maintaining an updated database, (3) collecting traces of different activities and users' groups "at the same time and space", and (4) recording their opinion and preferences, via text, video, sound or pictures. Furthermore, the chapter attempts to analyse distinct types of results produced by their use, based on different study cases where the digital tool has been tested. The data obtained in these places serve to demonstrate the features and type of data gathered. With these case studies, the chapter attempts to highlight the main potential of each platform as related to different stakeholders and users.

Keywords: Digital tools · Interacting with users · WAY-CyberParks · Ethnoally · CyberCardeto

C. Smaniotto Costa et al. (Eds.): CyberParks, LNCS 11380, pp. 278–293, 2019.
https://doi.org/10.1007/978-3-030-13417-4_22

1 Introduction

This chapter analyses how information and digital technologies (ICTs) can be used to improve public open spaces of our cities, and how new forms of communication can support different disciplines, in order to better plan and develop urban areas. The analysis is based on the work developed within the COST Action TU 1306 CyberParks. The CyberParks Project established an interdisciplinary research platform, including different specific groups working together to understand the dynamic relationship between ICT and the production and use of public open spaces, and its relevance to sustainable urban development (Šuklje-Erjavec and Smaniotto Costa 2015; Smaniotto Costa et al. 2015). This chapter is focused on the opportunities offered by three different digital tools: the WAY CyberParks; the EthnoAlly; and the CyberCardeto.

These digital tools are being developed, besides providing users contextual and interaction information, to monitor how people use public open spaces, and as an exchange interface between users and practitioners, decision makers, authorities. They aim to increasing the understanding of the usability of space and the call to improve it to meet people's needs. Additionally, all the three platforms are being developed with the intention of enabling planners to obtain data from different users and on specific issues related to a public open space. In this sense, the advantages of using similar digital approaches for monitoring and planning processes can be focused around the real-time data gathering, the maintenance of an updated database, the collection of different activities and users' groups 'at the same time and in the same space", and, finally, to record their opinion and preferences, via text, video, sound or pictures. These digital tools open up also the possibility to perform specific surveys.

Through this chapter, we intend to demonstrate the critical features of the three platforms and describe the functionalities and opportunities that each one offered. Different types of results produced through their use will be analysed, based on each different study cases where the digital tool was tested. By describing the case studies, our main goal is to argue about the main potential of each platform, related to different stakeholders and users.

This chapter is organised in five sections. In sections two, three and four the WAY-Cyberparks digital tool, CyberCardeto smartphone application, and EthnoAlly, are correspondingly described and discussed. In the last section, the chapter concludes with a critical discussion and lessons learned.

2 WAY-Cyberparks

The WAY-Cyberparks digital tool is one of the main outcomes of the COST Action TU1306, and it is a result of strong international transdisciplinary cooperation between ICTs developers, urban planners/designers/landscape architects, social and behavioural scientists. The main objective of this digital tool is to provide support to fieldwork activities, related to the understanding of the interactions between people and physical space, taking advantages of the potentiality behind the given mobile technologies.

2.1 Overall Description and Potential of the Digital Tool

In a nutshell, the WAY-Cyberparks consists of a smartphone application (APP) and a web platform, and it is developed with the intention of increasing the data and enhancing the insights on how citizens appropriate and use open public spaces, namely by tracking outdoor activities. Additionally, when users reach specific geographical points, the tool allows administrators to pose specific contextualized questions. Furthermore, users can also proactively send their suggestions and inquiries to the administrators, attaching different kinds of multimedia material. This collective method allows for the gathering of contextual feedback and significant information about the eventual use of public spaces. Moreover, the digital tool enriches the individuals' experience by providing contextual information and tools to socialize with others. The objectives behind the creation of these interactive contents is to make the exploration of public spaces more attractive and engaging, while fostering outdoor inclusiveness. By this way, the tool becomes more attractive both for place administrators as well as for common users. Additionally, the WAY-Cyberparks provides an off-line mode, allowing users to use it even when internet connection is not available.

The central architecture of WAY-Cyberparks is not the app itself, but rather the web platform where the administrator of each space can access all the available multimedia material gathered through the app, such as the participant's profile, their answers to the posed questions, their moving patterns in the place, the speed of movement, the stops enacted, their length, or even the weather conditions during the activity to better understand the complex user - space relationship. The administrator is also able to visualize information from the gathered material like the uploaded images, videos, audios and textual notes taken by the participants.

More specifically, the data gathered by the app can be divided into two groups. The first relates to the *direct data*, which includes the audio-visual material produced by the users while directly interacting with their surroundings. The second handles the *indirect data* classified as descriptive metadata. This second group of data is inferred by the app while it is running, gathering relevant information such as user's position, the actual time and the user's speed. The role of the material is important in better understanding users' behaviour, and to respond to their needs.

2.2 Case Studies Around the World

Up to date, the WAY-Cyberparks is specifically developed to function for many different cities attracting, at the same time, the attention of a remarkable number of professionals around the globe. Amongst these profiles we find teachers, educators, cultural heritage workers, urban planners, architects and local governments. It is being used in more than 25 cities spread all over the world (as shown in Fig. 1(A)), in European cities such as Barcelona, Lisbon, Ljubljana or Sofia; in Asian cities such as New Delhi; or South American cities such as Curitiba or Popayan. All these deployments have generated different data coming from more than 430 users. It should be highlighted that enable the digital tool for a specific place is a rapid process, coordinated by the University of Deusto with the administrator of this space.

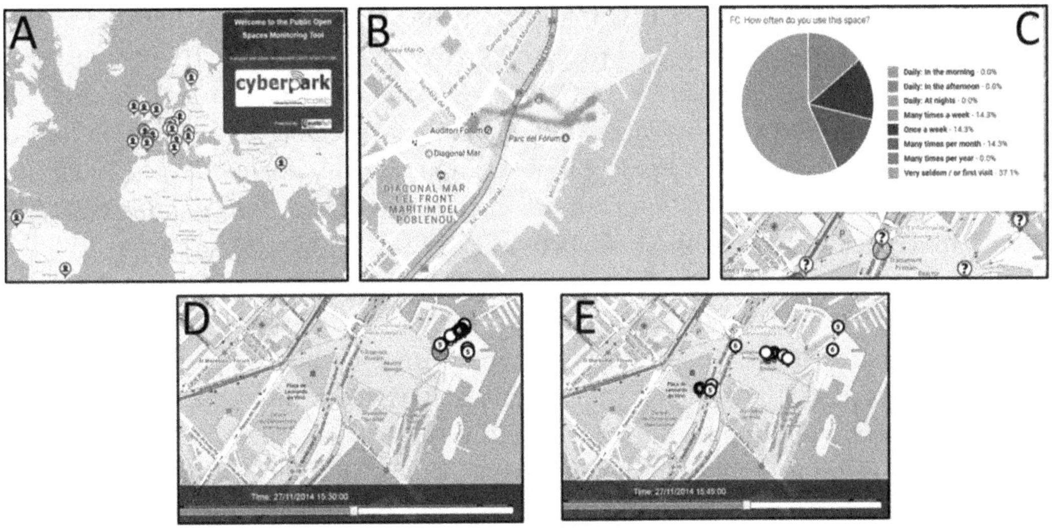

Fig. 1. (A) WAY-Cyberparks deployments all over the world. (B)–(E) Examples of some of the functionalities offered by WAY-CyberParks. Examples focused on the city of Barcelona.

The gathered data can be analysed in different ways by the administrators of each site. Among the various results obtained by the processed data we can highlight the development of behavioural heat map; the users' movement monitoring tool and the users' response analysis. The first one, the behavioural heat map, is a graphical representation of the activity carried out by the users. This graph is overlaid over the map of the study area, indicating the places with the most registered activity. One example of this functionality can be seen in Fig. 1(B), registered in the city of Barcelona.

The second functionality is the users' movement monitoring tool. The main motivation behind this monitoring tool is to trace how participants use an outdoor space - product of detailed planning and design - by recording their responses, behaviours and/or tracking their movement within the space. The aspects identified may help urban planners and decision-makers to investigate some crucial dimensions that can result to more responsive, stronger, safer and inclusive cities. An example of this functionality is demonstrated in Fig. 1(D) and (E), in which two different situations have been presented, showing the exact position of each user at two adjacent timestamps (with a difference of 15 min between them).

By the users' response analysis administrators can extract statistical data from the answers given to each question, and they can choose to receive graphical results from any of the questions posed, as showed in Fig. 1(C). At this point, it is important to highlight that all these functionalities can be filtered based on different criteria, such as the gender, occupation, education or age and that all this information can be taken from the user's profile.

2.3 Case Study Quinta das Conchas Park, Lisbon, Portugal

In this section, we explore the case study of the Quinta das Conchas Park in Lisbon. It was part of the activities associated with the European Researchers' Night which took place on September 25, 2015. The activity organised by the Portuguese team of

CyberParks (CeiED/ULHT and LNEC) set as main objective to test the digital tool WAY CyberParks. The results were processed, analysed and presented during the event.

The workshop was attended by 15 participants who, allocated in groups, used the mobile application WAY CyberParks. Beyond testing the tool, it was also an aim to open the opportunity to app users to propose improvements for its development and operation. During the event, administrators intended to collect information regarding specific functionalities of the WAY CyberParks. These can be categorised as follows: (1) the routes taken by each user (or group); (2) the information provided to the WAY CyberParks suggestion box; (3) the responses to the WAY CyberParks questions related to the visited space, and (4) a paper questionnaire on the usability and applicability of the tool WAY CyberParks. From these four functionalities, it was however not possible to collect the responses to the questions inserted in the application. The questions were uploaded and working online during the event. Due to technical issues related to a change of the hosting server of the tool, it was not possible to record the responses given by the users. Their routes allow to understand which parts of the spaces were more used. The Figs. 2 and 3 show an example of the route taken by a user and the behavioural map associated. This information, combined with possible suggestions and/or answers to questions, can show how the space is used, which areas have a greater or lesser occupation and the time space associated with journeys and stays.

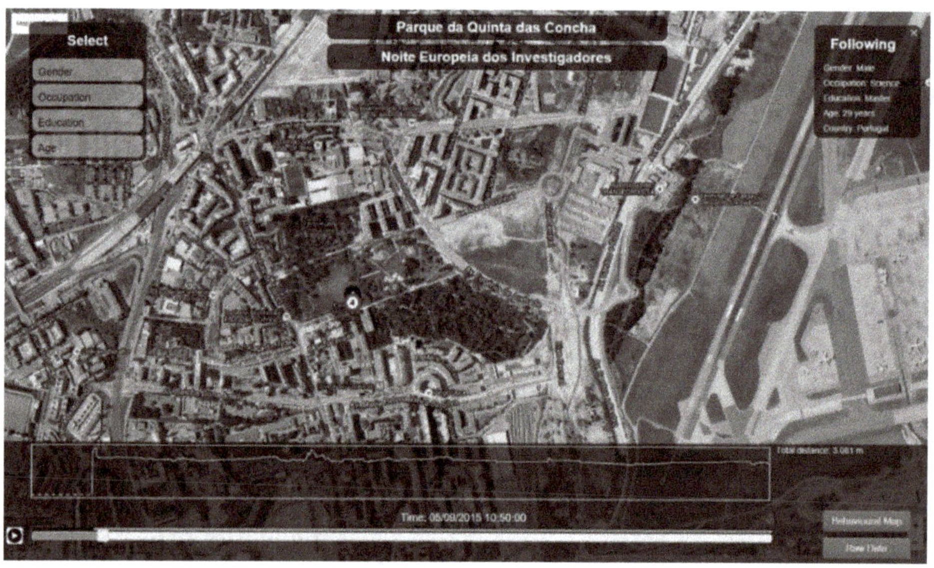

Fig. 2. Print screen website CyberParks (http://services.cyberparks-project.eu/): User path and distance travelled.

The "suggestion box" was a functionality widely used by the participants, with 17 interactions in total. The sound submission feature was not used and only one video was uploaded. Sending of suggestions was done mostly through text and image, and the use of text with illustration (image) in the same suggestion was the most commonly used option. Most of records are related to observing of negative points, corresponding to 65% of interactions (11 records). This functionality allows to ease and speed checking users' opinions about the visited space.

Taking advantage of a workshop with a previously registered group of people, and in order to obtain more information about the usability of the tool WAY CyberParks a paper questionnaire was prepared and submitted to the participants. It was provided to participants at the end of the event. Although the objective was not to tackle the results obtained by the tool, the users' opinions regarding the questions launched by the mobile application highlighted some suggestions for improvement, for example to add the functionality to allow the discovery of something new in the park.

As for the questions that were automatically launched, the participants point out their preference for, among other things, direct opinions while encouraging a closer observation of the surrounding area. Some suggestions for improvement have also been made, such as to offer the mobile application in Portuguese; the improvement of the interface and a system of notifications of questions to be launched automatically. It should be noted that these two main aspects highlighted by the users allowed to significantly improve the tool soon after the workshop. Regarding the raised question in terms of the aid that the mobile application might have given in the discovery of something new in the Park, most users answered affirmatively, as indicated by the less visited areas of the Quinta dos Liláses, an adjacent park to Quinta das Conchas.

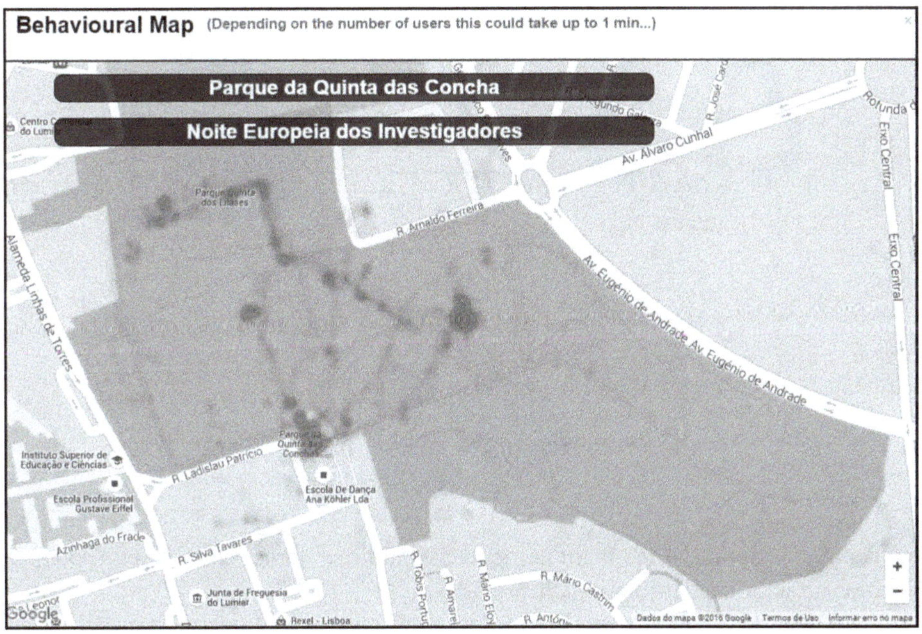

Fig. 3. Print screen website CyberParks (http://services.cyberparks-project.eu/): Behavioural map

3 CyberCardeto

The CyberCardeto application has been developed and tested in a real scenario to validate the feasibility of the mentioned paradigm of *Senseable Spaces* (Rati et al. 2006; Kostankos et al. 2010; Girardin et al. 2008), in terms both of giving and getting information to and from the users.

3.1 Overall Description and Potential of the Digital Tool

CyberCardeto is a mobile application developed with the specific aim of shaping the paradigm of a senseable space, defining this latter as this kind of space where there is a seamless exchange of information between the users and the technology installed on it. In fact, the application can be used once user gets into a public space, i.e. a park, since it provides contextual information about the environment with text and media hints. The user is geo-localised and can see her/himself located into the map of the park. The application is paired with sensors that have been installed in the park and that enable the activation of notification once the user gets into the radius of influence of each sensor. The sensors are also enabled to collect the information from the users' device, storing data in a remote repository for future statistical inferences. The architecture of the application in composed of three main elements. The first one is the mobile application, which provides contextual awareness services. The second consists of the active sensors installed within the park having the twofold purpose of providing the information and acquiring data. The data collection service is hence performed by a server, which deals with the task of storing the data coming from the activity of the users in the park. The overall architecture of the tool can be seen in Fig. 4.

Fig. 4. Overall description of the main components of the system architecture. The Application can communicate with the sensors which provides.

The application was designed to run on both iOS and Android device and it is available for free[1,2] download. The structure of the application is very easy and user-friendly, and it is mainly composed of a toolbar which brings the user into the main functionalities:

[1] https://play.google.com/store/apps/details?id=it.univpm.dii.cardeto&hl=es.

[2] https://itunes.apple.com/us/app/cybercardeto/id1219952063?mt=8.

- The Points of Interest (POI) which allow the user to get in-depth information about the main attraction of the park and are divided into two main categories: *natural* and *historical*. Once the user clicks over a POI, she/he is enabled to discover more details in terms of the flora found in the park, as well as its background history. Moreover, the user can express her/his attitude/preferences towards a single POI, so that the manager of the area can understand the visitors' behaviour within the park. Some possible paths are also suggested, being accessible from the map function;
- The Map is designed as to be essential and simple and it is enabled for GPS geolocation. The user can see her/his position inside the map and can also pick the POIs to reach the associated information. The path is designed as to suggest the POIs that are closer to her/him.

Some screenshots of the application running are depicted in Fig. 5. Inside the park, and in order to monitor visitors' movements, we installed active beacons arranged in a limited area. Beacons are BLE (Bluetooth low energy) based sensor, enabling smart devices to perform actions when they are close to them. These transmitters are commonly used for distributing messages at specific POIs (as in this specific case) and as part of an indoor/outdoor positioning systems. More specifically, the beacons used for this case study are the well-known Estimote Locations Beacons[3] which are commercially available sensors with a built-in bidirectional low energy BLE radio. These are medium range location transmitters, designed to be used in both outdoor and indoor locations. Active beacons were placed near the main "attractions" of the study area, with the dual scope of providing notifications and collecting statistics about each attraction. Beacons' ping is caught by the smartphones and the application is enabled to send data to the cloud via 3G/4G connection. This solution is particularly suitable for such kind of services, since it allows the cross-platform development, it is of low cost and it assures a long-life due to low battery consumption.

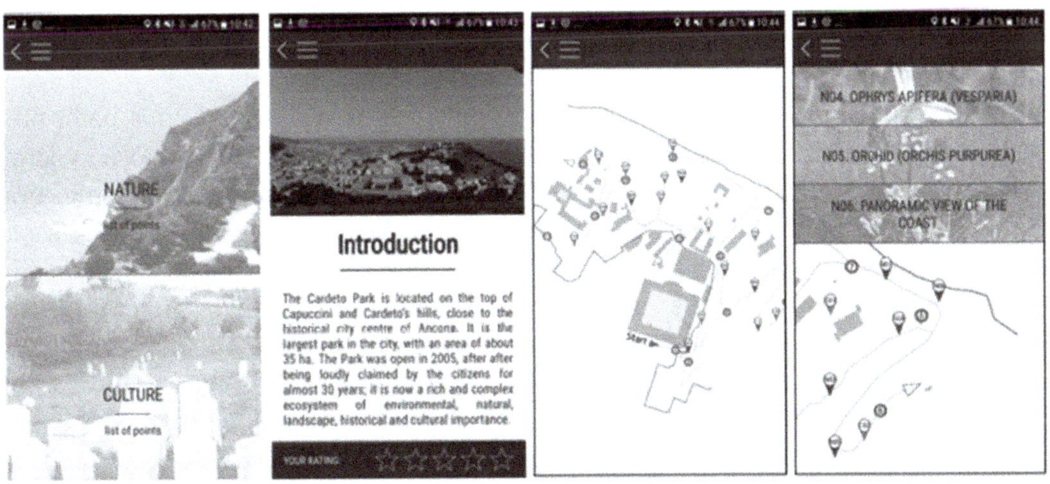

Fig. 5. Some screenshots of the application running. In particular on the right picture is depicted the interaction with the beacon, once the user gets within its area of influence. The nearest POIs are suggested.

---

[3] https://estimote.com/.

In the next section a more detailed description of the case study specifically designed to test the application and to validate the methodology for further investigations and uses is provided.

3.2 Case Study Cardeto Park, Ancona, Italy

The specific case study has been chosen to test the functionalities of the application within the premises of Cardeto Park in Ancona, an urban green space close to the city centre. It is one of the biggest city parks in Ancona with an area of 35 hectares. In its broad territory, the park includes numerous natural and historic places that attract a great number of users every year. Additionally, its proximity to the harbour, its natural landscape and the diverse views offered along the elevated coast makes it an attractive destination for local, as well as for tourists. The area of the Park can be ideally divided into three areas. The North-Western part of the Park located between the ruins of roman Amphitheatre and the Lighthouse including a small residential area close to the new lighthouse. The South-Eastern part of the park as a natural zone that includes places with panoramic views, jogging paths, lawn court for running and sports, ruins of the old Napoleonic fort, and rich botanic diversity. The middle part of the Park as an area of blended zones, from the historic-cultural cluster of the west part to the strong natural-botanic character of the south. This mixed-use area includes an English and a Hebrew cemeteries, old military buildings, to be restructured and assigned to further academic needs, and a play-ground. All these features make the Cardeto Park the proper scenario to validate the potential of the tools in terms both of behaviour analysis and efficiency for the visitors.

For testing the application, we chose the part located in the middle of the Park and, as it has been explained already, includes diverse elements identified by historic, cultural and botanic perspectives. The map of the area of interest is depicted in Fig. 4. The testing area is a territory of 9 hectares where nature and culture are inseparable, with two independent entrances from the city and the main road that connects the area with all the other parts of the Park.

The mobile application was designed to guide the user along the visit path, providing contextual information through the POIs and thus promoting a close synergy between visitors and the place. As said before, the main functionality of the application is the contextual notification of the attraction points. Moreover, to improve the capability of the park to "suggest a path" to the visitors, beacons have been also installed in bifurcation points leaving the user free to choose her/his own preferred path. Notwithstanding, other functions increase the user's experience. The localization service allows finding attractions in a virtual map. The list of POIs proved useful for the visitor that attempts to reach a point of interest. Discussing the cloud service, the data have been collected in the following way: once the smartphone is permanently into the operational range of the beacon (recording five consequent pings) the application performs two operations. The first is to notify the users with a welcome message, while the second is the sending of the data to the cloud automatically done after the first step. The same criteria are adopted to discard the device once the smartphone exits

Fig. 6. The map of the park with highlighted the study area

from the area of influence of the beacon. In this way, it is possible to collect a series of information like the overall time spent by the users in each POI, the interaction among groups of users, the preferred path and response to an attraction point as well as other statistical data that can be of great value for the managing authorities and planners.

4 EthnoAlly

The EthnoAlly is a digital tool developed to facilitate the work of the ethnographic researchers, allowing them to strictly focus on their fieldwork, while letting the tool do the hard and necessary job of recomposing the gathered material once the experience has finished. A large part of the ethnographic fieldwork consists in bringing together the various materials collected during a day in the field. This is a daily activity, and it is important to make it in a coherent and productive way. Only by this way the researcher can generate intelligible archives or documents for further analysis and consultation. In fact, the ethnographer needs to be capable of finding a way throughout the amount of materials gathered in a later time, once the direct memory of the events portrayed may have faded. Specifically, the laboriousness of this activity is especially important for those researches performed in semiotically dense environments, or in scenarios in which little time is left during the day to collect thoughts or materials. To help out of this, digital technologies are rapidly entering the work of ethnographers, shaping new ways by which they can conduct their daily fieldwork.

4.1 Overall Description and Potential of the Digital Tool

EthnoAlly is a digital tool specifically designed for conducting participatory audio-visual ethnographic research. Succinctly explained, EthnoAlly consists of two different elements. The first one is a smartphone/tablet app, which permits the users the collection of audio-visual material. The second component is a web platform. Its aim is to drawn information from the gathered multimedia material and to transform it into an understandable structure for further use. These two components are connected by an additional third element, which is the server in the cloud. This server acts as a bridge between the web platform and the app. In this sense, the server synchronizes, archives, and organizes the raw data gathered by the app and provides the data to the web platform for proper visualization and analysis. The architecture of the complete digital tool is depicted in Fig. 7.

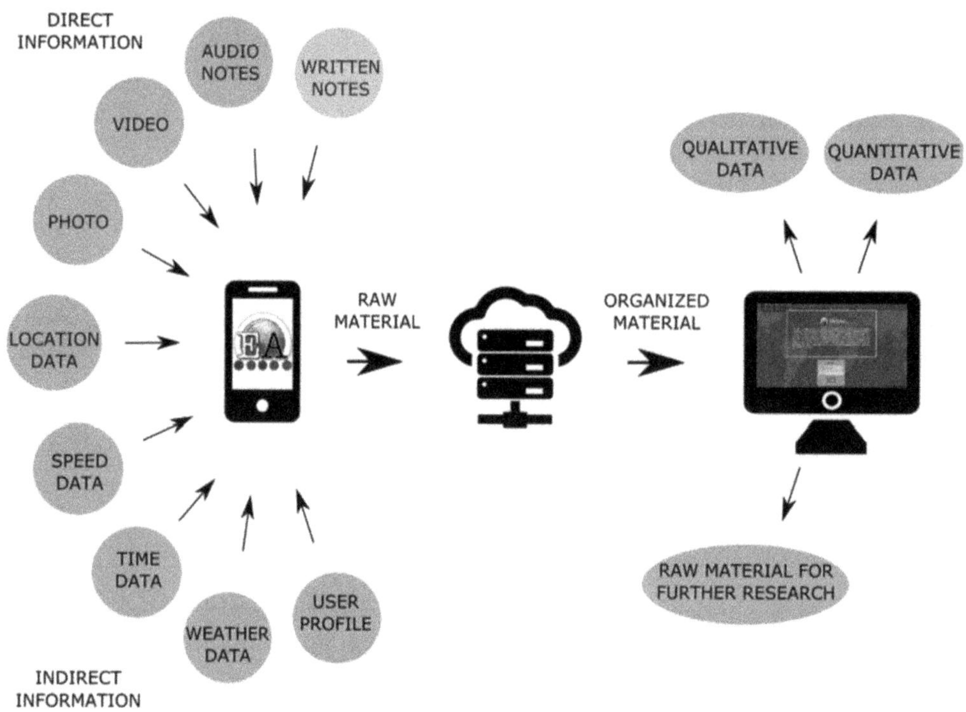

Fig. 7. Architecture of EthnoAlly digital tool with the three different elements depicted: The smartphone APP, the cloud and the Web Platform.

On one hand, the smartphone/tablet app, defined primarily as an audio-visual information gatherer, is able to collect different kinds of multimedia material such as photos, audios, videos, or text notes. All these data can be introduced by a user-friendly interface. In line with this, it is noteworthy to mention the full commitment of the digital tool with the user's privacy. In this regard, all the information gathered by a specific user cannot be seen by someone else apart from the material previously set as "public". Furthermore, EthnoAlly researchers have access to all the available data prior the consent confirmation of the users while all this information is completely untied from any personal identification. This makes it impossible to associate the gathered data with any specific user. Besides that, as in the case of the tool WAY-Cyberparks, the data collected by the smartphone/tablet app can be classified into two different groups: *direct* and *indirect* data. Direct data are these audio-visual materials that are directly produced by the users through her/his interaction with the environment and the application. This information represents the principal data that any EthnoAlly user can access. Additionally, the indirect information represents the descriptive metadata. In this sense, this material is inferred by the application while being used, even in the background. Some examples of this indirect data are the time, the position, or even the weather conditions. All this information has a remarkable importance for the proper contextualization of the direct data, and it greatly helps the researcher to completely understand the users' behaviour and response.

On the other hand, the main component of the digital tool is the web platform[4]. This platform is fed by the direct and indirect data gathered by the app and is stored in the above-mentioned cloud server. In this sense, the server is responsible for the organization of all gathered data. Afterwards, all this material is provided to the web platform for its proper presentation, facilitating any posterior analysis and visualization. Besides that, the most interesting functionality of this platform, along with the possibility of visualizing and analysing all the collected material, is the content search engine further presented in the following subsection.

4.2 Case Study Antwerp, Belgium

In this subsection, an example of how EthnoAlly has been used in a real scenario is discussed. In this case, the activities performed by one user in a single field work session in Antwerp, Belgium, are described. More concretely, this case study is focused on an interesting functionality implemented on EthnoAlly, which helps the user to recompose all the materials collected during the fieldwork. This feature is represented by the track - a concept related to the activity conducted by the user in a single session. In this sense, once a user activates the track functionality, all the direct and indirect information acquired by the app during that session is automatically associated to this path. Additionally, the user can also attach any direct material taken in any other moment, or through any other method or application. The end results of this process result to a route composed by all the materials found and attached to the specific track. Figure 8 shows some screenshots related to the track concept.

Once the work of the ethnographer has been finished, and after collecting different information, she/he can easily view all the performed activity throughout the web platform. As previously explained, all the collected material is perfectly contextualized, meaning that all the information appears superimposed on the map in the exact places where they were taken (as shown in Fig. 6, in a created track in Antwerp). Furthermore, all the information has additional contextual data associated, such as the weather conditions or the exact time they were collected. Additionally, taking the track as an example, the route may acquire other associated digital materials such as written notes,

---

[4] http://cloud.mobility.deustotech.eu/ethnoally.

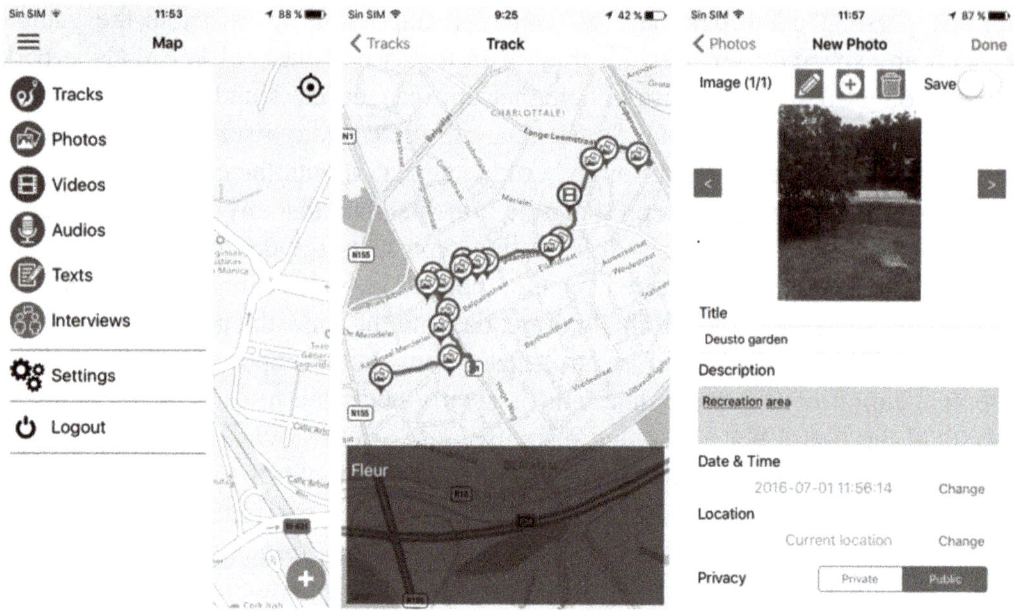

Fig. 8. Some screenshots of a field work session

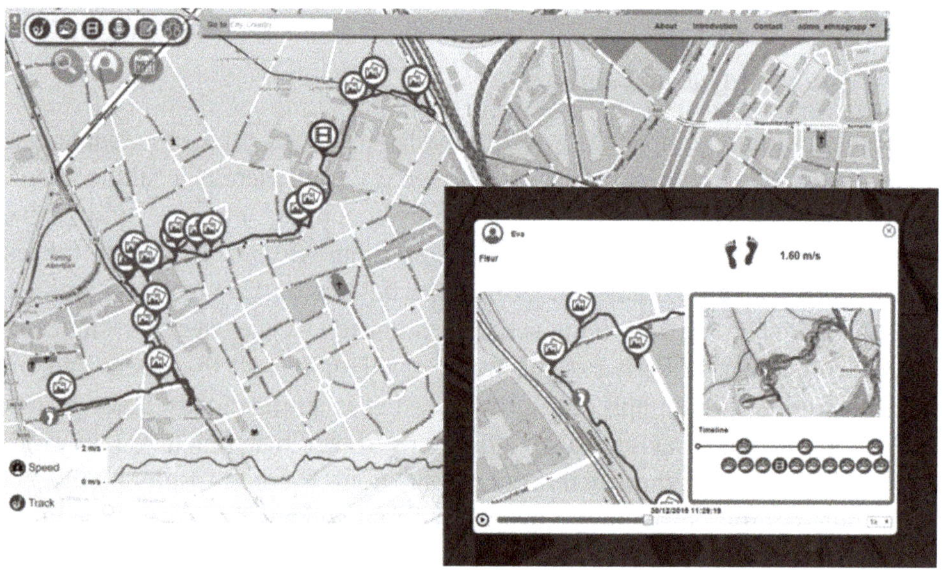

Fig. 9. Track functionality in the web platform

photos, videos or audios, which also appear in the exact places they were gathered. Besides that, as it is displayed in Fig. 9, all tracks can be visualized in an especially created video mode. In this mode, the user can reproduce step by step the followed routes. In addition, every time the route reaches a point in which a specific material has been gathered, it is automatically shown or reproduced.

Finally, to facilitate the retrieval of different content stored in the server, the web platform offers a user-friendly search engine. Using this engine, users can search any kind of content by keyword, user, or time-period. In Fig. 8, for example, a search by keyword of any type of direct content has been made (photo, video, audio or written note) inside the track taken in Antwerp. In this specific example, the search term was 'street', and one video matched with the search conditions. Additionally, searches based on users can also be made. In this case, users can search any other participant by introducing her/his name. Once the search is made, all the public content associated to the quested user is displayed, as seen in Fig. 10.

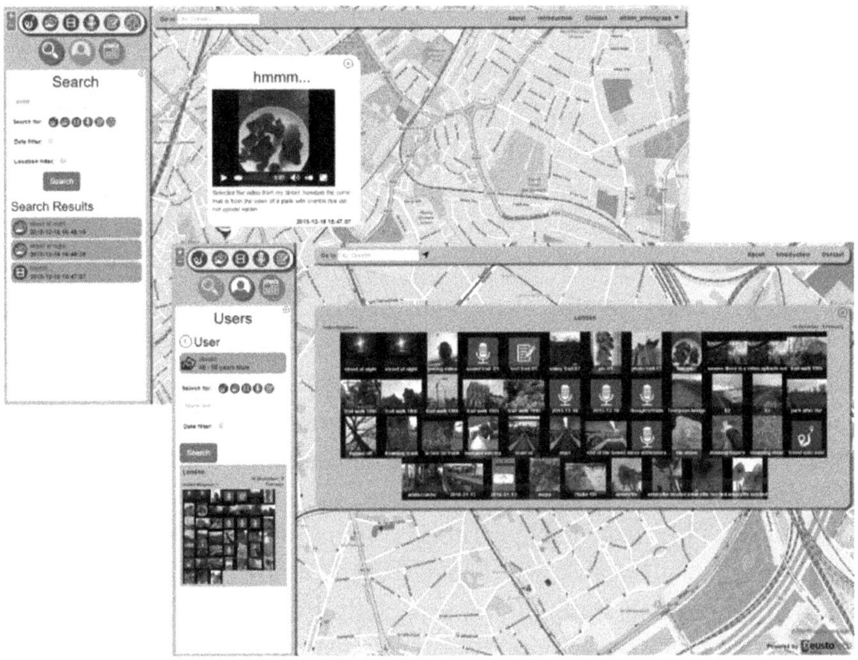

Fig. 10. Search function in the web platform

5 Conclusion and Lessons Learned

The use of ICTs allows for a new approach in the development of public open spaces in order to create more attractive and inclusive urban spaces. Throughout history, public spaces were reflecting the identity of the city, providing - from a social point of view - various functions. Increasingly, open spaces users have new needs, and planners have the responsibility to adapt and respond to these needs. Through the use of ICT, the main challenge is to promote interaction possibilities between users and decision makers, but above all promoting the coexistence of new groups (youngsters, adult, elderly people, tourists, researchers etc.). By enhancing public open spaces, we are encouraging healthier living behaviours, contributing to better living conditions in cities.

This chapter made possible a deeper understanding of the main functionalities and opportunities offered by the three different digital platforms: WAY CyberParks; EthnoAlly; and CyberCardeto. It allows the understanding of the main potential of each platform, related to different stakeholders and users. In brief, we can describe the WAY

CyberParks and CyberCardeto as tools that allow users to get dynamic contextual information related to space. Additionally, the first one allows different type of information to be transmitted using a suggestion box and a questionnaire available in each location. On the other hand, EthnoAlly is a digital tool born to facilitate the work of the ethnographic researchers, allowing them to focus strictly on their fieldwork, and letting the tool do the hard and necessary job of recomposing such material once the experience is finished. Being interactive tools, their use plays a relevant role not only in the development, but also in the maintenance and improvement of public spaces. They offer valuable resources to make a significant contribution to the study of public spaces. The type of results produced allows a quick and efficient collection of data that may prove essential in the development of new public spaces while improving existing ones. Basic advantages for different kind of users can be further highlighted. To refer some, in terms of planners and the public administration, we can foresee that a wider adoption of ICT tools might improve the tourism sector offering an economic boost by engaging higher numbers of visitors.

Moreover, the quality of the services can be improved, and new services can be tailored according to users' feedback and analysis. Finally, given the impervious layout of a park, the ICT can contribute to overcoming the physical barriers while restoring the vital connections and relationships between the park and the city. In addition, the visitors can benefit from such services. With pervasive, but not intrusive, services directly available for their own devices, users can achieve a better knowledge about their surroundings. Given the immense potential of the tools, it is also important to underline some possible drawbacks. Their systems are app based and are not so widespread. This is also because the app is based on BLE technology which is not popular so far. This presents a limitation, especially from the data collection viewpoint that is rather contradictory since by performing statistical inference about the behaviour of the user and the performances of the park, the bulk of data should in fact be increased.

Acknowledgements. This work has been supported by the Cost Action TU1306 CyberParks and the Spanish Ministry of Economy and Competitiveness under the ESPHIA project (TIN2014-56042-JIN). E. Osaba would like to thank the Basque Government for its funding support through the EMAITEK program. The authors would also like to thank the staff of UbiSive s.r.l. for the support in developing the CyberCardeto smartphone application.

References

Girardin, F., Calabrese, F., Fiore, F.D., Ratti, C., Blat, J.: Digital footprinting: uncovering tourists with user-generated content. IEEE Pervasive Comput. **7**(4) (2008)

Kostakos, V., O'Neill, E., Penn, A., Roussos, G., Papadongonas, D.: Brief encounters: sensing, modeling and visualizing urban mobility and copresence networks. ACM Trans. Comput.-Hum. Interact. (TOCHI) **17**(1), 2 (2010)

Ratti, C., Frenchman, D., Pulselli, R.M., Williams, S.: Mobile landscapes: using location data from cell phones for urban analysis. Environ. Plann. B: Plan. Des. **33**(5), 727–748 (2006)

Šuklje-Erjavec, I., Smaniotto Costa, C.: Cyberparks challenges exploring the relationships between information and communication technologies and urban open spaces. In: Places & Technologies, Nova Gorica, Slovenia, pp. 163–170 (2015)

Smaniotto Costa, C., Menezes, M., Mateus, D., Bahillo Martínez, A.: Podem as tecnologias da informação e comunicação contribuírem para capacitar o conhecimento das práticas e necessidades de uso de parques urbanos. In: XII Congresso Luso-Afro-Brasileiro de Ciências Sociais-XII CONLAB, pp. 7705–7713 (2015)

4.5

A Pedagogical Model for CyberParks

Philip Bonanno[1(✉)], Michal Klichowski[2], and Penelope Lister[1]

[1] Department of Leadership for Learning and Innovation, Faculty of Education, University of Malta, Msida, Malta
{philip.bonanno,penelope.lister.16}@um.edu.mt
[2] Faculty of Educational Studies, Adam Mickiewicz University in Poznan, Poznan, Poland
klichowski.michal@gmail.com

Abstract. This chapter discusses the recent conceptual developments about CyberParks and their educational potential. Key learning characteristics and pedagogical principles will be identified through a review of learning theories and studies from cognitive neuroscience. Relevant pedagogical models are reviewed to develop one that describes learning in CyberParks, which will be used to design and evaluate learning in such context. An innovative connectivist-inspired process-oriented pedagogical model is proposed to serve as a signpost in the process of developing adaptive expertise through which new pedagogies and innovative uses of CyberParks address the evolving needs of citizens.

Keywords: Pedagogy · Smart city learning · Design for learning · Connectivism · Cognitive neuroscience

1 Introduction

A cyberpark – the meditated public open space - can be considered as a hybrid urban learning space that combines natural with man-made features, the physical with the digital, the local with the global, formal with informal learning. Citizens use it for recreation and entertainment, to socialise, pursue healthy lifestyles, learn about themselves and their surroundings and participate in the development and use of their hybrid habitat (Klichowski 2017). Digital technologies and communication systems mediate, enhance and transform people's interaction in a cyberpark. The emphasis in literature about cyberparks and smart cities is more on the role of citizen-users and the enhancement of their quality of life rather than on the role played by physical and technological factors. Thomas et al. (2016) epitomises this in the concept of smart cities as place, people and purpose.

2 The Educational Potential of CyberParks

Cyberpark is smart physical learning environments exploiting the affordances of digital, context-aware and adaptive devices that promote better and faster learning through ubiquitous digital connectivity (Isaksson et al. 2017; Klichowski 2017). This enables

C. Smaniotto Costa et al. (Eds.): CyberParks, LNCS 11380, pp. 294–307, 2019.
https://doi.org/10.1007/978-3-030-13417-4_23

learners to connect in context-aware scenarios to a wider network of knowledge, experts and learning communities via their adaptive devices. For Hwang (2014) a smart learning environment, besides enabling learners to access digital resources and interact with learning systems in any place and at any time, actively provides the necessary learning guidance, supportive tools or learning suggestions. Buchem and Perez-Sanagustin (2013) propose four modes of learning (seamless learning, crowd learning, geo-learning and citizen inquiry) that emerge in such contexts manifesting users' interaction with the natural, historical, cultural, architectural and digital dimensions of the space. For Sharples et al. (2012) seamless learning is evident when a person experiences a continuity of learning across a combination of locations, times, technologies and social settings. Gros (2016) characterises learning in technology-enhanced environments (like in a cyberpark) as fundamentally personal, social, distributed, ubiquitous, flexible, dynamic and complex in nature. She states that one of the most important features of smart learning is that the data used serves as feedback for the learner to support personalised learning.

Hybrid environments like a cyberpark may trigger deep learning that change an individual's competence profile and epistemological conceptions. Interactivity extends the zone of possibilities providing new focussed learning instances (Cook et al. 2015). Buchem and Perez-Sanagustin (2013) contend that, when mediated through mobile technologies and locative media, the surrounding physical and the digital environment can be dynamically merged into augmented, ad-hoc personal learning environments. By interacting with these hybrid environments learners develop 21st century skills including efficient and effective access of information and knowledge, inquiry/problem-solving, creative, collaborative and communicative competences, and the ability to be innovative in using the surrounding habitat in culturally sensitive, globally aware and ethically responsible ways. Through networked technologies citizen-learners develop new interactional patterns with the various aspects of hybridity.

Cyberparks can challenge people to extend their learning boundaries through acquisition of new knowledge and skills, by sharing their understanding and by contributing to the distributed knowledge and networked experience (Klichowski 2017). The more citizens learn about technology and learn through technology the more empowered they become to interact with the surrounding environment. The situation is complex as it merges different epistemologies within one learning instance or calls on relevant epistemologies for different instances of learning. Consequently, different theories of learning serve as conceptual lenses through which interactions cyberpark can be analysed to identify the underlying learning principles and conditions.

3 Theories of Learning

Learning in a cyberpark is a composite experience involving intra-individual cognitive, affective and conative interactions together with inter-individual, networked, interactional processes. Anderson (2010) distinguishes between pre-net theories (developed before the event of the internet) and net-aware theories (characterising contexts rich in information and communication systems). Learning experience in cyberparks links to different theories according to the situation and conditions.

3.1 Pre-net Learner-Centric Theories

Behaviourist, cognitive, neurocognitive and socio-cultural theoretical perspectives describe manifested internal processes and external behaviours. Yet, while behaviourist pedagogies deliberately go no further than observable inputs and outputs, cognitivist approaches take into account the mental models and internal processes, building on a richer psychological understanding of learning and how it occurs (Dron and Anderson 2014). Mayes and de Freitas (2004), as well as Beetham and Sharpe (2007), describe three theoretical dimensions of learning – the associative, the cognitive and the situative. Learning in cyberparks may include aspects of the associative approach, for example when following prescribed learning activities to learn concepts or skills initially through basic stimulus-response conditioning and later by associating concepts in a chain of reasoning, or associating steps in a chain of activity to build a composite skill. The main focus is on the alignment of learning objectives, instructional strategy and assessment. This approach to learning is not concerned with how concepts or skills are represented internally, but how these are manifested in external behaviours and observable learning.

In contrast, cognitive approaches emphasise modelling of the processes of interpreting and constructing meaning. Knowledge acquisition is the outcome of interactions between new experiences and the relevant memory structures. The key cognitive challenge is to build a framework for understanding rather than behaviouristic strengthening of associations. It is also more authentic, contextual and social in nature, as these aspects are perceived more appropriate for equipping learners with the skills, they will need to participate in a constantly changing societal context (Conole 2014). Learning in cyberparks may have a constructivist orientation promoting understanding through active exploration of the hybrid environment. It can also involve constructionist activities when learners are engaged in creating something for others to see (Papert 1993). Learning by designing may result in effective participatory learning approaches and of embracing ways in which the web-service-based environment offers potential for learning (Beetham 2013).

Social constructivist learning results from achieving understanding through dialogue and collaboration with peer learners, tutors and experts who play a key role in developing a shared understanding of the task and provide feedback and support on the learner's activities and reflections, enabling learners to reach beyond what they are individually capable of learning. Situated learning emphasises social interaction within a community of practice through which one develops competences related to a particular role within the community progressing from novice to expert through observation, reflection, mentorship, and legitimate peripheral participation in community activities.

Cognitive neuroscience (in both behavioural and neuroimaging paradigms, see Klichowski and Kroliczak 2017) provides another learner-centric framework. Klichowski and Patricio (2017) show that learning in cyberparks combines two types of cerebral operations: motor and cognitive control. Many times, this involves learning with digital tools while on the move (Klichowski et al. 2015; Klichowski and Smaniotto Costa 2015). This cognitive-motor interaction requires an appropriate allocation of cognitive and motor resources for each operation. Figure 1 shows that the human brain does not cope well with this situation, which leads to an overload of central resources, and thus to destabilization of the course of cognitive and motor processes, the consequence of which is the weakening of both cognitive and motor tasks. Thus, using a smartphone while walking increases the risk of falling; performing arithmetic operations while driving reduces the accuracy of the result (Yamada et al. 2011). This effect is called dual-task cost (Takeuchi et al. 2016) and its implication for learning in cyberparks is that one should use technology for learning while stationary (sitting) but definitely not while walking. Experiment realised in a cyberpark by Klichowski (2017) use the two behavioural paradigms and the mobile electroencephalography method confirmed this. Thus, the idea of smart and immersive learning, in a sense, has to be revised.

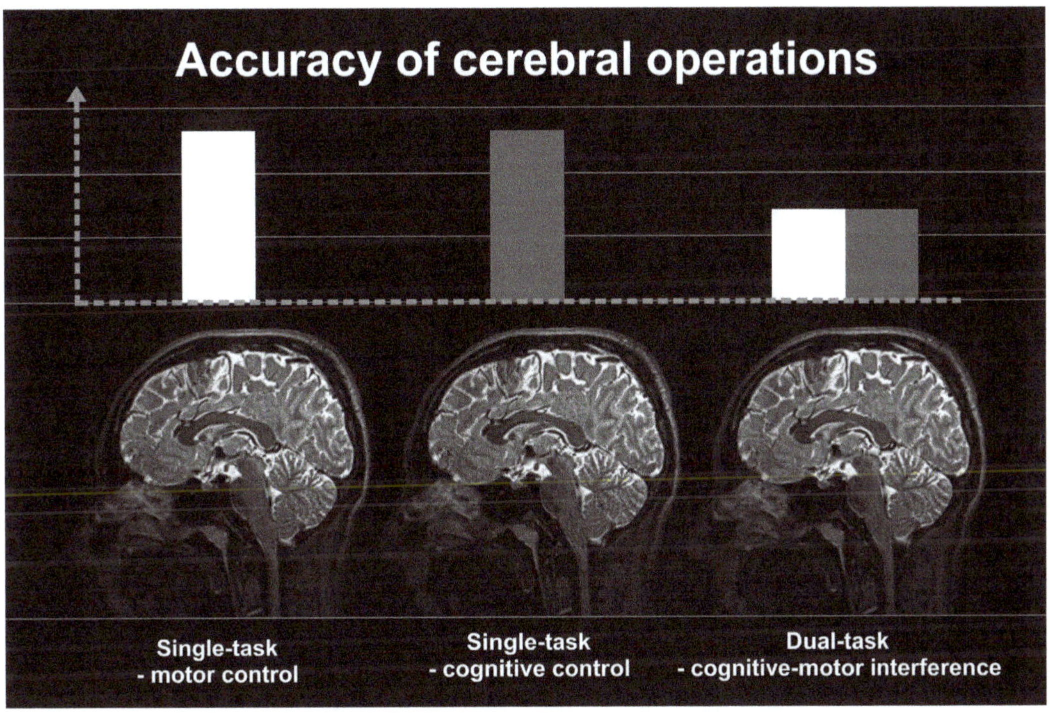

Fig. 1. The dual-task cost theory. The best cognitive or motor results are obtained when separating these processes. Their interaction weakens the results of both. Source: own work based on Pothier et al. (2014) and Yuan et al. (2016)

3.2 Post-net Networked Systems Theories

Gros et al. (2016) give three major categories of post-net networked systems theories: theories focused (1) on the network, (2) on social-personal interaction and (3) on the design of the network. The first category includes networked learning, connectivism and actor network theory (ANT). For Goodyear et al. (2004) networked learning involves the use of digital technologies to promote connections between learner-to-learner,

learner-to-tutors and learning community-to-its learning resources. Learning and knowledge construction is located in the connections and interactions between learners, teachers and resources, and seen as emerging from critical dialogue and enquiry. Such a perspective promotes learning as a social, relational phenomenon, and view knowledge and identity as constructed through interaction and dialogue.

In line with this theory, connectivism considers knowledge as a flow through a network of humans and non-humans (artefacts) comprising connections between nodes that can be individuals, groups, systems, fields, ideas, resources or communities (Siemens 2005). Downes (2006) considers knowledge residing not only in the mind of an individual but is also distributed across an information network or multiple individuals. Knowledge and learning can be defined in terms of connections: know where and know who are more important today than know what and know how (Siemens 2005). The connections that enable us to learn are more important than our current state of knowing. The claim that knowledge is held in the network and that the learning is the network is one of the most debated points of connectivism. Having transient knowledge residing in technical networks and learning externalised into human mediated distributed networks where it takes place and is, and not being restricted to a single individual to be internalised, contrast with the central tenets of previous learning theories. For Downes (2007) knowledge is literally the set of connections formed by actions and experience. It may consist in part of linguistic structures, but other digital media may play an important role in developing knowledge of a less linguistic, more affective and intuitive nature. Thus, learners need to develop skills in digital, information and media literacy, and critical thinking, alongside their understanding of how networks work.

Making no distinction in approach between the social, the natural and the technological, ANT proposes a socio-technical account that explores ways heterogeneous networks, of both human and non-human actors, are constructed and maintained, and focuses on tracing the transformation of these heterogeneous networks (Latour 2005). An actor is anything granted to be the source of an action, and is also a simplified network. There is no difference in the ability of technology, humans, animals or other non-humans to act. While it is possible to render social connections traceable in simple knowledge systems, there is no means to trace these or follow the actors or their actions in complex knowledge systems because these are uncertain, unexpected and often hidden and their connections are varied, ubiquitous and open (Latour 2005). For Gros et al. (2016) the main problem of this approach is that it reduces all actors into black boxes ignoring internal actions such as reflecting, self-criticizing and detecting/correcting errors, providing an incomplete, quasi-behaviourist explanation to the intra-individual and external interactions within hybrid environments like CyberParks.

The same authors discuss theories that focus on social-personal interaction considering learners who navigate through hybrid environments and through their own personal networks. Learning in cyberparks can be considered as part of the overarching lifelong and life wide self-determined learning, an approach in which learners take control of their own learning through self-management, self-monitoring and extension of their own learning (Tan et al. 2011). Heutagogy, another theoretical framework under the social-personal interaction category, is defined as the study of self-determined learning (Hase and Kenyon 2007) and developed as an extension to andragogy, or self-directed learning (Blaschke 2012). Compared to andragogy, heutagogy expands further upon the role of human agency in the learning process considering the learner as the key agent in learning (Hase and Kenyon 2007). Key concepts in heutagogy are:

- The instructor facilitates learning by providing guidance and resources, fully relinquishing ownership of the learning path and process to the learner, who negotiates the content and modality of learning.
- Involves double-loop learning and self-reflection. Learners consider the problem, the resulting action and outcomes in addition to reflecting upon the problem-solving process and how it influences learner's own beliefs and actions.
- There is a progression from andragogy to heutagogy, with learners likewise progressing in maturity and autonomy (Canning 2010). Being more self-directed, mature learners require less instructor control and course structure; less mature learners require more instructor guidance and course scaffolding (Canning and Callan 2010).
- Web 2.0 design supports a heutagogical approach by allowing learners to direct and determine their learning path and by enabling them to take an active role in their individual learning.

The last category of post-net networked systems proposed by (Gros et al. 2016) are theories focused on the affordances or design of the network. Learning as a network (LaaN) theory represents a theoretical framework for personal learning environment (PLE) models that is an emerging concept and a new vision of learning inspired by constructivist and connectivist learning models. It puts the learner at the centre and provides more autonomy and control over the learning experience (Klichowski 2017). LaaN views knowledge as a personal network and as inherently social. Learners need to be good knowledge networkers as well as good double-loop learners who can create and maintain external networks by identifying, integrating and elaborating knowledge nodes that can help to achieve better results, in a specific learning context. As a double-loop learner, one develops the ability to detect and correct errors and eventually change the theories-in-use according to the new setting.

This brief review of relevant learning theories points to key pedagogical factors that are at play in technology-enhanced learning environments. The following pedagogical model combines these principles for describing, designing and assessing learning in cyberparks.

4 Toward a Pedagogical Model for CyberParks

Bonanno (2011; 2014) uses a process-oriented model based on dimensions and levels of interactions for designing ubiquitous learning and learning within social networks. The dimensions of interactions are subject-content, technology, data networks and community. For learning in Cyberparks, this model can be extended by including the physical environment as another dimension.

Considering knowledge as distributed across networks of connections, Wang et al. (2014) developed a pedagogical model based on the characteristics and principles of interaction in complex connectivist learning contexts identifying three categories of connectivist learning activities: (1) personal knowledge acquisition from networked distributed knowledge, (2) social networked learning by building communities that form a network for knowledge sharing and connection, and (3) complex connectivist learning where learners prompt connection building and network formulation by contributing to distributed knowledge, to decision-making related to complex problems, and to the development of technological and pedagogical innovations.

Researchers about online learning identified dimensions of interactions according to technological affordances including student-teacher, student-student, student-content, student-interface, teacher-teacher, teacher-content and content-content interactions (Moore 1989; Hillman et al. 1994; Anderson and Garrison 1998). Through their social constructivist orientation, Web 2.0 and social technologies promote various forms of interpersonal interaction comprising group-content, group-group, learner-group, and teacher-group (Dron 2007), as well learner-content, learner-technology and learner-community (Bonanno 2011; 2014). Connectivist pedagogy, with its emphasis on the development and nurturing of networks as a major component of learning, extended the interaction possibilities to include groups, sets and networks (Dron and Anderson 2014. Besides dimensions researchers considered also levels of interaction such as learner-self, learner-resource (human and nonhuman) and a meta level learner-instruction interaction which guides the previous two types (Hirumi 2002; operation interaction, information interaction, and concept interaction, from simple to complex and concrete to abstract (Chen 2004; learner-content, learner-interface, learner-support, learner-learner, and learner-context (Ally 2004); pedagogical levels of acquisition, participation and contribution in relation to novice, experienced and expert competence levels in the domain, technology and community dimensions (Bonanno 2011; 2014).

Building on this literature about dimensions and levels of interaction researchers developed pedagogical models to facilitate the design, assessment and evaluation of learning in technology-enhanced contexts. Chen (2004) developed the hierarchical model for instructional interaction (HMII) in a distance-learning context, based on Laurillard's conversation framework. According to this model learners that shift from concrete to abstract and from low to high levels manifest three levels of interactions. The most concrete level, on which the other levels depend, is operation interaction, in which the learner operates different media and is interacting with the media interface.

The second level is information interaction, which includes learner-teacher, learner-learner, and learner-content interactions. In connectivist, networked environments characterised by fluid, complex and emerging knowledge, learners have to orientate themselves to filter, integrate, and extract information so as to make it coherent and understandable. Siemens (2011) proposed two means of information interaction and orientation in such complex online learning environments: wayfinding (orienting oneself spatially through the use of symbols, landmarks and environmental cues) and sensemaking (responding to uncertainty, complex topics or in changing settings).

The third level of HMII concept interaction is the most abstract and includes intra-individual cognitive and affective interactions that form neural networks. It stimulates the deepest cognitive engagement characterised by knowledge creation and growth

(Downes 2006; 2007). It includes creation of new learning artefacts individually or collaboratively and it is combined with learner-content interaction, but in collaborative learning environments (Wang et al. 2014).

These three levels of interaction can occur simultaneously and recursively, and are hierarchical with the operation interaction serving as the foundation of information interaction, while information interaction is the foundation of concept interaction. For (Chen 2004) the higher the level, the more critical it is to the achievement of learning objectives so that only concept interaction leads to meaningful learning. Merging Downes (2006; 2007) concept of innovation interaction with Bloom's revised taxonomy (Anderson et al. 2000) that proceeds from remembering to understanding, applying, analysing, evaluating, and creating as cognitive processes, Wang et al. (2014) superimpose four interaction levels onto the HMII. These are operation, wayfinding, sensemaking and innovation interaction. In operation interaction learners merely practice and remember how to operate various media to build their own learning spaces. In wayfinding interaction, learners have to master the ways to navigate in a complex information environment and connect with different human and nonhuman resources, thus reaching higher levels of understanding, applying and evaluating information and connection formed in this process. Sensemaking is a pattern recognition process, mainly involving applying, analysing and evaluating information. Innovation interaction focuses on the expression of ideas, models or theory by artefact creation and innovation to enhance and build new social, technological and informational connections. This engages learners at the deepest, creation level of Bloom's taxonomy.

Another process-oriented pedagogical model proposed by Bonanno (2011; 2014) integrates interactions along three dimensions (domain, technology and community) within three pedagogical levels of interaction (acquisition, participation and contribution). Table 1 show how this can be represented.

Table 1. Process-oriented pedagogical model proposed by Bonanno (2011; 2014)

Levels	Dimensions		
	Domain	Technology	Community
Acquisition Participation Contribution			

The acquisition level is similar to Wang's et al. (2014) operation interaction dealing with basic interactional skills in the domain (information categorisation), surface structure of digital tools and interpersonal interactional skills. The participation level is linked to the information interaction level comprising wayfinding and sensemaking within the domain and the learning community. The contribution level is identical to concept interaction and innovation interaction as it deals with learners' creations within the three domains.

Developed to consider interactions in on-line learning environments these two models do not capture all the dimensions of interactions evident in Cyberparks. Interactions of the different agents (persons, technology or data) with the physical environment are not considered. This shortcoming is addressed by including a fourth dimension – the physical environment. Another dimension (data) is being added considering Cyberparks as smart learning environments characterised by the utilisation and generation of data. To achieve more comprehensive coverage of the possible interactions in a CyberPark, the two models are merged into one, which is depicted in Table 2.

Table 2. A pedagogical model for CyberParks

Levels	Dimensions				
	Physical environment	Domain	Technology	Data/knowledge networks	Community
Operation interaction	Determining interactional potential of different areas of the CyberPark	Defining a domain-related PLE	Promoting digital and info competencies; developing effective HCI strategies	Identify data sources relevant to PLE	Nurturing interpersonal interactional skills within groups and networks
Wayfinding	Connecting specialized nodes or information sources related to CyberPark	Connecting key domain info and knowledge nodes to the different aspects of the CyberPark	Using digital tools that mediate learner connection with info, knowledge, resources and relevant people	Connecting to relevant data sources	Connecting with key people and identifying key features of mature identity
Sensemaking	Negotiation and argumentation to understand the different aspects of CyberPark	Negotiation and argumentation of domain related knowledge; developing an interdisciplinary knowledge structure	Linking technological affordances to learning modes	Developing an organizational network of data sources, types and capturing devices	Identity development; dialogic space analysis and expansion
Innovation interaction	Re-design of Cyberparks to address citizen evolving needs	Renovation of domain knowledge relevant to Cyberparks	Customize tools to interact in new ways with the hybrid environment	Generating data through creation of digital artefacts	Renovate and extend users' social networks and digital footprint

This final model captures most of the interactional possibilities that can take place in Cyberparks and can be used to design and evaluate smart learning activities. At the basic level operational interactions are possible in all five dimensions to build interaction spaces or PLE that merge knowledge and skill competence in different aspects of Cyberparks. Changing the physical environment into a PLE implies getting to know the interactional potential of each section of the place and linking these to ad hoc learning strategies. A smart learning journey, indicating relevant buildings, areas and any associated points of interests facilitates operational interactions in the physical environment. A PLE can be created in a particular domain (history, architecture, engineering, science or humanities) relevant to any aspect of the CyberPark, by identifying resources, support structures involving peer learners, experienced persons or experts, together with learning strategies that can be adopted.

Operational interaction involves connecting learners with different technologies through learner-interface interaction to support their further learning, by connecting with different knowledge and opportunities and by bridging learning across multiple learning and living contexts. Typical actions showing operational interactions with technology include play, download, search, read, view, listen and buy. Also, learners attempt to integrate other social and network-based media into their PLEs and connect with different groups of people and information nodes, to develop a collective distributed technological network. In data rich environments operational interactions enable smartphone users to connect with different data sources after rationalising relevant mobile app interfaces to obtain (and possibly contribute) data related to their learning endeavours. Along the community dimension interpersonal interactional skills have to be nurtured both with contiguous and on-line groups or networks. This develops operational competence with tools used for communication and social networking.

Wayfinding interaction involves finding and connecting the right information and people. Information about different sections of the physical environment are identified and made available for access. People and special interest groups related to the different areas are also identified, organising their means of contact. Learner-content interaction and learner-group interaction are also carried out within any field of knowledge related to the CyberPark, or any part of it, thus elaborating the relevant knowledge web, the learning community and the social networks. This linking and organisational approach is applied to any available or generated data. Typical wayfinding interactions include communicate (chat, rate, comment, message) and share (send, upload, publish).

Sensemaking interaction is a collaborative process that includes information sharing and discussion (Wang et al. 2014). Learners bring together concepts from different domains in a novel way to achieve a coherent comprehension of information and make decisions quickly. Thus, a detailed spatial plan and a global knowledge network serve to integrate the different sections of cyberparks. Knowledge organisation is also carried out in any field consulted, which in turn is linked to the other fields thus creating a final interdisciplinary knowledge structure. With regards to technology, sense making involves linking different digital tools used in various locations in cyberparks, such as QR code systems, augmented reality, geo-tagging and gaming, into a coherent functional system for promoting various modes of learning (Klichowski 2017). Similar patterns are established with regards to data, by creating a bird's eye view of data sources, data types and data capturing devices. Along the community dimension sensemaking interaction manifest itself in the development and sharing of learners' knowledge networks, network identities and social presence. Typical sensemaking interactions involve different modes of facilitation such as recommend, channel, tag, subscribe, filter and mentor. The outcomes of sensemaking interaction are organisational-networked patterns connecting tightly together nodes in geophysical, technological, data, social and conceptual (neural) networks which will eventually form the basis for personal contributions in innovation interaction.

Innovation interaction is the deepest form of learner interaction and cognitive engagement. Experienced learners show their knowledge and competence status through contribution, engaging in evaluative and creative activities (Bonanno 2011; 2014). They create (digital) artefacts or elaborate existing ones and share this innovation with others bringing more networking opportunities on the open network where they are both accessible and persistent (Wang et al. 2014). Cyberparks' users can propose new designs or re-designs of the existing space or parts of it, add or modify new knowledge about (aspects of) the cyberpark, or create/modify open educational resources relevant to some particular aspect or theme. New digital technologies or applications can be customised to interact in innovative or more elaborate ways with the physical, virtual and social environments. Cyberparks visitors use available data and generate new data as (multimedia) artefacts to communicate and share their ad hoc experience. New tools or elaboration of existing ones can be used to innovate and extend users' social networks and digital footprint. Thus, key innovation-interaction actions include customises, design, produce, contribute, program, model and evaluate.

This pedagogical model provides the necessary framework to design and assess formal or informal learning in cyberparks. It captures patterns of interactions characterising different learning instances or extension of one's knowledge and social networks. Each square of the grid represents a specific category of interactions that may be used to design focussed learning activities.

5 Conclusions

Anderson (2009) uses the tango metaphor: pedagogies and technologies are intertwined in a dance, where the moves of one determine the moves of the other. Cyberparks can serve as emergent hybrid environments where people, spaces, technology and purpose create the movement and rhythm of the dance. Nevertheless, a new approach needs to be adopted, to develop pedagogies for these emerging environments (Gros et al. 2016).

The proposed pedagogical model can serve as a theoretical lens and a practical guide for understanding learner experience in cyberparks. More than serving as a static instrument to fit and analyse learners' experience this model should serve as a signpost in the process of developing adaptive expertise. Gros et al. (2016; 15) claim that when "all the components of emerging pedagogies including technology, pedagogy, content and society are evolving, educators need to develop adaptive expertise to understand how these components interplay with and influence their own practices". This model is a proposal to address the continual challenge in developing new pedagogies based on innovative uses of technologies to fulfil the evolving needs and expectations of learners in contexts like Cyberparks.

References

Ally, M.: Foundations of educational theory for online learning. In: Anderson, T. (ed.) The Theory and Practice of Online Learning, pp. 15–44. Athabasca University Press, Edmonton (2004)

Anderson, L.W., et al.: A Taxonomy for Learning, Teaching, and Assessing: A Revision of Bloom's Taxonomy of Educational Objectives. Pearson, New York (2000)

Anderson, T.: The dance of technology and pedagogy in selfpaced distance education. Paper presented at the 17th ICDE World Congress, Maastricht (2009)

Anderson, T.: Theories for learning with emerging technologies. In: Veletsianos, G. (ed.) Emerging Technologies in Distance Education, pp. 23–39. Athabasca University Press, Edmonton (2010). https://doi.org/10.15215/aupress/9781771991490.01

Anderson, T., Garrison, D.R.: Learning in a networked world: new roles and responsibilities. In: Gibson, C. (ed.) Distance Learners in Higher Education, pp. 97–112. Atwood Publishing, Madison (1998)

Beetham, H.: Designing for active learning in technology-rich contexts. In: Beetham, H., Sharpe, R. (eds.) Rethinking Pedagogy for a Digital Age: Designing for 21st Century Learning, pp. 49–63. Routledge, New York and London (2013)

Beetham, H., Sharpe, R.: Rethinking Pedagogy for a Digital Age: Designing and Delivering e-Learning. Routledge, London and New York (2007)

Blaschke, L.M.: Heutagogy and lifelong learning: a review of heutagogical practice and self-determined learning. Int. Rev. Res. Open Distrib. Learn. **13**, 56–71 (2012)

Bonanno, P.: A process-oriented pedagogy for ubiquitous learning. In: Kidd, T., Chen, I. (eds.) Ubiquitous Learning: A Survey of Applications, Research, and Trends, pp. 17–35. Information Age Publishing, Charlotte (2011)

Bonanno, P.: Designing learning in social on-line learning environments: a process-oriented approach. In: Mallia, G. (ed.) The Social Classroom: Integrating Social Network Use in Education, pp. 40–61. IGI Global Publishing, Hershey (2014). https://doi.org/10.4018/978-1-4666-4904-0.ch003

Buchem, I., Perez-Sanagustin, M.: Personal learning environments in smart cities: current approaches and future scenarios. e-Learning Papers **35**, 1–14 (2013)

Canning, N.: Playing with heutagogy: exploring strategies to empower mature learners in higher education. J. Further High. Educ. **34**, 59–71 (2010). https://doi.org/10.1080/03098770903477102

Canning, N., Callan, S.: Heutagogy: spirals of reflection to empower learners in higher education. Reflective Pract. **11**, 71–82 (2010). https://doi.org/10.1080/14623940903500069

Chen, L.: A hierarchical model for student and teacher interaction in distance learning. Distance Educ. China **5**, 24–28 (2004)

Conole, G.: Designing for Learning in an Open World. Springer, New York (2014)

Cook, J., Lander, R., Flaxton, T.: The zone of possibility in citizen led hybrid cities. Position paper for Workshop on Smart Learning Ecosystems in Smart Regions and Cities. Co-located at EC-TEL, Toledo, Spain (2015)

Downes, S.: Learning networks and connective knowledge. Collective Intell. E-learn. **20**, 1–26 (2006). https://doi.org/10.4018/978-1-60566-729-4.ch001

Downes, S.: Learning networks in practice. In: David Ley, E. (ed.) Emerging Technologies for Learning, pp. 19–27. Becta, London (2007)

Dron, J.: Control and Constraint in e-Learning: Choosing When to Choose. Information Science Publishing, Hershey (2007)

Dron, J., Anderson, T.: Teaching Crowds. Edmonton, Athabasca (2014)

Goodyear, P., Banks, S., Hodgson, V., McConnell, D.: Advances in Research on Networked Learning. Kluwer Academic Publishers, Dordrecht (2004)

Gros, B.: The design of smart educational environments. Smart Learn. Environ. **3**, 1–11 (2016). https://doi.org/10.1186/s40561-016-0039-x

Gros, B., Kinshuk, Maina, M.: The Future of Ubiquitous Learning. Lecture Notes in Educational Technology. Springer, New York, Dordrecht, London, Heidelberg (2016)

Hase, S., Kenyon, C.: Heutagogy: a child of complexity theory. Complicity Int. Educ. **4**, 111–118 (2007)

Hillman, D.C.A., Willis, D.J., Gunawardena, C.N.: Learner-interface interaction in distance education: an extension of contemporary models and strategies for practitioners. Am. J. Distance Educ. **8**, 30–42 (1994). https://doi.org/10.1080/08923649409526853

Hirumi, A.: A framework for analyzing, designing, and sequencing planned elearning interactions. Q. Rev. Distance Educ. **3**, 141–160 (2002)

Hwang, G.J.: Definition, framework and research issues of smart learning environments – a context-aware ubiquitous learning perspective. Smart Learn. Environ. **1**, 1–14 (2014). https://doi.org/10.1186/s40561-014-0004-5

Isaksson, E., Naeve, A., Lefrère, P., Wild, F.: Towards a reference architecture for smart and personal learning environments. Innovations in Smart Learning. LNET, pp. 79–88. Springer, Singapore (2017). https://doi.org/10.1007/978-981-10-2419-1_13

Klichowski, M.: Learning in CyberParks. A Theoretical and Empirical Study. Adam Mickiewicz University Press, Poznan (2017)

Klichowski, M., Kroliczak, G.: Numbers and functional lateralization: a visual half-field and dichotic listening study in proficient bilinguals. Neuropsychologia **100**, 93–109 (2017). https://doi.org/10.1016/j.neuropsychologia.2017.04.019

Klichowski, M., Bonanno, P., Jaskulska, S., Smaniotto Costa, C., de Lange, M., Klauser, F.R.: CyberParks as a new context for Smart Education: theoretical background, assumptions, and pre-service teachers' rating. Am. J. Educ. Res. **3**, 1–10 (2015). https://doi.org/10.12691/education-3-12A-1

Klichowski, M., Patricio, C.: Does the human brain really like ICT tools and being outdoors? a brief overview of the cognitive neuroscience perspective of the cyberparks concept. In: Kenna, T., Zammit, A. (eds.) ICiTy – Enhancing places through technology, pp. 223–239. Lusófona University Press, Lisbon (2017)

Klichowski, M., Smaniotto Costa, C.: How do pre-service teachers rate ICT opportunity for education? a study in perspective of the SCOT theory. Kultura i Edukacja **4**, 152–168 (2015). https://doi.org/10.15804/kie.2015.04.09

Latour, B.: Reassembling the Social: An Introduction to Actor-Network-Theory. Oxford University Press, Oxford (2005)

Mayes, T., de Freitas, S.: Review of e-Learning Theories, Frameworks and Models. Joint Information Systems Committee, London (2004)

Moore, M.: Three types of interaction. Am. J. Distance Educ. **3**, 1–7 (1989). https://doi.org/10.1080/08923648909526659

Papert, S.: The Children's Machine: Rethinking School in the Age of the Computer. Basic Books, New York (1993)

Pothier, K., Benguigui, N., Kulpa, R., Chavoix, C.: Multiple object tracking while walking: similarities and differences between young, young-old, and old-old adults. J. Gerontol. Psychol. Sci. Soc. Sci. **70**, 840–849 (2014). https://doi.org/10.1093/geronb/gbu047

Sharples, M., et al.: Innovating Pedagogy 2012. The Open University, Milton Keynes (2012)

Siemens, G.: Connectivism: a learning theory for the digital age. Int. J. Instr. Technol. Distance Learn. **2**, 3–10 (2005)

Siemens, G.: Orientation: sensemaking and wayfinding in complex distributed online information environments. University of Aberdeen, Doctoral dissertation (2011)

Takeuchi, N., Mori, T., Suzukamo, Y., Tanaka, N., Izumi, S.I.: Parallel processing of cognitive and physical demands in left and right prefrontal cortices during smartphone use while walking. BMC Neurosci. **17**, 1–11 (2016). https://doi.org/10.1186/s12868-016-0244-0

Tan, S.C., Divaharan, S., Tan, L., Cheah, H.M.: Self-directed Learning with ICT: Theory, Practice and Assessment. Ministry of Education, Singapore (2011)

Thomas, V., Ding, W., Mullagh, L., Dunn, N.: Where's wally? in search of citizen perspectives on the smart city. Sustainability **8**, 1–13 (2016). https://doi.org/10.3390/su8030207

Wang, Z., Chen, L., Anderson, T.: A framework for interaction and cognitive engagement in connectivist learning contexts. Int. Rev. Res. Open Distrib. Learn. **15**, 121–141 (2014)

Yamada, M., Aoyama, T., Okamoto, K., Nagai, K., Tanaka, B., Takemura, T.: Using a smartphone while walking: a measure of dual-tasking ability as a falls risk assessment tool. Age Ageing **40**, 516–519 (2011). https://doi.org/10.1093/ageing/afr039

Yuan, P., et al.: Increased brain activation for dual tasking with 70-days head-down bed rest. Front. Syst. Neurosci. **10**, 71 (2016). https://doi.org/10.3389/fnsys.2016.00071

4.6

The Application of Advanced IoT in Cyberparks

Jamal Raiyn[1(✉)] and Jugoslav Jokovic[2]

[1] Computer Science Department, Al Qasemi Academic College, Baqa Al Gharbiah, Israel
raiyn@qsm.ac.il
[2] Faculty of Electronic Engineering, University of Nis, Nis, Serbia
jugoslav.jokovic@elfak.ni.ac.rs

Abstract. The diffusion of information and communication technologies (ICT) into public spaces is giving birth to a new type of public space: the cyberpark. ICT and the next generation of internet of things (IoT) impact the evolution of modern cities, changing traditional urban planning processes. The IoT with e-economy, e-government, e-medicine, e-learning, and e-society is believed to make a city more efficient and effective. Both IoT and ICT can be used to incentive people to use public open spaces and to spend more time outdoors. In order to attract people, public open spaces have to be attractive, easily accessible and inclusive. IoT can be used to manage the resources in mediated places, including the street traffic in conjunction with events offered in a particular place at a particular time for different user groups. IoT tools are implemented in public spaces to prevent crime and to increase the safety of users. Security services goes from smart cameras that are being installed in many places, to determining users' position and signal tracking with the support of smart mobile phones, GPS/GNSS, QR codes, web services, and Wi-fi. Furthermore, biometric of all types are considered an enhancement of visual surveillance. Biometric are already being used for identification and verification including fingerprint, face iris, speech, eye, and DNA analysis. Various IoT tools are used to design and to create virtual games based on augmented reality for different target such as, human interaction, information collection, and playing in abnormal condition. This chapter addresses IoT tools used in public places to promote their safer use.

Keywords: IoT · Surveillance · Privacy · Information security · Augmented reality

1 Introduction

The diffusion of information and communication technologies (ICT) into public open spaces is giving birth to a new type of public space: the cyberpark. ICT and the internet of things (IoT) have a strong impact on the evolution of modern cities, changing the traditional urban planning processes. The Internet of Things (IoT), also known as the Internet of Objects, refers to the networked interconnection of everyday objects. Today, the Internet of Things has become a leading path to the smart world of ubiquitous

C. Smaniotto Costa et al. (Eds.): CyberParks, LNCS 11380, pp. 308–321, 2019.
https://doi.org/10.1007/978-3-030-13417-4_24

computing and networking. The IoT is believed to make the e-economy, e-government, e-medicine, e-learning, and e-society of a city more efficient and effective. The major goal is to encourage people to better use the outdoor environment in a safe manner. Advanced IoT aims to promote the movement of people from virtual life to real life in society. In other words, information communication technologies and tools aim to free humans from the prison called virtual life and its predominantly sedentary behaviours. IoT can be used to incentivize people to use public open spaces and to spend more time outdoors. However, in order to engage people, public open spaces have to be attractive, easily accessible and inclusive. IoT can be used to manage the street traffic in cities in conjunction with events offered in a particular place at a particular time for different user groups, namely, the elderly, children and young people.

This chapter is focused on the improvement of human safety in cyberparks by introducing an encryption scheme. Encryption, a method that protects the communications protocol from cyber attacker, uses an algorithm and key to transform data at the source safety. In the secret-key encryption, the sender of the message uses an algorithm and a key to encrypt the message, and the receiver of the message uses the same key to decrypt the message. The receiver and the sender of the message must both agree on the key without any third party knowing, a method called key management. In former encryption schemes, the algorithm and the key were transmitted along with the data at the same time; however, such schemes were considered extremely unsecure. In today's encryption schemes, all communications involve public keys. The public keys for the two parties are published, but the private keys are kept secret. To retain and secure privacy, the biometric data in encryption mechanism are included.

2 IoT Technologies

This section introduces the IoT tools that can be used in cyberparks. Various IoT tools are being already used to monitor public spaces (Hachiya and Bandai 2014), with some of them summarised in Fig. 1.

2.1 Smart Video Cameras

Video cameras are being widely used to monitor traffic. Video surveillance systems have also been used in indoor and outdoor environments with the aim of preventing crime (Raiyn 2013). For years video surveillance systems have been used in streets and in public spaces to control, for example, drug-related criminality. Video surveillance is based on features of abnormal behaviour that are represented by energy: the velocity and disorderly features of the moving targets. Energy is a term used to express the relative positions of the moving targets. Current video surveillance systems have many limitations; systems face difficulties in isolating a number of people located at different positions at the same time, and in tracking those people automatically. The number of possibly targeted people is also limited by the extent of user's involvement in manually switching the view from one video camera to another. Furthermore, preserving personal privacy, the implementation of video surveillance is limited, and the private monitoring of public spaces is restricted. Nonetheless, video surveillance data analysis has proven particularly effective in solving crimes (Raiyn 2015a).

2.2 Mobile Networks

Location based services are offered by various IoT tools (Sekar and Liu 2014). A mobile station is needed to provide users with services related to their location. In some cases, like accidents, a person can call an emergency number but may be not able to give any information about the location of the occurrence. In such cases, the task of the IoT tools is to localize the injured person quickly and accurately (Smit et al. 2012). The user location can be easily determined based on the mobile phone service. In the last decade position determination through wireless network technologies has increased. Mobile and wireless communications systems increasingly offer this service. In a mediated open space (cyberpark), high quality location services can be used to provide more safety and security. A mobile station uses signals, transmitted by antennas to calculate its own position. In other words, the positioning receiver calculates the distance between the mobile station and the base station by signal measurements. Mobile phones mostly use wi-fi networks for internet access, or they use cellular systems to setup audio and video communication (Mok and Retscher 2007).

The cellular concept is a mobile network architecture composed ideally of hexagonal cells. The cells represent geographic areas. Inside the coverage area, the users, called mobile stations (MS) are able to communicate with the network while moving inside the cells. Each cell has a base station (BS), which serves the mobile stations. The coverage zones are however not hexagonal in real radio networks. Interference leads to missed and blocked calls due to errors in digital signalling. Between the transmitter (BS) and the receiver (MS), the channel is modelled by several key parameters. These parameters vary significantly with the environment (urban, rural, mountainous, etc.). The propagation of radio signals on both the uplink and the downlink is affected by the physical channel in several ways. A signal propagating through a wireless channel usually arrives its destination along a number of different paths, referred to as multi-paths. These paths arise from the scattering, reflection, refraction or diffraction of the radiating energy of objects in the environment. The received signal is weaker than the original transmitted signal due to phenomena such as mean propagation loss, slow fading and fast fading. The mean propagation loss comes from square-law spreading, absorption by water and foliage and the effect of ground reflections. Mean propagation loss is range dependent and changes very slowly even for fast mobiles. Slow fading results from a blocking effect by buildings and natural features and is also known as long-term fading, or shadowing. Fast fading results from multi-path scattering in the vicinity of the mobile. It is also known as short-term fading or Rayleigh fading, for reasons explained below. Multipath propagation results in the spreading of the signal in different dimensions (Raiyn 2014).

2.3 Satellite Technologies

There are several self-positioning systems, such as the GPS, GNSS, GLONASS, Galileo (Fernandez-Prades et al. 2011). The global positioning system (GPS) is a worldwide satellite-based radio navigation system (Huang and Pi 2014). It consists of three main segments: a space segment, a control segment and a user segment. There is a basic method for position determination-based cell identification. The cell identification method is based on an approximation of the position of a mobile handset by knowing in which cell the mobile station is located. This method is the basic technique; however, the accuracy of the method is rather low. Satellite navigation system such as the GPS and GNSS are tools well suited for collecting localization data such as a vehicle's speed and the direction of motion at regular time intervals. Satellite navigation systems have been used to manage real-time road traffic information in order to improve route choice decisions. When satellite navigation system data are unavailable, especially in developing countries, or outdoor, travel speeds can be computed on basis of the cellular network data. The GNSS has been used widely for outdoor services.

2.4 Interactive E-Services and Web Services

A cyberpark includes online services across different fields. Interactive e-services enable data collection and processing. Web based collaboration and mobile device applications actualize a user's location. In addition, some information is used to improve location-based e-services.

Developing web-based applications and services is assumed to make smart cities more efficient for citizens, such as e-services for hospitals, education, banking, events, transportation, tourism, security, to name a few. Similarly, Web services support social interactivity and cyberpark events.

Fig. 1. IoT technologies that can be used in a mediated public space

3 Surveillance in Cyberpark

People tend to use public spaces that are inviting, attractive, accessible, and above all safe. Crime in public places reflects a societal problem. It is a very complex issue with several aspects, and it cannot be solved by urban planning alone. Crimes consist of assaults, and threats and offenses against personal property. Various IoT tools and other techniques may help to create a safer environment. The use of IoT tools in public place is not new, cameras have been installed in many places around the world. However, their application in public open spaces and other natural settings is more recent, and therefore limited. IoT tools are increasingly being implemented in public spaces with the intention to prevent crime and to increase the safety of outdoor activities. Security services include position determination and signal tracking with the support of smart digital, mobile phones, GPS/GNSS, QR cod, web services, and wi-fi as listed in Table 1.

User location can be determined by these services (Patil et al. 2014). When a user requests information about a place from the location-based server, the server needs to know the location of the user, and a location information is normally requested. Furthermore, biometrics of all types are considered an enhancement of visual surveillance; biometrics are already being used for identification and verification including fingerprint, face iris, speech, eye, and DNA analysis.

Table 1. IoT-based services

IoT	Services\tasks	Feature	Reliability	
			Static	Dynamic
Digital camera	Monitor\surveillance	Image detection	√	
Mobile phone	Information	Signal		√
GPS\GNSS	Positioning, tracking	Altitude, longitude		√
WiFi	Internet connection	IP		√
QR code\web service	Information providing	IP/signal	√	
Interactive digital map	Visitor guide			√
Screen	Media playing		√	
Multimedia place	Calling, music, games		√	

To improve the safety in open spaces, an agent has been introduced (a cyberpark-agent) into the wireless video surveillance system, and a cyberpark agent based, multi-node, collaborative, wireless video monitoring scheme is proposed. The cyberpark agent is designed for target tracking, it can move among network nodes a designated path or on an independently selected path based on network conditions and cumulated information. The target will pass through multiple monitoring regions of nodes. Although aimed at the same target, each device obtains different target moving information, e.g., the target trajectory. Different cyberpark agents created for each target can be used to achieve continuous tracking. While the target switches between different monitoring regions, the cyberpark agent moves between different nodes, records target motion information, and accordingly reaches the goal of multi-node collaborative tracking. Videos, sensors and cellular networks are not sufficient for collecting data because of their limited coverage and expensive costs for installation and maintenance. To overcome the limitations of the tools mentioned above, GNSS can be introduced, as its application to monitor travel time has proven to be accurate. Its data are being used, for example, to monitor indoor areas and traffic congestions. GNSS products provide worldwide and real-time services using precise timing information, and positioning technologies (Bhuvana and Jiang 2014).

3.1 Privacy in IoT Technology

Information about users that is collected and stored should be kept secure. There are various algorithms for protecting information from possible cyber-attacks (Raiyn 2014). In general, cyber-attacks are actions that attempt to bypass the security mechanisms of computer systems. Cyber threats detection has been defined as "the problem of identifying individuals who are using a computer system without authorization and those who have legitimate access to the system but are abusing their privileges" (Bhuvana and Jiang 2014). To this definition the identification of attempts to use a computer system without authorization or to abuse existing privileges should be added (Karthikeyan and Indra 2010).

The main scientific challenge is to develop a multi-agent that detects, and tracks suspected cyber attackers (Maskat et al. 2011; Raiyn 2015b). Cyber security should be considered a top priority issue in the digital era since digital technology advancements seem to increase the incidence of criminal and terrorist acts. Moreover, we note that specific communities, like the Israeli society for example, suffers from frequent cyber-attacks. Since the inception of the internet the society and human life have become divided between the real and the virtual worlds. Large number of people spend their lives in the virtual world, many of them have misused internet. Criminal and cyber-attacks are increasing exponentially. To save people's life, we suggest setting ethical rules for the virtual world based on those of the real world. Furthermore, new security measures are required to protect privacy in the virtual world. Cyber-attacks attempt to bypass the security mechanisms of computer systems. According to Jerry Durlak (Smit et al. 2012), privacy is a human value consisting of elements he calls rights: the right to be alone without disturbances, the right to have no public personal identity, the right not to be monitored, the right to control one's personal information including the methods of dissemination of that information.

3.2 Information Security

In general, security can be considered a mean to prevent unauthorized access to information. It includes the integrity, confidentiality, privacy, availability, authentication, and authorisation of information stored and disseminated in servers, including information in files and databases and in transition between servers, and between clients and servers. The security of information can be ensured in a different number of ways. The most common are cryptography for information transmission and authentication. Cryptography, the science of writing and reading coded messages, forms the basis for all secure transmission. This is done through three functions: symmetric and asymmetric encryption, and hash functions.

4 Cyberpark's IoT Design Proposal

A mediated public space (cyberpark) can be designed in line with IoT services and what follows is our proposal to develop a safer open space. The cyberpark users have at hand several IoT tools to determine a user's location, as illustrated in Fig. 2. Users could also select and reserve social events a priori. The information received from the IoT tools is stored and the data obtained are organized in databases according to the type of IoT tool that is involved, and a cyberpark agent manages the data. Furthermore, to keep user information secure, the cyberpark (CP) agent protects the information from cyber-attacks. To manage the various IoT e-services resources in the cyberpark, a cyberpark agent that considers quality of service (QoS) and quality of experience (QoE) is put in place.

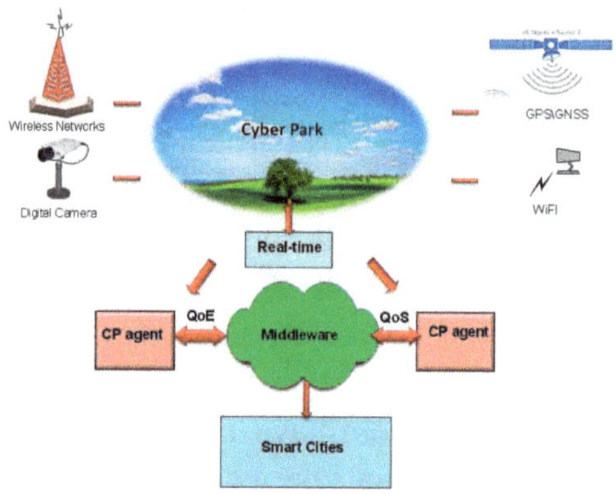

Fig. 2. The proposal for a cyberpark design

4.1 Cyberpark Agent

The cyberpark agent plays an important role in mediated places. It collects information about the activities of the cyberparks, updates the local information constantly, and takes the proper decision in terms of how to perform safely the selected activity. A cyberpark aims to increase the number of the users by applying the cyberpark agent. The cyberpark agent should have autonomy to work, in order to manage negotiation and take decisions (Fig. 3). Figure 2 depicts the decision-making process.

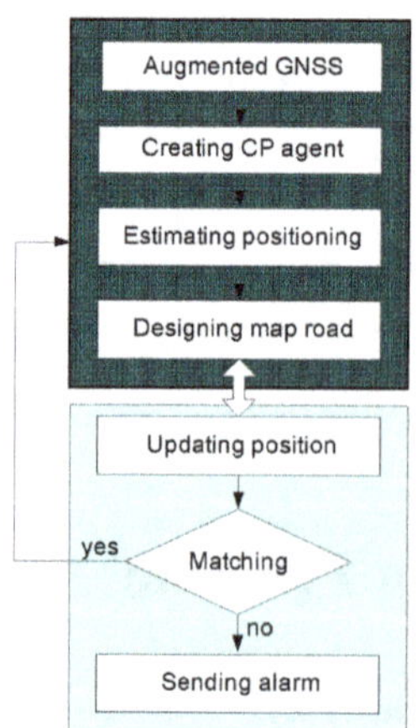

Fig. 3. Cyberpark agent strategy

4.2 Cyberpark Agent Communication

In this phase, the cyberpark agent collects information about the activities by using messaging exchange. The message exchange is secured based on biometric data. After that, the cyberpark agent sends request message to acquire an activity (Fig. 4).

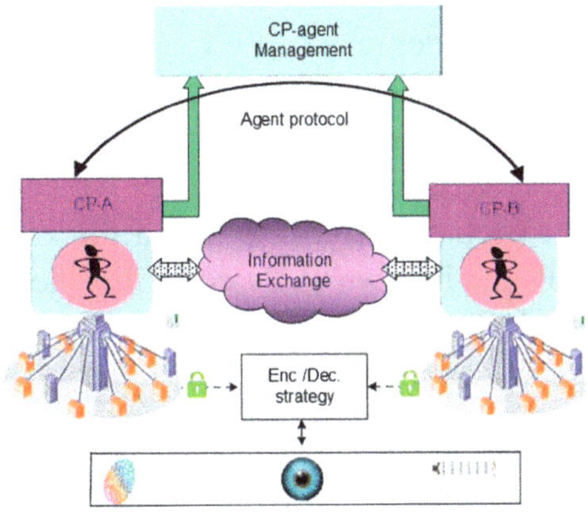

Fig. 4. Communication protocol

4.3 Information Collection

A new user who wishes to make use of cyberpark activities, is requested to register; a cyberpark agent is created to serve the user. According to the received information, a cyberpark agent offers activities suitable for the user's requirements and preferences. Furthermore, the cyberpark agent performs data analysis to improve the services based on quality of experience (Fig. 5).

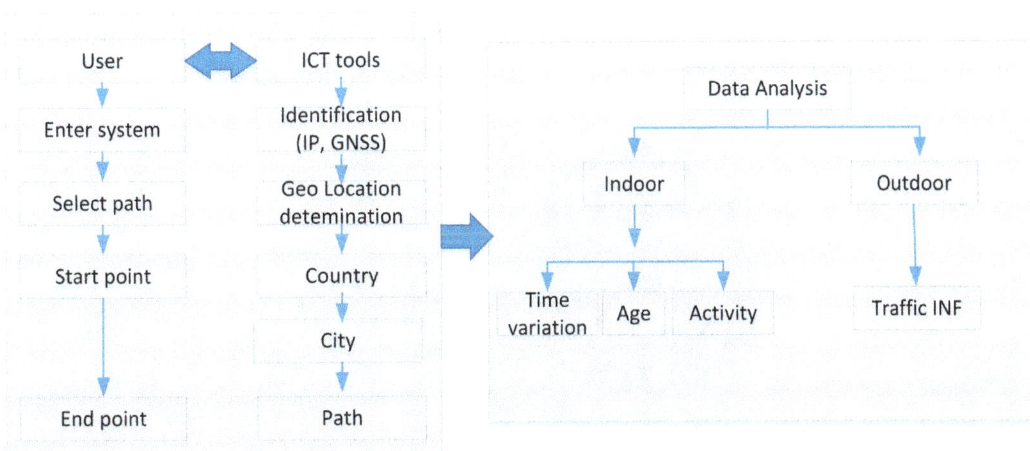

Fig. 5. The pathway of gathering information

5 Cyber Security with GNSS

This section addresses the currently available Global Navigation Satellite System (GNSS). The main task of GNSS is to provide localization and time synchronization services, for this it counts on three basic elements: the set of satellites, ground augmentation systems, and user equipment. Four main satellite technologies have gone live in recent years: Global Positioning System (GPS), GLONASS, Galileo, and BeiDou/Compass (Fernandez-Prades et al. 2011; Mok and Retscher 2007; Quddus et al. 2003). Among these technologies the GPS is the most commonly-used, especially for vehicle navigation and localization (Bernstein and Kornhauser 1996). The GPS data is transmitted via the Coarse/Acquisition (C/A) code, which is the unencrypted navigation data. The encrypted (military) signal is called the Precision-code, also broadcasted by every satellite. It has its own PRN codes, in the order of 1012 bits long. When locked onto the signal, the receiver will get the Y code, which is the encrypted signal with an unspecified W code. Only authorized users can decipher this information. Newly GPS satellites can perform further features.

To get a better estimation of a location, there are several methods of augmenting GNSS data. Three of these methods are: satellite-based augmentation systems (SBASs), assisted-GPS and differential-GPS (Greenfeld 2002). SBASs are commonly used in airplanes, especially for critical issues such as the landing phase. SBASs consist of few satellites and many ground stations, a SBAS covers only a certain GNSS for a specific area. For every GNSS, the accuracy is greatly dependent on and influenced by external factors, as propagation errors and "space weather" conditions (Langley 2000). These factors affect not only to GNSS applications, but all other wireless transmission applications. As the satellites are orbiting earth at a height of approximate 20.000 km, signals can be affected in many ways. According to Langley (2000), 'space weather' is greatly influenced by the sun, and this affects satellite signals too. GNSS requires however exact timing in the order of nanoseconds to determine a position. Furthermore, when the satellite signal reaches earth, it can be reflected on buildings and other objects, causing an increase in travel time. These factors have impact on the measurements. In order to overcome these issues and to increase the estimation of users' position outdoors, we combine augmented GNSS with biometric data, as Fig. 6 illustrates.

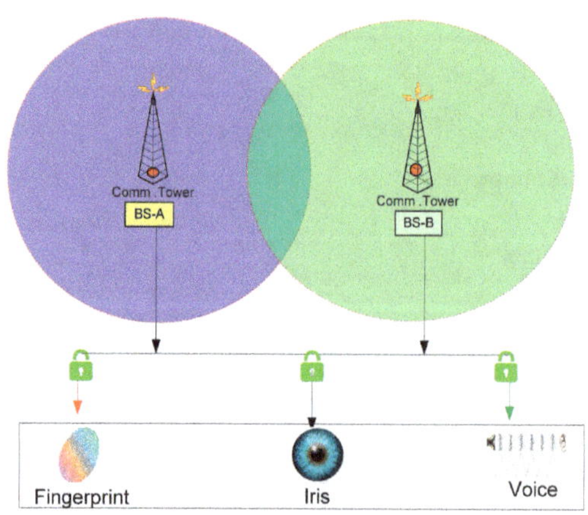

Fig. 6. Biometric data

6 Implementation

IoT tools can be a mean to invite and engage people in public spaces even seven days per week. When using public spaces, people consider the weather conditions and the time available. In this chapter, we introduce an application for interactive digital mapping based on the GNSS. Figure 7 illustrates the management of various resources in this application. Some resources, like e-services, are allocated in public spaces according to the date and time.

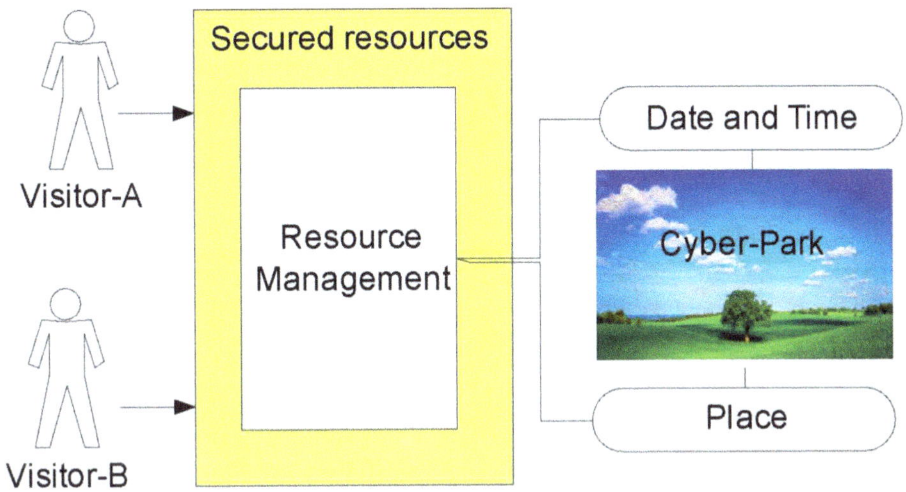

Fig. 7. E-services management

To use IoT tools outdoors, in a cyberpark, the user should log on the system as illustrated in Fig. 8. The system is protected by password authentication, also in data communication, authentication is used to ensure to the digital message recipient the identity of the sender and the integrity of the message. The authentication mechanism is based on cryptography use, either with secret-key or public-key schemes and mostly done via digital signatures based on biometric data, while the message exchange between users is secured with protocol supported with biometrics data, as shown in Fig. 9.

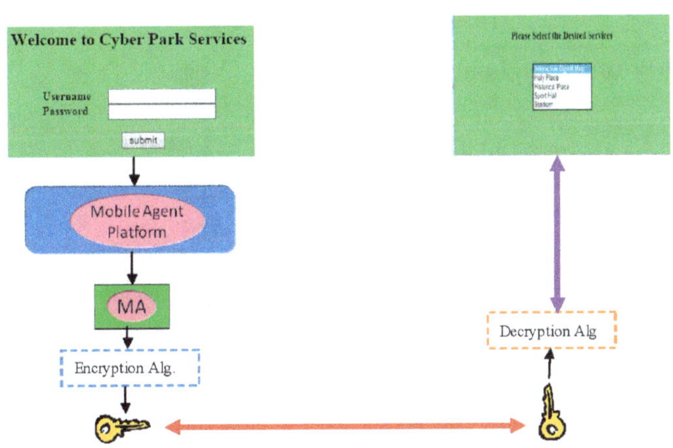

Fig. 8. The secured logon system

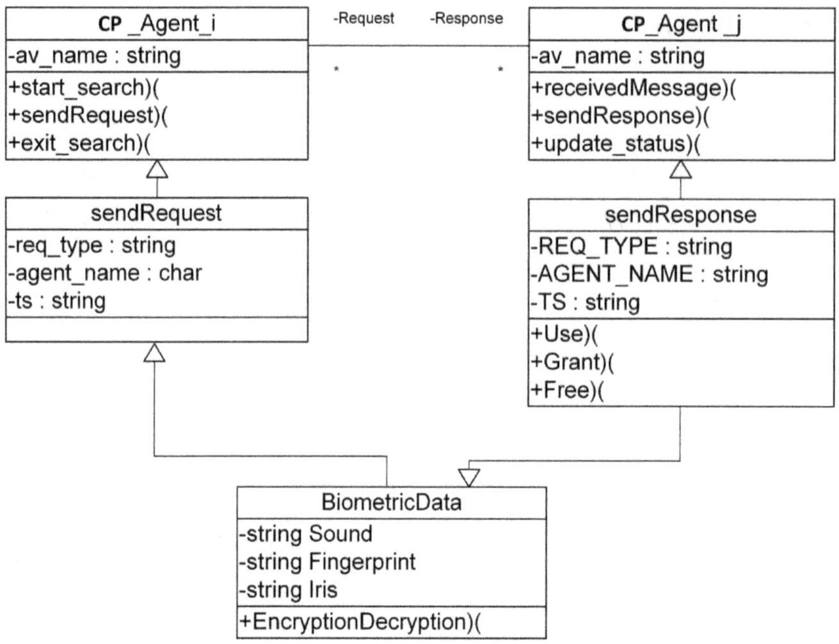

Fig. 9. Secured message exchange

7 Interactive Digital Map

In order to offer an enhanced service for users of a mediated public space, an interactive digital map can be installed as a station, or map can be displayed on a touch screen for people who do not carry mobile devices, or for those who have difficulties in using modern IoT devices. In this station users select a starting point and a destination for the trip and the cyberpark agent calculates the longitude and the altitude of the path as illustrates Table 2. Users have to provide some information in order to use IoT tools. Users start the trip by selecting a path, the system delineates the path, and tracks the users, as shown in Fig. 10. The tracking process can accomplish via various IoT tools. In this application, GNSS has been used to draw the trip path (Fig. 11).

Table 2. Location of nodes

Positioning	Longitude	Latitude	Velocity [km/h]
A	32.875902	35.187868	35.53
B	32.876271	35.191891	45.53
C	32.876866	35.197041	40.37
D	32.874280	35.197020	40.41
E	32.869117	35.200281	31.42
F	32.879540	35.203779	39.00
G	32.869838	35.207169	Final destination

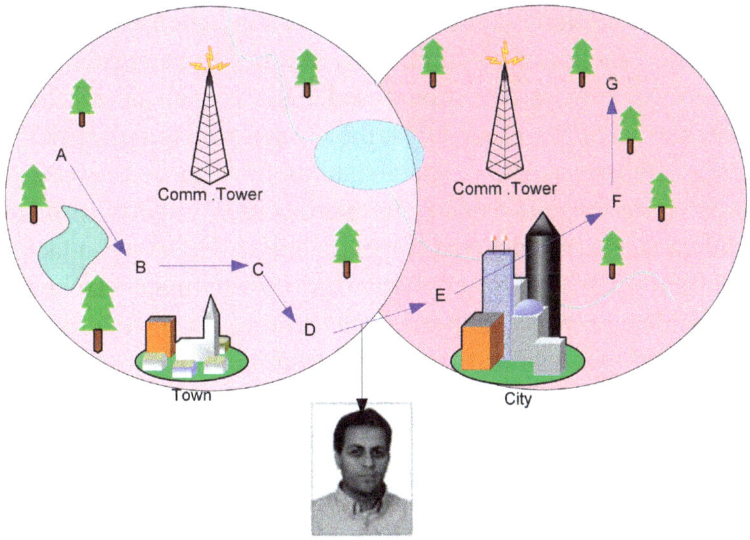

Fig. 10. Position tracking

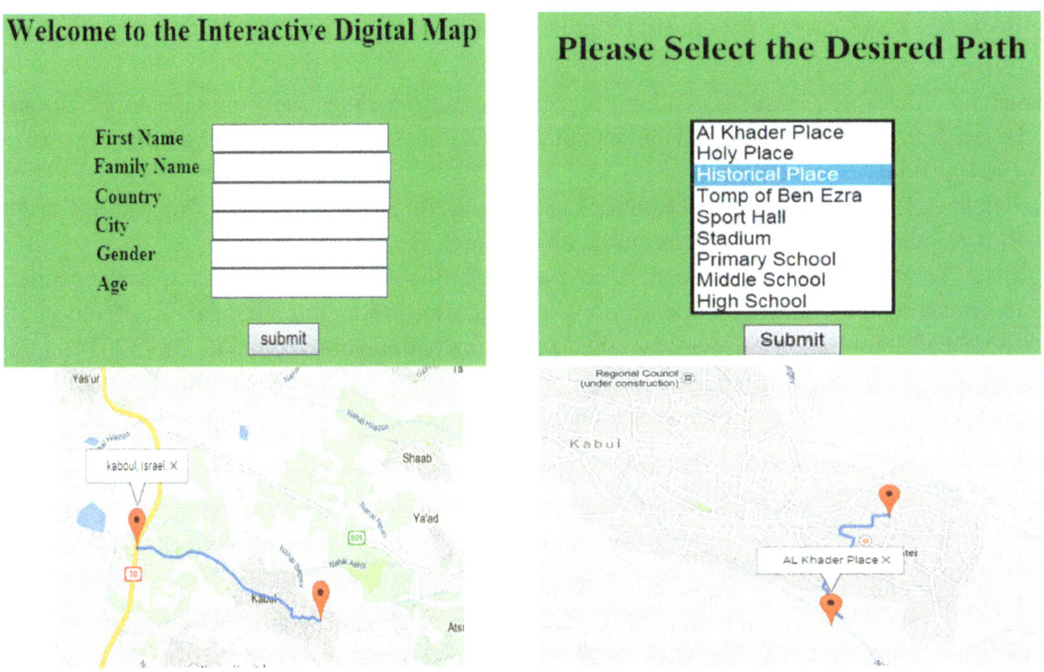

Fig. 11. Interactive digital map showing a fictive trip path

8 Conclusion

In this chapter some significant IoT tools were described and analysed. This analysis contributes to a broader understanding towards our primarily interest: developing a new scheme for securing the privacy of users in a mediated public space. Most cyber-attack detection schemes are fixed on use of authenticity strategies with session key agreement. However, traditional cyber-attack detection schemes do not satisfy current security requirements; and there are limitations in order to increase the threat defenses. The main limitation of misuse detection-based IDSs is that these schemes can accurately detect only known attack procedures; they are unable to notice unknown or novel attacks. Moreover, predefined attack specifications have to be provided to the IDS to enable misuse detection, which requires human security experts to manually analyse attack's related data and formulate attack specifications. However, attack specifications can be generated automatically by applying various automated techniques. In future work we will consider a novel cyber-attack detection scheme that is based on a cognitive security system. This system should act autonomously, analysing user behaviours, managing vertical handoff to track suspected cyber-attacks, moving over networks, considering anomaly detection, and handling cyber-attacks in real-time.

References

Bernstein, D., Kornhauser, A.: An introduction to map matching for personal navigation assistants. Technical report, New Jersey TIDE Center (1996)

Bhuvana, S., Jiang, B.L.: Location based mobile apps development on Android platform. In: IEEE 9th Conference on Industrial Electronics and Applications (ICIEA), pp. 2148–2153 (2014)

Fernandez-Prades, C., Presti, L., Falletti, E.: Satellite radio localization from GPS to GNSS and beyond: novel technologies and applications for civil mass market. Proc. IEEE **99**(11), 1882–1904 (2011)

Greenfeld, J.S.: Matching GPS observations to locations on a digital map. In: Proceedings of the 81st Annual Meeting of the Transportation Research Board (2002)

Hachiya, T., Bandai, M.: SmartLocService: place identification method using space dependent information for indoor location-based services. In: 28th International Conference on Advanced Information Networking and Applications Workshops, pp. 578–581 (2014)

Huang, P., Pi, Y.: An improved location service scheme in urban environments with the combination of GPS and mobile stations. Wirel. Commun. Mob. Comput. **14**, 1287–1301 (2014)

Karthikeyan, K.R., Indra, A.: Intrusion detection tools and techniques – a survey. Int. J. Comput. Theory Eng. **2**(6), 1793–8201 (2010)

Langley, R.B.: GPS, the Ionosphere, and the Solar Maximum. In: GPS World (2000). http://gauss.gge.unb.ca/gpsworld/gpsworld.july00.pdf (cit. on p. 19)

Maskat, K., Afizi, M., Khairuddin, M.A., Isa, M.R.M.: Mobile agents in intrusion detection system: review and analysis. Mod. Appl. Sci. **6**(5), 218–231 (2011)

Mok, E., Retscher, G.: Location determination using WiFi fingerprinting versus WiFi trilateration. J. Locat. Based Serv. **1**, 145–159 (2007)

Quddus, M.A., Ochieng, W.Y., Zhao, L., Noland, R.B.: A general map matching algorithm for transport telematics applications. GPS Solut. **7**, 157–167 (2003)

Patil, D.S., Gavali, A.B., Gavali, S.B.: Review on indexing methods in location based services. In: IEEE International Advance Computing Conference (IACC), pp. 930–936 (2014)

Raiyn, J.: Detection of objects in motion - a survey of video surveillance. Adv. Internet Things **3**, 73–78 (2013)

Raiyn, J.: A survey of cyber attack detection strategies. Int. J. Secur. Appl. **8**(1), 247–256 (2014). https://doi.org/10.14257/ijsia.2014.8.1.23

Raiyn, J.: Introduction to big data management based on evolution agent in cyberparks. J. Multi. Eng. Sci. Technol. 2(9), pp. 2432–2437 (2015a)

Raiyn, J.: Information security and safety in cyber parks. Global J. Adv. Eng. Technol. Sci. 2(8), pp. 33–38 (2015b)

Sekar, B., Liu, J.B.: Location based mobile apps development on android platform. In: IEEE 9th Conference on Industrial Electronics and Applications (ICIEA), pp. 2148–2153 (2014)

Smit, L., Stander, A., Ophoff, J.: An analysis of base station location accuracy within mobile-cellular networks. Int. J. Cyber Secur. Digit. Forensics (IJCSDF) **1**(4), 272–279 (2012)

Author Index

www.ingramcontent.com/pod-product-compliance
Lightning Source LLC
LaVergne TN
LVHW082116200926
848484LV00008B/1961